PIONEER HEALERS

◆PIONEER HEALERS

The History of Women Religious in American Health Care

**EDITED BY URSULA STEPSIS, CSA
AND DOLORES LIPTAK, RSM**

CROSSROAD • NEW YORK

1989
The Crossroad Publishing Company
370 Lexington Avenue, New York, N.Y. 10017

Library of Congress Cataloging-in-Publication Data

Pioneer healers: the history of women religious in American health
    care / edited by Ursula Stepsis and Dolores Liptak.
        p.   cm.
    Contents: Women religious in health care, the early years / Carlan
Kraman—In times of war / Judith Metz—In times of epidemic /
Duncan Neuhauser—In times of immigration / Judith G. Cetina—In
times of socioeconomic crisis / Edna Marie LeRoux—the transition
years / Mary Carol Conroy—Toward the twenty-first century /
Margaret John Kelly.
    Includes bibliographies and index.
    ISBN 0-8245-0894-7
    1. Monasticism and religious orders for women—United States—
History. 2. Medical care—United States—History. 3. Church work
with the sick—United States—History.   I. Stepsis, M. Ursula.
II. Liptak, Dolores Ann.
BX4220.U6P56 1988
271'.907'073—dc19   88-25657
                                                        CIP

To the women religious in health-care ministry,
past, present, and future

Contents

PIONEER HEALERS

Foreword

"Choose life then, that you and your descendants may live, by loving the Lord your God, heeding Yahweh's voice and holding fast to God" (Deuteronomy 30:19–20). The contributions of women religious to the healing ministry of Jesus during the nineteenth and twentieth centuries depict a story about choosing life. History is the teacher of life.

Some religious in Europe chose to come to America to embrace a new ministry, namely, to serve the pioneers, immigrants, and victims of war, epidemics, and natural disasters. Elizabeth Ann Seton wrote to Antonia Filicchi, "Could you but know what has happened in consequence of the little, dirty grain of mustard seed you planted by God's hand in America."[1] The beginning years of the Sisters of Charity of St. Augustine typify the struggles for many religious communities during the 1800s:

> Sisters Bernadine and Francoise obtained permission to return to France. The encounter with the hardships of a pioneer land, an unfamiliar language, a historically severe winter, and failing health were possibly the reasons for their departure. Two novices, Cornelie and Louise, decided to remain in Cleveland with the American postulants who had already been received into the new community.[2]

What enabled the religious to sustain these hardships? As you reflect upon the chapters of this book, you will note the mission and charism of the various communities. Vatican II urged religious to identify the special gifts of the Holy Spirit given to each community and to examine

1

and renew their life-style and spirituality in light of this charism. The Sisters of Charity of St. Augustine wrote:

> Out of the traditions of the past, we find meaning for the present and hope for the future, responding as our founding sisters did to the physical, emotional, intellectual, and spiritual needs of God's people. Nourished by a long tradition of meeting the charitable needs of the people, the Congregation continues, renewed and recommitted in this post-Vatican II period, to dedicate itself to works of health, education, and social services directing attention to those existing and emerging needs which are most critical.[3]

Jesus came to the world to make us fully human, to help us to realize our human dignity as creatures made into the image of God. Jesus came to bring the fullness of life. The example of Jesus and the attitudes of Jesus motivate religious of all time to minister to the poor and suffering that they in turn may have the strength to choose life. In their pastoral letter on "Health and Health Care" the American bishops state, "Health care is so important for full human dignity and so necessary for the proper development of life that it is a fundamental right of every human being."[4]

The story of the healing ministry of the women religious told in this book attests to the fundamental right of every human being to receive the care needed to live with dignity and respect. Medical science and technology make healing a complex task. The use of highly sophisticated medical equipment is an essential element of the health apostolate today. High touch must accompany high tech to realize the ideal of treating each person in a way that respects human dignity and recognizes the multifaceted causes of illness.

Poverty plagues our country: more than thirty-three million Americans are poor; by any reasonable standard another twenty to thirty million are needy. The burden of poverty falls most heavily on blacks, Hispanics, and Native Americans. Today, children are the largest single group among the poor.[5] Death will come to all of us with a degree of suffering but particularly to those who are poor. Religious involved in the healing mission of Christ render a unique service by bringing a faith dimension and a compassionate care to these crucial moments.

Women religious have the opportunity to choose life. Today the healing mission and ministry requires new linkages, new forms of involvement and dialogue, to build trust, to enable all of us to move beyond our security to address the needs of the medically indigent, the lonely, the homeless, the abused, and the displaced. All of us have been created to share in the divine life through a destiny that goes far beyond our human capabilities. God now asks us to sacrifice and to reflect on our reverence for human dignity and on our service and discipleship, so that the divine healing for the human family and this earth can be fulfilled.[6]

Jesus says: "I have come that all might have life and have it more abundantly" (John 10:10).

Joan Gallagher, CSA
Major Superior
Sisters of Charity
of Saint Augustine

NOTES

1. John R. Quinn, *Extending the Dialogue about Religious Life: Religious Life in the U.S. Church* (Ramsey, NJ: Paulist Church, 1984), p. 29.
2. Sisters of Charity of St. Augustine, Richfield, OH, *Constitution and Directory* (1985), p. 5.
3. Ibid., pp. 6–7.
4. National Conference of Catholic Bishops, *Health and Health Care* (Washington, D.C.: United States Catholic Conference, 1981), p. 5.
5. National Conference of Catholic Bishops, *Economic Justice for All* (Washington, D.C.: United States Catholic Conference, 1986), p. 8.
6. Ibid., p. 182.

Prologue

Not long after my book *American Catholics*[1] was published, a letter arrived at my door bearing the return address of a leading American Catholic health professional. I admit I opened the envelope with some apprehension. Surely she was going to take me to task for having written a history of American Catholicism and in the process virtually ignored one of the most significant ministries in which American Catholic men and women, lay and religious, have engaged. But no, there was no rebuke, only a request for help. The story of American Catholics and health care needed to be written—how could we go about it?

Right about that same time, Sister Ursula Stepsis, CSA, was thinking along the same lines. She conceived the idea of a collection of essays and statistics that would open up the whole question. The present book is the result of Sister Ursula's initiative. It does what she intended: it opens up the question. The story no longer lies buried in dozens of archives, obscure journal articles, and out-of-print books. At the hands of Sister Ursula and her collaborators, and with the capable editing of Sister Dolores Liptak, RSM, it has begun to come to light. We become acquainted with the sources. We learn the broad outlines of the story, along with enough detail to make it come alive. We learn of the monographs that have been published and of dissertations that will contribute to the tale. A boundary has been crossed, and I fully expect that this book will be the start of a library of fascinating studies illuminating the history of American medicine and American religion, and since it is so largely their story, the history of American women.

These essays focus principally on those American women, some native born, some immigrants, who heard and accepted a religious vocation to work in the ministry of health care. Most of them chose to live their lives as members of vowed religious communities. They were Catholic sisters, members of dozens of religious congregations, each with its own special charism. Different though each congregation might be in nuance or emphasis, their members shared a common motivation. It was well expressed by a physican in a Civil War military hospital who apologized to some sisters of St. Joseph because the patients referred to them as "sisters of charity." The internal intricacies of Roman Catholic religious community differences were too much for the wounded and sick soldiers to understand, "but you are all doing the work of charity, and that they *do* understand."

The story told in these essays is in the main that of Catholic sisters. As a beginning, that is fair enough. Catholic health care in this country has preeminently been a sister's story. Lutheran deaconesses and Episcopalian sisters paralleled Catholic efforts, and that is noted. A grand start on the history of Catholic brothers in health ministry has already been made by Christopher Kauffman in his two volumes on the Alexian Brothers, *Tamers of Death* and *Ministry of Healing*.[2] What still remains to be written is an overall study of American Roman Catholics and their involvement with the world of medicine, the physicians and the nurses and the technicians, the hospitals and medical centers, the specialized facilities for the handicapped, for foundlings and for the aged. This book is a building block in that effort. It tells about nurses and hospitals, and a great deal more besides.

It is always dangerous to categorize the past, to divide it up into neat little packages and try to fit it into cubbyholes. Somehow, history never seems to work that way. Human beings don't work that way. Situations, problems, attitudes, and solutions from one era lap over into another and, just when it seems time to close the book on one phase of the story, the pages fly open and we are back to where we started. That is very true in the tale told here. We find ourselves at the end of the story engulfed in the world of sophisticated health systems and high-tech facilities, but nothing is clearer than that the fundamental questions are still those with which we began, the need for health care that is wholistic and personal, that is informed by faith and hope and love.

With that caveat, I think it is possible to divide the history of Catholic health care in the United States into three major phases. It began as long ago as the American Revolution, with an initial spontaneous response to social need. Next came the extraordinary institutional development which accompanied the massive nineteenth-century immigrant waves that transformed American Catholicism. Religious pluralism, as it developed in the United States, encouraged American Catholics to open their own health-care facilities parallel to those of the state. The third phase, which has been emerging in the course of the present century represents a consolidation of past movements, and it has been marked in a particular way by increasingly refined emphasis on ethical concerns in the face of modern medical technology.

Dr. Benjamin Rush, one of four physicians to sign the 1776 Declaration of Independence, recorded in his commonplace book the story of Mary Waters of Philadelphia, a nurse in the hospitals of the Continental Army and who was later listed in Philadelphia city directories as a "doctoress" or "apotheycary."[3] She stands at the beginning of the American Catholic health-care tradition. In Rush's eyes she was something of a paragon, a skilled nurse, never out of sorts, who "told a merry story agreeably." She preferred acute-care cases and she took special pains to acquaint herself with "the character, manners, habits, etc., of all the physicians in town." What most fascinated the doctor was Mary Waters's sense of a religious vocation. She was a laywoman. She took vows in no religious community. But she was convinced, and Rush marveled at it, that her skill was nothing less than "a commission sent to her by heaven." She had a genuinely religious call to the work of health care. She responded by caring for men and women in time of war and in time of peace. With Mary Waters, health care as a religious vocation began in the United States. At the start it was quite simply a response to social need.

Social need took many forms. Canadian sisters nursed American soldiers of Benedict Arnold's invading army. Sisters of two dozen communities served both Union and Confederacy, winning the praise and support of both Jefferson Davis and Abraham Lincoln. Sisters of one community, that of Our Lady of Mercy of Charleston, managed the huge Confederate hospital at White Sulphur Springs, while their care for federal prisoners in their home city was such that after the war General Benjamin "Beast" Butler became the staunch advocate of compensation to them for war damages suffered in the siege of Charleston. During the Spanish-American War, sisters lost their lives in fever-ridden Florida camps, on hospital steamers returning the sick and wounded from Cuba, and with the troops in Puerto Rico. In a final flourish, Daughters of Charity—blue habits, coronets, and all—staffed a hospital unit with the Allied Expeditionary Force on the Italian front in World War I.

The sisters' wartime experiences were dramatic, but their nursing forays were scarcely limited to the battlefields. They were there in epidemics that periodically swept American cities and they aided victims of fires, floods, and earthquakes. By rail and stagecoach, on horseback and on flatbed wagons, they traveled to minister to the builders of our railroads and in the gold-, silver-, and copper-mining boom towns of the West. Hospitals and clinics were opened and closed as miners moved on to the latest strikes. Sisters nursed those caught in explosions and cave-ins and, in the anthracite mines, those who were victims of black lung disease. Working among lumberjacks as the northern frontier moved west they introduced some of the earliest forms of medical insurance. They worked among Native Americans, blacks, and migrants. In modern times, Appalachia has been the scene of clinics and home-nursing services. In many parts of the United States communities unable to support hospital services were able to have them because a community of Catholic religious women were willing to take on the task.

In that first phase of response to social need, Catholic American health-care professionals were carrying on a tradition with roots deep in the Middle Ages, when men and women hospitallers were the only organized groups caring for the sick and for society's outcasts. The medieval European world largely left to the church the care of much that in the modern world is the responsibility of the government. American religious pluralism demands a theory different from that of medieval Europe, but in actual historical fact the medieval tradition of religious response to social need has been alive and well—and welcomed in the strangest places—in the United States.

Religious pluralism led in this country to religious freedom, but it did not abolish bigotry. Pluralism is a condition in which toleration of divergent beliefs can and ideally does flourish. It was scarcely the mood that greeted most nineteenth-century Catholic arrivals from Europe. They met instead a fair measure of hostility. Public schools were used to mock their religion; priests were frequently denied access to their sickbeds in public institutions. The immigrants' answer shaped the Roman Catholic Church in the United States for generations to come. They created a whole alternative American way of life, and American Catholic way of life. It included schools on all levels, a uniquely American experiment, as well as health- and social-service institutions of every conceivable description. Daughters and sons of immigrants entered religious communities in impressive numbers; their lives and service made the system work. It was protective, supportive, and expressive of a confident Catholic identity.

Catholic health care grew in response to both social and religious need. It grew in the context of what those without the knowledge and wit to understand the situation liked to deride as "ghetto Catholicism." The cost in terms of money, of goals and orientations, and of dedicated human lives, was enormous. The schools and the hospitals responded magnificently to the needs for which they were fashioned. The essays in the present volume make it clear, if we still need convincing, to whom the credit is principally due, the successive generations of sisters who made up our religious congregations.

The third phase in the history of health care under American Catholic auspices is less easy to write about, but it is well handled here. Care standards have improved, but costs have escalated. Professionalization and secularization have seemed to go hand in hand. Conscious care has had to be taken to make sure that the poor and the outcast not be neglected, that what is personal and humane be safeguarded, and that "health-care justice" be maintained. Ethical directives need constant attention as new and unforeseen situations arise. Government and insurers have roles undreamt of in the era when our story began. All this and more is covered in the essays. Health care has indeed been one of the most significant ministries in which American Catholic men and women have engaged. This volume is a fitting tribute to them.

James Hennesey, SJ

NOTES

1. James Hennesey, SJ, *American Catholics: A History of the Roman Catholic Community in the United States* (New York and Oxford: Oxford University Press, 1981).
2. Christopher J. Kauffman, *Tamers of Death: The History of the Alexian Brothers, 1300–1789* (New York: Seabury Press, 1977), and *The Ministry of Healing: The History of the Alexian Brothers, 1789–1977* (New York: Seabury, 1978).
3. George W. Corner, ed., *The Autobiography of Benjamin Rush* (Princeton, NJ: Princeton University Press, 1948), pp. 201–2.

Preface

"All the difference in the world." In James Hennesey's view, these words, written by a Southern plantation mistress during the Civil War, not only best capture the attitude which sister-nurses inspired at that time but most correctly typify the composite long view of all the women religious who have provided health care to Americans during various episodes of our nation's history. All of us who have been associated with the writing and compilation of this study must surely agree with Father Hennesey. The procession of sisters about whom we have become acquainted during our research and writing were indeed an inspiring vanguard of health-care providers and worthy precursors of today's equally impressive corps of Catholic nursing professionals. Whether initially offering their services amid the squalor of the urban ghetto or in the crude wildernesses of the expanding West, these women religious fulfilled their vocation of service as though only they had been commissioned to do so. If their style of life and dress immediately set them apart from society in general, it clearly united them to the thousands whom they generously served. Their singleminded approach to healing meant new life and renewed spirits during the many decades before governmental agencies entered the field in earnest. By the mid-twentieth century, the efforts of these sisters had resulted in the creation of a vast, innovative health-care system that continues to command respect. Almost as one body—just as when they were merely known as the "Angels of Charity" or "of Mercy"—their service has made all the difference in the world.

In editing this book, I often found myself stunned to meditative silence as I read what these women accomplished. Sometimes I laughed aloud or sought out a willing listener to repeat some delightful episode

11

of courage or resourcefulness. Always I was amazed at the achievements of these women of God. The ugliest scenes of disease and disaster were not deterrents to their service. Bloody battlefields and operating rooms did not make them turn and run from the horrors of civil war. Down to the mine pits of Colorado or into the shanties of the immigrant poor they came, carrying food, bringing peace, easing pain—in countless ways, comforting those imprisoned by suffering.

Lest the memory of a ministry that stands unrivaled in scope, organization, and inspiration be forgotten, the plan of this book was conceived by Sister Ursula Stepsis, CSA, more than fifteen years ago. Now, through the sensitive efforts of several talented authors, the first broad strokes of the story of women religious in health care emerges. What each chapter has to tell us finds a second, and perhaps impressive, mode of expression in the statistical data and "milestones" of service that follow the narrative. Who can, for example, ignore the numbers of women, their early and consistent commitment to health care, as well as the vast geographical spread of their endeavors? Still another glimpse of skillful dedication is provided by the section devoted to the personal histories of just a few of the sisters who specially contributed to Catholic health care. As their story enfolds in these varied ways, it should become all the more clear how the energy of these women built such a solid foundation. The purpose of this book will be amply accomplished if our readers find in it the same inspiration, experience a similar appreciation for what has been accomplished, and recognize the place these women rightly hold in the making of American history.

Dolores Liptak, RSM

Acknowledgments

I wish to express my sincerest thanks and appreciation to Sister Joan Gallagher, CSA, Major Superior of the Sisters of Charity of St. Augustine, and to her Council, for their faith in and support of this project. I am also grateful to all the religious congregations in the field of health care, and their archivists, for providing the basis for this study; to our steering and marketing committee, for their advice and assistance; to the authors who, individually and as a group, made this book a reality; and, finally, to all those whose financial support made it possible.

There are innumerable persons and groups who deserve particular mention but who cannot be acknowledged here because of limitations of space. To all those women religious who served in the ministry of health care in the past, and to those who keep this history alive by their labors in the present, we acknowledge our everlasting debt and gratitude. And for those dedicated women of vision who will come in the future, we hope that this book will provide direction and ideals.

Ursula Stepsis, CSA

Congregation Coding

The numbers in brackets following the first mention in each chapter of every religious congregation refer to the codes assigned in *The Official Catholic Directory* of 1988, published by P. J. Kenedy & Sons, and are intended to be used in connection with Table 1, "Religious Congregations in Health Care in the United States," in Appendix 2 of this book. The code system was first adopted in *The Official Catholic Directory* of 1938. Prior to that time listing was in rather general terms, such as Sisters of Charity, Sisters of St. Francis, and so on. The lack of coding before 1938 and the frequent division of congregations into new autonomous communities have created difficulties at times in the proper identification of a few congregations.

13

✦ Women Religious in Health Care: The Early Years

CARLAN KRAMAN, OSF

Background

For centuries before 1800, women and religious congregations of women were involved in healing ministries and health care. Care of the sick from earliest days has been principally the work of women. Both women and men healers have known and used herbs and natural substances for the treatment of illness and disease. From ancient Egypt and Rome there is evidence that both men and women practiced the art of healing. In the medical annals of China, a female physician is mentioned as early as 260 B.C.

From the first century of Christianity, hospitality was given to travelers, the poor, the sick, orphans, and those handicapped in any way. Almost all of these places of refuge were connected to monasteries and religious orders and it is out of these that the hospitals of the Middle Ages developed.

Before the rise of monasteries of men and women, however, there were several notable houses which furnished public assistance to the sick. The first was founded in Rome in A.D. 390 by the matron Fabiola, who personally went out into the streets to find the most neglected and nurse them. Also in the fourth century, Basil the Great founded a type of hospice in Caesaria, and it is reported that there were even resident physicians and nurses. Basil's sister, Macrina (330–79), who founded a religious community of women, is known to have managed three hundred forty-seven such houses for the care of the sick in Constantinople.

The first truly monastic order of the West, the Benedictines, originated in the sixth century in Italy. Hospitality and the care of the sick

15

were always an important part of the Benedictine life. Benedictines were directed by their rule that "before and above all things, care must be taken of the sick." Benedictine abbeys of men and women spread rapidly throughout Europe between the sixth and tenth centuries.

The Hôtel Dieu of Paris was founded in the mid-seventh century; the original little band of laywomen who cared for the patients was organized into a religious community under Pope Innocent IV. They adopted the Rule of St. Augustine and thus are the oldest purely nursing order of sisters in existence.

Trotula and Abella are the names of two famous women physicians who served at the medical school of Salerno, which opened in the ninth century. Not only were women admitted to the medical school at Salerno but women physicians served on its faculty. Women physicians usually specialized in the diseases of women and children. As ruler of the Holy Roman Empire, Charlemagne (724–814) ordered hospitals to be attached to monasteries in rural areas of his kingdom and to cathedrals in the cities where the sick poor could be cared for.

By the year 800, every important city in the Moslem world had its own medical hospitals with trained physicians and substantial endowments, but Christian Europe accomplished this feat only in the thirteenth century, when almost every hospital was administered by religious orders of hospitallers.

Orders of hospitallers were established to give care to pilgrims, the poor, and the sick; they could be found in all the important cities of Europe. The Gilbertines, a group of religious women, worked mainly in England. Both the Antonines and the Order of the Holy Spirit began in France in the thirteenth century and spread throughout Europe in the ensuing years. The Knights of Malta were founded in 1108 to nurse the sick and tend pilgrims in the Holy Land during the Crusades; they affiliated hospitaller sisters to their order. St. Elizabeth of Hungary founded two hospitals: one in Eisenach in 1226, another in Marburg in 1228.

A Benedictine abbess of the twelfth century, Hildegard of Bingen, wrote books on medicine and was herself a physician. She has been called the most independent and learned of all medieval women. Her gifts and talents were extraordinary: she was an artist and musician, she wrote on physics and philosophy, and she recorded in words and in drawings her many mystical revelations.

By 1200 the medieval hospitallers were working under physicians trained at Salerno and Montpelier. When the orders of sister hospitallers came into being, the sick were treated as "masters of the house," and medical care in the Middle Ages was free to the patient.

The Renaissance brought renewed interest in the natural sciences, but had a negative effect on society by placing pleasure, leisure, and wealth above work, service, and devotion. The less fortunate were considered inferior and treated accordingly. During the Reformation, in the sixteenth century, Christendom was split and church properties confiscated, religious were driven out, and the sick and poor were left untended. With the dissolution of monasteries in England under Henry VIII the English hospital system virtually disappeared.

Gradually during the next century hospitals under municipal management appeared in London, Paris, and several German-speaking cities. A trend toward the study and teaching of medicine centered in the hospitals of this period was initiated in Holland with the introduction of bedside teaching at Leiden in 1626. Later, under the leadership of Dutch physician Herman Boerhaave (1668–1738), this trend was consolidated and influenced other medical centers, especially Edinburgh. By the beginning of the eighteenth century the character and concept of the hospital was changing, and there was a growing emphasis on its function of treating illness.

The development of hospitals in the "new world" began in the sixteenth century. The Spanish conquistadors established a hospital in Santo Domingo in 1503, and in 1524 Cortez founded the Hospital of Jesus in Mexico City, the oldest existing hospital on the American Continent. In Canada, the Hôtel Dieu de Precieux Sang was founded in Quebec in 1639; in 1644, another hospital was founded in Montreal. In the same century there were several hospitals for wounded and sick soldiers built by Dutch settlers in what was then New Amsterdam (present-day New York).

The Development of Active Orders

From the earliest days of Christianity, women chose the life of prayer and asceticism in order to devote themselves to the praise and glory of God and the salvation of their own souls. In monasteries set apart for spiritual purposes, they found new options. Not only did most religious houses provide opportunities for study, they also were training centers for domestic arts and for the development of such skills as weaving, tapestry making, and embroidery. Unhampered by the constraints of marriage and family, these women were less encumbered in their pursuit of wisdom, sanctity, and learning. On the other hand, all too often, active ministries which they also chose, such as the care of the sick and the instruction of the ignorant, were denied by the rule of the cloister that was imposed upon most religious houses for women from the sixth century onward. When, in 1298, strict cloister was required for all religious women by directive of Pope Boniface VIII, women religious were forbidden to do works of mercy outside the cloister, except in times of epidemics or disasters when their services were indispensable. Gradually, however, some abbessess and prioresses returned to the practice of permitting their nuns exemption so that they could attend to the ordinary needs of the neighboring populace. Yet, shortly after the close of the Council of Trent in 1563, Pope Pius V reinforced the requirements of strict cloister. Once again, the only exemption to leave cloister involved response to emergencies or to relieve such desperate cases as those suffering from epidemics, leprosy, or natural disasters.

Nonetheless, there were in every age, women who wished to move out of the cloister and commit themselves to serving the poor, the sick, and the ignorant while still living the vowed life in community. Attempts to do this were consistently obstructed by church law and the control of the hierarchy. One early venture to change conditions involved the Companions of St. Ursula, a congregation begun in 1535 in Brescia (Italy), under the direction of Angela Merici. A generation later, Milan's Archbishop Charles Borromeo transformed the group into a cloistered religious community. In 1609 Jane Frances de Chantal founded a community, the Order of the Visitation, with the intention of providing ministry to the sick and needy in their own homes, but in 1618 the bishop of Lyons modified their rule to eliminate external works of mercy and impose cloister. In England, Mary Ward tried to found a group of noncloistered women active in ministry in the same manner as the Society of Jesus, but without requiring the wearing of a distinctive habit. Her ideas were regarded as dangerously novel for the seventeenth century; by 1631, her institute was suppressed. Only as laywomen under private vows could Ward and some of her companions continue their apostolate.

Given such a history of reversal, the successful efforts of St. Vincent de Paul and St. Louise de Marillac to create and maintain a noncloistered religious congregation of women in France during the seventeenth century and beyond were all the more monumental. To achieve this purpose, Vincent had confided to Louise that he wanted them to view their monastery in ministerial terms: as though the women lived in "the house of the sick" where their cloister was "the streets of the city, your chapel, the parish church and your veil, holy modesty." Only in 1646, after thirteen years of service, principally in Paris, did Vincent seek a more formal status which proved more compatible with church policy for his order.

Vincent's attempt at bridging the gap between cloistered and active religious community became the American model. From the nineteenth century onward, the Vincentian spirit served the needs of the pioneer church in the United States; on American soil, on the mountain at Emmitsburg and in the backwoods of Kentucky, it took strong root, inspiring several American congregations of women. It would specifically inform the revised rule of the Daughters of Charity of St. Vincent de Paul [0760], whose motherhouse remained in Emmitsburg, Maryland. These women, together with a growing number of Catholic women who understood the challenge of a pioneering new nation, became the first organized corps of care givers upon which Americans could rely.

Medical Practice and Hospitals
in Colonial America (1607–1776)

There had been little structured provision for the needs of the sick on the American continent during colonial times. British Canada and French holdings in Louisiana proved minor exceptions to this reality. The New York and Pennsylvania colonies alone found means to respond to certain emergencies. The first quasi hospitals were actually those set up to care for the sick and wounded soldiers in service to European kings and queens. One hospital was founded by the Dutch of the East India Company on Manhattan Island in 1658. During the seventeenth and eighteenth centuries, almshouses were established by municipal officials in New York, Pennsylvania, and New Orleans. Philadelphia's almshouse, erected in 1731, was affectionately known as Old Blockley; New York's Bellevue functioned as an almshouse from 1736. There was also a health facility for New York's French colony, begun the same year. By 1737, New Orleans had begun the operation of St. John's. It admitted the poor but received payment from patients as well. Although most almshouses served primarily as institutions to care for the indigent of these cities, they usually provided multiple services, doubling sometimes as orphanages, sometimes for the confinement of criminals or the mentally ill. There were very few doctors. Whatever treatment was available took place either within these settings or at home.

Gradually, almshouses were separated from hospitals so that they could be used to isolate from the community those who were clearly undesirable. At the typical almshouse, the quality of care remained poor; there were often shocking abuses, especially involving those considered to be "insane." On the contrary, the "voluntary" hospitals provided better care because they were financed by contributions and by patients' fees. The first of these general hospitals was designated as the Pennsylvania Hospital in 1751; it was opened in Philadelphia in 1752. Under its founder, Dr. Thomas Bond, there were a number of firsts. It became, for example, the first colonial center to provide clinical teaching for medical students. On the eve of the American Revolution in 1776, wealthy New Yorkers could also resort to a voluntary hospital which had been founded in 1771. One of its chiefs of staff, Dr. Valentine Seaman, initiated the first instructional program for nurses in the United States. But the war itself interfered with the further education of nurses. These hospitals became the prototype of health-care institutions for Americans.

During the revolutionary war (1776–1783) health care took on another dimension. The wounded could anticipate care from a variety of sources, and for the first time some colonists came into contact with a corps of Catholic women whose religious inspiration motivated them to care for the sick. Protected by religious liberty in British Canada, these Catholic sisters were able to respond to the needs of the revolutionaries. Thus, New England soldiers serving under Benedict Arnold and ravaged by epidemics of smallpox and scarlet fever were nursed back to health by the sisters at the Hôtel Dieu hospital in Quebec. In a diary kept by one officer of the revolutionary army, an excerpt dated March 10, 1776 reads as follows:

> was removed to the Hôtel Dieu sick of the scarlet fever and placed under the care of the Mother Abbess, where I had fresh provisions and good attendance . . . when I think of my captivity I shall never forget the time spent among the nuns who treated me with so much humanity. . . . [1]

Later that year, other members of both the British and colonial forces who were involved in the Battle of Three Rivers (Vermont) were taken to a convent run by the Ursuline Sisters, where members of both armies were treated with compassion.

After the establishment of the United States, still more structured ways to care for the sick developed. Public hospitals were begun; and attention to health care could extend to the private domain and under religious auspices. In the improved religious climate, both Catholic and Protestant enterprises on behalf of the sick were encouraged. Furthermore, as health and surgical improvements made possible a different kind of medical care, Americans could view their obligations to provide for the sick in different ways. Except during certain local episodes of anti-Catholicism, which occurred during particularly stressful periods of economic depression, new groups of women religious founded in the United States and abroad fulfilled their religious commitment to serve God's poor.

Many changes in the provision of health services occurred as the new century began. For one thing, the United States Public Health Service began to function: it operated a marine hospital as early as 1798, where, by an 1804 act of Congress, every seaman in the merchant service was entitled to health care. New medical strategies, such as the use of morphine and the practice of isolation to prevent exposure to disease, were employed for the first time. During this period as well, Massachusetts General Hospital, which had been founded in 1807, became noted for its devotion to cleanliness and good nursing care. But, perhaps the greatest change developed because of the new need to respond to America's rapidly growing working class and immigrant population. At this point, a phalanx of women religious began to emerge; they were prepared to be the main health providers for their fellow Catholics in need, especially those devastated by the results of war, poverty, or communicable disease.

The First American Sisters' Response

Beginning with the establishment of native sisterhoods—such as the Sisters of Charity of St. Joseph, in Emmitsburg (1809), who were later known as the Daughters of Charity of St. Vincent de Paul; the Sisters of Charity of Nazareth [0500] (1812); and the Sisters of Loretto at the Foot of the Cross [2360], in Kentucky (1812)—a growing number of congregations of religious women began to provide service to the sick and poor, principally among the Catholics of their respective areas. These native sisterhoods included other American religious groups, such as the Congregation of St. Catherine of Siena (Sisters of the Third Order of St. Dominic) [1070], in Springfield, Kentucky (1822), and the Oblates of Providence [3040], founded by black Catholic women in Baltimore (1829). But soon they embraced such European-based congregations as the Sisters of St. Joseph of Carondelet [3840], established in Missouri (1836); the Sisters of Mercy [2570], whose early foundations were in Pittsburgh, Chicago, and San Francisco, as well as other immigrant communities whose members originally came to serve the needs of Catholics from France, Germany, and Ireland. As was written of Mother Elizabeth Seton, foundress of the original American congregation, this combined stream of women religious was to bring

> a new ideal to American life—the ideal of a band of women devoted to the care of their neighbors, through the same channels so well known in our own day: education of the children, asylum for the orphans, and hospitals for the sick.[2]

To be sure, care of the sick was to become a highly significant ministry, a most important way in which the nineteenth-century sister was to affect the future of both American society and the Catholic church in the United States.

The community which Elizabeth Seton (now St. Elizabeth Seton, the first American-born canonized saint) founded was clearly predisposed to consider the needs of the sick. Elizabeth was the daughter of a physician, Dr. Richard Bayley, a surgeon who was also a health inspector of the port of New York. Left a widow at age twenty-nine, Elizabeth recognized how the ravages of illness required compassionate care. Although her first ministry as a religious was to education, her commitment to health care was constant. When her congregation had sufficiently expanded, they were able to accept the invitation of the newly emerging University of Maryland to take charge of the Baltimore Infirmary connected to its medical department. In August 1823, her community, then known as the Sisters of Charity, began work in Baltimore; this historic date marks the beginning of the involvement of women religious in hospital work in the United States. According to a report in the *Giddings Baltimore Journal*, they provided care in eight wards, for seamen as well as for local patients (one of the four wards served the black population), all of whom they attended with "constant and unwearied attention" and "with a kindness truly sisterly, to the comfort of the sick."[3]

Yet, few records survive concerning the work of these religious women. Like most pioneers, these courageous sisters worked very hard and were not aware of the fact that they were "making history." Later, a doctor serving at Johns Hopkins would summarize the earlier time in terms of his own experience:

> Comparatively speaking, the nursing was excellent. The sisters worked under the immediate supervision of the attending physicians and the resident physicians. Many of the sisters were women of great intelligence, and for the time, superior education. The doctors held classes for the instruction of the sisters and the head sisters instructed their subordinates in the details of nursing technic [*sic*]. They did what the good nurse of the present day does—carried out the doctors' orders with promptness and intelligence.[4]

During the year that they had begun work at the Baltimore clinic, members of this congregation of the Sisters of Charity were asked to consider opening a hospital in St. Louis, Missouri, on land explicitly donated for that purpose by a Catholic benefactor, John Mullanphy. In 1828, four of the group (Sister Francis Xavier, as superintendent, and Sisters Rebecca, Francis, and Martina) would be the first of hundreds of nineteenth-century nursing sisters to serve in Catholic hospitals. Completed in 1832, St. Louis Mullanphy (now DePaul) Hospital was not only the first of its kind west of the Mississippi but it was also the first Catholic hospital in the United States. Only eight years after its opening, according to the 1840 *Catholic Almanac*, the number of patients had already exceeded one thousand and the first addition, "with very comfortable accomodations for lunatics," was completed.[5] The pattern of service was set. By 1834, the same sisters had also been asked to take charge of the Charity Hospital in New Orleans at the request of the governors of that state hospital. Wracked by twin disasters of hurricane and fire, the desperate directors of that hospital acknowledged that they could gain expert and devoted care for leprosy victims of all races from these committed sisters.

Only a few years after the Emmitsburg sisters had been organized under Elizabeth Seton and Bishop John Carroll for the Baltimore archdiocese, a second congregation, the Sisters of Charity of Nazareth, had been organized on the Kentucky frontier by Sulpician missionary Father

John Baptist David. For the cofounders of this community, Teresa Carrico, Elizabeth Wells, and Catherine Spalding, caring for the sick was also a preeminent concern. The constitution of the new congregation confirmed their bias; its ministry was to be for "the welfare of the neighbor, the suffering poor, the sick, the insane, the orphans in hospital and asylums, and the Christian education of youth, especially in parochial schools." From their "roomy cabin of unhewn logs in a corner of the seminary farm" these sisters regularly visited the sick—often on horseback.[6] Within two years of their founding in 1812, they were able to begin both a hospital (St. John's) and an orphanage in Nashville, Tennessee. In their work they were often assisted by some of the children they had raised as orphans.

When cholera hit Louisville, Kentucky, in 1832–1833 the Sisters of Charity of Nazareth found another way to prove their commitment to their fellow Americans. As death ravaged the adult population, they quickly sought provisions and beds for the newly orphaned; they expanded their own building for the sick children under their care. Their expertise was duly noticed; it did not prove difficult for them to establish a new facility, St. Vincent's Infirmary, that quickly "won the favor of the city physicians."[7] As the sisters' good reputation as nurses spread, the enterprise was again forced to move into larger quarters where, after 1853, their hospital became known as the St. Joseph Infirmary.

Another community—founded in 1829 in Charleston, South Carolina, by Bishop John England to educate Catholic children—soon turned to health care because of the great need in this center of immigration. From the start, the Sisters of Charity of Our Lady of Mercy [0510] were drawn into the work of nursing, providing medical care for homeless immigrants, aiding those suffering illnesses associated with joblessness, and nursing back to health those recently made victims of the epidemics of the 1830s. By 1839, these sisters had, in fact, been put in charge of a hospital financed by a lay brotherhood also established by the bishop to supply the needs of newcomers.

Given the general poverty of the Catholics to whom the various congregations of sisters ministered, the early success of these various communities is all the more remarkable. To be sure, the sisters were constantly plagued by poverty and insufficient funds to fulfill their religious goals. What made their endeavors possible was the constant encouragement and support of the bishops and priests who relied upon their assistance and of the Catholic poor who both needed and found ways to make their service possible. Yet, even this was not enough to avoid the scrutiny of those suspicious of their motives. Thus, if the sisters managed either to work for pay or to charge for their services, criticism was sometimes directed toward them. When the Sisters of Charity of Nazareth elected to be paid as "mercenary" nurses (the term used when the city of Louisville paid for services), they found it necessary to justify their decision. At one point, Mother Catherine Spalding admitted the terms of her accepting pay when she wrote:

> In the name of the society of which I have to be member, I proferred the gratuitous services of as many of our sisters (as might be necessary) in the then existing distress, requiring merely that their expenses should be paid. . . . [8]

Wherever possible, the services of nursing sisters were given freely. In fact, in order to keep the expenses of patients to a minimum, sisters often attempted to do all of the hospital work themselves—even when this was sometimes accomplished "under conditions which would have repelled many less zealous and stouthearted."[9] The first of the European-based communities to serve during this early period, the Sisters of St. Joseph of Carondelet, discovered this almost immediately. When these sisters did have to find ways to sustain themselves and their ministry, they had to take on a second work. As records kept by the sisters confirm:

> Some sources of income during these years were tuition charges (in the academies), art and music fees, and the charity of other Catholics. The Sisters did not hesitate to put their hands to any labor that would help them survive. In some cases this meant begging and taking collections.[10]

Fortunately, as health-care needs expanded and new medical procedures augured some positive improvements in the quality of American life, the problem of discovering ways to support the ministry of nursing became less accute. Besides, there was seldom a want of benefactors who understood the sisters' freely given commitment to God's people. More crucial during this early period of health care were questions involving the new areas of nursing into which the sisters should move as the nation underwent industrialization and modernization and as Catholic immigration rapidly increased.

Developments in Catholic Health Care: 1840–1880

As United States population expanded in the 1840s beyond seventeen million Americans to include hundreds of thousands of recent immigrants, especially those from Ireland and Germany, many aspects of American life changed. For one thing, procedures and practices concerning health issues changed dramatically. In particular, modern inventions and discoveries provided better health opportunities for Americans. Practicable coal furnaces and indoor facilities such as flush toilets, bathtubs, and efficient kitchens meant more healthful and sanitary conditions, even for recent immigrants and the urban poor. These improvements in the quality of life especially transformed the concept of establishing hospitals which would be equipped for specialized care, especially at times of epidemics and crises, and which would be staffed by trained personnel. Communicable diseases were isolated in certain wards; the mentally ill received special forms of treatment, as when Pennsylvania Hospital set up a separate department in 1841; surgery could be performed with the use of pain-killing drugs and anesthesia; and the sterilization of instruments made full recovery from surgery more certain.

In this improving mid-century health-care milieu, the career of nursing made its first steps toward acceptability and professionalism. Especially after the reforms set in motion by such stalwart women as Florence Nightingale, Dorothea Dix, and Clara Barton, the proper constructive moves toward providing for the health needs of Americans could firmly take root. During this same period as well, women religious became even more directly associated with the field of nursing and the organization of hospitals. Clearly stemming from motives of charity, these women continued to be an important source of service to American society and to the Catholic Church. Despite the fact that many of their accomplishments in nursing and in the establishment of hospitals had to be pursued during a period of intensified bigotry and nativism—despite the growing pains of an expanding nation, the carnage of the Civil War, and the immediate postwar crises—these women kept up their extraordinary efforts of courageous humanitarian service. Undaunted by these obstacles, they maintained the same momentum in providing health care during the equally trying years of reconstruction and westward migration.

Take, for example, the new direction in ministry which involved the Elizabeth Seton's Emmitsburg sisters, especially during the years in which their congregation expanded to more than twenty locations and became permanently affiliated with the Daughters of Charity of St. Vincent De Paul. In 1840 the sisters withdrew from the Maryland hospital where they had served from 1823; but their decision merely signified a move toward specialization. Asked to continue to care for some of the mental patients there, the sisters purchased land near Baltimore and built the Mount Hope Retreat, the first mental hospital in the United States under Catholic auspices. During the same decade, they were also busy opening six other health-care facilities. One of these, St. John's Infirmary (later St. Mary's) in Milwaukee, Wisconsin, demonstrated the change that was also taking place in the rationalization of health services. Judging from information quoted in the 1849 *Catholic Almanac*, St. John's was the first Catholic hospital to formulate policies regarding the operation of a Catholic health-care facility:

> As the Sisters of Charity are to be the only nurses and attendants in the house, none need fear the absence of sympathy and eager vigilance . . . Patients may call in any duly authorized medical man they please, but all food and medicine must be administered by the sisters. But this rule does not suffer them to deviate from the physician's advice. Any patient may call for any clergyman he may prefer, but no minister, whether Protestant or Catholic, will be permitted to preach to, to pray aloud before, or interfere religiously, with such patients as do not ask for the exercise of his offices. The fees for the keeping of patients either with or without medical attendance, may be known by application to the Sister Superior.
>
> Visits may be made at any time, Sunday excepted, from 10 A.M. until 6 P.M. But no rule, save such as a sense of delicacy to the sisters would dictate will, at any time, bar the entrance of immediate friends of the afflicted.[11]

In 1846, these same sisters founded St. Vincent's Hospital in the Bronx, New York, with Dr. Valentine Mott as chief surgeon. It became the first free hospital in New York to depend on voluntary contributions; the only other hospitals in the city at that time were New York Hospital and Bellevue, the latter of which was under direct city supervision. Meanwhile, in Buffalo, the sisters' approach to service highlighted another aspect of their desire to serve. There they had been asked to staff a hospital that was needed because the city had recently become a rail and canal terminus and, consequently, needed to serve victims of construction accidents or of the communicable diseases rampant among the underpaid laborers. Because most of their patients were poor and the sisters found it increasingly difficult to pay the bills for health care, they decided to apply to the state assembly for help in financing the hospital. This new trend in financing services became a matter of public debate. Almost immediately, an article by a Protestant minister appeared in the local paper to urge that "no appropriation by the state legislature should be given to the hospital, principally because it was sectarian in its character." The article also stated that "it was not conformable with our form of government to bestow appropriation on 'Romish institutions,' nor should Roman Catholics be the almoners of Protestant charities to the poor and destitute."[12] Never were any arguments raised which suggested either that the sisters were limiting their care to members of their own faith or that they were in any way attempting to proselytize.

Wherever they were to establish hospitals, the sisters were prepared for such challenges. Their ability to fulfill their mission of service prevailed. As a result, the sisters, known after 1850 as the Daughters of Charity of St. Vincent de Paul, remained in the forefront as pioneers in the establishment of general hospitals, maternity hospitals, and orphanages, or otherwise providing for the needs of Catholic immigrants. At the same time, they developed such programs as would improve the ministry they offered. Besides inaugurating allied programs involving health-care specialization, such as dietetics, they became one of the most important early advocates and sponsors of training schools for nurses.

Other congregations originally founded by Elizabeth Seton also contributed greatly to health care in the United States. The Sisters of Charity of Cincinnati [0440], which had become independent of the Daughters of Charity of St. Vincent de Paul [0760], was to provide remarkable service, especially in the western areas of the expanding nation. In the same year in which they separated from Emmitsburg, their archbishop, John Baptist Purcell, turned to them to organize Cincinnati's first Catholic hospital. That year he took over the city hospital and transferred it to the sisters' charge. Because their work since their arrival in Cincinnati in 1829 had been with orphans and in education, their acceptance of the episcopal invitation meant that they were launched into a new ministry. Within three years, St. John's Hospital des Invalides, as it was then called, had grown so much that it had to be moved to the site of their orphanage and academy. The hospital, equipped at the expense of four doctors and staffed by the faculty of Miami Medical College, became a model for other Catholic institutions. St. John's was the first Catholic hospital to have a teaching faculty connected with it.

During the Civil War, the sisters nursed the wounded servicemen at St. John's; several of the sisters also traveled with the army throughout the war caring for the wounded. One whose talents in this regard were widely acknowledged was Sister Anthony O'Connell. A year after the war's conclusion, Joseph C. Butler and Lewis Worthington, two benefactors who had been impressed by the devoted service of the sisters during the war, purchased a ninety-five bed hospital formerly used by the United States Marine Corps in Cincinnati and presented the deed to Sister Anthony as a birthday present. The donors asked that the name of the hospital be changed to the Hospital of the Good Samaritan. The deed captured the intention behind the name change. It specified that no applicant for admission should be preferred or excluded on account of religion or nationality. In October 1866, St. John's Hospital was abandoned and Good Samaritan opened its doors.

In the wake of the Civil War, Bishop Jean Baptist Lamy of Santa Fe, New Mexico, called upon these same sisters (whom he had come to know because of his previous affiliation in the diocese as well as his friendship with its archbishop, John Baptist Purcell) to assist him in his fledgling diocese. The sisters responded affirmatively and on August 21, 1865, a band of four young women left for the West. After an arduous journey, they arrived on September 13; immediately they set to work caring for the sick and orphaned. The first "hospital" in which they served was an adobe building with mud floors and ceiling which had been the residence of the bishop. Willing hands and hard work transformed the building's interior and St. Vincent's Hospital and Orphanage began its ministry. Besides hospital work, the sisters visited the sick, providing whatever remedies and supplies they could procure. Because of the poverty of the people, there was no source of income for the support of the hospital, and the sisters found ways to raise the funds themselves—even by going on begging expeditions to the mining camps. Under such devoted care, St. Vincent's Hospital, Sante Fe, flourished. It became a place where surgical and medical aid could be provided as the nation expanded to the southwest, especially for those laborers who were building the railroads.

Hospital care in Kansas can also be traced back to the ongoing apostolate of members of this community. Ministry there began as a direct outgrowth of the reorganization of the Sisters of Charity of Nazareth, whose career in nursing had begun twenty years before with their visitations to the poor in the backwoods area of frontier Kentucky. In 1851, six members of this community chose to separate and form an independent congregation in Nashville, Tennessee, and continue to work at St. John's Hospital in that city. At the same time that the sisters were considering still another relocation, one of their members, Mother Xavier, met Jesuit missionary Father Peter DeSmet, headquartered in St. Louis. Encouraged by him, she inspired her group to consider work on the frontier. DeSmet, in turn, urged the Jesuit vicar-apostolic of the Indian Territory of Kansas to invite the sisters of Leavenworth City to work among the Indians there. After disposing of their goods and re-settling some of the remaining orphans, fourteen sisters left Nashville in 1858 and moved to Leavenworth. Under the new title, the Sisters of Charity of Leavenworth [0480], they opened St. John's Hospital in that city in 1864; under Sister Joanna Brunner, who is acknowledged as the first trained nurse to practice in Kansas, the sisters carried out their remarkable hospital ministry in the nation's heartland and beyond.

Only six years later, in 1870, these same Sisters of Charity began another stage of their service to the frontier church, again at the invitation of Father DeSmet. They established an academy for girls in the Montana mining town of Last Chance Gulch, later known as Helena. Almost immediately they were directed toward health-care ministry, especially since there was heavy incidence of serious accidents in the mines. Even though the new community did not have enough sisters to manage the new venture, a group was sent to staff both a school and a hospital. On December 9, 1870, St. John's Hospital opened. Within a short time, again because of urgent need, facilities to care for the mentally ill were added. In the years to follow, hospitals in Denver, Colorado, and Butte, Montana, were also established by these pioneering women religious as they came to the aid of those Americans who continued in search of gold, timber, and land.

As was the experience of the diverse group of sisters specifically cited above, every one of the apostolic communities of religious women begun in the United States instinctively responded to the health needs of the Catholic poor. Yet, from the 1830s onward, it became equally clear that their help would still not be sufficient to cover the needs of Catholics, especially as immigrant populations increased dramatically. Thus, American bishops accelerated their search for new communities of women religious, especially those from Ireland, France, and Germany, whence most of the earlier immigrants also came. The first group of religious women who responded to the call of an American bishop were the Sisters of St. Joseph of Carondelet. At the request of the Bishop Joseph Rosati of St. Louis, eight weary sisters arrived in St. Louis from Lyons, France, on March 16, 1836, after a gruelling seventy-day journey. Two of the first sisters were immediately called upon to teach the deaf, a skill which had been recently developed in France. The remainder began the more generalized work of teaching and caring for the needy in Cahokia, Illinois, and Carondelet, a village outside of St. Louis. The poverty of these regions was extreme. The sisters had to find ways to support themselves. As has been noted, begging was not out of the question, but more creative means began to develop. Thus, sewing dresses for the ladies of St. Louis soon became their evening labor; it enabled them to spend their days in the works of charity, education, and mercy.

These sisters, formally known as the Sisters of St. Joseph of Carondelet, enlarged their apostolate to include hospital work when, in 1849, Bishop Francis Patrick Kenrick of Philadelphia asked them to open a hospital in that city, chiefly for the relief of the many fever-stricken Irish immigrants. Four years later, they were again on the move when Mother Celestine of Carondelet acceded to the request of Bishop Richard V. Whelan to send sisters to Wheeling, Virginia, to staff the first Catholic hospital. In the intervening years, another Sister of St. Joseph, Mother St. John Fournier, went to St. Paul, Minnesota, in 1851 accompanied by three other sisters to begin ministry there. They immediately set about founding schools while Bishop Joseph Cretin began building and planning for a hospital that the sisters soon added to their apostolate. After many difficulties due to scarcity of laborers and materials, a four-story hospital began to rise. An epidemic that spread rapidly through the city made the need for a hospital urgent. Soon every possible volunteer—including bishop, priests, and seminarians—made possible the opening of the hospital and the nursing work of the sisters. In the ensuing years, the Sisters of St. Joseph, expanding into regional provinces or separately organized within dioceses, established hospitals and orphanages and otherwise helped to provide leadership in Catholic health care.

Another European-based community of women religious who became particularly involved in the development of Catholic health care during these years was the Sisters of Mercy. A congregation founded in Dublin in 1831 by Catherine McAuley to serve the needs of working women, it was to spread rapidly in the United States after the sisters' first arrival in Pittsburgh at the request of Bishop Michael O'Connor, in 1843. Like other religious women, these amazingly energetic pioneers also had many trials at the hands of non-Catholics. Although they had to confront bigotry, their desire to help the Catholic poor left them little time for concerns over personal safety. From the start, they developed a reputation for mercy, based upon their response to the sick poor. To whatever Catholic neighborhood they were sent, the facts of disease and death were more important than any disapproval of their religion. Their immediate desire was to find ways to alleviate the daily misery they witnessed. In Pittsburgh, itself, the prevalence of what was known as "ship fever" (typhus) and the need for caring for the health of men employed on riverboats engaged in trade on the Ohio River induced the sisters to their first formal commitment to health care: they converted one of their buildings, known as the Old Concert Hall, into a hospital. Six months after the sisters opened this facility, the *Pittsburgh Post* could comment: "The institution is intended for the accommodation of persons of every creed and country, who will be attended with the most perfect tenderness, care, and cleanliness."[13] As in Ireland, the sisters continued to adapt the aims of their congregation to respond to every need of the immigrant poor. In the bustling new nation, they were attentive to such new concerns as the establishment of orphanages and homes for the elderly, and the development of networks of hospitals affiliated with the name of Mercy.

For the original Pittsburgh sisters, every aspect of their apostolate in health care was to prove a milestone. From the start, they were supported in several ways. The Catholic parishes of Pittsburgh did their share by providing financial assistance. But patients were also involved: charges for services were three dollars weekly in the general ward and five dollars for a private room. The personnel also supported the ambitious new project. At first, there were four physicians in attendance; these rotated their services free of charge on a three-month basis. From the start, all of the nursing was done by the sisters, who were themselves taught at the bedside by the doctors. Although they experienced their quota of blunders, heartaches, and joys, they remained constant in their dedication to the sick. Within the first thirteen months of their service in this simple setting of a converted concert hall, two hundred fifty-four patients had been admitted.

At the invitation of Bishop William Quarter, members of the same congregation of Sisters of Mercy were soon asked to move to Chicago where they could minister to the growing Irish-Catholic population there. By 1846, the first group of pioneer sisters had arrived; they were also to establish a number of firsts in providing for the needs of the immigrant population there as well. Not only did they open parochial schools, conduct adult night-school classes, and do prison work, they also nursed in the city's almshouses, at the county hospital, and at the marine hospital. By 1852, they were involved in plans for the erection of Mercy Hospital, Chicago, where they were to begin another first: the admission of medical interns.

In the midst of California's first gold strike, another contingent of Sisters of Mercy [2570] from Kinsale, Ireland, arrived at the invitation of the first bishop of the territory, Joseph Alemany, OP. Exhausted from their travel by sea and land routes—even through the overgrown forests of Central America—these indomitable women immediately took on the challenge provided by the bustling sprawl of San Francisco. After their arrival, in 1854, the sisters founded a number of convents and health-care facilities. In San Francisco, a land where "the rage for dueling, the passion for gambling, and barefaced depravity prevail to a frightful degree," they established their first hospital—an outgrowth of their instant involvement in the ravages of both "gold fever" and cholera.[14] In fact, hardly had the sisters settled in that city when the dreaded fever broke out. Because of their experience with the same epidemic back in Ireland, they were immediately put to work. According to one biographer:

> Their heroic charity in overcrowded hospitals, no matter what the creed or race of the sufferers, gained for them the love and respect of the people and helped to put down the animosity that had met them at every turn since their arrival.[15]

Still, even as the epidemic continued, the community became even more committed to their vocation to the sick. Renting a vacant building, they gave it the name St. Mary Hospital and continued their care there. After the epidemic waned, the sisters enjoined their newfound friends to help them enlarge the building. At different sites, the apostolate begun at St. Mary continued. Yet, from the start, as the first Catholic hospital on the Pacific Coast, St. Mary's was viewed as a clearinghouse for the work of the church and as a working base for much of the medical progress of California.

Another group of sisters to come from France at the invitation of an American bishop was the Sisters of Charity of St. Augustine [0580]. After their arrival in the United States in 1851 they first worked under the direction of Bishop Amadeus Rappe of Cleveland. Since there was no Catholic hospital or orphanage in the diocese, attention to these two ministries became their first concerns. Both tasks were well within the competence of the sisters; as Augustinians from Boulogne-sur-Mer, they were familiar with hospital work carried out since the thirteenth century at St. Louis Hospital. For one year, Mother Bernadine Cabaret and Sister Francoise Guillement and their two postulants, Louise Brulois and Cornelie Muselet, first lived with the Ursuline Sisters and performed their works of charity until the hospital and convent were completed. In 1852, St. Joseph Hospital opened; considered the first general hospital in Cleveland, it could accommodate forty patients. Despite the return to France of the original professed sisters, the nucleus of a new community formed around Mother Ursula, a sister recruited by Bishop Rappe, and the postulants. As the Sisters of Charity of St. Augustine, this newly organized group continued the ministry of their European founders. Although they subsequently closed St. Joseph, they joined Bishop Rappe and a local surgeon in making plans for the establishment of a new hospital, St. Vincent Charity Hospital, which opened in Cleveland in October 1865. Within eight years they had also begun a maternity hospital to care for unwed mothers.[16]

In 1858, from Aachen, Germany, came the Franciscan Sisters of the Poor [1440]. Their foundress, Frances Schervier, had the desire to serve the sick and poor from her childhood. A Third Order Secular Franciscan, she shared this ministry with four other committed women, and when a smallpox epidemic broke out in 1848 in Aachen, Frances and her companions opened their first infirmary, in a government-owned building, as their particular response to the crisis. In 1850, the infirmary became a hospital for incurables and the women became permanently involved in nursing and charity kitchen work. By 1851, Frances had gathered twenty-three associates; their mission to the United States began shortly after this when Bishop Purcell, the same bishop who had recruited the Sisters of Charity of Cincinnati, commissioned a friend to search throughout Europe for other willing congregations of women to assist him with his rapidly increasing Catholic immigrant population. Hearing of their good work while she was visiting Aachen, a recent convert and benefactor of the archdiocese, Mrs. Sarah Peter, told the sisters of the needs of the German immigrants of Cincinnati and persuaded the community to send sisters to the United States. Six sisters volunteered, arriving in Cincinnati in August 1858. One year later, with three more sisters from Germany, this immigrant community opened St. Mary's Hospital; in 1860, they established a second hospital, St. Elizabeth's, in a remodeled grocery store across the river in Covington, Kentucky. During the next few years, these sisters were invited to work with other dioceses which had large German-American Catholic communities; they opened hospitals in Hoboken, New Jersey, and Newark, New Jersey; in Brooklyn, New York City, and Quincy, Illinois. In the ensuing years, smaller houses, designed in the same manner as today's hospices, were opened. This ministry of healing has, in fact, continued to be the primary and impressive tradition of this congregation in its American foundation.

Because of the persecution of the Catholic church in Germany under Bismarck following the Franco-Prussian War, the Hospital Sisters of the Third Order of St. Francis [1820] sought refuge in the United States. Their desire to continue in service to the sick did not go unnoticed. With the approval of Bishop Peter Baltes of Alton (now Springfield), the sisters took up residence in Springfield, where they opened a hospital in 1875. This first hospital was so primitive that the sisters slept on the floor with only their cloaks to cover them. Even though they were strangers in a foreign land, unacquainted with the customs or even the language of the country, they managed to open other hospitals at Belleville, Effingham, and Litchfield, Illinois. Not knowing how to support themselves, they sought out benefactors among the clergy and laity from the start. As their records show:

> gifts were gladly and gratefully accepted because in order to be able to help the sick with greater success, the sisters were saving to build regular hospitals as soon as possible. They begged medicines and food and clothing for their impoverished patients and lived on what was left over after the poor were fed.[17]

Epidemics and hard times kept them ever occupied. In the late 1870s, there were many cases of scarlet fever, diptheria, and whooping cough; this made the work of these nursing sisters all the more indispensable. So, too, did economic progress take its inevitable human toll. But, in 1884, when the Wabash and the Missouri Pacific Railroads, the major employers in the area, decided to establish hospitals for their workers, they knew to whom to turn. Ironically these railroad hospitals provided something that the sisters had long denied themselves: the sisters were finally to receive a small salary, as well as free board and lodging.

Sometimes the rule of the Third Order of St. Francis was bestowed upon a congregation of women in the United States for purposes similar to the one which inspired the Aachen community to emigrate to Cincinnati. Thus, on April 9, 1855, St. John Nepomucene Neumann, then bishop of Philadelphia, invested three women with the habit of St. Francis: Marianna Bachman, Barbara Boll, and Anna Dorn. The express purpose was that the new religious congregation (known as the Glen Riddle Franciscans [1650], after 1896) would be particularly attentive to the needs of the German sick poor, orphans, and elderly of the Philadelphia diocese. Although the first work of the pioneers of this community was visiting and caring for the sick in their own homes, other charitable works were important ministries. The sisters nursed the sick during the epidemics that periodically ravaged the city; and in 1860 they opened St. Mary's Hospital in Philadelphia. By 1863, a branch of the community which had moved to Syracuse, New York, became an independent community, under the title Sisters of the Third Franciscan Order, Minor Conventuals [1490]. Remaining active in hospital work there, they also responded to another missionary call, sending sisters to serve the lepers in the Hawaiian Islands. To this day, these sisters run several leper hospitals in the islands, including the well-known one on Molokai.

As congregations of women religious expanded to serve the needs of the rapidly growing Catholic population in nineteenth-century America, women of Protestant and Episcopalian sisterhoods were making their special contribution to health care as well. One of the first Protestant groups to become involved in this ministry came to the United States at the request of William Passavant, an ordained Lutheran pastor who founded the Pittsburgh Infirmary. In 1849, he invited a group of Lutheran deaconesses from Kaiserwerth, in the Austro-Hungarian empire, to care for the sick of his parish. Within a year, they were at work there and had received a charter as "The Institution of Protestant Deaconesses of the County of Allegheny." These deaconesses, whose goals were "the relief of the sick and insane, the care of the orphan, the education of youth and the exercise of mercy to the unfortunate and destitute,"[18] also began hospitals in Milwaukee, Chicago, and Jacksonville, Illinois. Over the next few decades, other deaconesses had emmigrated from both Germany and Norway to work with sick children and the poor, especially those of German or Scandinavian background, in Philadelphia and St. Paul, and to staff several health-care facilities in the smaller cities of Minnesota, North Dakota, and Colorado.

During the same period, Episcopalian deaconesses and other sisterhoods, such as the Sisters of St. Luke, the Sisters of the Society of

St. Margaret, and the Sisters of St. Mary, came to the United States and took charge of a number of infirmaries and hospitals in such major immigrant centers as Baltimore, New York, and Boston, as well as in other American cities and towns. The Sisters of St. Margaret worked at Boston's Children Hospital; they also opened an orphanage in Lowell, Massachusetts, and were involved in parish ministry to the sick. The Community of St. Mary originated in the early 1860s in New York, where they had the interest of the homeless at heart. They provided shelter for women and for young girls who had already been forced into lives of prostitution. The orphanage which this community later began was aptly called Sheltering Arms. Another work begun in New York by these sisters was a hospital for children; it was widely known because of its skilled surgical department (one particular procedure initiated there, called skull trepanation, was lauded as a pioneering feat) as well as for the willingness of the sisters to admit acute cases regardless of ability to pay. In the postbellum era, this community started a school in Memphis, Tennessee, but also continued to work among New York's poor, where they staffed a second hospital and infirmary.

Thus, from the earliest decades of the nineteenth century, congregations of women religious, Catholic and Protestant, responded to the call of their churches and took upon themselves one of the most important challenges confronting American society: providing for the health care of a rapidly growing American society composed largely of immigrant families. From the visitation of the sick poor, their work quickly moved to the organization of hospitals and other health-care institutions. At the same time their services extended beyond bedside care to the instruction of nurses and providing other special services. By the third quarter of the nineteenth century, their efforts were not only accepted but even encouraged. That the mission which they assumed over this crucial span of years was eminently successful cannot be doubted. That the lives of these sisters provided something even greater—the strong presence of Jesus—is evident in the pervasive respect with which their ministry continues to be held.

"Angels of mercy" was once the name given the sisters as they served on the battlefields of the Civil War. Then and now it remains equally appropriate with respect to those women religious who provided the quieter day-to-day labor of loving service to the poor in crowded ghettoes or rural hinterlands at times of homelessness, hunger, and spreading disease. Entering into a society which had not yet developed a coherent strategy to care for the sick and the poor, this varied corps of women clearly embraced a challenge and began to organize what would become a vast and efficient network of hospitals, orphanages, and homes for the destitute and elderly. Yet, even as they preached the Gospel with their lives of service to the sick, the poor, the handicapped, and the abandoned, these sisters were also contributing specifically to the development of health care in the United States. Today the institutions they have sponsored are the testament to that achievement, and their mercy and their skill are with us yet.

NOTES

1. Ann Doyle, "Nursing by Religious in the United States, Part I, 1809–1840," *American Journal of Nursing (AJN)* 29, no. 7 (July 1929): 775–85; here p. 775. This is the first of a six-part article that appeared in consecutive issues of the *AJN*.
2. Peter Guilday quoted in Sister Mary Agnes McCann, *The History of Mother Seton's Daughters* (New York: Longmans, Green, 1917), p. xviii.
3. Doyle, p. 781.
4. Ibid., p. 782.
5. Ibid., p. 783.
6. Ibid., p. 778.
7. Ibid., p. 784.
8. Archives of the Sisters of Charity of Nazareth (22).
9. Doyle, p. 781.
10. Archives of the Sisters of St. Joseph of Carondelet (221).
11. Doyle, "Nursing by Religious in the United States, Part II, 1841–1870," *AJN* 29, no. 8 (August 1929): 959–69; here p. 963.
12. Sister Jeanette Rafferty, *Mercy Hospital, 1847–1972: An Historical Review* (privately printed), p. 6.
13. Archives of the Sisters of Charity of Buffalo (19).
14. Sister Mary Carol Conroy, *Historical Development of the Health Care Ministry of the Sisters of Charity of Leavenworth* (Manhattan, KS: Kansas State University, 1984), pp. 9–10.
15. James Hennesey, SJ, *American Catholics* (New York: Oxford University Press, 1981), p. 139.
16. Sister Mary Josephine Gately, *The Sisters of Mercy Historical Sketches, 1831–1931* (New York: Macmillan, 1931), p. 289.
17. Archives of the Hospital Sisters of the Third Order of St. Francis (72).
18. Doyle, "Nursing by Religious Sisters in the United States, Part IV, Lutheran Deaconesses," *AJN* 29, no. 10 (October 1929): 1197–1203; here p. 1198.

✦ In Times of War

JUDITH METZ, SC

Happy was the soldier who, wounded and bleeding, had her near him to whisper words of consolation and courage. Her person was reverenced by Blue and Gray, Protestant and Catholic alike, and the love for her became so strong that the title of the "Florence Nightingale" of America was conferred upon her, and soon her name became a household word in every section of the North and South.[1]

Critical times demand extraordinary responses. Wars are such times and women religious in the United States stood ready when the nation was in need. The first and most extensive activity of religious women was during the Civil War, which raged during the years 1861–1865. Sister-nurses also served in the Spanish-American War (1898) and World War I (1917–1918), but their service during the Civil War remains unparalleled.

The war between the North and South, when brother fought brother, stretched, principally, from Pennsylvania to Georgia. Fought over seemingly endless years, the casualties on both sides were higher than any other United States military engagement before or since. On April 12, 1861, as Confederate forces opened fire on Fort Sumter in the mouth of Charleston Harbor, both North and South were woefully unprepared to manage the affairs of war. Even though the storm clouds of war had been gathering for decades, neither side was psychologically or militarily ready to fight a protracted war.

Three days after the attack on Fort Sumter, President Abraham Lincoln called on the governors of each state to provide him with 75,000

39

militia for 90 days of service. There was a general expectation in the North that the war would be over "by Christmas." Instead the war became one of massive and inconclusive thrusts and setbacks. Before the summer of 1861 was over, Lincoln was calling for additional volunteers, this time requesting enlistment for three years. By January 1862 there were 450,000 Union troops in the field. Because the Southern army was smaller, in 1862 the Confederate government passed a conscription act to bolster their numbers. By the summer of 1863 Confederate forces reached their maximum of 261,000 soldiers. During the course of the war there would be 2,261 battles, engagements, and skirmishes. Yet during the first year of the war there was only one major battle. For the first two years the South held position in the eastern front with no decisive victories. Advantaged by their navy, on the other hand, the North could blockade the Confederate coastline, seize areas of the Mississippi Valley, and eventually invade the heartland of the Confederacy. The strategy caused most of the fighting to occur either on the eastern front in Virginia or in the campaigns throughout the Mississippi Valley.

If Fort Sumter shocked the nation, the army medical department headed by an eighty-year-old veteran of the War of 1812, Colonel Thomas Lawson, was unprepared even after the war broke out. He had no hospitals worthy of the name, no ward masters, nurses, or cooks except such as were detailed from the lines. An entire medical system for the Union troops had to be set up and put into operation after the war started. Consequently, in the early days of the conflict, care of the sick and wounded was conducted in an haphazard fashion. Churches, hotels, warehouses, or public buildings were refitted to be used as hospitals. In addition tent hospitals were erected adjacent to the military camps. In most cases, the administration of these left much to be desired. In both the North and South there were few trained personnel available; often convalescent soldiers doubled as the nursing staff.

As the carnage of war exacted its horrible toll, the largest medical problem faced in the camps of both sides was disease and infection. By the war's end more than twice as many soldiers had died of disease as had succumbed to battle-related injuries.

> The most common maladies were "looseness of the bowels," (diarrhea, dysntery, "flux," and scurvey), measles and malaria (generally called "the shakes"). Pneumonia, smallpox, yellow fever, and tuberculosis were of less frequent occurrence, but they resulted in many deaths. The principal killers on both

sides, however, were typhoid and intestinal infections. Typhoid probably was responsible for one-fourth of all the deaths from disease among Civil War participants.[2]

The high rate of sickness resulted from a combination of factors. Many of the enlisted men came from rural areas and had never been exposed to contagious diseases common among urban people. Thus, when these maladies struck, they did so with epidemic force. Another problem was the poor conditions that existed in many of the camps. The diet was not nutritious, the water in many cases was bad, and the lack of sanitation and elementary hygiene also contributed greatly to the health problems. In addition, once the diseases struck, there was a general ignorance as to how to treat them properly. Conditions in many of the hospitals were no better than in the camps. Lack of ventilation and general cleanliness as well as inadequate methods of handling the patients contributed to the already devastating situation.

In this first phase of modern warfare, the practice of medicine was in its infant stages. Amputation, for example, remained the cure-all for badly wounded limbs. Because anesthesia was not in general use until midway through the war, surgical methods and instruments used made the outcome of amputation surgery uncertain at best. Even if a person survived the operation, moreover, he had one chance in four of dying of infection.

Throughout the war, there was a tremendous shortage of personnel to provide medical assistance. Many of those who did work were volunteers without formal training. Almost ten thousand women served in one capacity or another during the course of the war— approximately nine thousand of these in the North. Some were independent volunteers, some worked with various relief organizations, many were employed in emergency situations to do menial chores. Approximately thirty two hundred served as military nurses and of these about six hundred forty were Catholic sisters.

Much needed to be done to improve the quality of health care that could be provided. To this end, on June 10, 1861, Dorothea Dix, the New England social reformer, was appointed by the Secretary of War to oversee women nursing volunteers. She began immediately to organize them into a corps of nurses, in the process often antagonizing army surgeons and nurses. Dix lacked diplomacy as well as administrative talent and found herself constantly at odds with most of the medical officers. She imposed some interesting requirements as well. She would accept no applicant under thirty years of age or attractive. In addition, those who were accepted had to appear "plain looking," wear simple brown or black dresses, and eschew all ornaments such as bows, curls, or jewelry. Hoop skirts were especially taboo. For pay they could expect forty cents per day, plus one meal. Many women ignored these requirements and nursed throughout the war without official recognition or financial compensation. Physicians sometimes refused to accept nurses assigned by their superintendent or treated them so badly that the women soon became ill or quit in disgust. For those who accepted the challenge, work remained constant and diverse, often including housekeeping, cooking, laundry, writing letters for the soldiers, or performing direct patient care. For this they might even be subjected to ill treatment and suspicion by both the physicians and soldiers. Common opinion was that women were not suited to this type of work. They were looked upon as unreliable, untrained, and undisciplined.

For the several hundred religious sisters who worked as army nurses, Dorothea Dix's influence also proved an obstacle to service. Her decidedly anti-Catholic attitude displayed itself particularly in her policies toward Catholic sister-nurses. Seldom would she approve a Catholic nurse applicant if a Protestant were available because she expected Catholics would proselytize the wounded and sick. Her prejudice became a point of contention among doctors who expressly requested the services of sisters, having had experience working with sisters in hospitals prior to the war. As a result, some physicians did all they could to obtain sisters for their military establishments even to the point of circumventing "official regulations." Often agreements entered into with those who requested the services of the sisters had clauses stating that sisters would work directly under the supervision of the army surgeons. When Dix and her associates became piqued at the obvious preference for sister-nurses and complained that Protestants were being discriminated against, one non-Catholic, Surgeon General William A. Hammond, retorted that nuns were sought after in many hospitals because they were good nurses.

The fact was that, when the Civil War began, Catholic sisters were almost the only women in America who had nursing experience. Even if the sisters were not trained as nurses, they could be counted on for their obedience, discipline, and selflessness. Their background, plus the willingness of various orders to serve in the war, made it natural for the sisters to be called upon. In several states, communities received appeals directly from the governor; some offered the hospitals they were operating for military use; some responded when battles took place in the vicinity of their convents and offered their facilities as emergency hospitals. Communities also responded to requests for their services from specific military authorities, or answered the need for nurses on the battlefield or on the floating hospitals equipped in the wake of battle. Despite the fact that twenty different religious congregations were active as nurses, the soldiers commonly referred to all these women as "Sisters of Charity." As one physician remarked to one Sister of St. Joseph working in Harrisburg, Pennsylvania, "It would be no use trying to explain to those around you the difference between religious orders. You are doing the work of charity, and that they understand."[3]

The types of work the sisters performed also ran the gamut of services: housekeeping, cooking, personal care, distributing food and medicine, assisting in surgery, supervising wards, and ministering to the wounded on the battlefield. What especially singled them out, however, was the encouragement they could offer in any of these circumstances, as well as their willingness to take on any type of work. In fact, they often volunteered for tasks which no one else was willing to assume. There are many instances, for example, where sisters volunteered to care for patients with contagious diseases, isolating themselves from their coworkers and risking contagion themselves. They took special delight in offering the sacrament of baptism to mortally wounded soldiers as testified to in numerous stories recorded of last-minute baptisms or repentances.

Sisters were present in every geographic area of the war. They made no distinction between Union or Confederate, Protestant or Catholic, in their ministrations. The sisters gained such a reputation for their unbiased and efficient service that they were favored by many of the army officers and government officials, even President Lincoln himself. Such was the level of trust afforded them that there are several examples of sisters from various hospitals being given carte blanche for supplies. The note given to the Sisters of Mercy [2570] of Baltimore at the Douglas Hospital in Washington, D.C., is one example:

> To Whom it May Concern:
> On application of the Sisters of Mercy in charge of the military hospital in Washington furnish such provisions as they desire to purchase, and charge same to the War Department.
> [Signed, Abraham Lincoln.][4]

In many of the congregations called to serve in the Civil War, the sisters were encouraged and assisted in their participation by their priest-superiors and local bishops. For the Sisters of the Congregation of the Holy Cross [1920] the request for nurses came to Father Edward Sorin, their director at Notre Dame, Indiana, who in turn took the message to the sisters at St. Mary's. In Cincinnati, Archbishop John B. Purcell was quick to relinquish the services of the priests and sisters in his diocese for the war effort. Accompanied by Mayor George Hatch, Archbishop Purcell personally visited the Sisters of Charity of Cincinnati [0440] on May 1, 1861, to deliver a request made by the governor of Ohio to go to a camp for sick soldiers (Camp Dennison) on the outskirts of the city.

The occasional reticence of local church authorities to allow the sisters to become involved in the war sometimes prevented the involvement of sisters. Archbishop John Hughes of New York was one of those church leaders reluctant to have sisters from his diocese participate. On May 9, 1861, in a letter to Archbishop Francis P. Kenrick of Baltimore, he stated,

> Our Sisters of Mercy have volunteered after the example of their sisters, toiling in the Crimean War. I have signified to them . . . that they had better mind their own affairs until their services are needed. I am now informed indirectly that the Sisters of Charity in the diocese would be willing to volunteer a force of from fifty to one hundred nurses. To this latest proposition I have very strong objections. . . . [5]

In other instances, priest-superiors even reprimanded the sisters for "violating cloister" or other points of rule in their response to the war conditions or demanded that impossible conditions be met by military authorities before the sisters were given permission to proceed with the work. These instances, however, were the exception rather than the rule. In almost every case the needs of the times took precedence over the rules and regulations of religious life. Much more typical was one religious superior who wrote to a Sister of St. Joseph of Philadelphia [3840] who was to be head nurse in a hospital:

> I suppose that you will be dispensed of a part of your prayers, and even Mass and Holy Communion through the week. Make a good meditation in the morning. Offer up all the actions of the day, attend to those poor people and I think Our Lord will be satisfied.

Later the same superior wrote to another group of sisters, "go to Holy Communion when you can have that favor . . . make your meditations in the morning after your prayers and be not troubled if you can say no other prayers of the Community, not even if you are deprived of Mass on Sunday."[6]

As the sisters embarked on their service during the Civil War, the country was emerging from a period of bitter nativism. Ignorance, fear, and hatred of Catholics had expressed itself in many forms of violence in the United States through the decades preceding the war. Although many Protestants had never had any direct experience with a Catholic sister, suspicion and bigotry was naturally transferred to them as visible symbols of the Catholic Church. This also complicated their nursing service. Thus, it was a common experience for the sisters to meet misunderstanding and prejudice when they first arrived to minister. According to one report,

> The soldiers at the hospital in Beaufort, South Carolina, many of them New Englanders well read in anti-convent literature, watched their sister-nurses very closely in order to catch any proselytizing that might be done. The steward of the hospital later confessed that he often watched them until one in the morning, expecting to find them poisoning patients, setting fire to offices, etc.[7]

Upon first contact, the soldiers were frightened and puzzled by the religious habit and often refused to cooperate with the sisters' efforts. This initial reaction soon turned to one of respect and admiration as the men came to know the sisters and appreciate their devoted care for them. Many took it upon themselves to become the "protectors" and spokesmen on behalf of the sisters. The multitude of tributes and testimonials to sisters range from simple letters and war diaries of common soldiers to expressions of gratitude—even from generals or presidents—on both sides of the conflict. Catching sight of some Mercy sisters one day after the war was over, Jefferson Davis approached them and said, "I can never forget your kindness to the sick and wounded during our darkest days. And I know not how to testify my gratitude and respect for every member your noble order."[8]

Northern Virginia became the initial battleground of the war, the first activity occurring in the one-hundred-mile area separating the District of Columbia and Richmond, capital cities for the two opposing sides. Even before the first major engagement, the Sisters of Mercy of Baltimore recognized the role they would have to play. They offered their Washington infirmary to authorities for use as a military hospital, the first of sixteen facilities pressed into service in the vicinity of that city alone during the course of the war. Within six months the sisters' building had been reduced to ashes and was replaced by "The Douglas" on I Street, a "hospital" which actually comprised three large residences—the main building being the mansion of Senator Stephan Douglas. The sisters remained on duty there for the duration of the war and beyond, not quitting their task until the convalescent soldiers were able to travel home. Several congregations of sisters also gave service in these hospitals.

In the South, sisters also responded to need. The Daughters of Charity of St. Vincent de Paul of Emmitsburg, Maryland [0760], were asked to assist at the military hospital located in Richmond, Virginia, in May 1861. The congregation responded immediately by sending a core of nurses to staff the facility, which would later be known as St. Anne's Military Hospital. Three hundred soldiers awaited the sisters. Richmond continued to be the hub of the Confederacy throughout the war and received the wounded from the numerous battles and skirmishes constantly taking place in the vicinity. The Infirmary of St. Francis de Sales, located in the same city and also operated by the Daughters of Charity, was the second facility utilized immediately for wounded and sick soldiers. According to one source,

> Other hospitals in and around Richmond were built, and as rapidly as they were made ready for use, the surgeons applied for sisters to take charge of them . . . The hospitals were often without the necessaries of life. For the sisters' table rough corn bread and strong fat bacon were luxuries; as for beverages, they could rarely tell what was given to them for tea or coffee, for at one time it was sage and at another herbs.[9]

Another area which was an initial site of military conflict was Charleston, South Carolina, the site of Fort Sumter. Immediately the small diocesan community of the Sisters of Charity of Our Lady of Mercy [0510], a group founded by Bishop John England, volunteered their services. Roper Military Hospital was one of the first post hospitals established during the conflict. The city came under seige in July 1863, and remained in that situation for the duration of the war.

Every day as the struggle continued, the number of soldiers requiring medical and surgical aid increased, and it became necessary to erect temporary hospitals on the outskirts of the city . . . There were between thirty and thirty-five sisters on duty at the Roper Hospital and its scores of affiliated tent hospitals.[10]

The *Charleston Mercury* commented during the seige:

There is probably no one in our midst whose eyes have not followed with interest the quiet and modest figure of some Sister of Our Lady of Mercy as she passed upon her rounds . . . Nor is the large kindness of these ladies solely displayed in the personal cares which they bestow upon the sufferer. They give generously from their limited means at the same time and many a want is then supplied which might otherwise have been left unsatisfied. Since the beginning of the seige of our city their presence has diffused its blessings in every hospital and their unmarred attentions to the soldiers have done incalculable good.[11]

In addition to their work in Charleston these sisters sent volunteers to White Sulpher Springs, Virginia, in December 1861. At the war's end they were still caring for over three hundred soldiers there. In an unusual, perhaps vengeful twist, the Union army refused to provide them with transportation back to Charleston. Undaunted, they traveled to New York with the assistance of the hospital chaplain. Through the kindness of some parishioners of St. Peter's Church in New York, they eventually made their way home. There they found their convent in ruins and their possessions lost or destroyed.

During the course of the war medical organizations expanded into new areas of health care. Many of the state governors took the responsibility of providing facilities for their military units. The Sisters of St. Joseph of Philadelphia [3840] were contacted in January 1862 by the Surgeon General of Pennsylvania, Dr. Henry Smith. In a letter to Mother St. John Fournier, the rationale for requesting sisters was clarified with the words:

whilst beset by applicants, he has refused every female nurse, being unwilling to trust any but his old friends, the Sisters of

St. Joseph . . . The living will be rough, the recompense poor, and nothing but the solace of religion can render the nurses contented.[12]

Three sisters left for Camp Curtain in Harrisburg, Pennsylvania, followed shortly by a second group bound for Church Hospital in the same city. Three thousand men were stationed in Harrisburg, where the hospitals were nothing more than temporary frame buildings roughly put together. During their stay, in an atmosphere charged with fear and suspicion that these experienced nurses from St. Joseph Hospital in Philadelphia would disturb existing conditions, the sisters quickly won the doubters over. In early February, Dr. Smith reported to Mother St. John:

> Already each hospital shows the blessing attendant on their presence. Everything is now neat, orderly, and comfortable. Sister P is "Captain of the Ward" in the camp hospital and has a drummer boy to attend her. Sister C in the kitchen is also in authority, and has a sentry at the kitchen door . . . Sister M is "The Major" and commands the surgeons keeping them in good humor by her kind acts.[13]

Within a few months, these hospitals, too, were temporarily closed, and the sisters moved to Fort Monroe at the mouth of the James River to care for soldiers being evacuated from Yorktown. There they served on two floating hospitals, the *Whilden* and the *Commodore,* making trips to Philadelphia with the wounded. When the U.S. government took over these state hospitals, these sisters saw their last active service in the war.

In 1862, because more than twenty major battles and innumerable skirmishes kept hospital needs urgent, Union leaders petitioned the Daughters of Charity to send sisters for service in Washington, D.C., hospitals. More than fifty sisters came to work at four area hospitals. The most concentrated scene of their labors was the Lincoln General Hospital where President and Mrs. Lincoln visited occasionally during the war. Many of the patients who at first feared or disliked the sisters were gradually won over and went out of their way to express their appreciation.

> One day a poor fellow obtained a pass and spent the entire day in the city and returned at twilight looking sad and fatigued.

A sister of his ward asked him if he was suffering and he replied: "No, sister; but I am tired and vexed. I received my pass early today and walked through every street in Washington trying to buy one of those white bonnets for you and did not find a single one for sale."[14]

That same year, the Sisters of Mercy [2570] from Pittsburgh's Mercy Hospital were invited by Secretary of War Edwin Stanton to take charge of Stanton Hospital in Washington. Eight sisters were assigned; their task was to care for both Northern casualties and Southern prisoners of war. The sisters also staffed a section reserved for soldiers suffering from mental problems. In addition to their work at Stanton, this congregation of Sisters of Mercy served at the state convalescent hospital, Western Pennsylvania Hospital in Pittsburgh.

Other East Coast cities also opened military hospitals. In September 1862 the New York Commission of the New Central Park offered a building on its property for use as a medical facility. The Sisters of Charity of St. Vincent de Paul of New York [0650] were requested to staff this hospital that, ironically, was housed in their former motherhouse, which they had been forced to vacate when the city exercised the right of eminent domain to create Central Park. They called the building St. Joseph Hospital and served there until the close of hostilities.

In 1862, the New York congregation of the Sisters of Mercy [2570] were asked to send sisters to Beaufort and later to New Berne, North Carolina. Nine sisters were assigned to a five-hundred-room former summer hotel. According to Mother Mary Carroll the hospital

> was so near the shore that at high tide the waves rolled in and out under the timber props on which it was erected. The place contained no furniture except a few miserable bedsteads, and was in a most desolate condition. There was only one broom and very few utensils . . . Along the shore were wrecks of pianos, tables, chairs, glass, etc. There were no candles or lamps, and everyone was compelled to retire before night.[15]

When supply requisitions were not filled the sisters threatened to withdraw. Soon the United States Sanitary Commission responded and the sisters remained in this area until April 1863.

Philadelphia was the site of Satterlee Hospital, one of the largest military hospitals. Over the four years of the conflict, some fifty thousand soldiers were cared for in this facility's thirty-three wards of seventy-five beds each. In 1862 the Daughters of Charity from Emmitsburg were invited to take charge. From then until August 1865, Sister Mary Gonzaga Grace ran the hospital with a staff of more than forty sisters. After each major battle, casualties were brought to her: from Bull Run, fifteen hundred; from Gettysburg, six thousand. If the wards became overcrowded, tents were erected to accommodate the rest of the wounded. The sisters' comment: "We had at one time not less than forty-five hundred in the hospital."[16]

Smallpox was a recurring problem at Satterlee and those afflicted were removed from the general wards to hospitals for smallpox victims, several miles from the city. "From November 1864 until May 1865 we had upward of ninety cases," states a journal kept by the sisters.

> We had, I may say, entire charge of the poor sufferers, as the physician who attended them seldom paid them a visit, but allowed us to do anything we thought proper for them . . . They often said it was the sisters who cured them and not the doctors, for they believed they were afraid of the disease. Our smallpox patients appeared to think that the sisters were not like other human beings or they could not attend such loathsome contagious diseases, which everyone else shunned. One day I was advising an application to a man's face for poison— he would not see one of the doctors, because, he said, the doctor did him no good—and I told him this remedy had cured a Sister who was poisoned. The man looked at me in perfect astonishment. "A sister!" he exclaimed. I answered yes. "Why," said he, "I didn't know the sisters ever got anything like that." I told him "To be sure they did. They are liable to take disease as well as anyone else." "To be sure *not!*" he said, "For the boys often say they must be different from other people, for they do for us what no other persons do. They are not afraid of fevers, smallpox, or anything else."[17]

Wheeling Hospital in West Virginia operated by the Sisters of St. Joseph [3830], whose motherhouse was located in the same city, was another hospital converted to military purposes during the war. In this border-state environment, the sisters used one wing of their hospital for both Union soldiers and Confederate prisoners who were received as private patients. By April 1864 the hospital was designated as a military hospital; at that point the sisters were hired as military nurses. In July of that year two hundred wounded arrived; rows of blankets were spread on the floor to receive these latest patients and the sisters moved their own belongings to the chapel. Sister Ignatius Farley recalled:

> As I opened the door of our temporary dormitory, I stood fascinated by the picture before me. In the dim light afforded by the small, perpetual flame of the sanctuary lamp which flickered in the temporary chapel just beyond the glass panels of the folding doors, I beheld my sisters—all seven of them— lying on the floor fast asleep. Each weary head rested on a pillow made of a coffee sack stuffed with leaves gathered from the hospital grounds.[18]

Often makeshift military hospitals were set up near the location of army camps or near battle sites. On February 15, 1862, the Sisters of Charity of Cincinnati received a request to manage military hospitals in Cumberland, Maryland. These "hospitals" were twelve converted hotels and warehouses spread over a three-mile area. Eight sisters set out from Cincinnati to look after thirty-two hundred soldiers suffering from typhoid, scurvy, and pneumonia. The soldiers were "unable to comprehend the devotedness, zeal, and unwearying patience of the sisters," reported the *Catholic Telegraph*. "The cleanliness of the hospitals, the improvement in the patients, the great changes for the better . . . are subjects of general remark by the patients."[19]

By June the army had moved on to New Creek; so too did the sister-nurses. After a month, all moved again to Culpepper Court House and then to Gallipolis, Ohio. This experience of following the army was also a common one for the Daughters of Charity in both Union- and Confederate-held territory. From Richmond, where the sisters staffed several hospitals they were sent on duty to various Southern battlefields. When they arrived at Manasses in August 1862 five hundred patients were waiting for them. "The wards of the temporary hospital were in a most deplorable condition and resisted the efforts of the broom, to which they had long been strangers. It was finally discovered that the aid of a shovel was necessary."[20] The Battle of Antietam (Sharpsburg, Maryland) the following month left twenty-four thousand casualties. The fighting covered a twelve- to fifteen-mile area and the sisters spent six days among the wounded.

> During the time the sisters remained on the battlefield they went from farm to farm trying to find those who were in most

danger. The sisters were in constant danger from bombshells which had not exploded and which only required a slight jar to burst. The ground was covered with these and it was hard to distinguish them while the carriage wheels were rolling over straw and dry leaves. The farms in the vicinity were laid to waste.[21]

As territories in Virginia and Maryland changed hands between the opposing armies, the Daughters of Charity continued to minister, irrespective of political or religious persuasion. They ministered in a litany of locations. In addition to cities and battlefields, they were present on the transports. "They were in the lower cabins which were lighted all day by hanging lamps or candles; the ceiling was very low; the space between the men's beds was so narrow that it allowed room only for one to stand or kneel."[22]

No situation was more brutal than the one experienced for three consecutive days beginning July 1, 1863, at Gettysburg, Pennsylvania. The bloodiest and longest battle of the war, it occurred just seven miles from the Daughters of Charity Provincial House in Emmitsburg. By the battle's end every large building in Gettysburg had been converted to a makeshift hospital; at least one hundred thirteen "hospitals" were used to nurse the more than thirty-five thousand wounded. Carrying supplies and food, the sisters were dispatched from Emmitsburg to assist in the enormous task of assuaging suffering. So few surgeons were available that many of the men received their first dressing from the sisters. Just as on the battlefield, where they tore up their petticoats for bandages when the supply ran out, the sisters offered every support—physical, psychological, spiritual—that they could. In one instance after a sister who was praying with a dying man began to prepare the corpse, a nearby soldier asked, "Was this man her relative?" "No," was the reply, "but she is a Sister of Charity." "Well," said one of the company, "I have often heard of the Sisters of Charity, and I can now testify that they have been properly named."[23]

If carnage created heroism in the eastern campaigns of war, the battles waged in the Mississippi Valley called forth the same kind of dedicated services. Thus, to Camp Dennison, seven Sisters of Charity were sent as early as May 1861 "to attend the sick soldiers" since "the worst form of measles had broken out among them and they needed immediate attention."[24] In Indianapolis, a military hospital was set up in May 1861 when the governor of Indiana acquired the service of the Sisters of

Providence [3360] of St. Mary-of-the-Woods for nursing purposes. As in Ohio, the first crisis was a measles epidemic followed by bouts with typhoid and pneumonia. Success in overcoming this crisis went to Sister Athanasius, the director, who oversaw the initial clean-up the building. She saw it as her objective to keep the hospital as sanitary as possible. To this end, she often met arriving flatboats carrying the contagious cases or visited these "separated brothers" at camps outside the city. She kept a room at the entrance to the hospital, her "fumigation station" she called it, and took every precaution not to carry contagion into the hospital upon her return. All these efforts were often accomplished in a climate of bigotry and suspicion; pamphlets appeared almost daily at the patients' bedsides detailing the evils of convent life.

In addition, two sisters took charge of an emergency hospital in Vincennes for several months. At the same time plans to open a temporary hospital in Terre Haute did not materialize due to prejudice against using the sisters as nurses.

In Kentucky, it was Bishop Martin J. Spalding who allowed the Sisters of Charity of Nazareth [0500] to do their share. As a result, twenty-three sisters worked in three large makeshift hospitals in the Louisville area for the entire course of the war. As Kentucky became a battleground in 1861 and 1862, these sisters responded to every request, ministering to Northern and Southern troops alike. They eventually served in a variety of areas of Kentucky, from Lexington all the way to the western tip of the state. When an army officer asked whether the sisters favored the North or the South, a Negro woman who worked as a domestic in the hospital set the matter in order: "De sisters dey ai't for de Noff nuh de Souf, deys for God."[25]

The Cincinnati area supplied its share of military hospitals to the cause. Cincinnati based, the Franciscan Sisters of the Poor [1440] and the Sisters of Mercy [2570], both newly arrived in this country, responded immediately. The Sisters of Mercy rented part of their convent so that it could be used by military authorities. The Franciscans assigned four sisters to the marine hospital in the city and converted their own hospitals in the area to military purposes. The locally based Sisters of Charity cared for wounded soldiers at St. John's Hospital. All of these hospitals were filled beyond capacity throughout the war. So close were they to the war arena that the sisters serving here witnessed suffering firsthand, experienced much hardship and deprivation, and came face to face with the reality of wartime legislation against the enemy. Sister Agnes Phillips reflected in her war diary:

It was here [at St. John's] that I witnessed the most appalling sights: men wanting arms, or legs, or both; pale, haggard faces, worn out with fasting and marching. We cared for Unionist and Confederates alike, we knew no difference, made no difference. The streets of this now flourishing city witnessed extreme suffering and misery. Frequently fine young men, seated on their own coffins, passed through on their way to execution on some neighboring hillside.[26]

As the military was laying the groundwork for their campaign, so too did the cities and states that lay in the path of the armies of the western front prepare for war's effects. In St. Louis, the task fell to the Daughters of Charity; in Jefferson City charge rested upon the capable shoulders of the Sisters of Mercy [2570]. The Dominican Sisters [1070] from Nashville who were serving in Memphis became involved at the Hospital of the Southern Mothers in November 1861. Until 1862, when General William T. Sherman occupied the city and pitched his tents on the grounds of the convent, the Southern wounded were continually brought into the hospital established there.

The Sisters of the Holy Cross from Notre Dame, Indiana, responded to a request for nurses from the governor of Indiana. From October 1861 to the close of the war, Holy Cross Sisters served the sick and wounded in Illinois, Indiana, Missouri, Kentucky, and Tennessee.

One of these locations, the Mound City Hospital was typical of many of these temporary sites. It was described by Sister Ferdinand as

a large unfinished block of twenty-four unfinished warehouses, which the government converted into commodious quarters . . . There were as many wards as there are letters in the alphabet . . . At times there were from a thousand to fourteen hundred patients under treatment, many of the sick being prisoners of war.[27]

As the campaign of 1862 began, the work of the sisters consisted in "nothing but dressing wounds from morning till night. On an average there were seven or eight deaths every day."[28] There were few sisters and many demands. Physical privations were the order of the day. Mother Angela Gillespie's dedication and administrative ability gained for the Mound City Hospital the reputation as the best military hospital in the United States. It was while visiting her that author Mary Livermore remarked, "The world has known no nobler and more heroic women than those found in the ranks of the Catholic sisterhoods."[29]

Service on the hospital boat *Red Rover* from 1862 until the close of the war brought the Holy Cross Sisters the recognition of being pioneers of a second branch of service, Navy Nursing Corps. Transporting casualties from the battlefields to the hospitals, they worked for fifty cents per day, ten cents more than army nurses received.

Gettysburg's counterpart was on the Mississippi-Tennessee border where in April 1862 one of the most severe military engagements on the western front was fought, the Battle of Shiloh; there were over twenty-three thousand casualties in this major conflict. Even the weather contributed to the misery. A cold drizzling rain followed by blinding hail and sleet left many wounded on the field of battle without even a blanket to shield them. Most were evacuated on hospital boats on the Tennessee River. These "floating hospitals" arrived from Memphis, St. Louis, Pittsburgh, and Cincinnati; somehow carrying as many as seven hundred wounded they made numerous trips up and down the river. Sister Theodosia, a Sister of Charity, recalls, "our boat's deck looked like a slaughter house—wounded everywhere! . . . There seemed to be scores of wounded and dying. I have seen Dr. Blackman cut off arms and limbs by the dozen and consign them to a watery grave."[30] Sister Anthony O'Connell commented,

> The Sisters of Charity went to the war as nurses but it sometimes fell to their lot to be assistant surgeons. After the Battle of Shiloh the young surgeons went off on a kind of lark, as they called it, to prevent blue mol. I became Dr. Blackman's assistant in the surgical operation. He expressed himself well pleased with the manner in which I performed this duty and indeed I was well pleased to be able to alleviate in any degree the suffering of these heroic souls.[31]

In another place she comments, "What we endured on the field of battle whilst gathering up the wounded from among the dead is simply beyond description. The battlefield of Shiloh presented the most frightful and disgusting sights it was ever my lot to witness."[32]

This remarkable woman received many accolades due to her work in the war. An eyewitness of this battle said of her:

> Amid the sea of blood she performed the most revolting duties for those poor soldiers. Let us follow her as she gropes her way

among the wounded, dead, and dying. She seemed to me like
a ministering angel, and many a young soldier owes his life to
her care and charity. Let us gaze at her again . . . as she picks
her steps in the blood of these brave boys administering cor-
dial or dressing wounds.[33]

Several congregations responded to the horrors of this battle. The
Chicago Sisters of Mercy served on the steamboat *Empress,* which
worked out of St. Louis. The Dominicans from Memphis cared for
many casualties; the Sisters of Mercy from Pittsburgh sent two vessels.
On other floating hospitals out of Cincinnati came Franciscan Sisters of
the Poor, Sisters of Charity, and Cincinnati Sisters of Mercy. The latter
were assisted by laywomen but, when smallpox broke out among the
soldiers, they became so terrified that they quickly withdrew leaving
the sisters alone in their labor of mercy. When the disease became
especially severe, Mother Teresa Maher is said to have "reserved for
herself the most repulsive offices."[34]

Simultaneous with the Battle of Shiloh was the naval move planned by
Flag Officer David Farragut up the Mississippi from New Orleans in the
Union's two-pronged move to divide the Confederacy geographically. As
the gunboats moved upriver, cities and towns fell under the control of the
Union. The Daughters of Charity hospital in New Orleans cared for
hundreds of sick and wounded on both sides while the Sisters of Our
Lady of Mount Carmel [0400] responded with an emergency hospital at
Thibodaux, Louisiana. After these battles, the Cincinnati Sisters of
Charity followed the army first to Corinth, then to Richmond, Ken-
tucky, on to Murfreesboro and then to Nashville, Tennessee, where they
remained working in General Hospital 14 until July 1865.

The Dominicans at St. Catharine, Kentucky, found the war at their
doorstep when the Confederate army thrust into Kentucky in the fall of
1862. Their guesthouse was used successfully as headquarters by opposing officers. After the Battle of Perrysville, Kentucky, in October, the
same sisters went to the battlefield; moreover they turned their convent
into a military hospital.

There are two decisive campaigns in the west that marked the turning
point for Northern victory. One was Grant's move, in 1863, against
Vicksburg, the last remaining Confederate stronghold on the Mississippi
River. After surrounding the city, he instituted a six-week seige that
resulted in its surrender on July 4. During this terrible experience which
affected residents of that city as well, the Sisters of Mercy, who had

established a convent there only a few years before, took charge of the sick and wounded and offered their convent as a hospital. They traveled with the retreating Confederate army, nursing "the sick and wounded at Mississippi Springs, Oxford, Jackson, and Shelby Springs, removing as the enemy approached."[35] At approximately the same time, while the city of Galveston, Texas, was under seige, the Ursuline sisters [4110] from Galveston offered their monastery and assistance to the wounded.

The second 1863 western campaign was an energetic Union move against the Confederate army at Chattanooga, Tennessee. In late September the two armies met at Chickamauga, just across the Georgia border from Chattanooga, in one of the most savage battles of the war, leaving thirty-eight thousand casualties. Despite a spirited Confederate effort, the Union army prevailed and solidified its hold on Tennessee.

As in the eastern campaign, the Northern successes of 1863 sealed the fate of the South. The following year saw General Sherman's move into Georgia and his famous march to the sea. From there he pushed north through the Carolinas toward Virginia where surrender was already occurring. On April 9, 1865, Lee surrendered his troops to Grant at Appomattox Court House, in Virginia. In both eastern and western campaigns from skirmishes to the fiercest battles, congregations of religious women were ready to do their share for the sick and wounded.

Many tributes were paid to the sister-nurses who served in the Civil War. From journalists and civic leaders to the simple and sincere thanks extended by the veterans themselves, the work of the sisters was publicly lauded. Captain Jack Crawford, a Civil War veteran, in a speech delivered after the war, summarized his feelings: "On all God's green and beautiful earth there are no purer, no nobler, no more kindhearted and self-sacrificing women than those who wear the somber garb of Catholic sisters."[36]

Following their heroic work, the sisters returned to the more normal routine of their ministries of mercy and justice. It was some thirty years before American sisters were again called upon to assist in the midst of war.

Wartime Service in the 1890s and After

During the 1890s the United States became involved in another war, this one of an entirely different character than the Civil War. At this time the nation became entangled in the Caribbean area, when dreams of building a canal and being a two-ocean power were emerging. European interest or control in the area were a major stumbling block to moving forward. Tension was high between Spain and the United States both over domestic conditions that existed in the Spanish colony of Cuba, and as a result of U.S. ambitions in the area. Several incidents occurred in early 1898 that resulted in a declaration of war by Congress on April 25. Within ten weeks the hostilities were over and victory was assured in what Theodore Roosevelt referred to as "the splendid little war." The U.S. had taken Cuba, Puerto Rico, and the Philippines from Spain and the Spanish colonial presence was removed from the Western hemisphere.

As at the outbreak of the Civil War, the United States Army was unprepared. Their forces consisted of sixteen thousand men; there were no plans, equipment, or supplies in readiness. During April and May 1898 two hundred thousand volunteers enlisted. Of these, no more than thirty-five thousand left the United States. The rest sat out the war in military camps. The military engagements of the war were minimal and those slain in combat or killed by wounds represented only 12 percent of the deaths resulting from this war. It was only after the close of the war that the major losses began to mount due to disease, mainly typhoid, malaria, and dysentery. In fact, 80 percent of the deaths from disease were attributed to typhoid. Disease in the army camps was so rampant that by August, 30 percent of the army's total strength had been struck by illness, a figure that had been increasing steadily since May.

At the outbreak of hostilities, army nursing was done entirely by members of the Hospital Corps. As in the past, there was resistance to using female nurses. Early in the conflict, however, Congress authorized the employment of contract nurses; both men and women could apply. Immediately women responded: the government received almost one thousand applications during the first month of conflict. On April 28, the National Society of the Daughters of the American Revolution offered to establish an examining board of female nurses. Dr. Anita Newcomb McGee and Miss Ella Lorraine Dorsey were placed in charge of the effort. They established the criteria that any nurses hired were required to be graduate nurses and take an oath of allegiance to the United States. They would receive thirty dollars remuneration per month. Interviews were conducted, and on May 10 contracts were signed with the first group of six army nurses. Before the episode was over approximately fifteen hundred women served in a volunteer corps which would soon develop into the Army Nursing Corps.

In an effort to expand the number of qualified nurses, Ella Lorraine Dorsey wrote to the superiors of several women's religious congregations asking for volunteers and enclosing qualification slips. In her letter she specified that sisters with hospital experience would be accepted despite their lack of formal credentials. Immediately the Daughters of Charity, the Sisters of the Holy Cross from Notre Dame, Indiana, the Sisters of St. Joseph of Carondelet from St. Louis, and the Sisters of Mercy of Baltimore volunteered. Eventually, the Daughters of Charity provided nearly two hundred sister-nurses out of approximately three hundred sisters who participated. Dr. Nicholas Senn, an army doctor who served during the war, gives this testimony:

> The Sisters of Charity stood in the front rank of volunteer nurses in the Spanish War . . . President McKinley became familiar with their efficient and faithful services during the Civil War, and gladly accepted the offer of the order to furnish nurses, made soon after the war broke out. All of the principal hospitals in charge of the Sisters of Charity sent representatives to the front. They were on duty in nearly all of the National Camps, in Cuba and Puerto Rico.[37]

Ironically, the first sisters to offer their services in the Spanish-American War were not actually nurses, but teachers. In April 1898, Sister Mary Florentine, superior of the Sisters of the Holy Name of Jesus and Mary [1990] at the Holy Name Convent of Mary Immaculate in Key West, Florida, offered the U.S. commander there the use of their convent and two school buildings. In addition, she offered the services of the sisters as nurses. Both were accepted and as the work of preparation for the war moved forward, medical stores and equipment were shipped to the convent. In order to professionalize their preparation for receiving patients, the twenty sisters attended a series of lectures on nursing. In addition, four trained nurses were assigned to direct the nursing efforts. On July 4, the Spanish fleet was destroyed at Santiago, Cuba. The next day casualties began to arrive in Key West. Initially the nurses had three hundred men in their charge; in all they cared for more than six hundred sick and wounded. One soldier, Mason Mitchell, who had been wounded in the Battle of San Juan was most fervent in his praise:

> I feel that I owe my life to the kindness and good care of the nuns in the hospital at Key West. Words fail me when I try to express my admiration for those noble women who devote their lives so unselfishly to the care of their fellow creatures who are in distress.[38]

The aftermath of the destruction of the Spanish fleet in Santiago harbor was felt in other areas of the U.S. also. In early July sixteen hundred Spanish prisoners of war arrived at the Portsmouth, Virginia, naval yard. The wounded and sick were taken to the naval hospital. The first Daughters of Charity to serve were sent from the central house in Emmitsburg, Maryland, upon a request from the chief surgeon. These five sisters were to be the night nurses at the hospital. They were given entire charge from six o'clock in the evening until six o'clock the following morning. Sister Victorine, one of the Spanish-speaking sisters, recalled an interesting aspect of her experience:

> As I was about to enter my ward on the first night, I was met by a nurse who told me that the Spanish soldiers had been swearing almost continuously. I listened and much to her surprise I said, "They are praying." En el nombre del Padre, y del Hijo y del Espiritu Santo. Amen. A hush fell over the place soon to be followed by, "Madre, Madre" as many of the prisoners wept for joy. They were delighted to see the sisters and to know that they would be with them during the night. Some of them wanted to go to Confession, but I told them that I could not hear confessions. "Tell God that you are sorry and wish to be forgiven and I will tell Him also."[39]

In the aftermath of this "splendid little war," the need for nursing service actually increased. Fort Thomas, Kentucky, was a site where hundreds of sick soldiers were cared for between August 1898 and February 1899. Twenty Daughters of Charity worked there. Typical of the telegrams received by Mother Mariana at Emmitsburg are the following two concerning camps at Montauk Point, Long Island, and Chickamauga, Georgia, two of the largest government facilities of this period. At Montauk Point over twenty thousand patients were handled; at Chickamauga there were three times that many.

Aug. 18, 1898
Washington, D.C.   1:35 p.m.

To Mother Mariana
St. Joseph's

Send thirty sisters immediately to Montauk Point, also order seven from New Orleans to Montauk, immediately.

Anita Newcomb McGee[40]

Aug. 20, 1898
Washington, D.C.   1:30 p.m.

To Mother Mariana
St. Joseph's

By order of the Surgeon General send nine sisters to Chickamauga immediately. Report to surgeon commanding Stern-
berg Hospital there taking this telegram with them.

Anita Newcomb McGee[41]

Sister Perboyce, a Daughter of Charity, wrote on August 25 describing Camp Wikoff:

The whole place is white with tents. Each sister has charge of
a tent, and there are forty-eight or fifty patients in each. I am
on night duty, and happy am I. I have a whole tent to myself.
A tent is called a ward . . . There are so many sick, but all are
so good, so patient . . . I am taking temperature, pulse, respi-
ration, getting drinks, administering hypodermics, and spong-
ing all night . . . All our sisters are equally busy. We hardly see
one another all day, each is so busy in her ward . . . All are so
kind to us, and we are very comfortable.[42]

Eventually one hundred twelve Daughters of Charity served here in
August and September 1898. They were put in charge of the "annex"
hospital, which eventually became larger than the "central" hospital, as
well as two wards in the general hospital. In addition, an operating tent
was erected and placed in working order with the assistance of two
Daughters of Charity and Acting Assistant Surgeon Greenleaf.[43] One of
the surgeons at the camp, Dr. S. P. Kramer observed,

Sisters do good work. There is with them no bickering with the
ward doctor, no fussiness, no refusing to perform menial work
when necessary, no desire to "shine" as is the case with the
"trained nurses." The Sister of Charity has no ambition but
duty; she obeys all orders quietly, with a prompt, orderly, and
willing manner. No sacrifice is too great, no service too menial. It has been a matter of general comment here that the
annex is a far superior hospital to the main branch, and in my
mind this is largely due to the presence of the Sisters of Charity
in the former.[44]

Camp Thomas at Chickamauga, Georgia, was the largest established during the war. Hundreds of typhoid cases were treated there. At first the sisters were excluded from the camp, but as the number of patients increased, authorities called upon the Daughters of Charity and Sisters of Mercy from Baltimore. The eleven Sisters of Mercy were sent to the third division hospital where they found appalling sanitary conditions. "There was an abundance of medical supplies, but no order or system prevailed in their distribution. The diet for patients was good; but was served most unpalatably."[45]

The Sisters of the Holy Cross also rendered excellent service during the Spanish-American War. Six sisters were called to Camp Hamilton, in Lexington, Kentucky, September 7, 1898. In her memoirs Sister Emerentiana describes the scene:

> About one o'clock we reached the camp . . . Some of the soldiers told us afterwards that our entrance into the hospital grounds was the most beautiful sight they ever saw; but the reality of what we were facing dawned on us at the sight of the long rows of tents, and so we did not feel fine at all . . . Not much preparation had been made for our coming . . . We were introduced to Major Stewart, who placed us in charge of the Typhoid Ward, containing over fifty patients, most of them very ill . . . We learned there were over six hundred sick, who were in tents all around us . . . The sisters went to the wards immediately after breakfast (six o'clock in the morning) and stayed till ten at night, barely taking time for their meals . . . Between ministrations, they wrote letters for the men.[46]

Within a few days, more Holy Cross Sisters arrived. Sisters of St. Joseph of Carondelet and Daughters of Charity also shared the work. "Doctor Hawkins said that he was amazed in the improvement in his patients since the sisters had come," reported Sister Emerentiana. Confidently she added that one of the officers told "the general that one sister was worth two hundred new men nurses . . . The work was hard, even disgusting, if one allowed nature to speak, but all worked willingly."[47] In the course of their service some of the sisters succumbed to typhoid and malaria and were taken to St. Joseph Hospital in Lexington.

When Camp Hamilton was closed and the soldiers were moved farther south for the winter, the Holy Cross Sisters were transferred to Camp Conrad near Columbus, Georgia. Sister Emerentiana continues her account,

Two ambulances were at the station to convey us to the camp. We learned on our way that ten Sisters of Mercy from Knoxville, Tennessee had arrived the day before . . . Soon we were settled comfortably, though it was cold and rainy. We had two small "Dewey" stoves and an oil stove to heat the large dormitory in which we all slept.[48]

Through the fall of 1898 the sisters continually migrated from camp to camp: as one disbanded, they were assigned to others. The Daughters of Charity, particularly, had a wide range of service. Besides the camps already mentioned, they served in Huntsville, Alabama; Jacksonville, Florida, and Falls Church, Virginia. In Jacksonville, they were joined by four members of a congregation of American sisters who worked in the measles and mumps ward at Camp Libre.

In addition to their labors at camps in the United States, Daughters of Charity saw service in Cuba and Puerto Rico and on transport ships where they answered the surgeon general's request for "immune nurses" to go to Santiago, Cuba. Sister Aloysia describes their arrival:

We reached Santiago on the morning of the nineteenth of August. A tug came to the steamer for us . . . We were taken to the place where our five sisters awaited us and then all proceeded to the convent of the Sisters of Charity in Santiago. The sisters, who were Spanish, were preparing to leave and go back to Spain. They thought we had come to take charge of the hospital of Spanish prisoners—in other words, to take their places. But we told them no, that we were American sisters come to nurse our American soldiers who were so ill at Camp Siboney.[49]

In fact, the sisters never made it to Camp Siboney. The evening of their arrival they were informed that a transport was leaving the next day with sixteen hundred soldiers, thirteen hundred of whom were sick. These nurses were given charge of the sick. One of the sisters wrote of the journey,

We are busy enough on this great wide sea. We seldom stop, for our hands are full and you must not expect letters. The men are suffering from fever and many from bowel troubles . . . One poor man died today. Sister Fortunata and Aloysia knelt beside him, cheering him to the last. Tonight we will be on American soil.[50]

Nineteen Daughters of Charity were assigned to Ponce, Puerto Rico, where they saw three months' duty nursing sick American soldiers stationed there. In a letter dated November 5, 1898, a Vincentian priest, Reverend L. Roura, comments, "as their labors were excessive and their privations many, two of the ten who came to attend the sick, fell dangerously ill and, the day before yesterday at 3 P.M., one of the two, Sister Mary Larkin, died."[51] Sister Mary was but one of five Daughters of Charity and one Sister of Mercy who gave their lives in this way.

The Daughters of Charity often served to boost morale. Hoping to provide some pleasure to the sick boys during the Christmas holidays, they

> procured some large banana leaves in which they cut out the words "Merry Christmas, Happy New Year." These were tacked around the walls. Knowing that a little extra at meals would not be amiss, Sister Raphael procured some condensed milk and eggs which she had made into a custard. Fortunately the government had erected an ice plant, so by means of an improvised freezer the boys had ice cream.[52]

Both Holy Cross Sisters and Sisters of St. Joseph of Carondelet worked in Cuba. In January 1899 some Holy Cross Sisters were ordered to go to Cuba on the transport *Panama*. They arrived in Matanzas only to have the same experience their counterparts had in Santiago a few months earlier. No sooner did they dock than they were informed that they were to return to the United States on the same transport because there were a sufficient number of Sisters of St. Joseph of Carondelet who could care for the sick.

The St. Joseph sisters set up a hospital in a large home which accommodated forty beds. One of the sisters contracted yellow fever and was quarantined. "She was put in a tent," recalled Sister Julitta, "erected on the roof of the house, and there she stayed for twelve days. We took her food up and left it at the door of the tent, but she would not let any of us get near her."[53]

In addition to service in the camps and abroad, some religious communities offered their hospitals for use by the government. A number of the Daughters of Charity hospitals cared for war victims, most notably, Providence Hospital in Washington, D.C., and St. Joseph's in Philadelphia. Others, like the sisters at Mercy Hospital in Baltimore, were never to have the opportunity, despite the fact that they were, as they wrote to the surgeon general, "willing to take charge."[54] The Sisters of Charity of Nazareth cared for pneumonia and fever victims at their infirmary near Chattanooga. Mother Annunciata of the Holy Cross Sisters sent letters to the governors of Indiana, Ohio, and Illinois offering the use of their hospitals in those states with the services of the sisters stationed there. Two sisters from Mount Carmel Hospital in Columbus, Ohio, responded to the request of the governor of Ohio to locate sick soldiers and accompany them home. In one instance they went on a thirty-coach train that started in Tampa and wound its way up through the South stopping at various camps. Another time they were assigned to a transport ship picking up thirteen hundred in Ponce, Puerto Rico.

The Sisters of St. Francis [1650] of Philadelphia also offered their hospitals for care of sick and wounded soldiers. St. Mary's and St. Agnes's were both utilized. Nearly five hundred soldiers were cared for at St. Agnes's. During a single night more than one hundred fifty ice baths were given to typhoid patients there.

Even during this brief war, the work of the sisters did not escape attention. One comment, in praise of the Daughters of Charity, could certainly apply to all the sisters who participated. Dr. L. Brechemin, surgeon at Chickamauga, wrote to Mother Mariana at Emmitsburg,

> I can hardly tell you in words strong enough how much of an assistance and comfort they have been to me—I worked hard for them and they did the same for me—never failed me. They took superb care of their patients. They helped me in every department of my hospital, and if it was a success a great part of the credit is due to them.[55]

By the time of the next United States military involvement, World War I, the Army Nursing Corps was well established and ready to respond. There was only one instance when sisters were able to serve as nurses with American troops. The organizer of United States Base Hospital 102, Dr. Joseph A. Danna had worked with the Daughters of Charity at Hôtel Dieu and Charity Hospital in New Orleans. In his new position, he asked that the nursing service in Washington be allowed to appoint these sisters as head nurses. Ninety other nurses appointed for this hospital came largely from training schools conducted by the Daughters of Charity in all parts of the United States. Early in July

1918, the nursing staff of the base hospital was mobilized for training. The sisters were permitted by special ruling to wear the dark blue cloth habit, white collar, and coronet of their order. They sailed from New York on August 4 on the Italian freighter *Umbria*, arriving at their destination Vicenza, Italy, on September 5. Their hospital, a converted school building, was fifteen miles from the firing line. Sara Babb, one of the nurses, described their situation in a letter:

> I shall never forget the opening of the great Italian drive. At midnight we heard the most terrific explosion . . . We have a great many medical cases, influenza, pneumonia, and gassed cases: since the offensive started, our surgical wards are filled and the operating rooms are busy . . . The roar of big guns is like thunder in a far-off storm . . . we are the nearest nurses to the Italian front![56]

Base Hospital 102 operated for seven months, until March 15, 1919, treating over three thousand patients. In her historical account of the hospital, Sister Catherine O'Rourke states,

> The food and fuel shortage was a real handicap, but it is also true that the U.S. Army Base Hospital 102 worked under conditions much more favorable than those of other hospitals in the vicinity. It was the only hospital in this section that had trained personnel and its equipment was far superior to that of similar institutions for many miles distant. Moreover, its nursing service was well organized: Sister Chrysostom was an efficient chief nurse and she had generous and capable assistants.[57]

With their work completed, the sisters and nurses sailed for home, arriving in New York on April 15, 1919. Another chapter in the history of sisters working in health services during times of war had been written.

Needless to say, hospitals sponsored by religious congregations also received patients from the military in less direct ways, and stood ready to cooperate in whatever way they could during both World War I and World War II. There are several instances in World War II where sisters' services were required in military situations, but no large-scale involvement was needed.

In summary, it is apparent that religious sisters' participation in wartime has been generous. In the Civil War, the most costly war in which the United States has ever been involved, there was an overwhelming response from religious congregations many of whom were in their own formative years at the time. When the outbreak of the Spanish-American War found the country militarily and medically unprepared for battle, religious responded willingly once again. This war saw the first steps in the organization of a permanent Army Nursing Corps. After that, the "Angels of Mercy" and "Sisters of Charity" relinquished their special wartime role. The nation was now prepared to meet its own needs in military conflicts. However, the record shows that religious women have a proud history "in times of war."

NOTES

1. George Barton, *Angels of the Battlefield* (Philadelphia: Catholic Art Publishing, 1897), p. 47.
2. Bill I. Wiley, *The Common Soldier of the Civil War* (Gettysburg, PA: Historical Times, 1973), p. 55.
3. Ellen Ryan Jolly, *Nuns of the Battlefield* (Providence, RI: Providence Visitor Press, 1927), p. 163.
4. Ibid., p. 245.
5. Barton, *Angels of the Battlefield*, pp. 6–7, quoting John R. G. Hassard, *Life of Most Rev. John Hughes, D.D.* (New York: Catholic Publishing, 1878).
6. Mary Ewens, *The Role of the Nun in Nineteenth Century America* (New York: Arno Press, 1978), pp. 207–8, quoting Sister Maria Kostkalogue, *Sisters of St. Joseph of Philadelphia* (Westminster, MD: Newman, 1950), pp. 121, 126.
7. Ibid., p. 231, quoting Mary Teresa Austin Carroll, *Leaves from the Annals of the Sisters of Mercy*, vol. 3 (New York: Shea, 1895), p. 163.
8. Ibid., p. 235, quoting Carroll, *Leaves from the Annals of the Sisters of Mercy*, vol. 3, p. 166.
9. Barton, *Angels of the Battlefield*, p. 16.
10. Jolly, *Nuns of the Battlefield*, pp. 288–89.
11. Ibid., p. 293.
12. Ibid., p. 161.
13. Barton, *Angels of the Battlefield*, pp. 209–10.
14. Ibid., p. 39.
15. Ibid., pp. 166, 167.
16. Sara Trainer Smith, ed., "Notes on Satterlee Military Hospital from 1862 until its close in 1865," *American Catholic Historical Society Records* 8 (1897): 401.
17. Ibid., pp. 405–6.
18. Jolly, *Nuns of the Battlefield*, pp. 174–75.
19. *Catholic Telegraph*, March 5, 1862, p. 72.
20. Barton, *Angels of the Battlefield*, p. 71.
21. Ibid., p. 78.
22. *Mother Regina Smith and Mother Ann Simeon Norris* (Emmitsburg, MD: St. Joseph's Provincial House, 1939), p. 104.
23. Barton, *Angels of the Battlefield*, p. 99.

24. Sister Anthony O'Connell, "Civil War Diary" (Mount St. Joseph, OH: Archives of the Sisters of Charity of Cincinnati).

25. Jolly, *Nuns of the Battlefield*, p. 7.

26. Sister Agnes Phillips, "Civil War Diary" (Mount St. Joseph, OH: Archives of the Sisters of Charity of Cincinnati).

27. Jolly, *Nuns of the Battlefield*, pp. 132–33.

28. Sister M. Eleanore, *On the Kings Highway: A History of the Sisters of the Holy Cross of St. Mary of the Immaculate Conception, Notre Dame, Indiana* (New York: D. Appleton, 1931), p. 235.

29. Barton, *Angels of the Battlefield*, p. 223.

30. Sister Theodosia Farn, "Civil War Diary" (Mount St. Joseph, OH: Archives of the Sisters of Charity of Cincinnati).

31. O'Connell, "Civil War Diary."

32. Ibid.

33. Barton, *Angels of the Battlefield*, pp. 43–44.

34. Sister Mary Eulalia Herron, *The Sisters of Mercy in the United States 1843–1928* (New York: Macmillan, 1929), pp. 228–29.

35. *Leaves from the Annals of the Sisters of Mercy*, vol. 4 (New York: P. O'Shea Publisher, 1895), p. 77.

36. Barton, *Angels of the Battlefield*, p. 225.

37. Nicholas Senn, *Medico-Surgical Aspects of the Spanish American War* (Chicago: American Medical Association Press, 1900), pp. 323–24.

38. George Barton, "A Story of Self-Sacrifice," *Records of the American Catholic Historical Researches* 37, no. 2 (June, 1926): 124.

39. Sister Victorine, personal interview at Emmitsburg, MD, November 27, 1947, quoted in Sister Gertrude Fenner, "The Daughters of Charity of St. Vincent de Paul in the Spanish-American War" (unpublished thesis, Villanova University, 1949), p. 15.

40. "Military Hospitals," vol. 1 (unpublished manuscript, St. Joseph Provincial House, Emmitsburg, MD, 1898), quoted in Fenner, "The Daughters of Charity of St. Vincent de Paul in the Spanish-American War," p. 39.

41. Ibid., p. 39.

42. Letter, Sister Perboyce to Sister Agnes, August 25, 1898, quoted in Barton, "A Story of Self-Sacrifice," pp. 164, 165.

43. Senn, *Medico-Surgical Aspects of the Spanish-American War*, p. 177.

44. Barton, "A Story of Self-Sacrifice," p. 167.

45. Sister Mary Loretto Costello, *The Sisters of Mercy of Maryland 1855–1930* (St. Louis: Herder, 1931), p. 146.

46. Eleanore, *On the King's Highway*, pp. 326–28.

47. Ibid., p. 330.

48. Ibid., p. 332.

49. Barton, "A Story of Self Sacrifice," p. 138.

50. Ibid., p. 140.

51. Rev. J. A. Harnett, CM, "United States, North America," *Annals of the Congregation of the Mission* 6 (1899):280, quoted in Fenner, "The Daughters of Charity of St. Vincent de Paul in the Spanish-American War," p. 50.

52. Fenner, "The Daughters of Charity of St. Vincent de Paul in the Spanish-American War," pp. 28–29.

53. *St. Paul Pioneer Press*, "Angels of Mercy in Black Robes," May 22, 1899.

54. Barton, "A Story of Self-Sacrifice," p. 108.

55. Letter, Dr. L. Buchemin to Mother Mariana, Sept. 27, 1898, quoted in Fenner, "The Daughters of Charity of St. Vincent de Paul in the Spanish-American War," p. 44.

56. Letter, Sara Babb to Miss Delano quoted in Lavina Dock, R.N., et al., *History of American Red Cross Nursing* (New York: Macmillan, 1922), pp. 671–72.

57. Sister Catherine O'Rourke, "Historical Account of the United States Base Hospital Unit 102" (unpublished manuscript, Marillac Provincial House Archives, St. Louis, 1946).

✦ In Times of Epidemic

DUNCAN NEUHAUSER

> It is in the time of stress and human suffering that the
> world learns to appreciate the sisters, but we of the
> household of the faith know that they are quietly doing
> this work day after day, ready to sacrifice themselves at
> any time for the love of Christ.
>
> Rt. Rev. John P. Farrelly, D.D.
> Bishop of Cleveland
> November 20, 1918

In 1975, it would have been almost impossible to describe to young Americans the terror of a nineteenth-century epidemic. With the recent appearance of AIDS, some of that fear can again be seen. Today, we hear of threats to families that inhibit them from sending their AIDS-infected children to school, and of doctors, nurses, and other health workers who refuse to treat such patients.

In times of epidemic, according to the written record, sisters put aside their daily routine work to go out into the world and help, sometimes at the sacrifice of their own lives. How did the sisters have the courage to help, not just once, but over and over?

There are four interrelated answers. The first is religious belief and mission, including care of the sick (Matthew 8:3). The second is the lack of immediate family responsibility. (A mother's first care is for her own children, and she does not leave her children uncared for to help others. A sister can replace that very focused love of immediate family with a diffused loving warmth for all people.) Third, there is the social and psychological support of the small group of like-minded people. Fourth, there is selection and self-selection of dedicated women who join congregations in order to serve. Together, these four characteristics explain the sisters' consistent role. Take any one away, and the sisters' role would not be the same.

69

The history of contagious disease and its treatment goes back to the time of Moses and the Old Testament, when the two most important measures of control were cleanliness and the isolation of patients with active disease. These two measures are still basic to the control of infection.

The history of epidemics in America can be divided into three periods. The first is the seventeenth and eighteenth centuries. Epidemic disease decimated the Indian population, making European settlement possible. Epidemic disease was frequent; often arriving by ship to American ports. Winter disease may have been made worse by problems of nutrition. Written description of epidemics and disease, from town records and diaries, were so poorly defined, that it is difficult today to tell what diseases were being described.[1] The toll of disease kept population growth slow, so that after two centuries of settlement, there were about two million people in 1800.

The second period begins in 1800, when Jenner's smallpox vaccination was first used in the United States of America. The medical profession became organized; medical schools were created; and medical knowledge improved, bringing clearer understanding of diseases, if not their cure. This era saw the start of the modern public-health movement. Local and state health departments were created, and the water and sewage systems of the larger cities were engineering and architectural wonders. By the end of the century, pure milk, better housing, sanitation, and fresh-air treatment for tuberculosis were being used.

The third era can be said to begin in 1900, when the debate over the miasmatic ("bad air") versus the contagious theories of disease was resolved.

The control over infectious disease is powerfully demonstrated by comparing the French Panama Canal Company's failure, in the 1880s, due to disease, and the success of the American effort in 1904–1914, when infectious disease was brought under control.[2] The introduction of X rays to several hospitals in the United States in 1896 (December 29, 1896 at Mercy Hospital in Pittsburgh),[3] and the introduction of aseptic surgery to control infection in 1876, resulted in a greater demand for hospital care. In 1873 there were about two hundred hospitals; by 1914 there were five thousand forty-seven hospitals.

Some infectious diseases have constantly been present, including tuberculosis, venereal disease, and the common cold. The epidemic diseases struck suddenly with little warning, stopped normal community life, ran their terrible and terrifying course, and disappeared.

The major epidemic diseases in the nineteenth century were smallpox, asiatic cholera, yellow fever, diptheria, variola minor (a milder version of smallpox), typhoid, and influenza.

Table 1 at the back of this chapter provides a chronology of major epidemics in the United States during the nineteenth century. This table could be misleading in two ways. First, it focuses on the larger cities. Epidemics were not limited to these places, although their effects were perhaps more visible and were more thoroughly documented. Second, the table lists only the more notable epidemics; minor outbreaks occurred constantly. Cities where sisters are reported to have played an active role in care are indicated, but this is only a partial list of the places where sisters cared for the sick. In many cases, sisters caught the infection and died as a result of caring for the sick.

Technological progress also changed the nature of infectious disease. In the eighteenth century, epidemic disease spread across land about as fast as a man could walk or ride. Crossing the seas could take months. Later with trains and steamships, disease spread more rapidly. This in part may explain the magnitude of this country's worst (in terms of numbers of deaths) influenza epidemic, in 1918–1919, which led to five hundred fifty thousand deaths in the United States and twenty million worldwide (some estimates say one hundred million).

In the twentieth century, more deaths have been due to heart disease, cancer, and stroke than to infectious disease. Progress was seen in the bringing of one infectious disease after another under control. The 1977 worldwide elimination of smallpox is surely a true landmark in human progress.[4] Polio, diphtheria, pertussis, and measles became preventable through immunization. In spite of this, these diseases have not been eliminated.

Overoptimism might have closed the books on epidemic disease in this century. But flu keeps changing, so that last year's innoculation may not stop next year's flu variant. Earlier optimism was undone with the arrival of AIDS, in 1981. Through the techniques of molecular biology, we know an extraordinary amount about AIDS, and also know there will be perhaps millions of deaths before there is a chance of its being stopped.

Following are some vivid examples of epidemics. The places, dates, diseases, and congregations differ, but a similar pattern prevails.

The cholera epidemic broke out in Philadelphia on July 5, 1832, and spread rapidly. By August, it reached Irish laborers working on the Pennsylvania Railroad track beyond Malvern. They were living in a nearby shack. Terrified neighbors refused assistance, except for an unknown blacksmith. When news of the men's plight reached Philadelphia, four Daughters of Charity [0760] volunteered nursing care. They drove out in a stage coach, but the driver refused to go any closer to the shack than Greentree. The sisters completed the journey on foot. Within a short period, seventeen railroad workers died and were buried there in an unmarked grave. On completion of their task, the sisters had to walk back to Philadelphia. They could find no one to drive them home: everyone admired the sisters' courage in caring for the stricken men, but all feared the sisters might have contacted cholera.

In 1832, at the Philadelphia almshouse, such was the appalling nature of the cholera that fear overcame every consideration.

> In one ward where the disease raged in all its horrors . . . the nurse and her attendants were in a state of intoxication, heedless of the groans of the patients and fighting over the bodies of the dying and the dead. . . . The few good nurses were broken down by loss of rest and fatigue, and the remainder abandoned the sick from fear of the disease.

These circumstances led the board of managers to ask for the Daughters of Charity to nurse the cholera patients. Thirteen sisters reponded to the appeal, and faced incredible conditions at the almshouse (later to become the Philadelphia Hospital).

In Baltimore in 1832, thirty-year-old Sister Mary Frances and nineteen-year-old Sister Mary George died of cholera, as a result of caring for the sick at the Cholera Hospital.[5] The mayor and city council set aside six hundred dollars to honor them with a monument "sacred to the memory of the Daughters of Charity . . . by the Corporation of Baltimore as testimonial for their benevolent services."A well-meaning physician had treated Sister Mary Frances with strong emetics and purges to induce vomiting, and with brandy and morphine. Steam treatments produced excruciating suffering. He recorded her intellect as clear; she died without a murmur. "Life's taper dies in its socket." With present medical knowledge and hindsight, we can see that the sisters' work of providing cleanliness, nourishing food, and humane comfort and solace did more for the health of patients than the too often harmful medication of the doctors in that age of "heroic medicine."

October 1832 saw the death of "Sister Antonina (colored), of the Order of Oblates at Baltimore [3040], a victim of charity during the cholera." The Oblates were established in 1831 as the Sisters of Providence in Baltimore, Maryland, "a religious society of colored women."

Epidemics were frequent in Pittsburgh when the Sisters of Mercy [2570] opened their Mercy Hospital there in 1848. The streets were unpaved, and muddy in bad weather. Hogs, rats, and dogs had the run of the city. Good drinking water was scarce. Some people had wells, while others had tanks in their backyards, which were filled with water purchased from vendors who peddled the water in barrels from door to door. The slum areas had no adequate sewage disposal. Tuberculosis and typhus were prevalent. The deadly type of typhus fever, known as ship-fever, appeared early in 1848 and continued to rage through the spring and summer. Night and day the sisters hung over the unfortunate sufferers. Because so many sisters died (including Sister M. Xavier Tierman, on March 8, 1848), the hospital had to be closed for two months.

There were cholera epidemics in Pittsburgh in 1849 and 1854. The 1854 cholera epidemic was particularly severe and the number of victims brought to the hospital was so great that it was impossible to provide a sufficient number of beds. The sisters relinquished theirs, since they were not using them. Their services were required night and day, and whatever rest they could get was taken in a chair. Patients were placed on mattresses on the floor when no better accommodations were available. During this time, the male attendants fled in panic. The only man who remained was a carpenter who made the hospital's coffins.

During the winter of 1872, the city of St. Louis was plagued with poverty and disease. The mortuary tables printed each week gave evidence of the extent and virulence of the disease. However, they did not show that this epidemic was confined, almost exclusively, to the most crowded, filthy, and squalid section of the city.

It was here that the Sisters of St. Mary of the Third Order of St. Francis (now known as Franciscan Sisters of Mary [3970]) went to nurse the smallpox patients on the day after their arrival in St. Louis. The sisters found it necessary to search their clothing for bedbugs and other vermin before going home from a day at the riverfront. In 1872 there were 3,789 cases of smallpox; of these 1,591 died.

There was a poor understanding of various types of infection. After the epidemic of smallpox in 1882, this misunderstanding worked a hardship on the Sisters of St. Francis of Perpetual Adoration [1640] of Mishawaka, Indiana, for many years people were afraid of them. The city had many red flags placed on the grounds about the hospital to warn people to stay away. The priest was strictly forbidden to say Mass at the church or hospital, but each morning he secretly brought Holy Communion to the Sisters.

After the epidemic of 1882, everything was burned—beds, bedding, and clothing—even the plaster was taken from the walls and replaced at great expense. The county in turn gave new beds and supplies to replace those that had been burned.

In 1890 an epidemic of smallpox broke out in Houston, and lasted until April 1891. All persons found with the disease were immediately sent to the city pesthouse, which was located in an old cemetery. The people were in such dread of the disease that few could be found who were willing to look after the patients. The Sisters of Charity of the Incarnate Word [0470] secured permission from Bishop Gallagher to nurse in Houston. The sisters knew the dangers they were facing. They were trained in bedside nursing and cared for patients in previous epidemics. All the sisters volunteered to go, and three were selected: Sister M. Angelique Aherne, Sister M. Andrew Bonjour, and Sister M. Ursula Haugh. These three sisters lived at the pesthouse while the epidemic lasted. Their main religious sustenance during this period was the Blessed Sacrament, brought to them thrice weekly by Father Hennessey.

The pesthouse became so overcrowded that tents had to be put up to accommodate patients. The sisters were on duty twenty hours daily, and the four hours allotted for rest were frequently interrupted. It was impossible to get more help; no one could be induced, at any price, to serve. Everyone was so busy during the day that burial of the dead had to be done at night. The gravediggers worked by the light of lamps held by the sisters; the latter often acted as stretcher bearers of the smallpox victims.

After the epidemic was over, the mayor and city council unanimously adopted a proclamation thanking the sisters for their "timely and efficient services rendered without money and without price and amid scenes of desolation calculated to appall the stoutest heart." The sisters had risked their lives and proved themselves "veritable angels of mercy" among the stricken sufferers.

The Sisters of St. Joseph of Orange, California [3830], began their health services ministry in response to the 1919 influenza epidemic. The sisters did not have a hospital at the time, so they cared for the sick at home and at their convent and school. The sisters who were involved in caring for the sick noticed a decrease in prejudice toward the congregation after the epidemic.

* * *

Although the history of medicine focuses on the understanding, cure, and elimination of disease, the great amount of health-care work is related to the care of the sick. Yesterday, today, and probably tomorrow, most care is provided to people with diseases we cannot cure. When one disease, like smallpox, is stopped, we turn our attention to other diseases, like heart disease and cancer. The history of the sisters and epidemic disease is the history of caring. A frequent complaint about today's hospitals is that the lost art of caring has been drowned in an expensive sea of technology.

During the nineteenth-century epidemics, caring for the sick must have been terrifying in a way that we cannot understand today. The human tendency must have been to run from disease. Overcoming such an innate response is heroic by definition.

During an epidemic, sisters could lead a very active life, as is shown by the following correspondence, related to the 1897 yellow-fever epidemic in New Orleans, which infected about two thousand people and caused about three hundred deaths.

September 22, 1897, telegram to Mother Mariana, Daughter of Charity, in Baltimore from Sister Agnes, Charity Hospital, New Orleans:

"BOARD (of health) DECIDED TO OPEN BRANCH HOSPITALS FOR FEVER PATIENTS AT ONCE. SHALL NEED SISTERS, MAY WE BORROW FROM SOME OF OUR HOUSES. ANSWER".

Letter to Mother Mariana from Sister Agnes, September 24, 1897.

My very dear Mother;

The grace of our Lord be with us forever. Knowing the great anxiety our telegram must have caused you, I hasten a few lines of explanation.

The prevalent fever, each day, is gaining ground, and our Administrators judging it unwise to convert the Hospital into a Pesthouse, petitioned the Mayor to give them a building for this purpose, in some more isolated portion of the city. He accordingly placed at their disposal a school house located on Canal Street. Board employees removed the furniture and at the same time, several furniture wagons were engaged in transferring beds, furniture, etc. from here; our carpenters are putting them up, and our girls are cleaning up and helping. Patients, in different parts of the city, were to be moved there this morning.

Two of our Sisters had gone to look after the help and at five o'clock p.m. I went out to see how all was coming. Just about this time, a mob began to gather, lit fires and made speeches; a delegation waited on our poor little Dr. Bloom who was also on the premises, and after some threatening language, told him they were going to interview the Mayor, and if he failed to give them satisfaction, they could satisfy themselves.

They asked one favor however, of the Doctor, that he would see that the Sisters and all connected with the Hospital would vacate the premises for the night. Fortunately, my dear Mother, no patients had yet arrived. Had they, the Sisters would have remained with them, but our arrangements had been made for this morning to go out under the protection of Our Lady of Mercy.

On leaving there last night (eight o'clock), we sprinkled the building with holy water, sticking the Miraculous Medal in many a crevice. At twelve o'clock the mob set fire to the place, several times cutting the firemen's hose to prevent saving it, but the out-houses (Porters Lodge) only were burned, the schoolhouse proper is uninjured, except by the water.

This morning Mr. Ponder went to look after our bedding, etc. and one of the policeman on duty showed him the bottle on the mantel-piece saying "That must be *holy water*, no wonder they could not burn it down." There is nothing but the kindest feelings for our Sisters, the most excited even were very, very nice with us, only anxious that something might not happen while we were there. The bitterest feelings are entertained for the Board of Health.

Shall write you later, as I get news of what we are to expect. We are so grateful for the many prayers you are having offered for us, we need them all, and only hope our good God may avert from us the terrible scourge.

Our dear Sisters are all well at present, dear Sister Louise well also but not yet fit for duty.

With best love and begging a little remembrance for your children of the old Charity, I am, most devotedly in our All.

(signed) Sister Agnes Slavin

One of the saddest results of this epidemic was the almost complete stagnation of business and labor. Hundreds of the laboring class have not the necessaries of life.

1918–1919 Influenza

After ravaging Europe, the Spanish influenza spread throughout the United States. Among the first victims were the crews of the French cruisers *Marseillaise, Conde,* and *La Gloire* who were admitted to the French Hospital. Some of them were so ill, and weakened by fever, that they barely gave signs of life. Fifteen received the last sacrament but eventually recovered. The stricken arrived in such quick succession that a large conference hall had to be used as a public ward, and still there was not sufficient room to accommodate those who sought admission. A friend of the hospital put his villa at the service of the sisters, and the next day twenty-four convalescents were transported to Far Rockaway, then a summer residential section of Long Island. They were accompanied by two sisters.

The sisters had the consolation of seeing many patients return to the practice of their faith, and the neighboring residents themselves were edified at the sight of these men, regularly attending High Mass at the parish church.

The congregations were active in many places during the Spanish influenza epidemic of 1918–1919. This included army barracks filled with American soldiers returning from the World War I battlefields only to be attacked by influenza. As U.S. army chaplain John J. Donovan, SJ, wrote from the Jackson Barracks, New Orleans, on December 15, 1919, to Sister Eugenia,

> When it was impossible to get nurses at any price, and my own men dying for want of proper care *Sister Stanislaus* at Charity Hospital (New Orleans) sent 12 Sisters trained nurses *Gratis* and a number of *Aides* for both day and night in our five hospital buildings. Thus was relieved a chaotic condition that had become desperate. We are demobilizing here now with our faces turned north and home, but we shall take and keep with us in grateful hearts the memory of what the good *Sisters of Charity Hospital* did for us during these trying epidemic days at Jackson Barracks."

The newspapers of New Orleans said nothing about the great work of the Sisters during that crisis, but we want you to know that the generous self-sacrificing and noble service done by your Order was greatly appreciated and loudly praised by every officer and enlisted man at this post."

When the influenza struck the city of Pittsburgh, panic followed. Deaths were frequent, even several members of a family were ill at the same time. Immediately Mercy Hospital was filled to overflowing. In October schools were closed. This enabled the teaching sisters to visit the sick. Many went at night to care for the sick so members of a family who were able to work could get to work or if they were caring for the ill, they could get some rest. Three of the nursing sisters at Mercy Hospital [2570] died; two teachers succumbed to the dreaded disease. Several of the sisters contracted the disease but survived.

In the towns near Pittsburgh (Hays, McKees Rocks, Homestead, Youngwood, Greensburg, and Carnegie), the Sisters of Charity of Seton Hill [0570] staffed emergency hospitals.

In Homestead the poor living conditions of the local steel workers offered a rich harvest for the devastating plague. According to the recollections of a sister who nursed patients:

> In a short time the hospital was filled and a hotel was requisitioned to take care of the stricken of all classes and conditions. The ranks of trained nurses were so exhausted and people were dying in their homes without care. Early in October the schools and churches were closed and all assemblies of people were prohibited by law.

> Reverend Hugh C. Boyle (later Bishop of Pittsburgh) offered the town St. Mary Magdalens parochial school as an emergency hospital and the teaching staff of eighteen sisters took care of the sick. The Carnegie Steel Company erected three large tents as a field hospital each with sixty beds which were kept full. Two excellent Catholic nurses were sent from Boston to superintend the full hospital and several sisters assisted them.

> Other sisters continued the home nursing daily, distributing to the sick broth and other nourishment provided by Carnegie Steel Company and charitable persons. Not only did they nurse patients, they also did duty as laundress, cook, and housekeeper. All found demands they could meet.

By the end of November the scourge was over and teachers returned to school.

As the following letter shows, the Sisters were appreciated.

Sister Mary Lawrence
Seton Hill
Greensburg, Penn.

Dear Sister Mary Lawrence:

Your devoted attention during the past ten days administering to our employees shall never be forgotten. The dreaded disease which was then absorbing the lives of so many of our good citizens was materially, if not entirely, stopped through the prompt and efficient help rendered by your dear self and Sisters Angela, Francina, Hortense and Marcelline. We extend our sincere appreciation for your assistance given to us and in further appreciation, we enclosed herewith a check for $100.00.

> The Kelly Jones Co.
> Manufacturers of Iron Pipe
> Fittings Etc.
> Greensburg, Penn.
> November 6, 1918.

The Jamison Coal and Coke Company of Greensburg thanked the Sisters with a gift of $400.

AIDS

This infectious disease was first diagnosed in 1981 and named in 1983. By 1987, St. Clare's Hospital in Manhattan was probably the largest inpatient AIDS treatment center in the world. At that time New York City accounted for a third of all the AIDS cases in the United States. Sister Palma Buccelli, SCH [0640], took a half-hour out of her busy schedule at St. Clare's to talk to the author. She entered the Halifax Sisters of Charity fifty years ago in Halifax, Nova Scotia, and since then has cared for patients with polio and tuberculosis. She volunteered to work at St. Clare's along with sisters from several other orders.

Prisoners at Sing Sing with AIDS had a special unit at St. Clare's Hospital. At the prison the inmates collected five hundred dollars and entrusted this money to the sisters to help the prisoners with AIDS. Five hundred dollars is an enormous sum for prisoners who earn ten cents for a day's work. With some of this money Sister Palma had bought bargain-price doughnuts, which she was about to take to sick prisoners. She said that when she arrived, some of the hospital staff were refusing to enter the AIDS patients' rooms. The food trays would be put on the floor and pushed into the rooms. Sister Palma walked right into the patients' rooms and by her example other staff followed. She expressed her quiet satisfaction about a dying AIDS patient who admitted his long lapse of faith to her and asked to see a priest.

I asked if she was afraid of infection. She said in the calmest way that she had cared for patients with infectious diseases before—if she did not die of AIDS she would die of something else. "The Lord says when I am going to die."

Sister Palma said it was comforting to sit and rest her tired legs, but I felt she was eager to get back to her patients—patients who as both convicts and AIDS victims are surely among today's most rejected people.

After my reading of the sisters' efforts in other days and their care for those with now rare and forgotten diseases, Sister Palma brought all this history to life for me.

Across the country, other congregations are deciding how they can best care for AIDS patients. Ancilla Systems, Elk Grove Village, Illinois, announced plans to begin operating a program designed specifically to care for AIDS patients at home. The project is funded by grants from the Illinois Department of Health, the Washington Square Health Foundation, and the Provincial Council of the Poor Handmaids of Jesus Christ [3230]. It will be operational by April 1, 1988. With a budget of four hundred thirty thousand dollars for its first year and four hundred seventy thousand dollars for its second year the home support care project anticipates capability of caring for over one hundred AIDS patients per year.

The epidemics have changed but sisters continue to help today as they did in 1832.

NOTES

1. John Duffy, *Epidemics in Colonial America* (Baton Rouge: Louisiana State University Press, 1953).

2. David McCullough, *The Path between the Seas* (New York: Simon and Schuster, 1977).
3. Sister Jeanette Rafferty, "Mercy Hospital 1947–1972: An Historical Review," vol. 1 (Pittsburgh: Mercy Hospital manuscript, 1972), p. 83.
4. Donald Hopkins, *Princess and Peasants* (Chicago: University of Chicago, 1983).
5. Sister Bernadette Armiger, "Two Sister-Nurses Claimed by Cholera," *Nursing Outlook* (September 1964): 54–56.

Table 1: Partial List of Major American Epidemics after 1800

Years	OCD Codes	Congregation	Cities
1832–1845 Asiatic Cholera	[3040]	OBLATE SISTERS OF PROVIDENCE Baltimore, MD	Albany, NY
	[0510]	SISTERS OF CHARITY OF OUR LADY OF MERCY Charleston, SC	Charleston, SC
	[0500]	SISTERS OF CHARITY OF NAZARETH Nazareth, KY	Louisville, KY
1847–1848 Typhus	[2570]	SISTERS OF MERCY Pittsburgh, PA	Pittsburgh, PA
1849–1854 Cholera	[2570]	SISTERS OF MERCY Burlingame, CA	San Francisco, CA
	[0580]	SISTERS OF CHARITY OF ST. AUGUSTINE RICHFIELD, OH	Cleveland, OH
	[3840]	SISTERS OF ST. JOSEPH OF CARONDELET St. Louis, MO	St. Louis, MO
	[3840]	SISTERS OF ST. JOSEPH OF CARONDELET St. Paul, MN	St. Paul, MN
	[0480]	SISTERS OF CHARITY OF LEAVENWORTH Leavenworth, KS	Nashville, TN
	[2570]	SISTERS OF MERCY Pittsburgh, PA	Pittsburgh, PA
	[1960]	SISTERS OF THE HOLY FAMILY New Orleans, LA	New Orleans, LA
1852 Typhus	[0650]	SISTERS OF CHARITY OF ST. VINCENT DE PAUL Bronx, NY	New York, NY
1855 Yellow Fever	[1960]	SISTERS OF THE HOLY FAMILY New Orleans, LA	New Orleans, LA
1858 Smallpox	[1650]	SISTERS OF ST. FRANCIS OF PHILADELPHIA Glen Riddle-Ashton, PA	PA
1864 Yellow Fever	[0460]	SISTERS OF CHARITY OF THE INCARNATE WORD San Antonio, TX	Galveston, TX

Years	OCD Codes	Congregation	Cities
1866–1867 Yellow Fever	[0470]	SISTERS OF CHARITY OF THE INCARNATE WORK Galveston, TX	Galveston, TX
1870 Yellow Fever	[0500]	SISTERS OF CHARITY OF NAZARETH Nazareth, KY	KY
	[3840]	SISTERS OF ST. JOSEPH OF CARONDELET St. Louis, MO	St. Louis, MO
1871–1872 Smallpox	[0500]	SISTERS OF CHARITY OF NAZARETH Nazareth, KY	KY
	[1440]	FRANCISCAN SISTERS OF THE POOR Brooklyn, NY	KY
1873 Yellow Fever	[0500]	SISTERS OF CHARITY OF NAZARETH Nazareth, KY	Memphis, TN
1873 Cholera	[2570]	SISTERS OF MERCY Nashville, TN	Nashville, TN
1874–1876 Yellow Fever	[0500]	SISTERS OF CHARITY OF NAZARETH Nazareth, KY	Warrington, FL
1877–1878 Yellow Fever	[3900]	SISTERS OF ST. JOSEPH St. Augustine, FL	St. Augustine, FL
1878–1879 Yellow Fever	[0400]	CONGREGATION OF OUR LADY OF MT. CARMEL Lacombe, LA	Mississippi Valley
	[3840]	SISTERS OF ST. JOSEPH OF CARONDELET St. Louis, MO	Memphis, TN
	[3970]	SISTERS OF ST. MARY OF THE THIRD ORDER OF ST. FRANCIS (now Franciscan Sisters of Mary) St. Louis, MO	Memphis, TN
	[2570]	SISTERS OF MERCY Cincinnati, OH	Vicksburg, MI
1890–1892 Smallpox	[0470]	SISTERS OF CHARITY OF THE INCARNATE WORD Houston, TX	Houston, TX
1898 Cholera	[0500]	SISTERS OF CHARITY OF NAZARETH Nazareth, KY	Lexington, KY

Years	OCD Codes	Congregation	Cities
1899 *Cholera*	[0240]	OLIVETAN BENEDICTINE SISTERS Jonesboro, AK	AK
1900 *Diptheria*	[3320]	SISTERS OF THE PRESENTATION OF THE BLESSED VIRGIN MARY Fargo, ND	SD
1918–1919 *Spanish Influenza*	[0440]	SISTERS OF CHARITY OF CINCINNATI Mt. St. Joseph, OH	Albuquerque, NM Bay City, MI Cincinnati, OH Cleveland, OH Colorado Springs, CO Cripple Springs, CO Cumberland Mts., KY Dayton, OH Denver, CO Jackson, MI Lansing, MI Lima, OH Marion, OH Middletown, OH Primero, CO Springfield, OH Trinidad, CO Army Camps & Student Training Corps: Albuquerque, NM Chillicote, OH Cincinnati, OH Oxford, OH
	[3970]	SISTERS OF ST. MARY OF THE THIRD ORDER OF ST. FRANCIS	Blue Island, IL Kansas City, MO Madison, WI
	[2580]	SISTERS OF MERCY OF THE UNION	Cincinnati, OH Lima, OH Detroit, MI Tiffin, OH Toledo, OH Troy, NY Washington, DC
	[0580]	SISTERS OF CHARITY OF ST. AUGUSTINE	Cleveland, OH
	[0960]	DAUGHTERS OF WISDOM	Cleveland, OH
	[3230]	POOR HANDMAIDS OF JESUS CHRIST	Donaldson, IN

Years	OCD Codes	Congregation	Cities
	[1070]	DOMINICAN SISTERS OF GREAT BEND, KS	Great Bend, KS
	[0570]	SISTERS OF CHARITY OF GREENSBERG, PA	Greensberg, PA
	[2160]	SISTERS, SERVANTS OF IMMACULATE HEART OF MARY	Hollidaysburg, PA Scranton, PA Throop, PA
	[2410]	CONGREGATION OF MARIANITES OF THE HOLY CROSS	Merrill, WI
	[1680]	SCHOOL SISTERS OF ST. FRANCIS	Milwaukee, WI
	[4100]	SISTERS OF THE SORROWFUL MOTHER	Milwaukee, WI
	[2230]	CONGREGATION OF THE INFANT JESUS	New York, NY
	[3830]	SISTERS OF ST. JOSEPH OF ORANGE	Orange, CA
	[2060]	SISTERS OF THE MOST HOLY TRINITY	Philadelphia, PA
	[2570]	SISTERS OF MERCY	Pittsburgh, PA
	[1070]	DOMINICAN SISTERS OF SAN RAPHAEL, CA	San Raphael, CA
	[1820]	HOSPITAL SISTERS OF ST. FRANCIS	Springfield, IL
Army Camps Where Sisters Cared for Sick Soldiers			Fort Niagara, NY Gettysburg, PA Camp Meade, MD New Orleans, LA
	[3840]	SISTERS OF ST. JOSEPH	Lewiston, ID
	[2160]	SISTERS, SERVANTS OF THE IMMACULATE HEART OF MARY	Old Forge, PA

✦ IN TIMES OF IMMIGRATION

JUDITH G. CETINA

In his volume *American Catholics* James Hennesey includes a chapter with the title "Immigrants Become the Church"; it is not likely that another phrase could more aptly describe the emerging character of the Roman Catholic Church during the years 1820–1920. At the end of the American Revolution the church had a largely Anglo-American constituency with its fewer than twenty-five thousand members living in Maryland and Eastern Pennsylvania, employed as planters and farmers. By 1815 there were some one hundred thousand Roman Catholics in the United States, but over the next five decades church membership would grow to include over three million persons by the end of the Civil War. This swelling in the American church's ranks can be attributed to the tremendous number of Catholic immigrants who arrived on this country's shores. During the years prior to the Civil War these Catholic newcomers were predominantly Irish and German and their reasons for seeking a new home in America were multifold. Not a new feature on the American landscape, even in 1790 there were nearly four hundred thousand persons of Irish birth or descent then living in the United States. Although a significant part of this Irish contingent was Protestant, the group included a large number of Roman Catholics.[1] Conditions in nineteenth-century Ireland, including an agricultural economy unable to support an ever increasing population, and the country's dependence on the success of the potato crop, encouraged and eventually necessitated the exodus of massive numbers of the Irish from the Emerald Isle. During the years 1820–1840, over two hundred sixty thousand Irish came to America; and following the dramatic failure of the potato crop, with the resulting famine, more than one million people left Ire-

86

land between 1846 and 1851.[2] Perhaps most significantly for the history of the church, the new Irish immigrants were largely Roman Catholic.

Germany, too, experienced a dramatic increase in population during the nineteenth century and its agricultural system was not able to support the growing populace. The Industrial Revolution also impacted on the German economy as the factory system began to displace the skilled tradesman. Thus before the Civil War over one million Germans had arrived in the United States; and it is clear that a significant percentage of them were Roman Catholic.[3]

Although the decision to leave home and family could not have been an easy one, the immigrant faced a more significant challenge in the attempt to survive the voyage to the United States. The conditions that prevailed on most of the immigrant ships, including overcrowding, inadequate food supplies, and a lack of proper sanitation, were sufficient to weaken severely many immigrants and to make them even more susceptible to illness and disease. A United States Senate committee report dealing with sickness and mortality on these passenger vessels reported that:

> During the last four months of 1853, 312 vessels arrived at New York from European ports, with 96,950 passengers. Of these vessels 47 were visited by cholera, 1,933 passengers died at sea, while 457 were sent to the hospitals on landing; there, in all probability, to terminate in a short time their miserable existence, making nearly 2 percent of deaths among the whole number of persons who had embarked for the New World, and nearly 2.5 percent if those who were landed sick be included.[4]

Conditions on German immigrant vessels were not much better than those on the British ships, as Simon Peter Paul Cahensly, the German Catholic champion of the cause of the immigrant, suggested when he commented on the scene he witnessed in the steerage section of a German sailing ship in the 1860s:

> A person could climb only with the greatest difficulty to the upper and rear places because of the small amount of free space which was usually barricaded with boxes and trunks. Besides, there was almost total darkness, and I became frightened when I thought that in these small rooms of indescribable

disorder and darkness hundreds of people should spend weeks and months.[5]

Thus the Irish and German immigrants arrived in the United States at one of the large ports, like New York City, Boston, or Philadelphia, along the Eastern seaboard, in bad health, and sometimes penniless. The Irish, without the financial means to travel further, and attracted by the hope of job opportunities in America's urban centers, frequently made their homes in the port city of arrival. As an editorial would report in 1876 speaking of the failure of the Irish to take up farming in the heartland of America:

> Of the Irish immigrants who have come to the United States since 1840, about 60 percent of the male adults were agriculturists in Ireland—farmers or laborers. The great majority of them have settled in the cities as day laborers or in some other menial employment. The present condition of this class according to Irish-American newspapers is one of great wretchedness and if we are to credit the said newspapers, the prisons and poor houses of the northern and eastern states have unfortunately too large a proportion of their inmates included from this population.[6]

German immigrants, often better off financially and primarily interested in farming, were more likely to move westward and settle in the area that came to be known as the German Triangle, extending from Cincinnati to St. Louis to Milwaukee. Other Germans, however, skilled artisans and tradesmen, as well as those Germans without money or skills, chose to seek a livelihood in the city. A letter from Father John Neumann, later Bishop of Philadelphia, to the Leopoldine Society of Vienna in 1841 suggested that German immigrants often faced severe hardships and many were destitute or heavily in debt.[7]

America's antebellum cities, crowded, dirty, disease-ridden, and dangerous, offered the immigrant, who was tired, sick, poor, and friendless, an empty welcome. Initial efforts to assist the immigrant poor represented a temporary, somewhat spontaneous, type of benevolence, but when poverty in United States cities became a problem "novel in kind and alarming in size"[8] schemes to ameliorate the most intolerable conditions gradually became organized and systematic. Local government often met the responsibility to care for its needy citizens by establishing almshouses or city infirmaries that served as institutions for the segregation of the poor, sick, and homeless from the rest of society. Father Martin Kundig made an account of conditions in the Wayne County poorhouse in Detroit, Michigan, in which he suggested the nature of such facilities:

> In the month of March, 1834, the Ladies Society, called "the Catholic Female Association for the relief of the sick and poor of Detroit," was informed of the pitiable situation in which the inmates of the Wayne County poor house were kept, and of the unfinished state of the building, which was only inclosed and no arrangements made in the interior, boarded partitions having only been put up in a temporary manner; the sick were therefore in a wretched condition.[9]

Some Americans, however, motivated by a higher sense of Christian concern, and a desire to remedy society's disorders, established and supported various private institutions to assist the sick, orphans, delinquent minors, and the mentally ill. But these antebellum social reformers were predominantly American Protestants and the organizations and asylums they created met the physical but not necessarily the spiritual requirements of the Catholic immigrant. They also attempted to proselytize the immigrant poor, inculcating Protestant-American values in the hope of separating the immigrant from his traditional religious beliefs. In many cities, priests were not permitted to visit Catholics in the public hospitals or asylums, and thus the faithful were denied the comforts of their religion in times of sickness and impending death. A striking illustration of this anti-Catholic feeling, as related by an eminent Catholic historian, is the story of a Catholic priest, who, while allowed access to an almshouse in Fitchburg, Massachusetts, in 1846, was denied permission to spend time alone with a dying man. The superintendent of the institution repeatedly insisted that he would not allow any "paddy superstition" to go on in a house under his control; while the priest was alleged to have responded "I'll allow no infidel or bigot to debar me from the exercise of my office." Eventually the priest's stubborn perseverance won out as he was able to prepare the man for death.[10] For the most part, the ability to assist one's fellow Catholics was frequently compromised by prejudice, mistreatment, misunderstanding, or lack of manpower.

Thus Americans typically feared, rather than pitied, the Catholic immigrant poor and viewed them not as suitable objects of Christian charity but as targets for efforts at social reform. Catholicism, the immigrant, and the city appeared, in the minds of many, to be linked in one shadowy conspiracy.

> That dark specter, the city, loomed evil on the horizon, and it was peopled by teeming hordes of odd-smelling, odd-looking, odd speaking immigrants. Too many of them ended up in the penitentiary and workhouse. They drank too much, and some even did so on Sunday. A startling percentage were Roman Catholics.[11]

It was within this social milieu that the Roman Catholic clergy found it necessary to develop its own network of institutions and social programs, to meet the needs of a largely immigrant flock. What they created was a system of charities that was to be based solely on Christ's dictates to feed the hungry, clothe the naked, and care for the sick and imprisoned. Clearly the unhealthful conditions that prevailed on the passenger ships, the unsanitary conditions in the urban home and workplace, and the frequent epidemics of contagious diseases like cholera and yellow fever kept the immigrant perpetually in poor health, and American bishops, in their efforts to care for the sick poor, sought the help of women religious to provide this much needed ministry. The hierarchy called for priests to instruct their flocks, to provide spiritual guidance, and to administer the sacraments, but saw the good sisters as those religious most suited to serve as Christ's ambassadors to the poor. Although some bishops and priests, from the very beginning, placed a priority on the delivery of health-care services to the poor and secured women religious for that purpose, other Catholic clergy initially sought the assistance of religious orders of women to respond to the totality of the immigrant's needs. John Carroll, the first American bishop, who realized that the church could not survive without works of charity— "the first fruits" of the faith—envisioned the primary responsibility of women religious to be in the area of education. In a letter circa 1810 to Mother Elizabeth Seton, foundress of the American order of the Daughters of Charity of St. Vincent de Paul [0760], Carroll wrote:

> A century at least will pass before the exigencies and habits of this country will require and hardly admit of the charitable

exercises towards the sick, sufficient to employ any number of the Sisters out of our largest cities; and therefore, they must consider the business of education as a laborious, charitable and permanent object of their religious duty.[12]

Mother Seton, however, had other ideas desiring that her sisters honor the "Lord Jesus Christ as the source and model of all charity, by rendering to Him every temporal and spiritual service in their power, in the person of the poor, the sick, prisoners, the insane, and others in distress."[13] Thus it was often the women religious themselves who first took the initiative in the area of health care by visiting the sick poor in their own homes or who opened hospitals to fulfill what they perceived to be a need for such institutions in their own communities of service. It is clear, however, that such action would not have been possible without the support and encouragement of the local bishops.

To illustrate some of the early achievements in the area of health care made possible by the collaborative efforts of clergy and women religious, one can consider the actions taken by the Daughters of Charity of St. Vincent de Paul on behalf of the sick poor. In 1823 they took charge of the Baltimore Infirmary, then affiliated with the medical department of the University of Maryland. With this move, their reputation soared. Only five years later, Bishop Joseph Rosati of St. Louis, Missouri, requested their services.

> I come to obtain through your intervention three Sisters of Charity for a hospital in St. Louis . . . Without having said one word, a very rich man offers me a very beautiful piece of ground with two houses in the city of St. Louis . . . But, he will not leave it in the hands of mercenaries; if we do not get the Sisters of Emmitsburg this establishment will fail.[14]

Their geographic outreach never ceased. By midcentury they were establishing hospitals from New York City to Detroit to Rochester, New York, and were providing health care to the homeless and sick poor in every region to which they were called.

Illustrative as well was the apostolate of the Sisters of Mercy [2570], whose American foundations, first in Pittsburgh, dated from 1843. Days after their arrival in any new locality, the sisters sought the sick and poor in their own homes, attending to both temporal and spiritual needs as "a vast field of neglected humanity spread out before them on every hand."[15] An excerpt from the 1851 *Laity's Directory* records that "the Sisters of Mercy visit the sick-poor every day and carry to them nourishment and clothing as far as their means admit."[16] Often, in fact, such service had begun on the very ships which brought them to the United States. One group, destined for Little Rock, Arkansas, sailed from Ireland in November 1850 with about three hundred immigrants. They commenced their work not only by providing religious instruction for the children but also ministering to the sick on board the ship.

But the ability of the Sisters of Mercy and the Daughters of Charity to respond so spontaneously and naturally when faced with the problems of the immigrant sick poor, through the implementation of programs of home nursing and the creation of hospitals to care for the ill, could not have been possible without the tacit support and active encouragement of members of the clergy. The women religious and their local bishops thus entered into an active "partnership," each playing an important role in bringing quality health care to the suffering and needy. Although the prior examples have emphasized the initiative taken by the sisters in caring for the sick poor, one can also cite a number of cases where women religious were specifically summoned to service by those farsighted and caring clergymen who saw the delivery of medical care to the poor as a priority.

A native of Bohemia, John Neumann, who became the fourth bishop of Philadelphia in 1852, was the first German-speaking bishop to govern an eastern diocese. Neumann had a special concern for the sick and suffering and he expressed this deep sense of caring by taking positive action on their behalf. The city of Philadelphia had one Catholic hospital, St. Joseph's, opened in 1849, and it was administered by the Sisters of St. Joseph of Carondelet [3840], an order established in the United States in 1836, who were first called from St. Louis to Philadelphia by Bishop Francis Kenrick to operate an orphanage. Two men, Dr. William Horner, a convert physician and dean of medicine at the University of Pennsylvania, and Jesuit Father Barbelin, are credited with primary responsibility for founding the hospital, and it is clear that the facility was created to relieve the sick Irish immigrants arriving in the city, many of them suffering from the fever.[17] Bishop Neumann was a frequent visitor to St. Joseph's Hospital, traveling through the wards and stopping at each bed to offer some words of hope or consolation to the sick and dying. According to Mother St. John Fournier, Bishop Neumann also asked the nuns who ministered to the sick to regard them as the suffering members of Jesus Christ, "and to lavish on them every care and attention."[18] But the bishop's concern for the sick did not end with his hospital visits. As one author suggests, "Bishop Neumann was alive to all wants of his diocese; he planned an Infant Asylum and a Hospital for Immigrants." The bishop also had fond hopes of bringing to the United States from Bohemia the Sisters of St. Charles to run the hospital he envisioned for Philadelphia; but due to a variety of circumstances the Sisters of St. Charles never came to Philadelphia nor was the bishop's hospital ever built. Yet despite his failure to open another hospital for Philadelphia, Bishop Neumann made a more important contribution toward the continuing care of the sick by establishing the Sisters of the Third Order of St. Francis [1650]. Although Neumann had plans to seek an order of Dominican sisters for service in Philadelphia, Pope Pius XI counseled the creation of a community of the Third Order of St. Francis. In the parish of St. Peter's Church in Philadelphia, the bishop soon found three worthy candidates for admission, and in April 1855 the new members were received in the order. Although the sisters initially earned a living by sewing, in response to repeated calls for help, they were later occupied by frequent visits to the sick and dying. The work of these Philadelphia sisters among the sick poor became known to others and in 1860 Father Richard Kleineidam, rector of St. Mary Church in Buffalo, New York, requested that the sisters establish a similar ministry in his community. With the permission of Neumann's successor in Philadelphia, Bishop Frederick Wood, and the encouragement of Bishop John Timon of Buffalo, who also was anxious to have some provision made in his diocese for the care of the poor who were old and sick, the Sisters of St. Francis came to Buffalo in 1861 with the purpose of establishing a hospital. The sisters' first act of charity, however, was the nursing of the sick poor in their own homes, although they did establish the St. Francis Asylum on Pine Street in Buffalo as a home for the elderly poor. While soliciting alms for the Pine Street Home in the city of Pittsburgh, two of the sisters were approached by the Reverend Francis Tschenhens with the proposal that they establish a hospital there. Again, with the encouragement of Bishop Timon, three members from the Buffalo community of the Sisters of the Third Order of St. Francis [1620] went to Pittsburgh in November 1865 and opened St. Francis Hospital on Forty-fourth Street. Thus the concern of Bishop Neumann for the suffering of the sick poor led to the creation of an order of women religious that administered hospitals and old-age institutions, and whose members also nursed the sick poor in their own homes.

But there were also many other American bishops who evidenced their strong concern for the plight of the sick poor—so many of them recent immigrants—by active efforts to solicit the assistance of women religious as ambassadors to the ill and suffering during the decades before the Civil War. And there were many other sisters who answered the call to minister to the needy.

One might first note the foresight shown by Joseph Cretin, who was consecrated bishop of St. Paul, a diocese that encompassed the entire Minnesota Territory. In his 1851 report to the Society for the Propagation of the Faith, the bishop recounted the conditions in his far-flung diocese, describing the population he was called upon to serve as "three thousand Catholics, one thousand heretics and twenty-seven thousand infidels";[19] and later anticipating the future needs of his diocese, the bishop suggested that twenty thousand immigrants, most of them from Catholic European countries, could be expected in Minnesota during the following season. Thus, with a growing immigrant population and the logistical problems encountered in reaching out to the sick in a large diocese, it is not surprising that Bishop Cretin, in his appeal to the Society for the Propagation of the Faith that year, listed a hospital, in addition to a sisters' school, a school for Indians, and an orphanage as the pressing needs in the diocese of St. Paul. Thus St. Joseph's Hospital was eventually opened in 1854 and placed under the management of the Sisters of St. Joseph who had been laboring in the St. Paul diocese since 1851, when first invited there at the call of Bishop Cretin. A newspaper account published in 1855 describing the "Catholic Hospital" in St. Paul commented that the sufferings incident to poverty and the pain of sickness were "removed by the tender solicitude of sisterly affection extended to them by 'those Angels of Mercy, the Sisters of St. Joseph, to whom the care of the distressed is a joyful trouble.' "[20]

In 1834 New York Bishop John DuBois called for the establishment of a Catholic hospital for the poor immigrants, particularly those from Ireland, that would offer them "the necessary relief, attendance in sickness and spiritual comfort, amidst the disease of a climate new to them."[21] Certainly New York City, a mecca for many immigrants, and an urban area that became a permanent home for significant numbers of these newcomers, also suffered in the antebellum era from a lack of medical facilities for the care of the Catholic poor. Catholics did, of course, seek aid in public hospitals but in New York priests were either barred from visiting them in such institutions or were generally unwelcome; and in response to this situation Bishop John Hughes in an 1847 pastoral letter urged the creation of a Catholic hospital to shelter his immigrant flock. In 1849 the Sisters of Charity of New York [0650], under the direction of Sister Mary Angela Hughes, the bishop's sister, opened St. Vincent's Hospital, and this small institution on Thirteenth Street soon become a haven for the sick poor. Although St. Vincent's extended its welcome to all, regardless of race, religion, or color, some Catholics did not feel totally at home there. German immigrants unable to speak the language preferred to seek necessary medical aid from those who spoke their native tongue. Thus in 1865 St. Francis Hospital was opened in a Redemptorist parish with a large German constituency on New York City's lower East Side, under the auspices of the Poor Sisters of St. Francis [1440], an order of religious women who had seven years before helped to found a hospital in Cincinnati. Their foundress, Mother Frances Schervier, remained steadfast in an apostolate which had begun in Germany in 1845 to care for the sick poor in their homes and in hospitals. Although the Redemptorist Fathers had hopes of making the hospital an exclusive preserve for the German sick poor of their parish, Mother Frances insisted that the hospital be open to all people. And as the impetus for the establishment of St. Francis Hospital in New York and St. Mary's Hospital in Ohio had developed from a desire of German immigrants to be cared for by German sisters, the demand by immigrants representing various ethnic groups to be treated medically by women religious of their own nationalities became more urgent and insistent in the years following the Civil War.

The postwar era marked a major transition in the history of United States immigration as the "old" immigrants were joined first by a trickle, and then by a flood, of "new" European newcomers, so that in 1896 statistics would reveal that while only 40 percent of immigrants were from northern and western Europe, 57 percent of the newcomers were from eastern and southern European countries. The decades after the Civil War also witnessed the second wave of German immigration as an increasingly industrialized Germany displaced a large number of farm laborers; between 1860 and 1900, three and one-half million Germans arrived in America.

The Italians and the Poles, as had the Germans and the Irish decades earlier, left their homelands in the late nineteenth century in search of economic opportunity. As population increased in size, and good land available for cultivation dwindled, immigration offered the only hope for survival. United States cities once again served as magnets for the new immigrants, who were predominantly Catholic, largely without skills, and in search of jobs. In 1920, for example, 84 percent of the Italian foreign born were described as city dwellers, and eight out of ten of these immigrants were unskilled laborers digging ditches, hauling cement, or loading ships for a livelihood. The Poles, also untrained, sought out the industrial cities of the Midwest, including Chicago, Cleveland, and Gary, Indiana, looking for work in factories, steel mills, and meatpacking plants; others sought employment in the coal mines of Pennsylvania. The fact that the Polish and Italian immigrants were poor and unskilled was not unexpected, but their distinctive languages, "strange" appearance, and unfamiliar customs, clearly separated the newcomers from other Americans and also served to create a barrier between them and the other Catholics who represented the more established immigrant groups. The "alien character" of the Catholic Church was increasingly reflected in the "halting conversations of the newcomers and displayed itself in strangely ornate architectural features in neighborhood ghettos and in the employment offices of both factories and foundries."[22] More established Catholics were offended by the initiative exhibited by the newcomers who argued for equality, and feared that cooperation with the strangers might result in a loss of their hard-won social and economic status in society. The new immigrants of the post–Civil War era, then, more clearly sought refuge within their own ethnic communities, where they were assured of finding acceptance.

But prejudice was the least of the immigrants' worries, as life in America's fast-growing urban areas posed the most serious threat to their survival. City sewer and water facilities were inadequate and municipalities provided poor fire protection and allowed garbage to pile high on city streets. The housing stock available to the immigrant was substandard and only intensified other problems linked with inadequate shelter, including disease, the danger of fire, and the eventual dissolution of the family that led to crime and juvenile delinquency. Sometimes the ghetto environment became the greatest threat to health.

> An infant pierces an eye while playing with scissors, a mother slicing bread for the family severs an artery of her wrist, a falling rock smashes a ditchdigger's legs, a child tumbles from a clothes pole and breaks his arm, a breadwinner is paralyzed, a rat bite causes gangrene, a firecracker explodes and shatters a girl's face, a mother becomes infected by the germ-laden fingers of a midwife, the wintry damp walls hasten a cold into pneumonia.[23]

But because of need, both public and private hospitals multiplied after the Civil War. If by 1871 there were at least seventy hospitals established either by or under the auspices of Catholic women religious, the development of Catholic hospitals really blossomed during the late nineteenth and early twentieth centuries as approximately two hundred seventy such institutions were opened from 1876 to 1906. By that time as well people recognized the value of seeking medical assistance in a hospital setting and were less traumatized by its association with the poorhouses where the inmates had provided the nursing services. But for those immigrants—including Germans, Poles, Italians, and others—who could not speak English, even the sound medical treatment and the good nursing care provided in Catholic hospitals could not compensate for the fact that the patients were unable to communicate verbally with the women religious who were attending them. Although during the decades before the Civil War American bishops had played an active role in securing the assistance of women religious to meet the specialized health care needs of the Irish and German immigrants, the hierarchy of the postwar era when faced with the more complex demands of the multiethnic new immigration was less sensitive to the needs of specific immigrant groups and adopted more generalized solutions to what they perceived to be certain universal problems. One author has suggested that the bishops commonly responded to the new immigration by creating national parishes within their dioceses.

> In an atmosphere where ethnic Catholicism was so poorly understood and where the very organizational structure of the Church provided no direct means of producing effective change, little seems to have been accomplished by immigrant protests. National parishes were established and immigrant priests were sought out, to be sure. But beyond this, there seemed to be little episcopal initiative. Apart from actively searching for trained clergy, or sometimes even sending seminarians abroad to be educated in the language and customs of immigrant Catholics, bishops did not appear to consider immigrant needs or to develop policies based upon them.[24]

Thus during the late nineteenth century the impetus for better healthcare services to meet the requirements of specific ethnic groups often had to develop from within the immigrant community; and it was the women religious, representing various national backgrounds, with the encouragment and support of sympathetic priests and bishops, who provided the leadership in a movement to ensure good health care, both in the home and in hospitals, for the sick poor.

Prior to the Civil War it was the German immigrant who first expressed uneasiness over entering Catholic hospitals that did not have German-speaking sisters, and thus the Poor Sisters of St. Francis were able to begin their health-care apostolate for the sick poor in the United States. But the desire of other communities of German immigrants to seek assistance in times of sickness from their own women religious continued during the late nineteenth century—and, perhaps fortuitously, came at a time when German sisters were anxious to leave their homeland to establish mission fields in other nations, including the United States. This exodus was precipitated by the *Kulturkampf* ("culture struggle"), actually a series of politically motivated measures taken by the German government under Bismarck that were aimed at the Catholic Church and resulted in the expulsion of the Jesuits in 1872 and the dissolution of all religious orders by 1875. Thus for example, Mother Mary Odilia Berger, originally a member of the Poor Franciscans of the Holy Family, a Bavarian order devoted to the care of orphans and of the sick poor in their homes, clearly saw the difficulties of continued service in her native land and therefore wrote to a former patient, one she had nursed during a smallpox epidemic who had immigrated to the United States, regarding opportunities for her sisters in America.

> The present state of affairs with regard to religious, and convents especially, is so discouraging that we feel inclined to cross the ocean also; therefore, I would ask you to make the acquaintance of some priests, Jesuits or Franciscans if possible, and inquire of them whether or not it would be advisable for five sisters who devote themselves to the care of the sick to come to America.[25]

With the encouragement of her former patient, Gustave Wegman, and the support of the Vicar General of the German immigrants of St. Louis, Monsignor Henry Muehlsiepen, Mother Mary Odilia and four other sisters reached St. Louis in November of 1872 to begin a ministry of nursing for the sick poor. The sisters found a home in the German parish of St. Mary of Victories, and came under the spiritual guidance of its pastor, Father William Faerber, a man dedicated to the cause of the

German immigrant. Mother Mary Odilia and her companions soon became known as the Sisters of St. Mary [3970].

The need for German women religious was clear, particularly in St. Louis, a city that in 1872 was home for a large number of Germans as well as a temporary haven for other immigrants traveling westward. The city's inadequate sanitary facilities as well as the absence of any comprehensive public health program contributed to the spread of diseases and illnesses that visited the immigrant community with great regularity.

> One contributing factor responsible for the increase in contagious diseases as well as the poverty in general was the heavy accession of immigrants, especially among the Germans . . . But there were also other reasons, the chief of them being the high birth rate, the industrialization of the eastern seaboard, with increase in municipal population and resulting overcrowding, bad housing, inadequate sanitary facilities, polluted municipal water supplies, contaminated foods, myriads of flies, and general prevalence of filth.[26]

The Sisters of St. Mary came to battle the poverty and disease of St. Louis, daily visiting and nursing the "poorest" of the city's poor along the banks of the Mississippi River.

> Down at the ferry docks, urchins in filthy rags as well as women of all ages, tawny queens of the slums, lugged great bags of coal up the levee into dark, dank hovels on Second Street and beyond.[27]

The poor suffered from a variety of sicknesses including consumption, cerebro-spinal fever, typhoid fever, diptheria, croup, measles, scarlet fever, and cholera; its victims were nursed in their homes by the Sisters of St. Mary, who often helped the sick by doing the washing, cooking, and cleaning during the times of prolonged illness.

As had earlier the Sisters of Mercy and the Daughters of Charity, the Sisters of St. Mary found it increasingly difficult to provide adequate medical care for the sick in the crowded, unsanitary tenement dwellings, and equally hard to reach all of those in need of their help scattered "in the tortuous alleys and lanes near the riverfront."[28] The establishment of a hospital in a more centralized area appeared an obvious solution and Mother Mary Odilia accepted the responsibility to make such an institution a reality. Although there were already six Catholic hospitals in St. Louis by the mid-1870s, the need for additional facilities was yet apparent. In 1872 public health officer Dr. William L. Barrett had called for additional hospitals to assist

> the helpless, destitute, and suffering, who daily arrived by steamboat or railroad, who have no means of support but charity, no shelter but a doorstep or awning, and no refuge but the hospital where they might be carried, or permitted to die in the streets.[29]

Although Mother Mary Odilia had hoped to open a hospital within St. Mary of Victories parish, thus remaining close to her spiritual advisor Father Faerber, she realized that a medical facility should be built in an area of the city free from filth and contagion. She thought that by removing the sick poor from their polluted environment they might be introduced to a new and more healthful way of life. Thus in 1877 St. Mary's Infirmary, under the administration of the Sisters of St. Mary was opened in an upper class St. Louis neighborhood. And the sisters did not confine their nursing of the sick poor at home or in hospitals to St. Louis: they expanded their health-care ministry to include foundations elsewhere in Missouri, for example at St. Charles and Kansas City, as well as in Wisconsin and Illinois.

The Sisters of St. Mary were not the only women religious who, forced to leave Germany as a result of the *Kulturkampf*, came to the United States so that they might continue to care for the sick poor, particularly those within the German immigrant community. One can also briefly cite the examples set in this regard by the Sisters of St. Francis Seraph of the Perpetual Adoration [1640], the Hospital Sisters of St. Francis of Springfield [1820] and by the Franciscan Sisters, the Daughters of the Sacred Hearts of Jesus and Mary [1240] (Franciscan Sisters of St. Louis). The point should be made, however, that these sisters did not necessarily limit their charity to German immigrants for many religious saw it as their duty to serve the larger community of the sick poor that often included persons representing a variety of ethnic groups.

In 1875 six Poor Sisters of St. Francis Seraph of the Perpetual Adoration fled from persecution in their native Westphalia, where they had been for the previous fifteen years nursing the sick poor in their own homes and caring for neglected children. The sisters found a home in the diocese of Fort Wayne, Indiana, and within eight months of their arrival a kind benefactor presented the women with two lots upon which they built St. Elizabeth's Hospital, their first health facility in the United States. In 1884 the Poor Sisters of St. Francis Seraph were invited to serve in the diocese of Cleveland by Bishop Richard Gilmour, upon the recommendation of the Reverend Kilian Schloesser, a Franciscan priest and pastor of St. Joseph's Church. The sisters settled in a strongly ethnic working-class Cleveland neighborhood, making their home in the former convent of the Poor Clares, on Broadway at McBride. Sisters Leonarda and Alexa came to Cleveland with the purpose of establishing a hospital in the industrialized Cuyahoga Valley, where the "numerous factories and mills, the several railroads, and the large population of the southeastern part of Cleveland rendered the hospital an urgent necessity." Their hospital, St. Alexis, was opened to the public in August of 1884, and the Poor Sisters of St. Francis Seraph made it clear through the policy adopted by Sister Leonarda that "those who can afford to pay can always find room elsewhere. Those who can't, we must manage to keep here."[30] At the end of the first year twenty-five persons were admitted to St. Alexis, all of them poor and unable to pay for their care or treatment. As the hospital's annual report for 1900 demonstrated, 732 patients paid full or partial rates, while 1,289 persons were admitted as charity cases. This clearly confirms Bishop Gilmour's contention that the hospital was to be devoted entirely to the care of the sick poor. It is also equally clear that a significant percentage of the sick poor admitted to St. Alexis shared an immigrant background. The hospital's annual report, issued circa 1895, documents that of the 1,217 persons treated during the year, 942 represented nationalities other than "American" and included about 41 percent Irish, nearly 25 percent German, and 7 percent Bohemian patients.[31]

The sisters' health ministry to the poor was not limited to hospital work as they also visited the homes of the sick on a regular basis. As an article published in Cleveland's *Catholic Universe* in October 1884 reported:

> This nursing order not only takes care of patients at the hospital but goes to their homes and cares for them, in both cases gratis—although donations are not refused. We know of one case where poor as these sisters are, they are actually paying for the medicine for their patient, who is being treated at home. Such a charity commends itself without many words.[32]

Twenty Hospital Sisters of St. Francis arrived in Alton, Illinois, in 1875, not unlike the Poor Sisters of St. Francis Seraph and the Sisters of St. Mary, fleeing from the excesses of the *Kulturkampf* with the express purpose of caring for the sick poor. The hospital sisters placed themselves in the service of Bishop Peter Baltes of the Alton disocese and began their work by visiting the sick in their homes. Soon after, however, the sisters obtained a residence that they transformed into a hospital later to be known as St. John's Hospital in Springfield, Illinois.

One final group of German sisters who arrived in the United States during the period of the *Kulturkampf* with the purpose of caring for the poor and the sick, were the Franciscan Sisters (Daughters of the Sacred Hearts of Jesus and Mary) of St. Louis, who came to the United States to administer a hospital planned by the Reverend Ernest Andrew Schindel of Carondelet, Missouri, for the needs of St. Boniface parish and its vicinity. Father Schindel had asked his colleague Father Brockhagen to return to their native Germany to seek sisters to undertake the hospital work he envisioned for them. Father Brockhagen secured the services of The Franciscan Sisters at Salzkotten and he accompanied the women religious to the United States, arriving in Carondelet in 1873. When the building was completed the sisters assumed the responsibility for the management of St. Boniface Hospital. Although this institution was forced to close in 1877 after a disastrous fire, the sisters remained totally dedicated to hospital work in Missouri, at communities including St. Louis and Cape Girardeau, as well as in Illinois, Iowa, Wisconsin, and Colorado.

Thus the period after the Civil War witnessed the prominent activity of German women religious in the field of health care, when conditions in Germany made it impossible for orders dedicated to the nursing of the sick poor to continue service in their own country. At the same time, the demand for such care was most insistent in United States cities, particularly in those areas with significant German populations. It seems as if these communities of German women religious had a special penchant for hospitals.

But there were yet other ethnic groups who clamored for their own "sisters" to meet not only health needs, but to teach and provide child care. It was only through the initiative and hard work of immigrant communities of women religious who first recognized the inadequacy of the existing social services available to their compatriots that hospitals and programs of home nursing were established to reach out to immigrant Poles, Italians, and other neglected nationalities, and to provide the medical treatment and care they demanded.

In 1874 Frances Siedliska, a Polish noblewoman, established the order of the Sisters of the Holy Family of Nazareth in Rome. By 1881, Mother Siedliska, who remained particularly mindful of the needs of other Poles, gained permission to send her sisters to open a mission field in the City of Cracow, Poland. At the same time Mother Frances recognized the need for women religious to serve the communities of Polish immigrants in the United States. When invited by Bishop Patrick Feehan of Chicago to send sisters to administer schools and an orphanage primarily for Polish immigrants, she not only agreed to answer his call but actually accompanied her Holy Family sisters, arriving in the United States in 1885.

Chicago had attracted large numbers of Polish immigrants and was an ideal location for a foundation of the Sisters of the Holy Family of Nazareth [1970]. The women made their first home in a small convent in St. Joseph's parish. Initially, the sisters restricted their efforts to the field of education, although they never refused to help the sick poor who came to them in times of need; and they did make routine visits to the homes of the ill and suffering. The sisters also visited those patients who had difficulty understanding English who were being treated in non-Catholic facilities. Not all of the patients were Poles and the sisters' ability to speak several languages allowed them to bring messages of hope and the consolations of religion to the bedsides of many. But it was the immigrant Poles who appeared most frustrated by their inability to communicate with hospital personnel and who missed the comforts of their religion in times of illness. Thus the Polish immigrants were the first to propose to the Sisters of the Holy Family of Nazareth the idea of establishing a hospital in Chicago for their care. The plan for such an institution caught the interest of many and various committees were soon active in raising funds for this purpose. The sisters even made visits to other facilities to become acquainted with routine hospital practices and procedures. Finally on May 6, 1894, the Holy Family Hospital was dedicated and the following day the first patient was admitted.

It should not be surprising that a city like Chicago, with its large Polish immigrant community, would attract other Polish women religious, dedicated to the care of the poor, sick, and elderly, or that such a new community would actually evolve and grow in its very midst. The economic depression of 1893 had a particularly devastating effect on the immigrant population of Chicago, as it followed so closely the brief period of prosperity that had characterized the city a year earlier, when the international Columbian Exhibition, celebrating the four-hundredth anniversary of America's discovery, had been held there. With the closing of the exhibition came mass unemployment and the Poles, inarticulate and powerless, were among the first to lose their jobs. The combination of "hard times" and cold weather made the winter of 1893 a particularly trying time for the city's Polish immigrants: many were cold, sick, and hungry, while others were also homeless. One author described the scene in Chicago during that winter of 1893 in this way:

> Thousands of the homeless roamed the streets; many suffered the pangs of hunger; others sought the shelter of railroad stations and public buildings, sleeping on the benches and in the corridors. Death came in the night to the starved and frozen who could not help themselves.[33]

When St. Stanislaus Kostka, one of the Polish national parishes in Chicago, was particularly hard hit there was at least one immigrant member of this community who was not only distressed by the suffering around her but also was motivated to do something about it. Josephine Dudzik had arrived in Chicago with her parents and other siblings in 1881 and settled in St. Stanislaus Kostka parish. By 1893 Josephine was living alone with her mother and earning money as a seamstress. But a concern for the sick and poor in her neighborhood occupied her mind and energies:

> this constant thought of how to serve the sick and the weak never left me, neither by day nor night, although I was unaware of the means by which this could be accomplished.[34]

Josephine Dudzik also stated that she had been considering how she might accommodate more comfortably "the poor, the widows, the sick, and the disabled, for frequently I sheltered too many of them, in the limited quarters of my home." A biographer further describes Josephine as one who would relinquish her bed, or who would sew throughout the night to earn extra money to buy medicine for the sick.[35]

Josephine finally resolved to purchase or rent a home within the St. Stanislaus parish where she might care for all of the sick poor seeking admission and she hoped to gather around her young women willing to "lead a common life of prayer and work for the support of this project."[36] This community of like-minded women that Josephine envisioned became a reality in December of 1894 with the creation of the Sisters of St. Francis of Blessed Kunegunda [1210] (Sisters of St. Francis of Chicago); and Josephine, known as Mother Mary Theresa, was elected the order's first superior. Although Mother Mary Theresa's abiding concern for the sick and suffering did not lead to the creation of another hospital for Chicago, her hard work, sacrifice, and stubborn refusal to abandon her poor neighbors in their struggle for survival, did open the doors of St. Joseph's Home for the elderly poor in 1898.

When considering the role Polish women religious played in responding to the needs of their own poor and unfortunate, one should not ignore the example set by the Felician Sisters of the Order of St. Francis, although their contribution was not strictly in the area of health care. The Felicians, an order established in Warsaw, Poland, in 1855, first came to the United States in 1874, arriving in Polonia, Wisconsin, at the invitation of Father Joseph Dabrowski, an early missionary among the immigrant Poles. The Felician Sisters [1170] distinguished themselves in the field of education, undertaking an apostolate, primarily among the Polish immigrants and their children, "seeking to guide them in the harmonious development of their triple cultural heritage as Catholics, Americans, and Poles."[37] For sixteen years the Felician Sisters from the Buffalo province also served St. Joseph's Home for Polish Immigrants on Ellis Island. The home was a charitable institution under lay sponsorship that helped Poles adjust to their new life in the United States and protected them against those who would take advantage of their naïveté. Although the Felician Sisters terminated their services on the Island in 1913, they later opened the St. Joseph's Home for Working Girls in New York City in 1923 as a shelter for young immigrant women. This institution also served as a hospice for Felician Sisters after they arrived in the United States. In addition to the Felician Sisters there were at various times as many as ninety missionary and immigrant aid societies active on Ellis Island.

Perhaps, however, one of the best known of the special homes or hospices for the new arrivals to the United States was New York City's Leo House, established for the care of German immigrants and operated under the auspices of the Sisters of St. Agnes [3710]. There were many in the United States, as well as in Germany, who had a deep concern for the fate of German immigrants who had to endure many hardships in order to reach America, beginning with their passage across the Atlantic, and continuing upon their arrival in the United States, often alone, without friends, and unable to communicate in English. One especially passionate defender of the German immigrant's right to safe passage and fair treatment, as mentioned earlier, was Peter Paul Cahensly, a

German merchant, who helped to establish the St. Raphael's Society in Germany in 1871 and served as its secretary. The society was formed to promote the welfare of the Catholic immigrant under the patronage of St. Raphael the Archangel, patron saint of travelers; and it pursued a three-point program: to assist the immigrant in every way before he sailed, during the voyage, and at the ports of entry. Cahensly himself came to the United States in 1883 to travel throughout America and visit those areas with significant German populations to encourage the establishment of a St. Raphael's Society. In 1883 a chapter of the society was formed in New York City with Bishop Winand N. Wigger as its president. In order to support its work on behalf of German immigrants, the society was in need of a mission station with a "chapel for spiritual exercises as well as board and lodging accommodations."[38] Although members of the society supported the establishment of such an institution and German newspapers voiced their approval, it took the concerted action of German-American priests in the United States to make the mission station a reality. At the first conference of the *Deutsch-Amerikaner Priester Verein*, in 1887, those in attendance agreed that it would be proper to collect money from German Catholics in the United States, and petition the Holy See for approval to use the funds to construct an immigrant station in honor of the Holy Father. Contributions were freely offered by many German Catholics and by the spring of 1888 fifty-two thousand of a seventy-five thousand dollar goal had been met. A building at 6 State Street in Castle Garden Park was purchased and fitted for use as the proposed immigrant station. Although Mass was offered in the chapel in August 1889, Bishop Wigger did not formally bless the new Leo House until December 7, 1889. Bishop Wigger, a member of the Leo House board of directors, and New York's Archbishop Michael Corrigan, honorary board president, desired to obtain the services of a community of women religious to manage the new hospice but failed to interest any order in the eastern United States in assuming this responsibility. William Schickel, a New York architect and Leo House board member who had designed the convent and chapel for the Sisters of Saint Agnes in Fond Du Lac, Wisconsin, was acquainted with Mother Agnes Hazotte, the order's superior, and recommended that these German-speaking sisters be asked to run the Leo House. The Sisters of St. Agnes were formed in Barton, Wisconsin, in 1858 by the Reverend Caspar Rehrl, a priest sent to the United States by the Leopoldine Society to work among German immigrants in Wisconsin, to assist him in his work. Mother Agnes, elected superior in 1864, at first demurred at Schickel's invitation in October of 1889 as her order's primary activities were in the area of education. However, Father Francis Haas, spiritual director of the Sisters of St. Agnes granted his permission for the new venture and Mother Agnes accepted the challenge on behalf of the Sisters of St. Agnes. In a Christmas letter to her sisters in Wisconsin dated December 18, 1889, Mother Agnes described the new Leo House in this way:

> There is a chapel in the house and a caplain [sic], so the sisters have Mass daily. The place is nicely situated near Castle Garden fronted by a beautiful park. The house was instituted for the protection of German immigrants, so that they might not be led astray. Sad experience teaches that many lost their faith for want of such an institution. Here they receive the sacraments and are directed to places where there are Catholic churches and schools. Girls who remain in the city are placed with Catholic families.[39]

An analysis of the social services provided by the Leo House suggests that from 1889 to 1890, 3,970 immigrants as well as 241 other guests were beneficiaries of the hospitality offered by the hospice, with 2,493 individuals receiving free meals and 845 people obtaining free lodgings.

The special homes and hospices operated by the German and Polish women religious for the benefit of the immigrants—newly arrived, lost, bewildered, and in need of a kind word in their native tongue and a warm bed or good meal—were much needed and undoubtedly helped to make the immigrant's initial adjustment to life in America easier. Nonetheless, they were only temporary havens and could not really assist the newcomers in their daily, ongoing struggle for survival. Nor could such places adequately meet the health-care needs of those poor who were dwelling in the depressed areas of America's big cities. Thus, for the Italians who arrived in the United States during the late nineteenth century in such significant numbers, the establishment of a St. Raphael's Home was not the answer for providing the medical care and treatment necessary for those who were ill or injured.

As the German immigrants had Peter Paul Cahensly to fight for their rights to a better life, the Italian people had Bishop Giovanni Scalabrini of Piacenza. Bishop Scalabrini took up the cause of the Italian immigrants, researching the nature of their plight and educating the public regarding their situation through lectures and publications. In 1888 the bishop founded the Congregation of St. Charles Borromeo, often called the Scalabrinian Fathers. The Scalabrinians began their work in New York City with only two priests and a lay brother, taking possession of a former Protestant church in the city and naming it in honor of St. Joachim. However, Bishop Scalabrini wanted to do more for the Italian immigrants and encouraged Mother Francesca Cabrini, foundress of the Missionary Sisters of the Sacred Heart [2860] (established in 1880), to open a mission field in America, and told her:

> Mother Cabrini, the spiritual and social plight of our people in America is beyond belief. Italian souls that have inherited many centuries of Christ's love are corroding and being seduced back to a dark pagan desert in the huge new America. America needs your Missionary Sisters of the Sacred Heart, for there are prodigious works of light to be done.[40]

Mother Cabrini, however, had a decided preference for missionary work in the lands of the Orient and reportedly told Bishop Scalabrini that New York City was too small a place for her. When the Bishop replied that she should find America large enough, she answered, "No, Monsignor. For me the whole world is too small."[41] Following an audience with Pope Leo XIII, when he informed her that her mission field was not in the East but the West, and instructed her to go to America and plant and cultivate the "beautiful fruit of Christ," Mother Cabrini dutifully agreed and accepted the invitation of New York Archbishop Michael Corrigan to help with Italian orphanage work there.[42] Mother Cabrini, despite her physical frailty, as well as disappointment over being denied the opportunity to labor in the mission fields of the Orient, channeled her great spiritual strength and boundless enthusiasm into her work with the Italian immigrants in the United States. Mother Cabrini and her Missionary Sisters set sail for New York in 1889 and almost immediately the women were called upon to minister to some fifteen hundred Italians on board the vessel *Bourgogne*. Although so many of the passengers, including the Sisters, succumbed to seasickness, Mother Cabrini remained strong in support of the weakened immigrants as she helped them, prayed with them, and simply kept silent beside them.

When they arrived in the United States, Archbishop Corrigan explained to the Missionary Sisters that upon further consideration he thought the time was not right to begin an orphanage for Italian children in New York City and he advised Mother Cabrini to return to Italy.

She remained steadfast, however, refused to go back home, and obtained the archbishop's permission to open a day school for Italian children in St. Joachim's Church. This small step in the area of education inaugurated Mother Cabrini's work on behalf of the Italian immigrant in America, a ministry that would eventually extend from the East to the West Coast of the United States. Although the Missionary Sisters did not originally intend any extensive involvement in health care (outside, of course, of their visits of mercy to Italian immigrants hospitalized in New York's public institutions), Bishop Scalabrini asked Mother Cabrini's Sisters in 1891 to work in the small hospital on East 109th Street that he had established for Italian patients under the direction of the Scalabrinian Fathers. Although there were other hospitals and health facilities in New York City open to the Italian immigrant, their problems with the English language and their limited knowledge of resources available to them combined to prevent their access to decent health care. As one author explains:

> The death rate was enormous, and only mysterious good luck could keep the immigrants healthy. When immigrants were injured or seriously ill, the language barrier, poverty, pride, ignorance, timidity, and the utter indifference of public officials denied them the aid that might have saved their lives. They simply remained stoically in the miserable beds of their dark squalid rooms. When primitive treatment of herbs, poultices, and leeches failed, they turned to prayers and votive lights, witchcraft and cabalistic incantations. Too often, death followed in the wake of agonies.[43]

An often repeated story regarding an illiterate man hospitalized for months in a New York hospital's public charity ward, who was unable to read a letter from Italy, helps to illustrate why a special hospital for the care of the Italian immigrant was deemed necessary. According to the account it was not until one of the Missionary Sisters visited him that the man was able to hear the letter, one that he was certain contained a message from his beloved mother, and only after the sister read the letter to him did the patient learn of his mother's death. Thus a stay for Italians, alone and friendless, in a public health facility could be devastating, and although their "sick bodies received some attention; the fact that they had still sicker souls was rarely thought of."[44] It is often suggested by Mother Cabrini's biographers that the incident involving the sick Italian patient was an important determinant in her decision to enter the field of health care. Thus ten of Mother Cabrini's daughters were assigned to work in the small New York Italian hospital; and the Missionary Sisters managed and operated the institution, often begging alms on the city's streets to pay off its mounting debts. By 1892, despite the best efforts of the Missionary Sisters, the hospital was threatened with foreclosure, and the uncooperative attitude exhibited by the Scalabrinian Fathers, who expected the sisters to work without pay and to rescue them from debt, led to a parting of ways between the two Italian religious communities. Mother Cabrini then assumed the initiative, and with the small sum of two hundred fifty dollars rented two adjoining houses on East Twelfth Street and transferred ten of her patients from the old hospital to the new location. She named the facility the Columbus Hospital after Christopher Columbus, the first Christian immigrant and pilgrim to "plant the cross of Christ in America."[45] This same name was also applied to the other hospitals Mother Cabrini would later establish in Chicago, Seattle, and other cities.

It is clear, then, that German, Polish, and Italian women religious played a most prominent role during the late nineteenth century in establishing hospitals designed primarily for immigrants of their respective nationalities. But this is not to suggest that hospitals managed by women religious for the care of other ethnic groups, those that constituted a smaller percentage of the immigrant population, did not also exist and flourish, as the activities of the Sisters Marianites of the Holy Cross [2410] and the Sisters of St. Casimir [3740] will illustrate.

In 1881 the French Benevolent Society, an organization established in 1808 for the welfare of poor French persons, founded the French Hospital in New York City. The President of the Society, Charles Renaud, was dissatisfied with the lay management of the hospital and thus sought the advice of New York Archbishop Michael Corrigan regarding the procurement of women religious for service there. Corrigan suggested that he seek out the help of an order already active in the archdiocese and Renaud, who was acquainted with the work of the Marianite sisters working at the St. Vincent de Paul Orphanage and Industrial School, contacted the order's foundress for permission to obtain Marianite sisters for service in the French Hospital. The first United States foundation of the Sisters of the Holy Cross of LeMans, France, was made in 1849, when four sisters arrived in New Orleans, Louisiana, to manage an orphan asylum as the Sisters Marianites of the Holy Cross. With approval of the foundress, the Sisters Marianites began their work in the French Hospital in December 1885 and reportedly their presence in the facility "caused great satisfaction to the French quarter of New York City." The hospital was not only of service to the French immigrants but also cared for the sailors and crews of French passenger and merchant ships who felt particularly welcome "in a hospital where French-speaking sisters were happy and ready to care for them." The French Hospital was open to all, regardless of nationality, and made special provisions for the care of the poor.[46]

Large numbers of Lithuanians began to arrive in the United States after the Civil War, with between fifty thousand and one hundred thousand coming to America during the nineteenth century. Many settled in the coal-producing areas of Pennsylvania, and in 1907 the Sisters of St. Casimir were established in Scranton, Pennsylvania, to teach children of Lithuanian birth and descent. In 1911, however, the motherhouse was transferred to Chicago, Illinois, and although primarily active in the field of education, the Sisters of St. Casimir were asked to administer Holy Cross Hospital when it opened in Chicago in 1928. The hospital originated as a revenue-producing measure to assist the Lithuanian Catholic Alliance, an organization dedicated to the care of poor and needy Lithuanian immigrants in the United States. During the Great Depression, Holy Cross Hospital offered medical care to the unfortunate and also provided meals to the people of the neighborhood.[47]

Catholic health care during the late nineteenth century became increasingly institutionalized, as hospitals, staffed by women religious, served as the primary care givers, and as medical facilities were more frequently established to meet the requirements of specific ethnic groups. Yet there was a need within various communities for women religious who would continue to visit the sick poor in their own homes. One such order of religious was the Sisters of Bon Secours [0270], invited by Archbishop James Gibbons to serve in the city of Baltimore. An account of the Archbishop's visit to the Bon Secours community in Paris in 1880 stated that instead of taking the sick to their house and creating a hospital, the Sisters of Bon Secours went to the homes of those in need of nursing and remained there. Indeed, the Congregation of Bon Secours was founded in Paris in 1824 with the purpose of caring for the sick and helpless in their own homes. The sisters accepted the new mission and in 1881 arrived in Baltimore, a city that was home to an increasing number of immigrants as well as to a significant population of industrial workers, most of them poor and living in depressed areas of the city. Appeals for trained nurses to go into the homes of the sick poor in Baltimore were frequent; as for those living in poverty, the "sickroom" was their hospital, and their home the place where they had to recover and learn again to live healthfully. Almost immediately following their arrival in Baltimore the Sisters of Bon Secours were called upon to nurse the sick poor and although their services were available to all, regardless of economic status, religion, or nationality, their first recorded care was offered to a French woman. While the Bon Secours specialized in private-duty nursing in the home, visiting nursing and social work among the poor remained an important part of their daily activities. One source suggests that a certain number of sisters were appointed to conduct the visitations in response to calls from physicians, clergy, and laity. The sisters were identified by the black bags they carried filled with all sorts of food, medicines, and tonics for the comfort of the sick. Thus the Bon Secours traveled through the slums of South and East Baltimore, going from home to home, ministering to the sick and poverty-stricken families, cheering and uplifting many types of people with whom they came into contact during their daily round of duties. One of the superiors of the Bon Secours, Mother Urban, appointed in 1898, also made every effort to feed and clothe the poor, and when possible provide them with fuel. The services of the Sisters of Bon Secours were not confined to Baltimore: they later served in Washington, D.C., and Detroit, Michigan. It was not until 1919 that the Bon Secours were presented with their own hospital in Baltimore.[48]

The Bon Secours were not the only women religious devoted to home nursing care. The Order of Sisters of the Infant Jesus [2230] (known in the United States as the Nursing Sisters of the Sick Poor) was founded in France in 1835 for the education of the poor and the care of the sick. These sisters arrived in Brooklyn, New York, in 1905 and first enjoyed the hospitality of the Little Sisters of the Poor [2340]. The Nursing Sisters were persuaded to remain in Brooklyn at the invitation of the bishop to care for the sick poor. The sisters did not restrict their ministrations to one particular nationality or parish but served all the needy of the diocese. In 1913 the bishop called upon the Nursing Sisters to establish the first Catholic hospital, Mercy Hospital, on Long Island, New York. The hospital was welcomed by local Catholics, and it became a "spiritual solace in a time of suffering and death, birth, and life."[49]

The discussion thus far has centered on the health needs of the Catholic immigrant and the work of Catholic women religious in the area of health care. Not all immigrants were Catholic, and Protestant women also provided medical assistance to the poor in the late nineteenth century through the deaconess movement. To better understand the nature of the health-care ministry offered by the deaconesses to the poor one can cite the example of Elisabeth Fedde's work on behalf of Norwegian immigrants. Fedde was born in Norway in 1840 and was trained in the Deaconess Institute in Oslo, the first training school for nurses in Norway. After serving in the State Hospital, and working on private cases as well, Elisabeth Fedde came to Brooklyn in 1883 to help her fellow Norwegian immigrants. Fedde began her work, as did so many Catholic women religious, by visiting the sick poor in their homes, and she also regularly stopped at the immigrant hospital in Castle Garden as well as the Ward Island Hospital, to comfort ailing Norwegians. Her experiences in the public facilities helped to convince her that Norwegians should be treated in their own health facilities where they would not feel like strangers. In 1885 the Norwegian Relief Society rented a house in Brooklyn that contained nine hospital beds and this institution became the Deaconess Home and Hospital of Brooklyn. Using this hospital as a base Fedde went to the homes of the bedridden, helping them with household chores and looking after children. A larger hospital was later erected, and in 1892 was named the Norwegian Lutheran Deaconesses' Home and Hospital, eventually becoming the Lutheran Medical Center. Fedde also opened a similar deaconess hospital in Minneapolis.[50]

Despite the obvious parallels in the work of the Catholic and Protestant women religious there was a basic difference between the health-care activities of Catholic sisters and Protestant deaconesses and this can best be illustrated by examining the underlying purposes that motivated their acts of charity. Catholic women religious simply desired to alleviate the suffering of the sick, including men, women, and children, and to bring them spiritual consolation during times of illness and impending death. The motivation behind the work of the Protestant deaconesses was more evangelical in nature, that involved the delivery of the good news to women by women. Their work among the poor women in America's big cities had religious conversion as its primary goal, but the deaconesses believed that the "basic needs of food, work, and family had to be met if spiritual change was to follow." In the late nineteenth century, middle-class Protestants looked to the deaconesses as agents of social control to tame and civilize the ignorant immigrant masses, and thus to save America's cities. The work of the deaconess most commonly involved the establishment and management of various charitable institutions including hospitals, schools, and settlement houses for the poor.

The women thought of their responsibility as a "restoration" of the New Testament office of deacon or servant; and the sisters lived together in a parent or motherhouse but did not take vows.[51]

Thus the methods of delivering health care to the immigrant poor seemed to come full circle during the nineteenth century. In the decades before the Civil War, the natural response of the sisters—for example, the Sisters of Mercy—when confronted by the needs of the sick and suffering immigrant population, was to seek them out in their homes, offering medical treatment and spiritual consolation. As one author suggests, these religious communities were established for charity work of one sort or another. Thus the "design of their founders in most instances was that they should minister unto the poor in their own homes," and any further institutions they established were "incidental" to their basic work of home care. Also, those hospitals that were established under the auspices of women religious—under, for example, the Daughters of Charity of St. Vincent de Paul and the Sisters of St. Joseph —were created to provide good nursing care for the poor, regardless of ethnic background. It is equally clear that during the antebellum era, it was the local bishops, as illustrated by the examples of Joseph Cretin, John Neumann, and Joseph Rosati, who were often the first to recognize the need of the immigrant, frequently in poor health, for good medical treatment, and who actively sought the assistance of women religious to serve as the care givers. Although the women religious may not always have initiated ministries of health care, they served the poor gladly and willingly, joining in partnership with the bishops, sacrificing their own material comforts and frequently begging for alms, so that the sick could be treated either at home or in hospitals. But in the post–Civil War era, the sisters, after finding that the poor could not be nursed properly in the crowded dark tenement houses they called home, institutionalized their efforts by caring for the sick in a hospital setting. While the women religious never refused to admit a patient because of race, sex, or national origin, the Catholic hospitals the sisters established in the late nineteenth century were often planned and designed to meet the health-care needs of specific immigrant groups. The members of the religious orders charged with the management of such hospitals were often themselves immigrants who had come to the United States to help their own compatriots. Also, the movement to provide good health care for the immigrant poor during the late nineteenth century was led by several exceptional women religious, including Mother Francesca Cabrini, Mother Mary Theresa (Josephine Dudzik),

Mother Mary Odilia Berger, and Mother Agnes Hazotte, whose drive and energy as well as devotion to the cause of the immigrant poor made possible the creation of good hospitals, hospices, and health-care programs in America's urban areas.

The late nineteenth century witnessed a resurgent demand for women religious to institute programs of home nursing and visitation to complement the work performed by other sisters in Catholic medical facilities. Even at the dawn of the twentieth century there were many poor who feared entering a hospital, viewing such an act as the final step before death and preferring to remain in their own home during times of ill health. Thus the services of the Sisters of Bon Secours and the Nursing Sisters of the Sick Poor were often in demand in America's major cities. Although the manner in which health care was extended to the sick poor in America may have varied, the commitment of women religious to an active health-care ministry never wavered, as they offered Christ all "temporal and spiritual" services in their power to care for the poor, the sick, and others in distress.

NOTES

1. See James Hennesey, "Immigrants Become the Church" in his *American Catholics: A History of the Roman Catholic Community in the United States* (New York: Oxford University Press, 1981). Also see Aaron I. Abell, *American Catholicism and Social Action: A Search for Social Justice* (Garden City, NY: Hanover House, 1960), p. 11; Jay P. Dolan, *The Immigrant Church. New York's Irish and German Catholics 1815-1865* (Baltimore: Johns Hopkins, 1977; University of Notre Dame edition, 1983), p. 2; and Jay P. Dolan, *The American Catholic Experience. A History from Colonial Times to the Present* (Garden City, NY: Doubleday, 1985) p.128.

2. Dolan, *The American Catholic Experience*, pp. 128–29.

3. Ibid., p. 130.

4. *Report of the Select Committee of the Senate of the United States on the Sickness and Mortality on Board Emigrant Ships*, Washington, D.C., 1854, p. 9, as cited by John O'Grady, *Catholic Charities in the United States: History and Problems* (Washington D.C.: Conference of Catholic Charities, 1930), p. 40.

5. Colman J. Barry, *The Catholic Church and German Americans* (Milwaukee: Bruce Publishing, 1953), p. 22

6. *Catholic Mirror* of Baltimore, 6 May 1876, as cited by O'Grady, *Catholic Charities in the United States*, p. 53.

7. Dolan, *The American Catholic Experience*, pp. 137, 145; and O'Grady, *Catholic Charities in the United States*, p. 46.

8. John A. Garraty, ed., *The American Nation: A History of the United States* (New York: Harper and Row, and American Heritage Publishing, 1966), p. 341.

9. George Pare, *The Catholic Church in Detroit, 1701–1888* (Detroit: Gabriel Richard Press, 1951; reprint ed., Detroit: Wayne State University, 1983), p. 659.

10. John Gilmary Shea, *History of the Catholic Church in the United States*, 4 vols. (New York: John G. Shea, 1886–1892), vol. 4, p. 154.

11. Hennesey, *American Catholics*, p. 118.

12. O'Grady, *Catholic Charities in the United States*, p. 10.

13. Elinor Tong Dehey, *Religious Orders of Women in the United States, Catholic*, rev. ed. (Hammond, IN: W. B. Conkey Printers, 1930), p. 75.

14. O'Grady, *Catholic Charities in the United States*, p. 25.

15. John Rothensteiner, *History of the Archdiocese of St. Louis: In Its Various Stages of Development from A.D. 1673 to A.D. 1928*, 2 vols. (St. Louis MO: Press of Blackwell Wielandy, 1928), vol. 2, p. 32.

16. Sister Mary Eulalia Herron, *The Sisters of Mercy in the United States, 1843–1928* (New York: MacMillan, 1929), p. 32.

17. O'Grady, *Catholic Charities in the United States*, p. 187; Ann Doyle, "Nursing by Religious Orders in the United States: Part II, 1841–1970," *The American Journal of Nursing* 29 (August 1929): 962; and John J. Delaney, *Dictionary of American Catholic Biography* (Garden City, NY: Doubleday, 1984), p. 33. For another view, see James F. Connelly, ed., *The History of the Archdiocese of Philadelphia* (Philadelphia: Archdiocese of Philadelphia, 1976), p. 223.

18. Connelly, *The History of the Archdiocese of Philadelphia*, p. 223.

19. Sister Helen Angela Hurley, *On Good Ground: The Story of the Sisters of St. Joseph in St. Paul* (Minneapolis: University of Minnesota Press, 1951), p. 17.

20. The article appeared in the *Pioneer* on 26 January 1855, and is cited by Hurley in her *On Good Ground*, p. 78.

21. Dolan, *The Immigrant Church: New York's Irish and German Catholics 1815–1865*, p. 130.

22. Dolores Ann Liptak, *European Immigrants and the Catholic Church in Connecticut, 1870–1920* (New York: Center for Migration Studies, 1987), p. 12.

23. Pietro Di Donato, *Immigrant Saint: The Life of Mother Cabrini* (New York: McGraw Hill, 1960; Dell Publishing, 1962), pp. 101–2.

24. Liptak, *European Immigrants and the Catholic Church in Connecticut*, p. 14.

25. Sister Mary Gabriel Henninger, *Sisters of Saint Mary and their Healing Mission* (St. Louis, MO: Sisters of St. Mary of the Third Order of St. Francis, 1979), p. 4.

26. Henninger, *Sisters of St. Mary*, p. 7.

27. Ibid., p. 6

28. Ibid., p. 23.

29. Ibid.

30. "History of St. Alexis Hospital," unpaginated from the collection of the Archives of the Diocese of Cleveland, OH.

31. *Ibid*; "The Annual Report St. Alexis Hospital, Cleveland, 1900," p. 22, in the papers of Bishop Ignatius Horstmann, the Archives of the Diocese of Cleveland, OH; and see "Annual Report St. Alexis Hospital, January 1, 1895–January 1, 1896," in the same collection.

32. Taken from page 230 of the scrapbook prepared by Monsignor George F. Houck, in the Archives of the Diocese of Cleveland, OH.

33. Henry M. Malak, *The Apostle of Mercy from Chicago* (London: Veritas Foundation Press, 1962), pp. 52–54, and Malak, ed., *The Apostle of Mercy from Chicago Bulletin* 1 (January 1962): 3, in the papers of Bishop Edward F. Hoban, Archives of the Diocese of Cleveland, OH.

34. Malak, *The Apostle of Mercy from Chicago*, p. 56.

35. Malak, ed., *The Apostle of Mercy from Chicago Bulletin*, pp. 3–4.

36. Malak, *The Apostle of Mercy from Chicago*, p. 56.

37. The Felician Sisters, *Magnificat: A Centennial Record of the Congregation of the Sisters of St. Felix* (November 1955), pp. 7–8.

38. Barry, *The Catholic Church and German Americans*, pp. 30–31, 39–41, 97–98.

39. Amadea Wirtz, *Haven for the Homeless: The Story of the Leo House* (Congregation of the Sisters of St. Agnes, 1985), pp. 10–11.

40. Di Donato, *Immigrant Saint*, p. 56.

41. Thomas Maynard, *Too Small a World: The Life of Francesca Cabrini*, The Science and Culture Series (Milwaukee: Bruce Publishing, 1945), p. 4.

42. Di Donato, *Immigrant Saint*, pp. 59–60.

43. Ibid., p. 102.

44. Maynard, *Too Small a World*, p. 165.

45. Di Donato, *Immigrant Saint*, pp. 103–4.

46. See archival material on the French Hospital provided by the Sisters Marianites of the Holy Cross, or the Marianites, New York, NY; also see Dehey, *Religious Orders of Women*, p. 851.

47. See the archives of Holy Cross Hospital, provided by the Sisters of St. Casimir, Chicago, IL.

48. Sister Mary Cecilia O'Sullivan, *The Sisters of Bon Secours in the United States, 1881–1981: A Century of Caring* (Paris: Congregation of Bon Secours 1982; York, PA: The Maple Press) *passim.*

49. Dehey, *Religious Orders of Women*, pp. 763–64; Archives, Nursing Sisters of the Sick Poor, Brooklyn, NY.

50. Cecyle S. Neidle, *America's Immigrant Women* (Boston: Twayne Publishers, 1975), pp. 76–78.

51. Rosemary Skinner Keller, "Lay Women in the Protestant Tradition," in *Women and Religion in America*, vol. 1, *The Nineteenth Century: A Documentary History*, Rosemary Radford Reuther and Rosemary Skinner Keller, ed. (San Francisco: Harper and Row, 1981), pp. 243 and 249.

✦ In Times of Socioeconomic Crisis

EDNA MARIE LEROUX, RSM

In the archives of religious communities throughout the United States a plethora of source material awaits writers of fiction, history, and biography. Here, in books, manuscripts, and old newspapers are stories as unique as that of Sister Joanna Bruner and her companion who found three men hanging from a lamppost as they entered Laramie, Wyoming; or Sister Amata, dubbed "Sister Lumberjack," who baked pies for men in Minnesota's lumber camps; for the Franciscan Sisters who drove their jeep into the mountains of Arizona to bring medical assistance to isolated Indians and their sick animals. Page after page recounts the experiences of dedicated women who, motivated by love of God and their neighbor, traveled to pioneer missions in America's early years, and every page seems to predict the work of women religious who serve the sick, poor, and neglected today.

During the frequent periods of social and economic crises in the United States, these women, members of many different religious communities in the Catholic church, endured great hardship to bring health care and assistance to victims of disasters and economic depressions. Throughout the nineteenth century they sought out minority groups suffering from prejudice, poverty, and illness; they responded to the health needs of men in railroad and lumber camps; they aided oppressed coal miners; and they traveled miles to care for victims of disease and accidents during and after the California gold rush.

In Mines and Camps

In the West a crisis in health care began when gold was discovered in California in 1848, and word was spread that all one needed to gather

118

a fortune was a pick, shovel, and pan. Men streamed into California from all parts of the United States and abroad.

The blacksmith dropped his hammer, the carpenter his plans, the mason his trowel, the farmer his sickle, the baker his loaf, and the tapster his bottle. All were off for the mines, some on horses, some on carts, and some on crutches.[1]

Boom towns sprang up overnight "roaring with life and death . . . brimming with sap and mischief and vice."[2] In a land where the boundaries of Mexican and American jurisdictions were at first not clear, law-abiding citizens were few. In sprawling boom towns and crowded camps, miners frequently quarreled, injuring or killing one another in gunfights and brawls. Besides living in this dangerous environment, miners, in order to reach gold deposits, often had to descend into deep shafts by means of fragile cages operated by chains that often broke. As plunging cages crashed down the shaft, men were injured or killed.

Despite danger and disease prevalent in the camps and mines, little care was at first taken to prevent accidents or illness, and many miners suffered permanent disability or died from lack of proper care. Gradually, communities of women religious became aware of the situation. Sometimes miners themselves turned to the sisters for assistance. From the 1850s through the end of the nineteenth century, many religious communities responded to these requests. Among them were the Sisters of Charity of Leavenworth, Kansas [0480], who opened a hospital in Deer Lodge, Montana, in 1873; the Congregation of the Sisters of the Holy Cross [1920] from South Bend, Indiana, who established hospitals in both Lead City and Deadwood, in the Dakota Territory, in 1878; the Sisters of St. Joseph of Carondelet [3840], who founded a hospital in Georgetown, Colorado, in 1880; and the Sisters of Mercy from Denver (now part of the Omaha Province, Sisters of Mercy of the Union [2580]), who opened a hospital in Cripple Creek, Colorado, in 1894. Usually only a few sisters could be spared to set up hospitals, perhaps begun in abandoned buildings or log cabins with meager equipment and little or no outside help in addressing the needs of the area. It was not unusual for sisters to visit the sick in camps and then also function as administrators, nurses, and menial workers in the hospitals.

As miners moved from place to place in search of precious metals, requests for women religious to organize hospitals multiplied. In the 1860s, for instance, Colorado miners who had previously met the Sisters of Charity of Leavenworth on their trips, begged them to open a hospital in Leadville. Soon three sisters were on their way. To reach this city of twenty thousand people they traveled by rail, stagecoach, and flatbed wagon in subzero weather. Once in Leadville, new problems loomed. For one thing, the terrain was so rugged that materials to build the hospital were frequently delayed, and even before the structure was finished, almost thirty patients had been admitted.

These early hospitals near mines were often financed by an insurance plan. The miners paid a small fee, from five to twelve dollars a year, and in return received free hospital care when injured or ill. Sisters and priests also solicited funds from generous miners who appreciated the sisters' care and concern for their physical and spiritual welfare. In Butte, Montana, for example, where the Sisters of Charity of Leavenworth agreed to operate a hospital in 1881, two sisters went about on horseback soliciting contributions. Catholic and non-Catholic supported their efforts. When the hospital was built, private patients and county patients received "careful nursing in clean, well-ventilated rooms."[3] The chief means of support, however, was the miners' payment of monthly subscriptions for care. But as the population in boom towns decreased when the source of wealth in mines was depleted, many hospitals closed; others endured for over a hundred years, and some continue today.

Coal miners were as greatly in need of medical care as were miners of precious metals. Their plight was equally dangerous; their work conditions oppressive. Some measures had been taken to prevent worse conditions, but progress was slow, particularly during the throes of industrial growth. Before the unions became effectively strong in the twentieth century, miners were paid low wages for dangerous and exhausting work and were constantly exploited. In some areas they were compelled to buy only from the company store, using twenty dollars in scrip every month; otherwise, they were laid off until that amount was spent. A stanza by Merle Travis expressed in dark humor the miners' frustration:

> You load sixteen ton and what do you get?
> Another day older, and deeper in debt.
> St. Peter, don't you call me, because I can't go
> I owe my soul to the company store.[4]

Caught in a web of poverty, malnutrition, and illness, the miners could expect little. In the poorly ventilated mines, coal dust polluted the air, methane lights ignited volatile gas, and frequent cave-ins buried miners.

Near coal mines as well as near gold mines, religious congregations sought ways to provide adequate care. For instance, in Wilkes-Barre, Pennsylvania, called the geographical center of the largest anthracite coal fields, tragic accidents and horrible injuries were common. The Sisters of Mercy [2580] from Scranton (now of the Scranton Province of the Union) answered the request of several young physicians and established the Wilkes-Barre Mercy Hospital in 1889. From their motherhouse the sisters commuted daily to treat victims of mine disasters as well as the poor and sick in the area.

More recently, in 1979, in Memphis, Tennessee, an article in a diocesan newspaper records a different but related type of health service. When twenty-six men died in twin methane gas explosions in 1976, two congregations of women religious, the Sisters of Loretto at the Foot of the Cross [2360] and the Sisters, Servants of the Immaculate Heart of Mary [2170], both congregations holding stock in the Blue Diamond Mines in Letcher County, Kentucky, sued the coal company for not recognizing them as stockholders and not notifying them of all meetings. By this action sisters were able to effect change by emphasizing the social responsibility of corporations in preventing injuries to their workers.

But camps and settlements near coal or gold mines were not the only areas which needed health care. During the westward movement in the nineteenth century, the lumber industry also boomed. As lumber camps dotted the forest, lumberjacks suffered many serious injuries when they felled trees or rolled logs downriver to the saw mills. Although the lumberjack himself was usually young, powerfully built, and unmarried ("a lad who ranged three thousand miles through the forests of Maine to Oregon, steel calks in his boots, an ax in his fist, and a plug of chewing handy"[5]) he was assured of a job only so long as he remained healthy.

But disease and the danger of injury and death were always present in the northern forests from Maine to the Pacific Northwest, and Paul Bunyan was not around as lumberjacks hewed and sawed through thick trunks of towering trees, where a sudden wind could cause a tree to fall the wrong way and crush anyone in its path, flying splinters could pierce an eye, and hands could be severed by dangerous saws. In the bitter northern winters hands and feet were frozen, and in milder weather men could be hurt or drowned while rolling logs down the rivers. Many lumberjacks were crippled for life or died for want of intelligent care.

To provide care and build hospitals, members of religious congregations came to lumber camp areas. For instance, in Michigan, scene of many lumber camps and saw mills, the local pastor visited the camps and, appalled by the sad condition of lumberjacks who suffered from accidents or were victims of disease, requested the Sisters of Mercy from Grand Rapids [2580] (now part of the Detroit Province of the Union) to found a hospital near the camp at Big Rapids, a thriving center of lumbering industry. Although the Sisters of Mercy in Grand Rapids were teachers, Mother Mary Joseph Lynch, foundress of the Grand Rapids Sisters of Mercy, had had nursing experience with Florence Nightingale during the Crimean War. With a few Sisters of Mercy she came to Big Rapids in 1879, prepared to help the lumberjacks.

A hospital fund had been accumulating before the sisters arrived, and a plain wooden frame structure "that was ceiled [sic] up inside and protected from the cold by a layer of sawdust in the walls"[6] was built. Inside were wards for the lumberjacks, for until about 1899 the care of the patients was almost the sole responsibility of a few sisters whose duties included not only nursing but also the hospital's financial affairs, food service, and menial work. During the first four years sisters admitted over two thousand patients, most of whom had paid only five dollars yearly for health care. For this amount the lumberjack received a ticket which entitled him to "a home, with board, medicine, doctor's fee, and care of the sisters." In accepting patients, the sisters made no distinction regarding creed or country of origin; all were welcomed and treated equally. There were, however, a few restrictions on the reverse of the insurance ticket which stated that it was not transferable, must have the Mercy seal, and was not good for admission to any other hospital. The hospital would not admit anyone under the influence of liquor, nor "any person affected with disease of indiscretion . . . unless on payment of an extra fee, and then by advice of the physician only."[7]

By 1905 the ticket charge was eight dollars a year with the same services provided. Without the ticket, the charge was one dollar a day. By this time, the old hospital building had burned and a new brick-veneer building, the "pride of Big Rapids," had taken its place. Unfortunately, in 1908 this building also burned, and the sisters took over the old Northern Hotel in Big Rapids and converted it into a hospital. When fire destroyed this structure in 1919 and five lives were lost, the sisters, although encouraged to remain, could no longer risk building another hospital because of inadequate water facilities in case of fire. Meanwhile, however, the Sisters of Mercy had established other hospitals farther north and west in Michigan—in Manistee, Grayling, Cadillac,

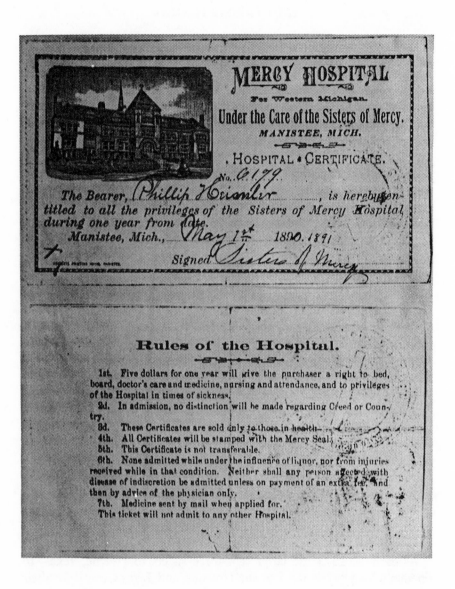

Copy of an "insurance" certificate purchased by a lumberjack. Original in Archives, Sisters of Mercy of the Union, Detroit Province, Farmington Hills, Michigan.

and Muskegon—all near lumber camps and mills. Today, the Sisters of Mercy of the Detroit Province continue to sponsor all but one of these hospitals.

Over time, other religious communities of women became involved in supplying health needs for lumberjacks. In the 1870s the Franciscan Sisters, known also as Sisters of the Third Order Minor Conventuals [1490], from Syracuse, New York, traveled by freight train and sled to the Adirondacks to solicit funds for their hospital; in 1874 the Daughters of Charity [0760] staffed a hospital for lumberjacks in Saginaw, Michigan; and in the 1880s a Benedictine sister from Duluth [0230], Sister Amata, known as "the Lumberjack Sister," walked or rode by "tote team or railroad caboose" from camp to camp selling insurance tickets to lumberjacks to finance hospitals in northern Minnesota. As lumberjacks moved north and west, members of religious congregations moved to new locales to set up hospitals and provide health service for lumberjacks. Many hospitals originally built near lumber camps remain viable institutions today.

In the nineteenth century another critical need for health care arose as railroads began inching across the United States. Many immigrants—Chinese, Italian, German, Mexican, and others from different parts of Europe—joined with Indians and other Americans to find employment with the powerful railroad companies that began linking cities throughout the United States. Workers, subject to disease and serious injury while blasting through rocks, pounding spikes with huge hammers, or forging rails in mills set up along the tracks, lived in temporary camps near the rails as they moved across the states and territories sometimes far from cities and hospitals. Railroad companies, bishops, and priests soon realized the urgency of providing workers with access to adequate health care and began requesting the services of such religious congregations as the Sisters of Charity of the Incarnate Word from Galveston, Texas [0470].

As early as 1871 the latter sent three sisters to Hearne, Texas, to operate a hospital donated by the Houston and Texas Central for their employees. St. Theresa's Hospital, as it was named, was destined to be short-lived, for Hearne lost importance as a railroad center later in the year, and the sisters returned to St. Mary's Infirmary in Galveston. However, a few years later St. Mary's Infirmary itself became the center for treatment of injured and sick railroad employees of the Gulf, Colorado, and Sante Fe Railway Company. When this railway's offices and activity moved east to Temple, Texas, employees of the railway urged the company to staff the new hospital with sisters from St. Mary's Infirmary. Complying with their request, Mother Mary Joseph Roussin and four sisters went to Temple in 1891 and organized a twenty-bed hospital in a little frame house. For over sixty years the Sisters of Charity of the Incarnate Word staffed this hospital and saw to its expansion.

Another religious congregation, the Sisters of Charity of Leavenworth, Kansas, also administered a hospital for railroad workers at the request of the pastor of Laramie City, Wyoming, the county commissioners of the poor, and the manager of the Union Pacific Railway Company. Although for the first two sisters who arrived in Laramie City, Sister Joanna Bruner and Sister Martha Meade, the sight of three men hanging from a lamppost had occasioned shock and distress, they remained in this Wild West area to organize a twenty-four-bed hospital in a renovated building for all who needed care. Even this old building, however, soon proved inadequate. To gather funds the sisters took to the road once more. On railway handcars, with "black habits and headdresses billowing in the winds, they . . . headed for the camps to solicit funds to finance the new hospital."[8] At mining camps and railroad camps, men responded generously and the new hospital was built. For almost a decade the Sisters of Charity of Leavenworth labored in Laramie City. Then in 1895 they sold the hospital to the diocese and withdrew.

Other religious congregations of women responded to railway managers' requests to staff hospitals for their employees. Among them were the Hospital Sisters of the Third Order of St. Francis [1820], who provided nursing service from 1884 to 1906 for a total of six railroad hospitals serving both the Wabash Railroad and the Missouri Pacific Railroad in Illinois; the Sisters of Mercy from Kansas (now in the St. Louis Province of the Union [2580], who organized a hospital in Fort Scott in 1886 and another in Kansas City, Kansas, in 1893 for the Memphis Railway Company; the Sisters of Mercy from California (now of the Sisters of Mercy, Burlingame [2570], who contracted with the Southern Pacific Railway Company in 1897 to admit railway cases to already existing hospitals in Prescott and Nogales, Arizona; and the Congregation of the Sisters of the Holy Cross [1920] from South Bend, Indiana, who opened two hospitals, one in Ogden, Utah, in 1887 for the Union Pacific Railway and another in Springfield, Missouri, for the St. Louis and San Francisco Railway in 1899. Usually railway companies paid salaries to the sisters and sometimes added room and board. Many companies also offered some type of insurance for their workers for as little as fifty cents a month. In other situations sisters themselves initiated an insurance plan or persuaded societies to finance health care for ill or injured railroad workers, as did Sister Joanna Bruner, who persuaded the Society for Hospital Care to allocate part of their funds for this purpose.

Railroad hospitals continued their service even after the construction of railroads was finished, for in the early years of railroad travel many accidents occurred: men working on the lines were caught between cars or slipped under the wheels, and frequently crews and passengers were injured or killed in train wrecks. But as the urgency for health care lessened in some areas, hospitals phased out their operations and women religious moved elsewhere. Occasionally, residents expressed public recognition for sisters' services—sometimes many years after they had left. Because of Sister Joanna Bruner's accomplishments, a street in Laramie, Wyoming, was named after her by the county commissioner a hundred years after her work there. It was the first street in Laramie not only named for a woman, but certainly the first named for a member of a religious congregation.

Among Minority Groups

Throughout the nineteenth and twentieth centuries religious congregations of women made their services available not only in areas experiencing a crisis in health care near mines and camps, but also in areas where minority groups—especially Indians, blacks, the poor of Appalachia, and migrants—had settled or worked. In fact, one congregation of women religious, the Sisters of the Blessed Sacrament for Indians and Colored People [0260], founded in 1891 by Katherine Drexel (an heiress to the Drexel fortune), has for its main focus the care of the sick among blacks and Indians and the education of their children.

In the nineteenth century the sad condition of the American Indians, gradually displaced and often shuttled off to live an unnatural way of life within the confining limits of reservations, became a major concern for many religious congregations. Without a knowledge of good hygiene, Indians were easy prey for communicable diseases, such as smallpox and other debilitating illnesses. At the request of missionary priests or bishops, religious congregations sent sisters to the Indian missions, beginning in the late 1840s. Among the sisters who were engaged in Indian missionary work were the Sisters of Loretto at the Foot of the Cross from Kentucky, who went to the Osage Indian mission in Kansas as early as 1847 to teach children and visit and care for the sick; the Sisters of St. Joseph of Carondelet, who in 1851 established a mission for the Winnebago Indians in Long Prairie, Minnesota; and the Sisters of Charity of Providence from Montreal, Quebec [3350], who began to work at St. Ignatius Mission in Montana by the late 1850s. Other congregations active among the Indians were the Sisters of Mercy from Manchester, New Hampshire, who went to Maine to help the Abenaki Indians near the Penobscot River in 1878; the Congregation of the Sisters of the Third Order of St. Francis of Perpetual Adoration [1780] from La Crosse, Wisconsin, who worked at the Chippewa mission in Odanah, Wisconsin in 1883; and the Ursuline Sisters [4110] from Montana, who labored at Indian missions during the nineteenth century in various areas in Montana and eventually extended their services to natives of Alaska in 1905.

Life for the missionaries on Indian missions, particularly in the nineteenth century, was not easy. The Sisters of St. Joseph of Carondelet described the scene of many missions as "having a basic lack of water alternating with washouts from floods."[9] The missionaries experienced long days of manual labor, along with classroom instruction and visitation of the sick and dying Indians in their homes—wigwams, lodges, hogans, and cabins. Many times, to reach their patients, sisters would have to crawl on hands and knees through openings serving as doors. Once inside they would need an interpreter to understand their patients. In areas where few priests were regularly available, sisters acted as quasi pastors—baptizing, assisting the dying, and officiating at funerals. Not only were physical conditions trying, but occasionally the bigotry of white people added to their hardship. Angry medicine men, too, often resented the presence of sisters who cared for the sick: in one particular instance, several sisters would have been murdered if they had not been warned.

In the twentieth century more women religious, aware of the poverty and disease prevalent on Indian reservations, became available to care for Indians. For example, the Hospital Sisters of the Third Order of St. Francis from Springfield, Illinois, continued to send sisters to the Navajo Reservation at Lukachuka, Arizona, as the mission grew. In 1953 they began to attend to the health of the Indians twice weekly. Later, as the number of patients increased, they established a residence and opened a dispensary in two hogans. By 1954 the sisters were treating almost fifteen thousand patients annually, and in 1956 they had to build a new dispensary with a few beds for patients. Later this building would be converted into an outpatient clinic serviced by volunteer doctors. The sisters also reached outlying districts by jeep, where, as word of their arrival spread, Indians brought not only their sick for treatment, but sometimes even their sick animals. In more recent times, as direct links with the public health departments became more typical, the sisters added an obstetric clinic and began operating such adjunct services as used-clothing shops. Unfortunately, circumstances forced the sisters to withdraw in 1980.

While work among the Indians was strenuous and exhausting, work among the blacks, particularly in the South, had a meaner dimension because of the presence of deep-seated prejudice. Before the advent of civil rights legislation and federal entitlement programs, segregation was typical in public facilities, including hospitals. Black patients were often placed in damp, dark basement rooms where only black nurses could care for them; moreover, no black physicians were allowed on the staff. For the most part, black employees did menial work only.

This was the state of affairs when the Springfield Dominicans, also known as the Congregation of Our Lady of the Sacred Heart [1070], took over a public hospital in Jackson, Mississippi, in the 1940s and named it St. Dominic's. So pervasive was the prejudice they encountered that they immediately examined their alternatives of service. They realized that to be too aggressive in breaking down prejudice would result in exclusion from effective health service to blacks, but to be too timid would signify approval of unjust laws. The only feasible tactic, the sisters decided, was compromise. They developed a moderate but persistent policy to promote equal treatment for black patients and respect for blacks as individuals. Among the changes the Springfield Dominicans were able to make were decent accommodations for black patients, the integration of every area in the hospital not forbidden by law, and the employment of qualified blacks throughout the hospital, where sisters encouraged them to advance professionally. When later a hospital addition was needed and was submitted for approval by the American College of Surgeons, the sisters' application for federal funds was blocked by the Mississippi Commission on Hospital Care. Once more, the sisters had to use every means to fight prejudice. Only the assistance of a few influential citizens, untainted by local prejudice, effected the completion of the building. A decade later, the administrator of St. Dominic's was finally able to sign the federal Assurance Compliance Form, indicating that the hospital would completely integrate. At that point, finally, the transition was almost without incident. Few employees resigned.

As in the Mississippi example, many southern hospitals and nursing homes at first refused to admit blacks. When the Hospital Sisters of the Third Order of St. Francis opened a nursing home for the aged in Louisiana, they were also advised to limit admissions to white persons. Their alternative was particularly ingenious. To insure proper health care to blacks, the sisters used the nursing home as a supply center. From here they provided nursing service to blacks taking medicinal supplies and providing health care to blacks in their own homes. Later they were able to reserve a section of the nursing home for blacks. Gradually they managed to have white and black patients share rooms without incident.

Another example of mean-spirited prejudice occurred in Jonesboro, Arkansas. There the Olivetan Benedictine Sisters [0240] had actually been ordered not to admit black patients. However, when a tragedy occurred in a nearby quarry and many blacks were trapped in a landslide, the sisters ignored the order and sought out the victims, admitting workers who were severely injured and required surgery. Almost immediately there were threatening letters, and worse than threats—the resignation of all but one of the doctors. The remaining doctor's courage and the sisters' insistence that they would serve the blacks, gradually broke down enough prejudice so that the sisters were able to maintain a reserved section in the hospital for blacks.

Injuries to blacks and whites during race riots often brought about ironic situations. In the 1908 race riot in Springfield, Illinois, the hospital administered by the Hospital Sisters of the Third Order of St. Francis became so overcrowded with riot victims that mattresses had to be set up on the floor to supplement the available beds. There, sharing a common misery, black and white patients, lying adjacent to each other, forgot their prejudice and antagonism. St. Mary's Hospital, administered by the Poor Handmaids of Jesus Christ [3230], also became a refuge for both black and white during a race riot in East St. Louis, Illinois, in 1917. Other similar incidents are recorded during more recent race riots in Detroit, Newark, and other cities.

In the nineteenth and twentieth centuries the welfare of blacks has been one of the primary concerns of a number of congregations of women religious. The Sisters of the Blessed Sacrament for Indians and Colored People [0260], the Franciscan Sisters of St. Joseph [1470], the Congregation of the Sisters of the Holy Cross from South Bend, Indiana, have all stated that service to blacks is one of the aims of their congregation; and certainly it is the purpose of two congregations of black women religious, the Oblate Sisters of Providence [3040], founded in

Baltimore in 1829, and the Congregation of the Sisters of the Holy Family [1950], founded in New Orleans in 1842.

Although less overt than prejudice against blacks, prejudice against migrants continues to exist in many areas. Migrants, many of whom are Mexican-American or Mexican, live a nomadic life as they move from farm to farm to harvest seasonal crops. From their southern home base, they form a "migrant stream" moving north in the spring and another returning south in the fall; never are they able to remain very long in one locality. This impermanence, along with their background and nationality, leads to less than fair treatment. Living at the poverty level, they are at the mercy of their employers and usually cannot benefit from the support of certain unions (the Taft-Hartley Act specifically denies farmworkers the right to organize). Therefore, they seldom engage in collective bargaining. Dependent on middlemen, they hope to obtain employment at a fixed minimum wage. The work is backbreaking, the hours are long, and there is no extra pay for overtime or compensation for layoffs during bad weather or mechanical breakdowns. Living conditions are equally bad; they must settle for overcrowded, dilapidated houses with inadequate, and even contaminated, water supply, and with inadequate refrigeration and food-storage facilities. Few are the employers who provide decent living quarters and a just wage.

Because of these substandard living and working conditions, migrants are subject to diseases that seldom affect established Americans—tuberculosis, parasitic infestations, diarrheal disease, and nutritional deficiencies. Preventable accidents are frequent; health problems are compounded by contact with pesticides and lack of proper sanitation in work areas. To receive health care at times of illness migrants sometimes have to travel great distances, despite inadequate transportation. Even if they have good transportation, they may find clinics closed after work hours.

Since 1909 the United States government has commissioned reports, formed commissions, and held conferences concerning conditions for migrants. Unfortunately, effective implementation of recommendations has never become a reality; today the problems endure. Some improvement in migrants' health care, however, has been made by the federal government, especially by the passage of the Migrant Health Act in 1962, which appropriated funds, however inadequate, for migrant clinics. To fill the gap, religious congregations that operate hospitals have for years provided free hospitalization and treatment to migrants. For example, at Mercy Hospital, Bay City, Michigan, the Sisters of Mercy of the Detroit Province admitted and treated migrant patients, often free of charge; visited camps; donated medicine, clothing, and basic supplies; and sent volunteer doctors and nurses to examine and treat patients suffering from a variety of illnesses.

But perhaps the greatest and most effective service women religious have given to the migrant cause has been the formation of the National Migrant Worker's Council, created by religious of different congregations who belong to the National Council of Religious Superiors (now known as the Leadership Conference of Women Religious). Spearheaded by Sister Maurita Senglelaub of the Sisters of Mercy of the Union, Detroit Province [2580], the organization, incorporated in 1978, began a pattern of recruiting professional personnel—nurses, health aides, and others who could serve migrants during peak crop seasons in fifteen states along the East Coast, and during the winter at the migrants' home base in Florida. Through Sister Mary Maurita's efforts substantial funds for the project were appropriated by the Division of Health Service of the Department of Human Services of the federal government and by other organizations. More recently founded is the Midwest Migrant Health Project, which serves midwestern states in a somewhat different capacity and operates out of the Midwest Migrant Health Information Office. The Catholic Consortium for Migrant Health contributes annual funds to this initiative. The consortium is composed of six Catholic health systems, each sponsored by one of six different religious congregations—the Sisters of St. Mary of the Third Order of St. Francis [3970], St. Louis, Missouri; the Franciscan Sisters, Little Falls, Minnesota [1310]; the Congregation of the Sisters of the Holy Cross, South Bend, Indiana; the Sisters of Mercy of the Union, Detroit Province, Farmington Hills, Michigan; the Sisters of Providence [3350], Seattle, Washington; and the Sisters of Charity of Nazareth [0500], Louisville, Kentucky.

Another deprived minority group, the resident poor of Appalachia, continue to be in urgent need of adequate health care. Describing the indigence and deprivation prevalent in this area in the early 1960s, an author and social activist stated:

> Being poor is not one aspect of a person's life in this country, it is his life. Taken as a whole poverty is a culture. Taken on a family level, it has the same quality. These are people who lack education and skill, who have bad health, poor housing, low levels of aspiration and high levels of mental distress.[10]

Such were the conditions when Sister Rachel, a member of the Glenmary Sisters [2080], formally known as the Home Mission Sisters of America, and her three companions came to Hayesville, North Carolina, in 1958 and opened a clinic and home-nursing service. It was an area where few jobs were available; where families lived in patched, tar-paper cabins; where people, black and white, weak from lack of proper nutrition, lived mostly by subsistence farming on worn-out land. There were no hospitals or nursing services, and the people were ill, lonely, and discouraged. Here the sisters lived among the people in this mountainous area amid scenes of breathtaking beauty, marred by strip farming and scarred by poverty. They visited the poor in their shacks, treated the sick, took blood pressures, arranged for trips to the clinic, encouraged good nutrition, and tried to dispel loneliness and discouragement.

At first the Glenmary Sisters were apprehensive. Hayesville and Clay County were only .5 percent Catholic; they knew there would be obstacles. However, after six years they were completely integrated into the community and were able to cooperate with the area's redevelopment program. Through the gift of a mobile clinic the sisters and doctors were able to give emergency hospital treatment in remote mountain districts. By the end of the first year the sisters made over four hundred home calls and serviced more than one thousand patients in the clinic. Although the Glenmary Sisters no longer reside in Appalachia, they continue to sponsor volunteers and lay nurses who work in many areas of Appalachia doing social work and providing health care.

Although in the 1980s the U.S. government passed the Appalachian Regional Development Act and expended about 1.2 billion dollars for road projects and other improvements, and while local organizations also have given assistance, the same conditions remain widespread today. But the efforts of religious communities continue to be effective. In addition to the Glenmary Sisters, who currently sponsor lay personnel, other religious congregations continue their work in this area giving health care, educating adults and children, and doing social work. Members of four different communities of Sisters of Mercy collaborate in doing social work and rescue-squad work in Pocahantas, Virginia; a second group of Sisters of Mercy—three from the Detroit Province of the Union and one from Plainfield, New Jersey—work in Rosman, North Carolina; the Sisters of Divine Providence from Melbourne, Kentucky, operate a number of hospitals; and religious and laypeople work out of the Big Sandy Hospice in Prestonburg, Kentucky, visiting terminally ill patients and their families.

In the Midst of Disasters

Not surprisingly, members of religious congregations have been among the first to assist the injured, homeless, and hungry at times of natural disasters and to make available their homes, schools, and hospitals to all who needed care or shelter. They have visited the suffering and the dying, giving them medical attention and consolation. These women religious have been ready for service when tornadoes, fires, floods, and earthquakes have spread destruction over cities and surrounding areas.

To mention earthquakes is to visualize the devastation wrecked on San Francisco by the terrible quake of 1906. But even before this date, earthquakes in San Francisco and in other areas have terrified residents. As early as 1868, a Sister of Mercy from the San Francisco community (now Sisters of Mercy, Burlingame) described a fairly severe shock as feeling "like a monster dog getting up from sleep."[11] Not as destructive or as extensive as the later San Francisco quake of 1906, it nevertheless was severe enough to collapse buildings, buckle sidewalks, and send terrified people rushing from buildings. Those who were unable to return to their homes slept in public squares for weeks afterward. Many who were injured were brought to St. Mary's Hospital, administered by the Sisters of Mercy, which was not affected by the quake. As many patients as the hospital could accommodate were cared for here. The sisters also visited and nursed the sick and injured who lay in parks and streets or in their own homes.

Then came the great earthquake of 1906. It struck San Francisco and destroyed half the city, splitting buildings, tumbling walls, and snapping or burying the city's water pipes. When fire broke out shortly after the quake, it could not be contained and raged three days and two nights. Injuries were devastating; people were burned, crushed, or struck by falling buildings and debris. Rough estimates of death and destruction range from four hundred fifty to seven hundred persons killed, with loss of property and possessions up to two hundred million dollars.

In the midst of this chaos and devastation, a number of congregations of women religious, among them the Dominican Sisters, Congregation of the Most Holy Name [1070], from San Rafael and Sisters of Mercy (now Sisters of Mercy, Burlingame) set up temporary hospitals and dispensaries in empty school buildings and in other structures still standing. Because starting fires for cooking was not allowed indoors, stoves were placed on sidewalks to boil water and heat soup for patients.

The sisters, assisted by the Red Cross, fed and nursed the injured and frequently gave up their mattresses to the sick. They also visited the sick in their homes and brought them medicine and food.

Meanwhile, the same St. Mary's Hospital which had withstood the 1886 earthquake became a refuge for victims of the 1906 quake, but for only a short time. When flames threatened to engulf this seemingly secure refuge, the Sisters of Mercy and other hospital personnel evacuated some three hundred patients, transporting them to the shore of San Francisco Bay, where they boarded the boat *Modoc*. As the boat moved across the bay to Oakland, all watched the hospital burn until only the cross, outlined in fire, blazed against the blackened sky. The hill upon which St. Mary's had stood then became known as Red Cross Hill. When residents were permitted to return to San Francisco, the sisters searched for a suitable building which might serve as a hospital. Disappointed, they hired two double-team wagons and drove around San Francisco until they had collected fifty tents, cots, and assorted blankets. To help equip what would become a tent hospital, the Presido Hospital donated utensils and a field range, and the U.S. government provided food and medicine. Volunteers helped set up the make-shift hospital so that the sisters could move patients and dependents back to San Francisco. This temporary tent hospital operated for about two months until the sisters were able to rent an old sanitorium. Later, after five years of nursing in this dilapidated building, they acquired sufficient funds to build a new St. Mary's Hospital on Hayes and Slanyon streets—significantly, on the same site as the former tent hospital. The Sisters of Mercy from the Burlingame community, which now includes the San Francisco community, remain its administrators today.

The services of women religious had also been offered during one of the most tragic and destructive fires ever to occur in the United States—the Chicago fire of 1871. Flaring up on Chicago's West Side, it raged for two days, destroying everything as it swept through the city: it ravaged 194 acres on the West Side, to the South Side business district, and on to the North. Almost two hundred persons were killed, about one hundred thousand were made homeless, and almost two hundred million dollars in real estate was lost. Waterworks and gas lines were shattered.

The hospital in Chicago then able to accommodate large numbers of patients was Mercy Hospital. Located near Lake Michigan and well out of range of the fire, it was immediately put to use: its capacity was stretched to admit 266, more than twice the figure it was equipped to serve. Victims of the disaster occupied every possible space from cellar to attic; Sisters of Mercy, who administered this hospital, and doctors often had to give up their beds to make room for the next emergency patients. But the extent of the disaster was apparent not only in numbers but in the severity of the suffering. Patients were brought in so blackened by soot, smoke, and burned flesh, that it was often impossible to distinguish black from white. Many were in excruciating agony with faces and hands disfigured and swollen, and clothing still adhering to their skin. Others suffered from smoke inhalation, broken bones, or other injuries. Space and services were further taxed when sailors from the burned-out Marine Hospital were admitted. Navy officers suggested there be police surveillance of these men, who tended to be unruly, but the sisters refused. The sisters' trust was well-founded. The sailors proved to be docile and cooperative patients. When the Marine Hospital was rebuilt, many preferred to remain in Mercy Hospital.

The effects of the fire were long-term. Besides suffering permanent physical disabilities, many endured severe emotional scarring as family members were separated or brought to different nursing areas. A frantic search for the missing too frequently ended in the tragic news that a father, mother, or child had died in the fire. Many children were orphaned and months went by before some were claimed; one child, unclaimed for three years, was finally adopted by the sisters at Mercy Hospital. Then, too, despite money and supplies sent from generous donors and help from local relief societies, the fire was a financial disaster. Bills could not be collected and the sisters had to sell mortgaged property at a great loss; they were left with only a few hundred dollars in the bank and an accumulation of bills to pay. Still the hospital was able to survive through donations, particularly that of the Chicago Relief and Aid Society, which endowed forty Mercy beds, at one thousand dollars each, in gratitude to the sisters for their care of the greatest number of patients during the fire. As a result, thirty to forty patients were supported on this fund for more than five years. Today, the Sisters of Mercy, now part of the Chicago Province, continue to administer the hospital.

During disasters caused by fires, many other religious congregations actively assisted the homeless, injured, and ill. For instance, in 1845 Sisters of Mercy from Pittsburgh [2570] aided victims of a fire which destroyed a large section of that city; in 1851 the Sisters of St. Joseph of Carondelet assisted victims of a fire in St. Louis that destroyed three-fourths of the city. Much later, in 1937, when the dirigible *Hindenburg* burned at Lakehurst, New Jersey, an Alexian Brother [0120], a member of the only congregation of men completely devoted to nursing the sick, drove the first ambulance to arrive at the scene of the disaster and transported victims to nearby Alexian Hospital in Elizabeth, New Jersey.

One of the first times that congregations of women religious in the United States were able to help victims of floods was in 1861 in Sacramento, California, when the American River flooded the city to a depth of eight feet. Thousands had no shelter. Families scrambled to reach upper stories in their homes; others took possession of deserted houses. The Sisters of Mercy (now of Burlingame) were victims of the flood; they were forced to move up to the second story of their flooded convent. From here they rowed a boat to other residences, set up planks from the prow of their boat to the second- or third-story windows of flooded homes, and climbed across to help the sick and dying. Mother Mary Baptist Russell, foundress of the California Sisters of Mercy (now of Burlingame), and a group of sisters worked day and night organizing shelter for the destitute and homeless. Sisters came from San Francisco to help, and San Francisco authorities sent bedding, food, and clothing. The sisters also went daily to a large building that was opened to receive the sick, injured, or homeless poor.

About two decades later, Cincinnati, Ohio, experienced one of its worst floods, the Great Flood of 1883, when the Ohio River overflowed and submerged the lower areas of the city. So deep were the flood waters that a fleet of steamers cruised canals where streets had been and brought food and supplies to residents living in upper stories of their homes. The flood provided an opportunity for the Sisters of Charity of Cincinnati [0440] to shelter the homeless and open a soup kitchen. One parlor in the House of Mercy was converted into a dispensary. All religious in the area helped care for the injured, ill, and destitute.

Another major flood, described as the worst flood since the 1889 Johnstown flood, was the 1913 flood in Hamilton, Ohio, located a few miles north of Cincinnati, which left more that one hundred dead and thousands of families homeless when, on March 25, a huge reservoir two miles north of the city burst, and the Great and Little Miami rivers overflowed. At Mercy Hospital, Hamilton, the lowest floor was flooded before warning could be given, and personnel and Sisters of Mercy (now in the Cincinnati Province of the Union) hastily carried supplies to the fourth floor. As the water rose, the hospital was cut off and lacked safe drinking water and heat. Friends rushed in supplies and more sisters came from Cincinnati to help in the emergency. Sisters used the three upper floors of the hospital for patients and refugees. There they fed the hungry, prepared surgical dressings for the injured, furnished medicine, and filled prescriptions for doctors. Outside, waters flowed around the hospital and rescue work continued as boats moved from home to home. Today, almost eighty years later, Mercy Hospital in Hamilton, greatly expanded, is a viable institution still administered by the Sisters of Mercy.

Religious congregations have frequently assisted victims of tornadoes in the United States, where each year more than six hundred tornadoes are reported. Ironically, one of the most destructive tornadoes indirectly initiated the foundation of the internationally famous Mayo Clinic in Rochester, Minnesota. In 1883 the town of Rochester, then comprising only sixteen hundred inhabitants, was struck by a devastating tornado which seemed to rush through the city like a sudden invasion of hundreds of freight trains. In the solid black of the storm, punctuated by flashes of lightning, the town was torn apart; within an hour one out of every three homes was demolished, twenty-six persons were killed, more than sixty were severely injured, and a hundred were hurt. Almost immediately a congregation of Franciscan Sisters (Sisters of the Third Order Regular of St. Francis of the Congregation of Our Lady of Lourdes [1720]) who operated a boarding school in Rochester turned the building over to Dr. William Worrell Mayo, a local physician who had been appointed by the city council to oversee treatment of the injured. Dr. Mayo requested the sisters to help take care of the tornado victims. Even though the sisters were teachers, they complied with his request, worked in their own convent school and in an empty dance hall, which had also been transformed into a temporary hospital. Under Dr. Mayo's direction, the sisters nursed the sick and injured in the temporary hospitals and visited other victims in the city, distributing food and clothing and giving help and consolation wherever needed.

Sometime later, when the town was returning to normal activity, Mother Alfred Moes, foundress of Rochester branch of the Franciscan Sisters, began to recognize a new mission for her congregation: in a small town like Rochester there should be a hospital prepared to admit victims of emergencies, and sister-nurses there to staff it. Her vision clear, she approached Dr. Mayo with the suggestion. So great was her enthusiasm that his initial reluctance gave way to assent. Dr. Mayo agreed to take charge of the future hospital if the sisters provided the building and equipment. Begun in 1888 and financed by the work of the Franciscan Sisters, St. Mary's Hospital was completed in 1889. Dr.

Mayo took charge, and later his two sons, both doctors, continued his work. From this modest beginning, envisioned by Mother Alfred, St. Mary's Hospital, the initial unit of the Mayo Clinic, grew rapidly in size and fame, and Dr. William Mayo's sons, the Mayo Brothers, became equally famous almost overnight. The Franciscan Sisters of Rochester still sponsor St. Mary's Hospital today.

In Times of Economic Depression

The Great Depression of 1929–1941, vividly recalled by many older citizens, was only the last in a series of national economic depressions in the United States during the nineteenth and early twentieth centuries. Economic depressions have been as capable of creating the same trauma and destitution as natural disasters. During these periods of suffering and deprivation, religious congregations in the Catholic Church responded generously, giving support and comfort where possible and providing health service in hospitals or in homes.

From 1873 to 1896 a long wave of national depressions, alternating with short periods of prosperity brought suffering to the majority of Americans. Bankruptcies, business failures, plunging prices, and a low national income marked these periods of depression. To meet the many social problems, churches and institutions fostered numerous charitable societies among laypeople. But the Catholic clergy also encouraged the founding of hospitals and orphanages, the majority of which were administered and staffed by women religious—among them the Sisters of Providence, whose Mother Joseph established fifteen hospitals throughout the Northwest, and various branches of both the Sisters of Charity and Sisters of Mercy. It is for this reason—assisting the sick poor—that most Catholic hospitals were at first located in working-class neighborhoods, areas that were most adversely affected by depressions. From the start, however, most hospitals recognized outreach potential. Thus, they fed hundreds of persons, young and old, who stood in lines at kitchen doors. For instance, at St. Mary's Hospital in San Francisco, between 1876 and 1877, the hungry were so numerous that Sisters of Mercy (now of Burlingame) set up a pavilion on the grounds and used a large boiler for hot soup to feed the hundreds of people who came for food. Over two thousand families applied for help at the House of Mercy, and the sisters continued their service for years. The sisters also visited homes of the sick and poor, gave medication, and even paid overdue rent.

During the late 1890s another lengthy depression meant widespread unemployment and distress across the United States. Because social legislation had not yet been enacted and labor organizations were still somewhat ineffective, the laboring class suffered great hardship, while hospitals and charitable institutions strained to provide assistance. In October 1893 about eighty men came daily to St. Mary's Hospital, San Francisco, for food; by the end of the year the number had risen to five hundred daily, and charity patients also increased. In Michigan, Sisters of St. Joseph of Nazareth [3830] accepted county patients for seventy cents a day; their hospital, Borgess Hospital, furnished medical and surgical care, food, nursing, and other services.

Depressions of less severity followed economic boom cycles or occurred locally when mines and forests were depleted or major industries closed down. But no depression in the history of the United States could equal the extent of suffering and long years of poverty spawned by the Great Depression of 1929–1941, since it affected not only the working class, middle class, and poor, but also the many wealthy who became the newly poor. After the stock-market crash of November 1929, the fortunes and savings of millions of Americans were wiped out, and a period of panic, poverty, suffering, and despair began. By 1932 twenty-seven and a half million Americans were without regular income, and most considered themselves among the ranks of the poor. By 1933, when Franklin D. Roosevelt began his first term of office, 25 percent of the population was unemployed. Many cities, like Detroit and Toledo, printed their own scrip, and businesses and families often exchanged merchandise, produce, or services as payment. Despite government funds for banks and other recovery measures organized during the Roosevelt administration, signs of poverty and suffering lingered for years. Farmers burned their crops for fuel or destroyed their harvests and moved into cities, even though jobs were usually unattainable. In cities, the jobless sold apples, polished shoes, or tramped the streets looking for employment. Lines to soup kitchens stretched out from doors of charitable organizations, churches, hospitals, monasteries, and convents; "Knights of the Road" roamed from city to city; and whole families were on the move. The total migratory population between 1929 and 1932 may have reached one million.

Because of unemployment and impoverishment, illnesses increased in number and intensity. Many who were ill could not afford doctor's fees or hospital care and allowed their sickness to become critical rather than request charity. Others, men especially, became mentally ill through worry, anxiety, and frustration when they were unable to provide for their families because they could find no jobs. Admissions to state hospitals tripled in the two-year period from 1930 to 1932 over the eight-year period between 1922 and 1930. The greatest number of illnesses, however, resulted from people being ill-fed and poorly clothed. In 1931, for instance, almost one hundred of New York City's citizens were admitted to local hospitals suffering from malnutrition. On the streets people fainted from hunger. Due to poor diet, cases of rickets, scurvy, and pellagra increased. Social-service organizations were overburdened, and many were forced to close.

Through this crisis, Catholic organizations opened their doors and endeavored to assist those who came asking for food and help. The hungry stood patiently in long lines at the doors of Catholic institutions, especially hospitals, since food was more readily available there. In New York City at the French Hospital operated by the Marianite Sisters, formally known as the Congregation of the Marianites of the Holy Cross [2410], many unemployed came daily to pick up sandwiches, while neighboring families arrived each evening. The Marianite Sisters also gave many free meals to employees. Sisters of St. Joseph in Wheeling, West Virginia [3830], delivered food to the destitute recuperating at home after hospitalization. The Congregation of Bon Secour Sisters [0270] in Detroit dipped into their building fund to feed the poor. The Hospital Sisters of St. Francis in Springfield, Illinois, gave soup, sandwiches, and coffee to men in their breadline. When the line grew longer and food ran out, county officials offered help. In Pittsburgh, Sisters of Mercy noted that it was common practice for different members of large families to take turns for one good meal a day. In Pontiac, Michigan, Sister Mary Xavier Shields, a Sister of Mercy of the Detroit Province of the Union and administrator of St. Joseph Mercy Hospital, arranged for sisters to cook for unemployed General Motors workers. As she states, "There was GM-owned farm land across from the hospital, and General Motors allowed its unemployed workers to farm it. . . . They'd bring the food to us and we'd cook it and feed them."[12]

But stretching food supplies to feed the hungry was not as difficult as stretching budgets to operate a hospital during this depression. With admissions decreasing and forcing many hospitals to close empty floors, income was at a minimum. Patients, never too eager to be hospitalized, delayed even longer and entered hospitals only when there were no other options. Many of these patients could not afford to pay or could pay only in part. During one year at St. Bernard's Hospital in

Jonesboro, Arkansas, for instance, of 881 patients discharged only 344 paid in full, 103 were charity cases, 16 were part charity and 24 received free service. In the Cincinnati archdiocese in depression years as late as 1939 and 1940, when conditions had become less severe, the total free care given by seven Catholic hospitals equaled one million dollars; in the Archdiocese of Detroit, during the same years, nine hospitals and two sanitoria provided one and a quarter million dollars in services to destitute patients.[13] As a result of their policy of providing care and food for all in need, Catholic hospitals became deeply in debt, not being able to satisfy creditors and yet refusing to turn away the destitute.

Nonetheless, survival means were not entirely lacking. When possible, hospitals accepted payment in produce and meat from farmers or merchants, or permitted patients to pay in installments of one to twenty-five dollars a month and discounted large bills. At times members of patients' families worked for the hospital to pay off bills or gave other services in lieu of cash. To help both patients and sisters, many doctors and nurses treated patients without charge, especially in clinics. Generous donors supplied funds in financial emergencies, and board members organized drives, furnished necessary equipment, or kept equipment in repair through their businesses. Women's auxiliaries, leagues, and other groups supplied patients with necessities and otherwise earned extra money for the hospital. Many creditors carried hospitals on their books for years as payments trickled in.

For the sisters, the depression meant an increased work load and longer hours (twelve to fourteen hours a day being the norm), tested their creativity, and in most cases delayed further education. Since they could not afford sufficient help for nursing and household work, they often assisted in the laundry, kitchen, or switchboard, in addition to their full-time jobs as administrators, floor supervisors, nurses, pharmacists, and other health professionals. Conversations with older Sisters of Mercy of the Detroit Province of the Union yielded further details of the hospital situation during the Great Depression. To save money, sisters repaired worn shades in patients' rooms, used feed sacks as sheets for cribs and curtains in the nursery, and salvaged, washed, and sterilized gauze for reuse. In some instances they made their own distilled water, saline, and glucose solutions, which they tested by using themselves as guinea pigs. Living was frugal and food was simple but usually sufficient, for many Mercy hospitals had gardens and sisters canned vegetables and fruit for their own and hospital use.

Stringent means of economizing extended to employees, many of whom were thankful to have jobs even at minimum wages, which were all the hospitals could afford. Some employees, including nurses, were content to work for room and board. On the other hand, rates for hospital services were also low, as were prices in general during the Great Depression. To continue to survive financially, as did the Sisters of the Humility of Mary [2110] at St. Elizabeth Hospital in Youngstown, Ohio, hospitals pared staff to a minimum, even to the point of having only one registered nurse per floor and no interns or orderlies. One of the most difficult situations to arise, however, was the necessity of refusing work to men who desperately needed income to provide for their families.

Many Catholic hospitals were caught by the depression while in the midst of a building program to replace or enlarge old hospitals. In practically all locations construction was halted or delayed. In 1930, for example, Alexian Brothers had begun a new wing on their St. Louis hospital to expand facilities for special services and to enlarge the area for mentally ill patients, but after managing to finish this first phase of a major building program, they were forced to delay plans. Paradoxically, the Sisters of St. Joseph of Orange [3820], California, founded four hospitals during these depression years at extreme financial burden to the religious community. One of their bookkeepers, Sister Redempta Girard, watched creditors pacing in front of the hospital, waiting for the morning mail, hoping to benefit from incoming payments. Other religious communities managed to enlarge their hospitals, as did the Sisters of St. Joseph of Carondelet in Great Bend, Kansas, where they treated many of the lung diseases so prevalent in that area during the 1930s. In general, however, building plans were postponed until the late 1930s, when the depression was less severe and local residents encouraged religious communities to build and initiated fund drives to support the project.

The majority of Catholic hospitals survived the Great Depression and continue to maintain their policy of admitting patients of all creeds, races, nationalities, and financial means, whether in "the best of times" or in "the worst of times." Buildings have been enlarged or replaced and many hospitals have been grouped together to form health systems. Insurance programs, Medicare, and Medicaid underwrite large percentages of patients' bills. However, there remain hundreds of patients without insurance and without adequate income who must rely on the charity of religious congregations who administer or sponsor these hospitals.

It is evident, however, that throughout the nineteenth and twentieth centuries, even before modern health systems and insurance plans were initiated, members of religious communities of women in the United States reached out to those lacking adequate health care—to miners, lumberjacks and railroad workers; to ethnic minority groups; and to the victims of natural disasters and economic depressions. Their motivation was love of God and their neighbor, and a dedication to service that allowed little time to record their activities. Although many more pages recounting the varied services of women religious during times of crises and economic depressions remain stored in archives, no religious communities have ever fully chronicled their history of service, and archives and interviews will never be able to reveal the complete story.

NOTES

In addition to books listed in footnotes, other valuable references include Jay Dolan, *The American Catholic Experience* (Garden City, NY: Doubleday, 1985); James Hennesey, *American Catholics* (New York: Oxford University Press, 1981); Mary Annrene Brau, RSM, *Mercy in the Heartland* (Kansas: Sisters of Mercy, 1986); Mary Loyola Hegarty, CCVI, *Serving with Gladness: The Origin and History of the Congregation of the Sisters of Charity of the Incarnate Word, Houston, Texas* (Houston, TX.: Bruce Publishing, 1967); Helen Johnston, *Health for the Nation's Harvesters* (Farmington Hills, MI.: National Migrant Worker Council, 1985); Mary Athanasius Sheridan, SM, *And Some Fell on Good Ground: A History of the Sisters of Mercy of California and Arizona* (New York: Carlton Press, 1982); and Dixon Wecter, *The Age of the Great Depression, 1929–1941* (New York: Franklin Watts, 1975).

1. Walter Cloton, USN, *Three Years in California* (New York: S. A. Rollo, 1850), pp. 242–53, quoted in Richard C. Brown, *The Human Side of American History* (New York: Ginn, 1962), pp. 114–15.

2. Alistair Cooke, *Alistair Cooke's America* (New York: Knopf, 1975), p. 155.

3. Mary Carol Conroy, SCL,"*The Historical Development of Health Care Ministry of the Sisters of Charity of Leavenworth*" (1984 doctoral dissertation, Kansas State University, Manhattan, KS.) p. 75.

4. Studs Terkel, *Hard Times* (New York: Pantheon, 1960), p. 198.

5. Stewart H. Holbrook, *Holy Old Mackinaw: A Natural History of the American Lumberjack* (New York: Macmillan, 1956), p. ii.

6. *The Pioneer*, Big Rapids, Michigan, 1903 (Archives of the Sisters of Mercy of the Union, Province of Detroit, Farmington Hills, MI.).

7. Ibid.

8. Conroy, p. 75.

9. Melita Ludwig, FSPA, *A Chapter of Franciscan History* (La Crosse, WI: Sisters of St. Francis), p. 242.

10. Michael Harrington, *The Other America*, as quoted in Glenmary Sisters' publication, *Kinship* (summer 1964): 3.

11. *Leaves from the Annals of the Sisters of Mercy*, vol. 4 (New York: P. O'Shea, 1895), p. 47.

12. "An Enduring Angel of Mercy," *The Grand Rapids Press*, June 24, 1983 (Archives of the Sisters of Mercy of the Union, Detroit Province, Farmington Hills, MI).

13. Information used with permission of Roman Godzak, director of the Archives of the Archdiocese of Detroit.

✦ The Transition Years

MARY CAROL CONROY, SCL

The preceding chapters record the response of Catholic religious women to the health-care needs of the immigrant church. As has been consistently noted, care for the sick initially took place in the home. A visiting physician diagnosed ailments and prescribed treatment, but it was the task of female family members or servants to meet the daily needs of the sick. Yet, even in early times, there were public hospitals for people who were homeless, destitute, or simply had no one to care for them; these were, however, considered to be last resorts.[1] Those who were cared for in these facilities found the medical practices of physicians wanting in many respects. Sanitary conditions in the hospitals were poor and, thus, mortality ran high. In fact, medical care and treatment were often worse than the illness. In many cases, whatever nursing occurred was of poor quality, because those who took on the task of nursing during the early 1800s often came from degrading circumstances themselves. The public hospitals at this time provided mainly custodial care and employed workers who were often drunkards and prostitutes. Nursing itself was viewed as an inferior kind of work; often the status of nurses was lower than that of domestic servants.[2]

Yet, as we have seen, during the first decades of the nineteenth century, new workers emerged who would challenge the prevailing categories and sterotypes. Comprising members of religious congregations of women, a procession of women committed themselves to the service of the poor and the sick, reaching out in loving care to their Catholic brothers and sisters in need. In increasing numbers and with growing competence, women religious began to respond to the health-care needs of the immigrant church. Initially, their missionary spirit prompted them to visit the sick in their homes. As the number of people in need of health care increased and care at home became more unrealistic, a few hospitals under religious auspices were established. This occurred especially along the East Coast, where the first waves of Catholics tended to settle, and then along the Mississippi, Missouri, or Ohio rivers and in the French and Spanish areas added to the United States in the early decades of the nineteenth century. Although the hospitals begun in these burgeoning communities by religious congregations were utilized mostly by Catholics, they quite often became havens for the general public as well. In some cases, in fact, Catholic hospitals were the only providers of health care for a region; in others, they emerged alongside city, county, or state hospitals.

From the start, however, Catholic facilities were staffed exclusively by sisters; it was at these hospitals where most of the nursing provided by sisters was done. There a cadre of religious nurses worked, in close collaboration with physicians, sharing their knowledge and providing care. Accounts of the experiences of religious women in the pioneer days reveal a pattern of collegial interaction between physicians and nursing sisters.

Like most pioneer women, nursing sisters developed their nursing expertise out of sheer necessity and through the experience of dealing with actual crises. Both their involvement at the times of epidemics and their heroic service during the Civil War provided what proved to be the most effective preparation for nursing. The skills manifested by both sisters and lay nurses in the midst of epidemics and combat converted hearts inured to anti-Catholicism and reinforced the favorable opinion which had developed during other times of crises. Because of the witness of sisters who volunteered at these times, nursing began to be viewed as an important and honorable endeavor. It also began to attract people of greater culture and education. The efforts of sisters and lay nurses especially during the Civil War, led to the elevation of the status of the nursing profession in the United States.[3]

One important result of the new postbellum attitude toward nursing was that, especially during the last decades of the nineteenth century, hospital care could be approached as a respectable form of human services. At this point, minimum standards for hospitals were introduced and hospitals took on a greater semblance of organization. Patients were now admitted to hospitals because of chronic illness, injury, general neglect, or because they were suffering from mental illness. In general, they came to the hospital to die. At this stage, however, it was still not necessary for patients to be admitted by a physician in order to receive hospital care. Moreover, during these years, medicine and medical education began to evolve from a base of folklore and trial-and-error procedures to a more scientific methodology that included training through preceptorship.[4]

Training schools for nurses, as they were called then, under both Catholic and public auspices were established, especially in the East and Midwest, and, in time, were patterned after the Nightingale Schools of London but adapted to the needs of American society.[5] The guidelines Miss Nightingale developed for nursing education indicated that a school for nurses should be associated with a medical school in a teaching hospital. Secondly, the residence for the nurses should be suitable for the formation of discipline and character. One designated person, referred to as the Matron, should have the final authority for the entire program, which included practical instruction and experience and specified living conditions for the students.[6] Although disease prevention and health maintenance were seen as important functions of nursing, training in caring for acute illnesses became the priority in the nursing curriculum.[7] Finally, because Nightingale was convinced that, "regardless of the auspices under which it was practiced, nursing must always be carried on in a deeply religious manner," a spiritual atmosphere for hospitals was encouraged.[8] Thus, Nightingale's ideas on nursing education remained compatible with the aims of those religious congregations that sponsored hospitals.

The American continent was further developed by the close of the nineteenth century with the building of the railroad, which contributed to the opening of the West. Frontier settlements gave way to towns and cities. New York and Chicago became great urban and manufacturing centers. West of the Mississippi River there were extensive agricultural and mining developments, with rough trails becoming major roads and terminals. Especially in the North, urbanization was the reality of the times. After the Spanish-American War, furthermore, the United States began to play a greater part in world affairs, bringing a broader world view to the American people. These, plus other developments in the early 1900s, were to have a definite influence on medical practice, hospital care, and the involvement of Catholic health-care providers.[9]

Formed in 1847, the American Medical Association was the national organization which was to make the first important and necessary changes in health care. Under its auspices, stricter educational and licensing practices were developed; it became effective in reducing and eventually eliminating "self-made" or worse, "quack" doctors.[10] The Association of Hospital Superintendents, founded in 1889, was a second organization established to be a charitable and educational association to improve the care supplied by hospitals and hospital personnel. Under a new title, the American Hospital Association, this organization took the initiative concerning the unregulated increase in hospitals: the one hundred seventy-eight hospitals of 1873 had grown to an astounding figure of more than twenty-five hundred by the turn of the century.[11]

Concerns regarding medical education grew more cumulative toward the end of the nineteenth century. To investigate the basis of complaints about the preparation of health providers and the care given by those involved in medical settings, a study was sponsored by the Carnegie Foundation. Conducted by Abraham Flexner, it examined one hundred and fifty-five medical schools then functioning in the United States and Canada. When the Flexner Report was released in 1910, it brought about the closure of some schools and the abrupt reform of many others.[12] Most of the schools surviving its critical investigation developed affiliations with universities and became nonprofit institutions. Despite this, many schools were reluctant to update or improve the education which they provided; their futures were seriously jeopardized.

The formation of the American College of Surgeons in 1913 also directly affected the development of hospital policy. Realizing the haphazard manner in which hospitals were managed, medical personnel renewed efforts to bring about needed and effective reforms. In 1918, this group developed minimum standards for hospitals which, over time, stimulated a major revolution in the manner in which both private and public hospitals conducted business throughout the nation.[13] It was at this point that physicians became the ones to decide upon who could be admitted to hospitals.

In similar fashion, St. Louis University served as a staging ground for another organizational attempt at coordinating Catholic health-care policies. At a meeting held there in 1914, the Reverend Charles B. Moulinier, SJ, a regent and professor of the university, was instrumental in organizing the Catholic Hospital Association. At its first convention, Father Moulinier identified the task of the organization:

> Our watchword should be work, work, work . . . in working
> for hospital efficiency, in working for the welfare of the sick,
> in trying to reach an ideal of perfection, we are doing God's
> will just as when we are on our knees saying our prayers.[14]

As the concept of hospitalization became more acceptable to both non-Catholic and Catholic health providers, the need for trained nurses became even more pressing. Quick to respond to the new situation were members of a number of religious congregations of women who had earlier established hospital schools of nursing. That such programs had already been in existence for decades, however, was made clear in a paper presented as early as 1869 by a Lutheran physician at the American Medical Association meeting in New Orleans. In his address at that meeting, the physician paid tribute to Catholic nursing, stating:

> It is remarkable that the subject in question [nursing] should hitherto have been singularly neglected by all denominations except Catholics whose noble deeds in preparing nurses for the sick and infirm of their own church reflects so much upon their charity and philanthrophy.[15]

Like the nursing programs in public hospitals, the curriculum offered at the sisters' schools during the post–Civil War period was oriented to apprenticeship. The doctors did the teaching and controlled the curriculum, setting a structure of the medical model focused on diseases as the basis of nursing school curricula. This model continued for decades.

In 1886, the Hospital Sisters of St. Francis [1820] established the first nursing program, the St. John's Hospital Training School, in Springfield, Illinois.[16] In 1896, the Sisters of Charity of Cincinnati [0440] established the Good Samaritan School of Nursing.[17] Other congregations to establish schools during this period were the Sisters of Mercy [2580] in Chicago, and the Daughters of Charity [0760] in Buffalo, New York, and at St. Mary's Hospital in Brooklyn, New York. However, admission to these and most other schools of nursing established at the turn of the century were restricted to members of the respective religious congregations. St. Joseph's Hospital School of Nursing in Denver, Colorado was established in 1900 and was open to lay women from the beginning, and according to the school's by-laws, at least one lay nurse was to be included in the school's faculty to provide a balance for the students.[18]

By the early 1900s, religious women owned and operated 59 of the approximately 393 nursing schools in the United States and 3 of some 25 in Canada. About half of these early Catholic schools of nursing in the United States were established by congregations springing from Mother Seton's Emmitsburg, Maryland, foundation: 21 were begun by the Daughters of Charity; 7 by three separate foundations of Sisters of Charity. The year 1931 was to represent an all-time high for Catholic nursing schools: there were 403 schools of nursing functioning at that time.[19] Following World War II, extensive changes in curriculum, consolidation of the small schools, and efforts to achieve national accreditation altered the programs and decreased the number of Catholic nursing schools.

Recognizing the significant contribution that Catholic schools of nursing were making to American society, the Catholic Hospital Association supported the development of the Conference of Catholic Schools of Nursing (CCSN) in 1948 as a voluntary association to promote the interests of Catholic schools of nursing in the United States and to foster the professional and spiritual ideals of Christian nursing. The members who encouraged this intervention represented schools of practical nursing operated by hospitals, colleges and junior colleges with associate-degree programs, hospitals with diploma programs, colleges and universities with undergraduate and graduate nursing programs, and sponsoring religious congregations.[20] Some of the most prominent nursing-education leaders of the Catholic schools of nursing during this era were Sisters Agnes Miriam Payne, SCN, Kathleen Mary Bohan, SCN, Eugene Teresa McCarthy, SCL, and Mary Zoe Ahern, SCL. Gradually the rate of growth of these schools declined, in the process of updating and realignment. Thus, in 1951, there were 351 diploma schools of nursing; in 1963 the number had once more decreased to 308.[21]

By 1946 records indicate an increased number of nursing programs in Catholic institutions of higher education and a gradual decline of Catholic hospital schools of nursing. St. Xavier College, Chicago, Illinois, is believed to be the first Catholic college to assume, as it did in 1935, full responsibility for a curriculum leading to the baccalaureate degree and eligibility to write the licensure exam for registered nurses.[22] Later, nursing leaders in other religious congregations incorporated similar measures into their schools of higher education; they also took additional steps to establish nursing as a profession. Their continued efforts had the greatest impact when the American Nurses' Association took the following stand:

> Education for those who work in nursing should take place in institutions of learning within the general system of education. The American Nurses' Association believes that: (1) the edu-

cation for all those who are licensed to practice nursing should take place in institutions of higher education; (2) minimum preparation for beginning professional nursing practice at the present time should be baccalaureate-degree education in nursing; (3) minimum preparation for beginning technical nursing practice at the present time should be the associate-degree education in nursing; and (4) education for assistants in the health-service occupations should be short, intensive preservice programs in vocational education institutions rather than on-the-job training programs.[23]

The position paper quoted above divided the nursing profession on the basis of the distinction made between the professional and the technical nurse. At this time, registered nurses were still prepared on three levels: the two-year associate degree; the three-year diploma; and the four-year baccalaureate nursing program. At the present time, the academic setting continues to be the one preferred by professional nurse leaders for the education of nurses—this despite declining numbers at all nursing schools.

The historical development of the nursing profession, whether under religious auspices or not, clearly indicates that the nursing profession, while steeped in military discipline and practice, had always been structured from a religious and philosophical base. Emerging from the Crimean War and the American Civil War, nursing had readily adapted such military features as ranks, rules, and regimentation of dress and conduct, as well as rigid regimes of discipline. At the same time, the influence of religious groups—who were in some ways adhering to the same kinds of disciplinary constraints—made an alternative impact on the profession through their open acknowledgement of moral and humanistic beliefs concerning the dignity of persons, the significance of work, the meaning of suffering and illness and belief in an eternal destiny, and through their testimony to the responsibility they believed each person must show toward the neighbor in need.

When the profession of nursing moved into the academic setting, however, often the natural compatibility between religious belief and health care became blurred. Consequently, some of the early practices of devotion, such as morning chapel services, receded, even in schools under religious auspices. After nursing education entered most completely into the educational mainstream, the philosophy and objectives of Catholic-sponsored nursing programs lost much of their earlier religious influence. Today the educational and professional practice of nursing has assumed a more secular and scientific base. Although the transition has evolved gradually, questions regarding the wisdom of this move, especially with respect to Catholic health-care providers has begun to emerge as an issue; it will probably need to be confronted in the future as our "high-tech" society seeks more personal and humane kinds of care giving. Concerns about the value of the person have already surfaced among members of the profession in response to the materialistic focus of our present health-care system.

Advances in medicine and the emphasis on professionalism by the nursing profession have occasioned other philosophical problems as well, giving rise to concern for the curriculum used by the sisters engaged in the ministry of nursing education. Critics of present instruction under Catholic auspices have observed that the view of health care that was learned through training and apprenticeship under the direct guidance of sister-nurses does not appear to be consistent with newer professional views where nursing knowledge is gained mainly through classroom education. Adaptations in the schools to a more educational orientation in some instances resulted in stressful conditions. Sisters whose primary concerns were patient care had to contend with those sisters in the schools of nursing whose interests were geared more toward the academic education of the nursing students. Conscious of this conflict of interests, especially after 1940, sisters worked diligently to reinforce their religious and philosophical beliefs and practices within their schools of nursing. This had to be accomplished in a way which would not sacrifice the credentials needed by their students and could satisfy the needs of graduates who later desired to seek baccalaureate degrees in nursing. In the light of these changes, a number of Catholic diploma schools of nursing were phased out after 1960.

Through the many decades when Catholic hospitals sponsored nursing schools, the sisters had, of course, continued to instill in their students a Christian concern for the dignity of the human person in their care of the sick. This was more easily accomplished within the setting of the Catholic nursing school; it could be easily witnessed through the example given by the hospital sisters. Another indirect effect of closing diploma schools of nursing has been the loss of role modelling as well as the reinforcement of Catholic ideals as previously supplied by the sisters. In effect, there is no longer a cadre of sister-nurses to act as mentors for students in Catholic hospitals. Another loss is that decisions about nursing education may not be determined with regard to religious motivation and the care of the sick—concerns which formerly influenced the actions of those directly involved in the service provided—rather by the dictates of the changing health-care system itself. Regardless of what influenced future decisions, however, nursing education has become quite different from the expansive and varied educational enterprise previously experienced.

Still another change that confronted Catholic hospital providers after the 1940s came about as a result of the Hill-Burton federal grants which allowed patients access to certain kinds of hospital treatments never before affordable. This federal law was meant to be a means of providing equal access to hospital care. The program also prompted the construction and expansion of hospitals through massive grants and subsidies for increases in hospital capacity. Expansion resulted in an increased patient census and greater access to newer therapeutic measures. Thus, the nation's hospital system mushroomed. This legislation also impacted Catholic health-care providers.

As new technologies continued to increase, new specialists in health care were required and new equipment and facilities had to be added. No longer was the aim of hospitals—Catholic or other— simply to serve the acutely ill. By the late 1940s and early 1950s, not only were patients suffering from chronic illnesses coming to the hospital for treatment, surgery, or relief of pain, but for the first time patients were also being admitted to hospitals in order to prevent or forestall disease or illness. The focus of hospitals became one of preventive medicine, and outpatient service centers were added to acute-care facilities. At this point, new skills had to be acquired and educational services had to be updated in order to provide specialized information for both physicians and nurses. In some facilities, research departments were needed to further health care delivery. This change in the scope of health care was confirmed by the ready response of the general public to the new directions. Following World War II in particular, entire families began to participate in a variety of voluntary health-care insurance programs.

As the function of hospitals changed, the sisters who had traditionally staffed almost every department of their hospitals continued as a visible presence within their facilities. In the face of the continuing changes in health care, however, the sisters who were supervisors of nursing units, educators in the schools of nursing, or heads of hospital departments, finally had to face the consequences of diversification and specialization of services. Formerly they had been totally responsible for the management and operation of their departments on a twenty-four-hour basis.

The sister supervisor in the nursing units, for example, made rounds with the doctors, addressed all problems, managed the nursing staff, and directed all care of the patients in her unit, as well as seeing to the needs of their families. She expected to be called upon for every emergency. Little thought was given to the need to prepare lay nurses—who, by this time, were also numerous—to develop their abilities in comparable areas. But as the ratio of lay nurses to sisters increased during the 1950s and the need to adapt to new demands became more pressing, the pattern of collaboration and interdependence had to be reexamined. Would the lay nurses who would have to assume some of the expanding supervisory positions in hospitals, for example, be as able to develop the same collaborative relationship which the sisters had achieved? What of the emergence of new occupations within the hospital setting, such as the position of nurses' aide, which was introduced in the 1940s? Would these maintain the same importance in nursing units? As sisters became more involved in planning and coordinating staff as administrators or as clinical instructors, furthermore, the question arose of what would become of the sisters' traditional place, involving visiting and praying with patients or preparing the dying for eternity. If these had once been the most important tasks of sisters, what could now preserve this aspect of their ministry in the face of the greatly enlarged scope of work?

The same questions remained to be answered well into the 1960s. New advances in medical science and techniques occurred. Major strides in plastic and reconstructive surgery during World War II and the Korean War contributed to corrective and rehabilitative procedures; the therapeutic aspect of medical care became an important part of overall medical care. So too did such drugs as cortisone, steroids, tranquilizers, antihistamines, and antimicrobial agents that contributed to the management, control, and, in some instances, prevention of health problems. Studies to combat heart disease, cancer, and strokes also yielded beneficial results and required specialized training. Federal funds were allocated for further research as consumer groups became more vocal in their demand for improved health care.

As the public pursued a better quality of health care, most Catholic hospitals joined public agencies in the utilization of federal funds—particularly those that enabled the construction and expansion of facilities which were designed for the new medical advances. In turn, the public, especially those aided by new health-care insurance, turned to hospitals in increasing numbers in order to take advantage of new possibilities. Still another change occurred as hospitals expanded their services: they became the major employers in their respective locations. In turn, the role of the sisters further diminished. In the new circumstances, furthermore, the sisters became less involved in the ongoing decision-making activities of their hospitals and more and more of the sister-nurses worked on the same level with other nursing personnel in specialty areas of the hospital. Yet the National Labor Relations Board viewed the same sisters as management personnel because they were constituents of the corporate body that owned the hospital. In other words, most of the sisters not in administrative roles became "evaluated employees" of their respective facilities.

There were other confusions with regard to hospital roles resulting from the changing times. Having entered religious life while in their late teens, nursing sisters knew both the rigors of structured religious life as well as the kind of training pursued in the typical three-year diploma schools. Following their profession of vows, they were assigned to a hospital school, where they quickly matured in the face of the realities of life and death. After completion of their hospital training program, however, they had to undergo still another transition in their life-style: suddenly they were named supervisors of patient care in one of their congregation's hospitals. Then, when this hospital structure succumbed to changing times, the sister was required not only to assume new administrative and nursing functions, but she might even have to consider returning to school in order to develop additional specializations, as, for example, a dietician, pharmacist, X-ray and medical technologist.

In addition to changes caused within the structure of hospital care, major alterations were also taking place in society during the turbulent 1960s that focused on the individual vis-à-vis the established systems and structures of the times. These would also affect the profession of nursing and Catholic health care. Life took an a more global perspective as the Vietnam War, race riots, and civil rights movements at home and abroad became realities not to be ignored amid television's graphic displays.[24] In these troubled years, a return to idealism seemed all the more necessary. While a new sense of mission was evidenced by thousands of young people who volunteered to serve the underdeveloped nations of the world as members of the Peace Corps, the Catholic Church also sponsored volunteer programs for the sake of social justice, including the Papal Volunteers. Both civic and religious groups were attractive to innumerable young men and women who were eager to serve those less fortunate at home and abroad. During the first phase of this period in particular, religious congregations of women were in the forefront of recognizing the signs of the times. But they also had to put these into the perspective of another phenomenon that directly affected decisions within the congregations: for all too brief a period, they, too, were experiencing a tremendous growth in numbers. Insight into the correct response to these dramatic changes was provided by the Sister Formation Conference, which had been established in 1954 by the Major Superiors of Religious Congregations in the United States and which advocated better educational and spiritual preparation of sisters.[25]

By the end of the decade, however, what had begun as a cry for peace and love by many of the most vocal advocates of social justice, ended in disillusion, the overuse of drugs, and a greater incidence of crime. Idealism waned; even vocations to religious life soon began a precipitous drop. Despite these changes, the restructured Great Society and its legislation, enabling the wide redistribution of goods, remained essentially in place and continued to be supplemented by the acts of both Democratic and Republican congresses.

One of the most important measures to affect national health care was the Medicare program, established in 1965. Designed for citizens over sixty-five, this federal intervention along with its medical-care program Medicaid, was to have great salutary effect for those in need of financial assistance.[26] But Medicare was to have negative effects as well. The status of Catholic or other nonprofit hospitals was dramatically changed by governmental oversight in many ways. In particular, the immunity of nonprofit hospitals from litigation on the basis of their charitable donation to society was slowly eliminated. Religious congregations had to face the implications of becoming indebted to the federal government. It must be pointed out that recent changes in reimbursement methods and regulations have decreased inpatient utilization of acute-care facilities significantly and increased outpatient activity. The severity of acute-care patients in acute-care hospitals has also increased, with the majority of these patients being elderly and having complex health problems. The needs of these frail elderly, especially their home-care needs, are among the most serious issues of this time. The increased life span of the population must be addressed in relation to its impact on society's healthcare systems.

The most significant event affecting all aspects of the American Catholic Church, however, was the convocation of the Second Vatican Council by John XXIII. Meeting in four successive sessions between 1962 and 1965, the council aimed at seeking renewal in the church and promoting the unity of Christians.[27] Indirectly its effects would alter every aspect of Catholic institutional life, including the delivery of health-care by Catholic providers. Since Vatican II, clerical and lay leaders have demonstrated considerable concern and action in meeting the needs of the poor, oppressed, and disadvantaged of society. The Conference of Major Superiors of Women, which is now the Leadership Conference of Religious Women (LCWR), became engaged in determining the degree to which the decisions of the council were being reflected within religious congregations of women.[28] Evidence of this was seen in the number of conferences and chapters held by sisters that resulted in legislation or policy changes with respect to many aspects of the life and service of religious congregations.

Beginning in the mid-1960s, however, a great exodus of sisters from religious congregations began to occur. This would, of course, bring about another change in the way religious congregations would continue to address their social ministries. Because a considerable number of those who left their religious communities at this time were engaged in the ministry of nursing, many aspects of hospital administration and personnel were affected. The loss in numbers also meant changes in terms of hospital planning. Finding new ways to provide for the spiritual care of patients became a realistic concern; solutions to this precipitated still another change in the relationship within Catholic hospitals between lay and religious staff. For the first time, pastoral departments which were especially aimed at providing a coherent plan of addressing the spiritual aspect of health service were inaugurated. In these, members of the laity were asked to share the work traditionally carried out by the clergy and religious. In a new collaborative style, the field of pastoral ministry emerged, with its own sophistication, knowledge, and skills. Nursing sisters, whose predecessors had generally spent their semiretirement attending to the spiritual care of patients, now found that, instead of anticipating this as their final contribution, they must rely upon other trained personnel, whether lay or religious, who were more prepared to take on this important responsibility.

Nursing sisters were also newly challenged by their interaction with health personnel on the federal and state levels, especially with regard to the legislative changes imposed by the Great Society. Whether working in hospitals of the congregation or in other agencies, for example, they now had to work under contract and follow the personnel policies of the respective agencies or institutions. The majority of the sisters still on the staff of hospitals of their own congregations were often in peer positions in contrast to the supervisory roles of an earlier time. As the hospitals owned and operated by these sisters were renovated and expanded, long-range plans had to be initiated; these also changed the roles of the sisters.

As personal income declined in the late 1970s, additional considerations came into focus, changing the nursing apostolate for women religious. Health care became a major expenditure for most people; the effects of this had to be evaluated in terms of strategic planning for the future. But the reality of major financial costs and debts created immediate problems for both patients and hospital personnel. Once again, hospitals began to be viewed by some as institutions of last resort; even those who were acutely ill now found that they had been restricted to limited stays. As a result, new options of health care, including home care, assumed renewed importance. A surplus of physicians became another factor in occasioning change. Among the more important consequences of these changes was a more open competitive spirit among health-care providers. Furthermore, the drive for excellence within Catholic hospitals tended to become even more explicitly tied to the drive to maintain financial solvency. Marketing efforts for new structures emerged, including such programs as Preferred Provider Organizations (PPOs) that teamed physicians with hospitals by contract. Health Maintenance Organizations (HMOs), providing managed health-care systems, also became common options. These various strategies for maintaining fiscal strength preoccupied planning sessions at both Catholic and public hospitals.

Because of the need to compete successfully with public health-care facilities, religious congregations that owned hospitals were required to become more and more involved in innovations in health-care provision. As a result, some inaugurated separate surgical centers for outpatient surgery and free-standing emergency centers. The creation of multihospital chains also became a typical means of response to competition, as they had the advantage of limiting the number of procedures in hospitals and, in the name of efficiency, could contribute to fiscal soundness as well as quality of care. There has also been a move toward diversifying revenue sources. Thus, some hospitals under religious auspices began to develop for-profit businesses to support their hospital work. If many public hospitals have purchased motels, shopping centers, or similar businesses, so too did private hospitals begin to consider similar sources of revenue, albeit ones consonant with their own express mission.

Greater freedom of selection of ministries has also resulted in fewer women religious selecting administrative roles in institutional settings.

This has precipitated another complicating change in the complexion of hospital personnel. As the number of religious women actively engaged in health care diminished, qualified lay personnel were appointed to leadership positions; other members of the laity have been named to hospital boards. In some cases, the business and professional expertise of the sisters themselves has been put to use in this new way, enabling the sponsoring religious community the continued opportunity of meeting the challenges of providing health care. Moreover, the employment of lay personnel has served the salutary function of freeing women religious so that they can upgrade their health-care ministry in general. What has been learned by resorting to these departures from custom is that it is necessary for health-care facilities to remain flexible so that they can respond appropriately to the rapid changes occurring in technology, medicine, and, especially, in society.

Finally, the continued pattern of complex change affecting Catholic-sponsored health-care institutions has prompted a number of religious congregations to organize their health-care facilities into a unified system based on a common philosophy. The single corporate management of the past held overall authority and responsibility for policy formation and operation decisions. This also provided a means of protecting the assets of facilities for the total congregation. Since 1979, there has been a continuous evolution and development of Catholic-sponsored health-care institutions into some form of multi-institutional system. A sponsoring group, as defined by the Catholic Health Association, refers to "a religious congregation and/or diocese, which has responsibility for a health-care facility based on the moral right and duty to control property, establish a philosophy, and set policy."[29] By 1985 there were more than fifty such arrangements. Four models are generally used to describe the organization of Catholic health-care facilities along these lines. Unified systems tend to be organized along one of several models, as illustrated in Figure 1.[30]

**Figure 1: Models of Organization
of Catholic Health-Care Facilities**

Traditional Model	*Characteristics*
	Institution owned/sponsored by religious congregation or diocese which controls assets/philosophy and mission of the institution.
	No professional management group or services involved.

A full- or part-time coordinator or
overseer is common.
May have some shared services.

Multi-Institutional System

Corporate Model

Characteristics
Separately incorporated.
Management organization is separate from
sponsoring group.
Management group responsible for management
control of all health facilities of
sponsoring group.
Management group reports to sponsoring group
through its board.
Professional staff and a separate budget
directed only to management of the health
care institution.

Key/unique feature
of this model:

Health-care institutions report to the
management group rather than to the
sponsoring group.

Consultation/Shared
Model

Characteristics
Professional staff of three or more persons
with or without health-care or related
backgrounds who serve as managers of shared
services for the health care institutions.
Staff spends 80% of time on health-care
institution matters.
Has a CEO but reports directly to the
sponsoring group, as does the
consultant/shared service organization.
Management group serves in staff capacity
with the relating bodies requesting their
services.

Multiunit Holding
Company Model

Characteristics
Represents joining of two or more provinces,
sponsors or systems and creation of
diversified holding companies of
health-related or non-health-related
services provided under profit or
not-for-profit subsidiaries.
Generally involves separate governing boards
and staff for each subsidiary.
All subsidiaries report to a holding company
management team that is responsible to the
sponsoring group.

The development of these systems was inevitable. Organic changes due to the growth and complexity of health-care delivery changed dramatically because of the greater volume of patients utilizing acute-care facilities. Thus, newer and more effective and efficient methods and systems were needed.

But no system is perfect, as is reflected in Figure 2, which compares some of the strengths and weaknesses of the past health-care delivery methods with those currently in use.

**Figure 2: Strengths and Weaknesses of Catholic
Health-Care System—Past Versus Present**

PAST

Strengths	*Weaknesses*
Religious control.	
Religious women highly visible.	
Catholic chaplain.	Other denominations generally not represented.
Spiritual care primarily for Catholic patients.	
Medical-moral directives clearly defined and followed.	
Resources set aside for charity after all expenses met.	
Few employees aside from nursing administrative personnel.	Sister-nurses carried major responsibilities of their hospitals 24 hours per day, 7 days per week, 12 months of the year.
	Life of total dedication.
Schools of nursing provide staff of hopsitals.	Loss of nursing schools diminished resources for delivery of nursing care.
	Auxillary personnel were needed and were often less prepared, i.e., nurse aide.
	Fewer role models to emulate.
Lay nurses more involved in nursing within Catholic Hospitals following World War II.	

Figure 2: continued

PRESENT

Strengths	Weaknesses
Corporate access to capital. Mandated budget controls.	Continued increase in health-care cost.
Lay involvement at all levels of administration/staff; both men and women prepared for administrative roles.	Religious much less visible, if present at all.
Advanced scientific technology.	Emphasis on technology, science, and equipment versus patient in need of care.
Some medical-moral dilemmas addressed.	These advances complicate medical-moral issues and resolutions are complex.
Concepts of caring and service emphasized more directly in absence of visible religious presence.	Marked decrease in religious due to aging process and/or choice of ministry—further decrease of role models.
Specialty services provided.	Duplication of specialty services.
Professional buildings with physicians' offices on or near hospital grounds.	Competition for patients and services offered.
Multiple roles and categories of employees.	Loss of identity of some traditional roles and "chipping away" some roles and functions of professional nurses by ancillary/support service personnel.

As a result of the changes which have occurred in health-care delivery, both sisters and lay personnel within Catholic-sponsored facilities have worked together to carry out the philosophy, goals, and objectives of their respective health-care facilities. But they have also learned to face the new problems which are bound to emerge. They recognize the fact that the latest challenges to their ministry actually stem from overcoming the deficiencies created by incorporating these new action plans into their overall hospital planning. Questions have arisen as to the wisdom of the new choices; these indicate the degree to which the revolution in health care in American society has transformed ministry within the American Catholic Church.

As Catholic leaders in health care project future needs, their primary concern will continue to be their response to "the preferential option for the poor."[31] They realize that this will make it necessary sometimes to assume responsibility for health care in the place of unresponsive government. In fact, administrators of Catholic hospitals and allied facilities, as well as heads of multisystem networks of health-care operations, recognize that they must respond in this way even as delivery systems continue their move toward precluding moral and humanistic considerations. The future challenges for all Catholic practitioners in the field, as well as for the recipients of their care, will definitely be very different from today's system. A health-care system has yet to develop in which the individual will be able to participate in a manner appropriate to need and irrespective of ability to pay. Nor is it possible in the present circumstances for the provider to continue service to the poor and needy when these are unable to supply insurance to cover costs. To seek the most equitable solution is, nevertheless, a key responsibility of those religious congregations who have traditionally been devoted to health-care ministry.

Other considerations complicate health-care provision today. Health care remains a major expenditure; in fact, catastrophic debt as a result of illness or accident has become a far-too-common occurrence. Such debt can even result from ordinary illness and become a problem even for those with financial resources. As more and more sophisticated means of diagnoses continue to advance rapidly, these add not only to the cost of care but can raise many difficult medical-moral and legal issues. As the decisions are made regarding who will receive what treatment, even greater problems for Catholic hospitals will emerge. The major responsibility of the Catholic hospital in the present age is to incorporate the principles of Christ in the midst of expanding and often overwhelming scientific knowledge and technology. Catholic health providers must continue to strive to preserve the Christian ideal of personalized care. Especially in the realm of medical-moral issues and concern for human life, women religious engaged in health care must proceed in such a way that they can influence decisions appropriately. To preserve quality facilities, moreover, there is an even greater need for courageous and clear thinking in the midst of medical research and the advance of medical opinions and options which may have important moral implications. Religious congregations must not only be personally prepared to provide moral leadership but they must also provide ways to assist in the formal preparation of Christian lay leaders in Catholic health-care facilities. And they must be ready to provide greater recognition of the laity as collaborators in carrying out their mission in the church.

There is no doubt that those pioneer religious women who established the foundation of ministry to the sick ever envisioned changes in health care that would lead to the present level of institutionalization and management of hospitals. Yet it happened. So, too, sisters presently engaged in the health-care ministry who demonstrate a spirit of dedication that remains vibrant cannot predict the future needs of God's people. But willingness to take risks and share common problems, as demonstrated by the sisters during the transition years of the 1950s, augurs well for the future. The growth of medicine, nursing, and hospitals as a result of scientific advances, coupled with the extensive stabilization and ultimate retrenchment of the hospitals and schools of nursing established by religious women that occurred at that time, reveal that energy, inspiration, and creativity can weather challenges and changes over the years. Religious women and members of the laity collaboratively engaged in the health-care ministry must continue to trust that they can carry forward the same concerns for the dignity of the human person, an equal responsiveness to a variety of practical needs, as advocates for the sick, the suffering, the poor, and any neighbors in need in keeping with the healing ministry of Christ.

NOTES

1. Writers Program of the State of Kansas, *Lamps on the Prairie* (Emporia, KS: Emporia Gazetter Press, 1942), pp. 70–71.

2. Grace L. Deloughery, *History and Trends of Professional Nursing* (St. Louis, MO: Mosby, 1977), pp. 1–24.

3. Margaret E. Parsons, "Mothers and Matrons," *Nursing Outlook* 31 (September/October 1983): 278. It was not until 1940 that a monument was erected to honor all of the sister nurses who served during the Civil War.

4. Joellen Watson, "The Evolution of Nursing Education in the United States: One Hundred Years of a Profession for Women," *Journal of Nursing Education* 16 (September 1977): 31.

5. Josephine Dolan, "Nurses in American History: Three Schools 1873," *American Journal of Nursing* 75 (June 1975): 988-92.

6. Anne L. Austin, *History of Nursing Sourcebook* (New York: Putnam's, 1957): 262–63.

7. Ina Madge Longway, "Curriculum Concepts: An Historical Analysis," *Nursing Outlook* 20 (February 1972): 117.

8. Lucille E. Notter and Eugenia Spalding, *Professional Nursing: Foundations, Perspectives, and Relationships*, 9th ed. (Philadelphia: Lippincott, 1976), p. 7.

9. Samuel P. Hays, *The Response to Industrialism 1885–1914* (Chicago: University of Chicago Press, 1957), p. 170.

10. Erwin H. Ackerknecht, M.D., *A Short History of Medicine* (New York: Ronald Press, 1955), p. 209.

11. Philip A. Kalisch and Beatrice J. Kalisch, *The Advance of Modern Nursing* (Boston: Little, Brown, 1973), pp. 162–64.

12. Abraham Flexner, *Medical Education in the United States and Canada* (Carnegie Foundation for the Advancement of Teaching, 1910) pp. 3–185.

13. Joint Commission on Accreditation of Hospitals, "Accreditation Manual for Hospitals" (Chicago, 1982), pp. ix-x.

14. "The Catholic Hospital Today," in *A History of the Catholic Hospital* (Cincinnati, OH: Standard Textile Co., n.d.), p. 6.

15. Kalisch and Kalisch, *The Advance of Modern Nursing*, p. 81.

16. M. M. Foley, "Nursing, Catholic Schools," *The New Catholic Encyclopedia*, 2nd ed. (St. Louis, MO: Thomas Nelson, 1983), p. 578.

17. Sister Mary Virginia Dryden, "History of the Good Samaritan Hospital School of Nursing," 1941 master's thesis, University of Cincinnati.

18. St. Joseph's Hospital School of Nursing, Denver, CO: Sisters of Charity of Leavenworth Archives, Leavenworth, KS.

19. Foley, "Nursing, Catholic Schools," p. 578.

20. Catholic Hospital Association, Conference of Catholic Schools of Nursing, *Nursing Education and Catholic Institutions* (St. Louis, MO: Catholic Hospital Association, 1963), p. iii.

21. Foley, "Nursing, Catholic Schools," p. 579.

22. Ibid.

23. American Nurses' Association Committee on Nursing Education, *A Case for Baccalaureate Education in Nursing* (New York: American Nurses' Association, 1979), p. 4. Commonly referred to as the "Position Paper."

24. William O'Neill, *Coming Apart: An Informal History of America in the 1960s* (Chicago: Quadrangle Books, 1971), pp. 25–28.

25. Sister Rose Dominic Gabisch, SCL, Ph.D. Personal file, February 1982, Sisters of Charity of Leavenworth Archives, Leavenworth, KS. Sister Gabisch served as national executive secretary of the Sister Formation Conference, Washington, D.C., from 1964 to 1967.

26. DeLoughery, *History and Trends of Professional Nursing*, pp. 141–45.

27. Austin Flannery, OP, ed., *Vatican Council II: The Conciliar and Post-Conciliar Documents* (Wilmington, DE: Scholarly Resources, 1975), pp. 388–89.

28. Sister Rose Dominic Gabisch, SCL, "The Story of Sister Rose Dominic Gabisch, SCL" (February 1982), pp. 200–203. Sisters of Charity of Leavenworth Archives, Leavenworth, KS.

29. Catholic Hospital Association of the United States, *Evaluative Criteria for Catholic Health Care Facilities* (St. Louis, MO: Catholic Hospital Association of the United States, 1980) p. 61.

30. Catholic Health Association of the United States, "Introduction," *Profiles of Catholic Multi-Institutional Systems 1985–1986* (St. Louis MO: Catholic Health Association of the United States, 1985).

31. Catholic Health Association of the United States, *No Room in the Marketplace: The Health Care of the Poor*, Task Force Final Report (St. Louis, MO: Catholic Health Association of the United States, 1986).

◆ Toward the Twenty-first Century

MARGARET JOHN KELLY, DC

The last three decades of the twentieth century will undoubtedly go down in history as the era of greatest change within the Catholic Church and within the health-care field. The major and perhaps the single most precipitating event within the church was Vatican II. The revolution in health care is principally attributable to the rapid acceleration in the development of scientific knowledge and medical technology; the improved standard of living for most Americans; the change in United States demographics, including the growing populations of both the elderly and the poor; and a pluralism of moralities, as well as of religions. Both the church and the health field have also experienced a growing awareness of global responsibility and national interdependence.

At the close of the 1980s, we can see the directions for the new millennium, and we can, with relative assurance, project the Catholic health-care ministry into the twenty-first century. It appears that the church's long-standing tradition of providing quality health care, supporting state-of-the-art facilities, and promoting wholeness will continue. As it continues, religious sponsors will lead the health ministry to:

1. higher consciousness of church identity and increased involvement of the laity,
2. broader patterns of consolidation and collaboration,
3. greater corporatization that combines Gospel emphasis and efficient structures,
4. stronger political advocacy for justice for the poor, and
5. greater international involvement.

These projections derive from trends that already have significantly focused and directed the ministry. While somewhat optimistic, they are shared, for the most part, by many leaders in the ministry who have contributed their reflections to this essay.[1]

Before projecting into that future, however, it is profitable to review the dominant post–Vatican II trends of the 1970s and early eighties as the matrix for the evolution of the ministry. Five major trends, to a large extent in response to Vatican II directives and post–Vatican II sensitivities, have coalesced to bring Catholic facilities to their present status. First, both internationally and nationally, there has been a higher level of papal and episcopal involvement in the Catholic health ministry. Second, there is an awareness of the significance of responding to the new ethical issues that have developed from advances in scientific knowledge and technology, and that have been and will continue to be most deeply and pervasively experienced within health care. Third, a large body of literature on sponsorship and Catholic identity has developed. Fourth, religious congregations have experienced a major decline in membership but have modified their views of ministry and their governance structures to compensate for that numerical decline. Finally, in the post–Vatican II period, the laity have come of age and have expanded into every level of service, management, and governance in health care, often becoming equal partners with members of religious congregations.

Higher Level of Papal and Episcopal Involvement in Health Care

Vatican II remained silent on the issue of Catholic health care; the documents of the council include no specific reference to this significant ministry. Since the 1960s, however, the hierarchy has become increasingly vocal and involved at the international, national, and local levels. John XXIII and Paul VI developed blueprints for economic justice that encompassed the individual's right to health care. Their observations form the basis of a variety of subsequent social documents. John Paul II, like Pius XII, has seized many opportunities to support the role of the church in health care, and in *Redemptor hominis* he challenged the ministry to stress "the priority of ethics over technology, the primacy of persons over things, and the superiority of spirit over matter." In 1984 he encouraged participants in the First International Congress on Catholic Health Affairs to make every effort to provide health services in a manner faithful to Jesus' healing and his Gospel message. In 1985 he formed an International Commission on Health Affairs and encouraged the publication *Dolentium hominum,* which chronicles issues of health care from the international perspective.

At the Roman curia level, the Congregation for the Doctrine of the Faith has issued two significant documents that have been widely discussed in the secular press as well as within health-care facilities and by religious sponsors. In June 1980, the "Declaration on Euthanasia" was presented, and in March 1987 "Instruction on Respect for Human Life in its Origin and on the Dignity of Procreation" was issued in response to the growing number of reproductive technologies that are now becoming more generally available.

Although, in the past, American bishops have not jointly attempted to exert direct influence over the evolution of Catholic health care (the sponsorship of facilities having been maintained by congregations or religious institutes), this has changed since the 1960s. In fact, one of the documents developed and updated in the 1970s by the National Conference of Catholic Bishops, "The Religious and Ethical Directives for Catholic Health Facilities" (revised 1975), has been a major force in policy formation in the Catholic facilities. Furthermore, in 1977 the bishops published the Vatican response to the National Catholic Conference of bishops (NCCB) request for clarification on sterilization. In a further move to reinforce this new involvement, the bishops joined the National Conference of Catholic Charities (NCCC) and the Catholic Health Association (CHA) in the Joint Task Force on Future Health Care Directions, in 1980. Even though disagreement on the issue of national health insurance caused the group to disband, the bishops' deliberate entry into the arena where health-care issues are addressed testified to changing episcopal attitudes. The U.S. bishops' attendance at the annual educational program conducted by the Pope John XXIII Center for Medical Moral Research and Education, for bishops of the U.S., Canada, Mexico, and the Antilles, testifies to their interest in ethical issues.

In 1981, moreover, the bishops took their first joint stance when they issued a health-oriented pastoral, "Health and Health Care." In this document they acknowledged health-care professionals with gratitude but proposed four challenges even as they committed themselves, both *personally* and institutionally, to do their part "in maintaining and developing a Catholic institutional presence within the health-care field in our country."[2] Taking this lead, the Catholic Health Association's Task Force on the Poor recently requested a further update of this pastoral as continuing evidence of episcopal support during this challenging period.

Although there is no distinct office for health affairs at United States Catholic Conference (USCC), the Office for Social Development handles health-care issues and oversees health programs.

In addition to several pastorals issued individually by diocesan bishops as a follow-up to their 1981 pastoral, many bishops have become more actively involved with the health-care ministry within their diocese. This represents a major change, since contact between congregationally sponsored facilities and the bishops previously had been almost exclusively limited to relations less intrinsic to Gospel orientation, such as fundraising or matters of protocol regarding participation in cornerstone-laying ceremonies and other social functions. Now, with growing regularity, bishops are convening the sponsors and the chief executive officers of the Catholic facilities within their diocese to share perspectives on the ministry and in many cases to facilitate collaboration. One of the most dramatic examples of this has occurred in Chicago, where Cardinal Joseph L. Bernardin regularly convenes the leadership of the sixteen religious congregations sponsoring the twenty-three hospitals of the area as well as the chief executive officers. These meetings have led to the formation of an alliance with a full-time director to facilitate archdiocesan collaboration. Thus, an outcome of this was Cardinal Bernardin's ability to encourage the Missionary Sisters, Servants of the Holy Spirit [3530] of Techny, Illinois, in 1987 to reject a for-profit system's offer for the Catholic Medical Center in Waukegan and to accept an offer by a Catholic system, the Franciscan Sisters of the Sacred Heart [1450] of Mokena, Illinois.

During the same year the Cardinal John J. O'Connor of New York was able to form an alliance which will ultimately include the seventeen Catholic hospitals of the archdiocese as well as its fourteen nursing homes, sixteen child-care agencies, and three home-care agencies. It is expected that the administrative structure which will evolve from this effort will be a model for other dioceses since it sets the stage for new designs of diocesan/congregational collaboration along a wholistic model of service. Two years earlier, under the direction of Cardinal Bernard Law, the Archdiocese of Boston incorporated the Caritas Christi Health System for its own four hospitals; subsequently it accepted the affiliate-membership of a hospital historically tied to the Bon Secours [0270] congregation. At the same time Cardinal Law encouraged the development of the Catholic Hospital Council, which includes the chief executive officer of each of the eleven Catholic hospitals in the archdiocese and the seven religious congregations involved in health care. In many dioceses, including those as varied as Green Bay, Oklahoma City, Sioux Falls, Indianapolis, and Baltimore, the bishops have spearheaded efforts to animate and coordinate health-care activities within their dioceses. These efforts are not directed at episcopal control but rather appear to be motivated by a desire that, despite possibilities of retrenchment, the health ministry within dioceses and archdioceses will continue.

Another very interesting and inspiring example of episcopal interest in health care was generated in late 1984 by Archbishop (now Cardinal) James A. Hickey of Washington who solicited the help of over one thousand Catholic physicians in his archdiocese to assist with the health-care needs of the poor. Hickey was successful in developing a volunteer network of one hundred seventy physicians and thirty dentists to collaborate with various archdiocesan agencies and institutions to address the needs of the poor. They have been particularly effective with the growing "homeless" population. It is significant that in 1987 both the American Medical Association and the American Bar Association contributed a joint editorial to the *Journal of the American Medical Association* urging each of their members to supply *pro bono* service of fifty hours annually. This type of voluntarism can be a powerful assist to the congregations' efforts to serve the poor.

The trend toward increased episcopal involvement is apparent as well on the state level, where a number of bishops have urged diocesan Catholic conferences to become more active in addressing health-care issues. As a result, regional Catholic conferences have not only become involved in medical-moral issues, including euthanasia, abortion, and surrogate parenting, but they have also become extremely active in pursuing health-care justice for the poor. Conferences in New York, Pennsylvania, Texas, and Wisconsin have achieved outstanding results at the advocacy level; they also benefitted from the solidarity engendered by these joint stands. Since 1987, for example, the Health Affairs Office of the New York State Conference has been able to educate regulators and legislators on the necessity for sponsors to retain certain reserved powers.

The Office of Diocesan Coordinator of Health Affairs, first developed in 1939 and staffed at the National Catholic Welfare Council (NCWC) in 1942, has evolved to become more focused and more standardized. In many cases, staffing on the diocesan levels has been upgraded to full-time participation. By 1987, approximately half of the dioceses in the United States had chosen to maintain such offices on a permanent basis. Their principal function has been to facilitate communication between the bishop of the diocese and health-care facilities so that diocesan-wide policy issues could be coordinated. This communication and coordination have become increasingly necessary because, while some dioceses traditionally serve as sponsors,[3] most hospitals (95 percent) are owned and administered by religious congregations. Efforts at collaboration and communication with other Catholic providers are surfacing with greater frequency. Some diocesan sponsors are exploring the feasibility of affiliating with an existent regional or national system of congregational sponsorship, or are establishing their own. Because free-standing facilities are particularly vulnerable, religious congregations that have developed successful systems can assist diocesan providers. However, there have already been some situations where competition rather than collaboration has pointed to the need for great cooperation.

Growing Complexity of Ethical Challenges

The rapid acceleration of scientific knowledge and medical technology has sensitized the bishops to their responsibilities as moral leaders and has forced sponsors and hospital administrators to upgrade ethical education at the corporate and local levels. It has made everyone more aware of the tremendous influence the Catholic health ministry can have as a platform for a Christian response to the ethical issues spawned by medical advances. It is not an exaggeration to claim that the major ethical issues of these last two decades of the twentieth century and well into the twenty-first century will be played out in the arena of health and medical care. While reproductive and genetic issues have long held attention, the current issues which will grow in importance are euthanasia, access to care for the poor, and the allocation of medical resources at both the "macro" and "micro" levels. In addition, many church leaders have recognized that, in the spirit of "The Church in the Modern World," the Christian perspective on the person must be brought to bear on such emerging issues as brain research and personality modification through chemical interventions.

While the American bishops did not directly allude to the pathogenic nature of poverty in their recent pastoral on economic justice, many now appear to recognize that health status is closely correlated with economic status and that the two issues must be related in their discussions of human rights. Two recent studies conducted by the American Hospital Association and the American College of Health Care Executives with Arthur Andersen Co. identified allocation, access to services, and other medical-ethical issues as major concerns in the 1990s. All of this suggests that the dialogue on ethical issues must proceed at a pace even more vigorous than that of technological advances. Effective dialogue between sponsors and bishops will assist the magisterium to adopt a proactive rather than reactive stance, and will provide for a unified approach to legislative and judicial initiatives which have ethical implications. The Catholic health ministry has already shown such leadership in the development of local ethics committees and in appointing corporate ethicists to assist in policy making.

Church Sponsorship and Catholic Identity

In the areas of sponsorship and Catholic identity one sees a very dramatic change in Catholic health care over the past twenty years. Sponsorship did not become a major issue until the mid 1970s, largely because of the identifiable presence of religious workers (usually sisters, but in some cases brothers) and because religious symbols seemed to preclude the need for Catholic identity and ownership discussions. It was the Maida-McGrath controversy of the early 1970s that set the stage for the exploration of the concept and the clarification of the term *sponsorship*. That controversy probed the precise legal relationship of church entities with their incorporated apostolates. The contention of one of the disputants, Father Adam J. Maida, now bishop of Green Bay, was that congregations held property as stewards for the church;[4] on the other hand, Father John McGrath maintained that the assets of a Catholic hospital did not belong to the church through the congregation but were in fact public property.[5] The controversy became more acute during this period because religious congregations were experiencing a rapid decline in personnel and were facing the issue of retrenchment of works. Furthermore, an anti-institutional bias had begun to cause congregational discussions and voting chapters to question the role of religious congregations in maintaining church institutions. Some religious seemed drawn to divest themselves of large institutions, which, they argued, were incompatible with the Gospel call to servanthood and poverty.

Prior to Vatican II, sponsorship had been focused principally in the presence of numerous and identifiable members of the sponsoring congregation serving within the facility and a religious chief executive officer. In some cases, hospitals were not separately incorporated from the congregation itself. For the most part, congregational leaders maintained but had no need to exercise civil and canonical control through the governance structures. The philosophy and value system of the sponsor was lived out by the numerous religious who held the major supervisory positions and taught in the nursing schools which provided the major personnel source. Modeling became the principal mode of transmitting the values of the sponsors and was educationally very effective.

In the 1970s, however, the experience of declining religious personnel, caused by the decreased number of applicants and the increased attrition by death and withdrawals, forced religious congregations to assess the nature and value of their relationship to their sponsored institutions. Unfortunately, in this analysis, some concluded that sponsorship was not a high value and attempted to divest themselves of their facilities. A few others opted to separate the financial and mission areas of sponsorship and yielded the major responsibility of business affairs to lay boards, retaining responsibility only for formation and pastoral care within the facility. Both of these approaches were well motivated, but they often influenced adversely the religious value system of these institutions, in effect "secularizing" some facilities. During the 1980s many congregations gradually reevaluated their decisions to divide responsibility, and again assumed sponsorship obligations. Unfortunately, some discovered at this point that the ease with which a congregation can regain sponsorship powers is conditioned by the role the religious played in the intervening years and the willingness of boards to relinquish powers and autonomy to the congregation. Some of the struggles that resulted from this attempt to return control to the congregation have polarized congregations and lay boards and at times have even involved the local bishop in public discussions.

One good outcome of this confusion over the nature of sponsorship is that since the 1970s religious congregations have become aware of the civil and canonical aspects of sponsorship and have discovered new ways to be effective stewards of the ministry developed by their foremothers. Since the physical presence of members of the sponsorship group within the facility could no longer be relied upon as an effective means of transmitting the corporate culture of the sponsor or of retaining the necessary control, it became increasingly apparent that *physical presence* would have to be replaced by the stronger force of *moral and legal presence*. It also became clear that this presence could be achieved at two levels: The first would be through strong corporate documents and legal structures that reserved the essential sponsorship powers to the religious institute. The second method would be through formation programs for boards, administrators, and staffs, so that the value system would be taught to and internalized by all associated with the sponsor's work. The original driving force and religious inspiration of a congregation—its "charism"—also received major attention at this time because of Vatican II's mandates to rediscover "the founders' spirit" and interpret "the signs of the times."

Integral to the notion of sponsorship was the concept of Catholic identity. At the same time the sponsors were looking within, the Catholic Health Association conducted a major self-study which in 1977 concluded that Catholic identity was the major issue facing the entire Catholic health-care ministry. One of the major activities of this study group was to convene a task force of theologians and others associated with the Catholic health-care ministry to study the meaning of Catholic identity in regard to health facilities. (Tangentially, it is interesting to note that the same kind of study was conducted in the early 1980s by the National Conference of Catholic Charities and the National Catholic Education Association as they sought the meaning of being Catholic in the social-service and educational worlds.)

To assist sponsors and health-care personnel, the CHA study group in 1980 generated the seminal document *Evaluative Criteria for Catholic Health Facilities.*[6] This publication, praised by the American bishops in their 1981 pastoral "Health and Health Care," presented to the ministry an overall statement of Catholic health-care philosophy that subsumed eight basic principles which were subsequently developed fully in the eight chapters of the book. This document quickly became a tool for sponsors, local boards, and administrators to study and evaluate their own Catholic identity. The sponsorship concept, highlighted in the earlier Maida-McGrath discussions, now had taken flesh in this educational workbook. While that document was used extensively and successfully within the ministry from 1980 through 1984, it was subsequently withdrawn by the Catholic Health Association. The question of Catholic identity, however, remained relevant at the national level because a theological narrative, *Catholic Identity and Health Care in the United States: Theological Framework*, was published by CHA in 1987 as a substitute preliminary document.[7] This document focused on the sacramental quality of the Catholic health care, but its humanistic, adenominational approach did little to illumine the understanding of what ministry, which is both catholic and Catholic, entails.

One of the problems in defining the essence of Catholic health care was the continuing stress on the pluralism of American society and of

Catholicism within the United States and its subsequent effect upon health care. Because some sponsors encouraged a collaborative approach, they began to insist that Catholic institutions stress their "Christian" rather than their "Catholic" identity. They argued this on the basis of the religious heterogeneity of their patients and staff. In the end, both positive and negative ramifications of such thinking resulted. More important consequences were the appreciation of the differences and the realization of the need to shore up First Amendment rights and to guarantee Catholics their right to exercise their distinctive ministry. While there still remains some disagreement, the greater number of sponsors appear convinced that unless their facilities do have a unique quality and are distinctive, they should not exist. These discussions are very pointed in towns where there are two facilities, one Catholic and one public.

The experience of church groups in seeking to consolidate services and facilities with nonchurch groups is very instructive. Because in most cases the Catholic facility has the more restrictive ethical code, the more permissive institution must concur with the Catholic ethical stance or distinct operations must be maintained. When the Sisters of Charity of St. Augustine [0580] consolidated their St. John Hospital with West Shore Hospital, two distinct delivery towers were maintained. While the diocese of Allentown and Sacred Heart Hospital had temporarily arranged a consolidation, they eventually had to disband the plan because of ethical disputes. In very recent efforts of DuBois Hospital, sponsored by Mercy Sisters [2570] of Erie, Pennsylvania, to arrange a consolidation with Maple Avenue Hospital, an innovative trust arrangement has been introduced. Many other examples could be cited to demonstrate the great challenge of collaborating when there is great diversity in ethical perspective about particular medical procedures. While in the past the point of controversy generally focused on the reproductive issues, it is fair to assume that in the future the struggle will surround termination of treatment and attitudes toward euthanasia.

These Catholic identity and sponsorship issues have continued to be major discussion points. This can be easily documented by a quick review of the various educational programs conducted at the local, state, and congregational levels or of the bibliographies of contemporary health periodicals. A review of many board agendas in that same period shows a major shift from legal and financial issues to a blending of mission-oriented concerns with the legal and financial questions. This reflects the growing awareness on the part of women religious of the ramifications of the stewardship of mission as well as stewardship of economic resources. Sponsorship statements then came under the scrutiny of legislative chapters and other congregational conventions. In a CHA interview survey conducted in 1982, 60 percent of the sponsors polled reported that they had made a formal commitment to sponsorship..

During this same period, there was a large increase in the number of persons directly involved in responsibility for seeing that the *mission* of the congregation is carried out. In 1980 only three of the then approximately twenty-eight Catholic multihospital systems had a staff person involved in mission projects; in 1984 well over half of the forty-eight systems had an individual whose major focus was sponsorship or mission. A 1985 CHA survey with a 65 percent return from the fifty-five systems, showed that twenty-four out of thirty-six systems had a person in mission effectiveness or sponsorship. This same trend was emerging in local facilities as well and was greatly strengthened by the growing number of health systems, as well as by the increased networking at the state and national levels of persons involved in these areas.

A major impetus was given to sponsorship when the Catholic Health Association followed up its surveys with specific programs. From 1981 forward CHA offered membership to both the sponsors and their systems. This action expanded CHA membership to three categories from the long-standing single institutional category of hospital or nursing home. This type of convening and expanded CHA membership opened the way for many subsequent developments in sponsorship networking and affiliating that grew from the improved communication among the leadership of the sponsoring congregations. Surveys published by *Hospital Progress* in 1981 and 1983 revealed the attitudes and reactions of the sponsors to some of these activities and documented congregations' growing concern about being faithful stewards. The short tenures of congregational leaders requires that orientation programs in sponsorship be regularly available, especially for leaders of multiministry congregations.

Interest in sponsorship has continued. Despite a low response, a 1987 survey conducted by CHA showed that 62 percent of the respondent group identified a need for assistance in carrying out the mission and philosophy while 51 percent requested help in stewardship orientation programs. Furthermore, a new publication, *Ministry and Mission Alert*, appeared in July 1987. It can be viewed as a revitalization of an earlier publication, *Ministry and Mission* (1981–1984), which was developed specifically to assist sponsors. Together with another CHA publication,

Health Care Ministry Assessment : A Basic Accountability Process for Sponsors of Catholic Health Care Facilities (1983), which assisted sponsors to initiate a self-study, these two documents are again being used to identify the nature of sponsorship and the role of Catholic health-care facilities today. To be sure, sponsorship came of age in the 1980s and will remain the critical focus throughout the nineties because of the internal climate of religious congregations and the external challenges to their ministry.

Decline in Religious Personnel

Before the Second Vatican Council, there were over two hundred religious congregations in acute health care, some dedicated exclusively to health care. Since the council, however, there has been a rapid decline in the number of religious personnel available to the ministry and the number of communities able to be involved in health ministry. In a 1981 survey conducted by Sister Ursula Stepsis, CSA, for the Catholic Health Association the following statistics were compiled.[8]

	U.S. Religious	Number of religious in acute care	% of congregational membership in health care
1968	176,538	15,977	18%
1972	143,189	11,047	14%
1976	130,929	8,944	13%
1980	122,771	7,131	11%

While one admits that these statistics are not totally representative of health services because they are limited to women-religious personnel in acute care, one does see that the number of sisters in acute care decreased dramatically and that the percentage of the membership involved in health care also decreased. The decline continues. By 1986, the number of religious women in the United States was set at 114,000; their ministry in acute-care facilities also underwent a proportionate decline.

Such statistics need not, however, be viewed in a totally negative light. For example, many religious are now involved in hospital governance rather than in service positions. In these policy-making positions they have already been able to render great service—a trend which may continue. Sisters are also being appointed as full-time chairpersons of boards with greater frequency. The ministry of trusteeship and governance has allowed other religious who have their primary apostolic ministry in education or social service to become involved at the leadership level in health care. This type of collaboration within the sponsoring congregation contributes to a sense of ownership of the health ministry within the institute or congregation. Furthermore, as retrenchments are being made, some congregations are giving priority to their health ministry because of their special sponsorship responsibilities for these "owned" facilities.

Increasing Involvement of the Laity

Simultaneous with the decline of religious personnel and the growing interest in sponsorship, the role of Catholic laymen and laywomen in health care has expanded. Vatican II's document on the laity became the authoritative guide for those studying ministry issues in health care. Even though the laity had significantly outnumbered religious in the health-care field from the late 1930s, religious women held the most important positions. A survey of the percentage of lay hospital chief executive officers illustrates this growth. Lay CEOs held 3 percent of the top hospital positions in 1965; 23 percent in 1970; 38 percent in 1975; 51 percent in 1980; and more than 60 percent in 1985. The 1987 Catholic Health Association's annual report indicates that while the percentage of lay chief executive officers has remained constant, the number of Catholic hospitals has actually decreased. While the laity have assumed more than half of the chief executive posts in Catholic hospitals, members of religious congregations hold the majority of positions in Catholic multi-institutional health systems. This may represent a congregational shift from an emphasis on institutional administration to positions of system administration and governance.

An increase of lay administrators can also be seen in other areas formerly dominated by religious, such as nursing service, dietary, and pharmacy. This change grew out of discussions, particularly during the 1970s and early 1980s, as to the manner in which the laity should and could collaborate at various levels of the ministry and which institutional positions should be reserved for the members of the sponsoring congregation. Today these discussions have moved to the question of how to utilize the talents of all for the church ministry. On the part of religious congregations, there is some concern over losing flexibility in "placing" their own members within their institutions because of justice to lay incumbents.

Finally, while a few congregations still attempt to fill all or, at least a majority of trustee positions with their own members, the greater number of trustee boards of Catholic health-care facilities and health systems have a good representation of fully enfranchised laity. Despite some lingering reservations about the value of "nonreligious" on boards, this broadening of membership has allowed a wide range of expertise to be added to that of the sponsoring congregation and is generally not only appreciated but demanded.

Traditionally, the role of sponsor has remained within the domain of congregations and dioceses as public juridic persons. However, the Catholic Health Association has recently developed alternative sponsorship models which allow the laity to move into the position of sponsors of health-care facilities, either as private juridic persons or as lay associations. These models permit lay groups to have sponsorship rights equal to those inherent in the public juridic person. In late 1987, St. Frances Hospital in Memphis pioneered with the private association of the Christian faithful model. St. Joseph, Elmira, New York, is in the process of adopting the second alternative model, the private juridic person. Time will determine the effectiveness of these models. Some believe that, because sponsorship by a religious congregation provides continuity, stability, and unity of vision, it will always be the preferred model of canonical sponsorship. Others are fully confident that lay sponsorship can be equally effective and declare that the movement within the church is toward full partnership models. The American Catholic Lay Network, formed in 1985 to facilitate lay participation and collaboration within the church, has developed a special program for lay-religious bonding. Undoubtedly its growing influences, coupled with the efforts of religious sponsors, will advance partnership in ministry and may generate other models of sponsorship.

Summation

We have come almost two and a half decades since the close of Vatican II, and it is apparent that in those years religious institutions and their health ministries have experienced dramatic change. It is also apparent that their present situation is characterized by vigor, commitment, and strength. Unifying the elements of change is a greater awareness of health care as a *ministry of the total church*. This is seen in the broader interest of the pope and the bishops of the United States as well as in the full participation of the laity. It is revealed as well by an increased commitment to sponsorship and depth study of Catholic identity and it is also marked by the growing sensitivity to the importance of the Christian ethic at a time when health care is experiencing the technological stage of a "perfection of means but a confusion of goals." Through all these changes health care has been richly maintained in this country by women religious who have taken seriously Cardinal Bernardin's challenge that the "ministry be both leaven and leverage": providing witness to Gospel values and exerting influence in policy-making arenas.

Toward the Next Millennium: Five Major Trends Forging the Future of Catholic Health-Care Ministry

Before introducing the five major trends that will probably take us into the twenty-first century, it seems appropriate to look at the quantitative survey of the ministry from the historical perspective. While we must allow for a margin of error, the following statistics drawn from the *Official Catholic Directory* are revealing and provide a context for these future trends. It is also necessary to recall that religious institutes of women sponsor well over 90 percent of the institutional services, but these statistics do encompass works of dioceses and of nine congregations of men as well.

	1966	1976	1986
General hospitals	803	660	634
(Bed capacity)	(149,000)	(162,000)	(170,000)
Specialty hospitals	140	90	103
(Bed capacity)	(13,000)	(7,800)	(5,800)
Homes for the aged	399	458	615
(Residents)	(38,000)	(53,000)	(77,000)
Schools of nursing	331	135	114
(Students)	(35,000)	(19,700)	(20,100)

While the number of hospitals has decreased, their scope of service has increased significantly. As indicated by the increase in general hospital beds and the decrease in the bed capacity of specialty hospitals (pediatric and psychiatric, for example) there has been much integration in the acute-care setting. These statistics do not reveal the very large expansion of services through outpatient and other ambulatory services that began in the midseventies and is still in an upward trend. The *CHA*

1986 Guide reported thirty-four million such visits in Catholic facilities, 15 percent of the national total. Because of changes in medical practice and delivery sites, bed capacity or inpatient service is no longer the valid measure of health-care activity.

The statistics reveal other major changes. One that has been viewed quite negatively by many, particularly with the current nursing shortage, is the relative disappearance of nursing schools under Catholic hospital auspices. However, to gain an accurate picture of what has occurred in nursing education, we would need to examine the number of Catholic nursing programs that are now in collegiate settings. The statistics also reveal an increase in homes for the aged, which is a direct response to the needs of this growing segment of the population.

In summary, this statistical overview suggests a vibrant, responsive ministry that in 1986 accounted for 10 percent of the total hospitals in the nation and for 16 percent of hospital beds. In addition, the most recent *Modern Health Care* surveys show that Catholic systems are growing in the number of facilities owned and managed and indicates that there are some Catholic systems that rank among the top twenty hospital and long-term care systems.

Trends generated by Vatican II and the health-care environment are now sufficiently clear to make projections concerning Catholic health care in the next millennium. The observations made in this chapter reflect the author's viewpoints but have, as indicated before, been validated in most instances by the observations of several health-care leaders. In our view, Catholic health care in the twenty-first century will be marked by:

1. a higher consciousness of church identity;
2. continuing major sponsorship by religious congregations with a variety of configurations of collaboration within and among those congregations and with the laity;
3. acceptance of the need for greater corporatization but resistance to any structures that do not yield measurable benefits or that reflect the values of a secular corpocracy rather than the Gospel;
4. increasing advocacy efforts to achieve justice in health care; and
5. greater involvement at the international level in assisting underdeveloped nations.

Higher Consciousness of Church Identity

Two principal realities, one ethical and one political, will motivate the Catholic health ministry to sustain the Vatican II awakened efforts to be faithful to the mission of continuing the healing ministry of Jesus. First, the high-technology trend that contributes to depersonalization and that will bring on the advent of the "quartiary" facility (high-tech care) will underscore the need for Catholic health care to be wholistic and personalized. Second, the struggle to preserve First Amendment rights and tax-exempt status has the potential to unify and mobilize all church entities. Educational efforts could produce greater national consciousness of the phenomenal service network provided by the church through its health, education, and social-service agencies. This heightened consciousness may also evoke greater collaboration among various Christian health groups because all are now struggling to retain their rights in this pluralistic society.

A hostile economic and moral climate encourages greater cooperation among churches and within the church. The current trend of health-care sponsors and providers meeting at the local church level (diocese and archdiocese) can be expected to increase as further retrenchment is required by changes in delivery models. Also as legislation and adjudication at the state level (regulation, governance, reimbursement, medical practice, and bioethical areas) increase sponsors will interact more with state Catholic Conference staffs. In fact, it may prove to be more feasible for the regional and state Catholic hospital or health associations to dissolve some of their organization and fund staff for work at the state Catholic Conference level. While Catholic leaders will strive to prevent the health-care facilities from becoming ghettoized, and thereby losing their opportunity to impact the pluralistic service organizations, creeping secularism will require greater solidarity and advocacy among persons of like moral stance. As in the past religious sponsors can be depended upon to provide leadership within such groups. Congregations whose facilities are located in several diocese will need to discover new methods of congregational participation because of the resources required to participate meaningfully in several dioceses.

This higher consciousness of church identity and the emphasis on ecclesial collaboration may also move the church into a more wholistic model of delivery. Traditionally health care and social service have followed a medical model of service while the field of education being more of a ministry that is social, wholistic, and preventative. The stronger church identity in health care may well revolutionize the manner in which sponsoring congregations provide health service and encourage a new wholistic model of delivery. The multi-ministry congregations, because of their experience and their broad expertise, are in a unique position to give leadership to this movement. As a result, in place of the fragmented medical model currently in place, the church may well develop a social model of service that will offer prevention and wellness programs from the wholistic perspective. This new model may require the elimination of the current charities and educational services at the diocesan level or the addition of health care on an equal footing, although this presents many problems because of the difference in sponsorship. Central to the wholistic model is a conviction that the family must be the basic unit of service. This new thrust could add to the community experience so desired in our consumer-oriented, materialistic society.

A related challenge to Catholic sponsors, along with many other Christian denominations, will be to develop their wellness programs with a spiritual focus. Physical models developed in the 1980s (nutrition, exercise, and stress control) need to be expanded into wholistic programs that deal with the more basic influence of personal spirituality on one's physical and mental health. Current trends in traditional and alternative treatment modalities support this move and resonate with the feminine desire for the natural.

To implement this social model, hospitals will have to establish new working relationships with parishes, especially with regard to support groups, wellness programs, home health services, and pastoral care. The reduced number of priests, the shorter terms patients spend in acute-care facilities, and the very serious issues of chronicity will create a need for institutional pastoral-care departments to train personnel and coordinate services rather than provide service. Lay ministers, paid and volunteers, will be major providers of pastoral care. Sponsors will have to support these programs morally and perhaps financially as well.

While such unified, collaborative efforts reflect the lessons of Vatican II, two related trends could inhibit this unifying of ministry within the church. The first is the current proliferation of organizations and projects within the overall Catholic ministerial canvas. The second is the apparent lack of a corporate memory which prevents today's care givers from learning from the experience of their predecessors.

Because of the number of distinct congregations sponsoring health facilities, and the size of the nation and the ministry itself, any plan to secure and mold the future of the ministry must coordinate the major decision makers. However, the past decade has seen a proliferation of organizations seeking the same worthwhile goal. The greatest obstacle to true advancement of the ministry appears to be the current lack of centralized strong national leadership to develop a unified plan of action for the total ministry. Organizations proliferate in such a leadership vacuum. Two examples of this are the 1985 formation of Consolidated Catholic Health Care, a Chicago-based organization encompassing twenty-two Catholic hospital systems, and the Commission on Catholic Health Care Ministry, established in April 1987. Goals of the two groups are quite similar although their mode of operation, functions, and target populations are quite divergent. In a letter to the American bishops, the president of Consolidated Catholic Health Care described the goal of the organization as follows:

> To explore with some specificity how Consolidated Catholic Health Care might work with hospitals in the dioceses to facilitate a stronger Catholic health ministry, we are reaching out beyond our current membership to work with all interested parties in reaching the goal we share: to ensure the long-term viability of Catholic health ministries.

The Commission on Catholic Health Care views itself as "the corporate mechanism for offering a national vision of the future of the Catholic health-care ministry in the United States with options and strategies for advancing that vision." When one places these purposes against those of the Catholic Health Association, founded in 1915 under the impetus of the Sisters of St. Joseph of Carondelet [3840], one must question the advisability and the feasibility of this fracturing of efforts to advance the ministry in the absence of national leadership to coordinate efforts and reduce unnecessary duplication.

Interpretations of why this situation has occurred vary. It is the opinion of some that lack of communication between sponsors and administrators at both the local and system levels has in fact caused this proliferation and led to the formation of the Commission. Others suggest that the Catholic Health Association failed to provide appropriate leadership and support services to special-interest groups that then formed their own organizations. Most agree that the next few years are critical to reunifying the ministry. Again, religious sponsors can seize this opportunity and move toward unification of all these efforts, either through a revitalization of the national Catholic Health Association or by supporting a new organization. The ultimate control, and thus, the future of the Catholic health ministry lies in the hands of the sponsors, the greatest number of whom are women religious. They must provide the leadership.

Related to this trend of proliferation of organizations is the lack of a corporate memory in regard to past efforts in unifying and strengthening the ministry. Efforts of organizations like the Commission give hope because they focus on the future. But they also create despair because they appear, like so many church ventures, to ignore the past by failing to build on the wisdom and progress of the past. The goal undertaken by this new commission has been addressed at a national level twice before. Those experiences should be very instructive.

In 1975, the Catholic Health Association developed the Catholic Leadership Program for major superiors. While the program was ahead of its time (and thus, unsuccessful according to the terms envisioned by its designers), it did develop readiness for the events of later years. The many articles written and programs developed by the Catholic Health Association at that time established the readiness and created the climate for the Catholic identity/sponsorship orientation of the 1980s.

From 1981 to 1984 a blue-ribbon group called the Stewardship Task Force addressed the vision and the future of health-care ministry.[9] Its goal was "to identity, develop, and assist in the implementation of processes, standards, and systems required to maintain the strength and viability of the Catholic health-care ministry in the United States." As one reviews the specific goals adopted by this task force, along with its products and its eight recommendations, one hopes that the work of the newly formed national Commission on the Catholic Health Care Ministry will build on the findings and proposals of the past and not fall into the proverbial "committee syndrome" of reduplication and inability to create effective new options. Some of the task force's recommendations, such as the care-of-the-poor project, have had dramatic impact on the ministry while others are only now being addressed by the Catholic Health Association. Still others appear not to have been considered in planning.

While the 1980s have been dynamic years and have witnessed great advances in sponsorship, there will have to be formation programs for congregational members as well as for lay collaborators if this momentum is to be sustained and unified. It is hoped that the Christian formation programs offered by St. Louis University, St. Louis; Xavier University, Cincinnati; and St. John's University, New York, will become syndicated national programs. These could be made available through a church university of the air providing specialized programs in a wide range of topics, from health-care theology for board members to ethical issues for physicians and nurses.

Collaboration in Sponsorship and Programming

A study of the sponsorship trends of the late 1980s reveals a variety of collaborative models. Early in the 1980s many predicted that collaboration was moving the ministry toward a limited number of megasystems or even to one national megasystem that would encompass a wide range of institutional services and business entities provided by Catholic sponsors. Some projected a Catholic Health Corporation of America to coordinate the more than six hundred hospitals and four hundred long-term care facilities. These projections grew out of the rapid acceleration of system development that began in the mid-1970s with congregations unifying their separately incorporated facilities into shared services operations or into integrated health systems. From 1979 to 1987 the number of Catholic systems grew from twenty-eight to fifty-five; now they encompass over two-thirds of the Catholic hospitals.

In the early 1980s commentators saw four guiding foci in the development of multihospital or multi-institutional health-care system:

1. Organizing systems by congregation
2. Organizing systems by charism
3. Organizing systems along regional lines
4. Organizing systems along specialty lines, such as systems for rehabilitation or chemical dependency

The first three have emerged as the basic models of system development (congregation, charism, and region) and will perdure into the next millennium just as they have experienced great growth in the 1980s. These arrangements came of age with the advent of the prospective payment system in 1983. At that time, single free-standing facilities sought out means to profit from economies of scale in such areas as purchasing, insurance, risk management, and quality assurance, and found affiliation with a system not only feasible but necessary. The first steps in collaboration occurred within a congregation or between provinces as congregational systems were formed. In 1986, the Daughters of Charity of St. Vincent De Paul [0760] unified their five geographic areas and two regional systems into the largest nonprofit system in the nation.

In the early 1980s many predicted that intercongregational collaboration would also be guided by charism because of an assumed compatibility between congregations. Networking and alliance building along charism lines has indeed been a major type of collaboration. The Franciscan Sisters, with thirty-nine distinct congregations involved in health care, collaborate with the eight systems and the other facilities in the Franciscan network. In the hospital ministry, Franciscan facilities account for over 15 percent of all Catholic facilities, so they have tremendous potential to exert influence and to achieve economies of scale. The Sisters of St. Joseph (CSJ and SSJ) formed an alliance in the late 1980s that encompasses four major systems with approximately forty facilities spanning the whole United States; two other St. Joseph systems affiliate with this alliance. During the 1980s the Mercy sisters moved toward federation at several levels to strengthen community and ministry. In addition to several existing Mercy systems in the Midwest and Farwest, in 1986 some of the eastern provinces of Mercy sisters formed an eastern Mercy system that embraces nine facilities. Some of the subsidiary corporations of the Farmington Province system serve Mercy facilities throughout the country. Undoubtedly, similarity of charism and geography caused the Sisters of St. Joseph of Concordia, Kansas [3830], to transfer their three hospitals to the Sisters of St. Joseph of Wichita, Kansas [3830].

Another emerging trend which is setting the stage for greater collaboration is the actual merging of governmentally distinct congregations which have identical charisms. Some of these mergers are for ministry purposes only and affect only the health ministry, while others are fully canonical. In 1986 two independent Mercy health systems located in Auburn and Burlingame merged the systems and became Catholic Health Care West. In 1988 the system became intercongregational with the addition of the Adrian Dominicans. In 1986 two Missouri Franciscan groups which had once formed a single community, the Sisters of St. Mary, in St. Louis, and the Sisters of St. Francis, in Maryville, reunited and are now Franciscan Sisters of Mary in St. Louis [3970]. The long-standing health system of the larger group (fourteen facilities) accepted the two facilities of the smaller group. During the same period, the Sisters of St. Joseph of Superior, Wisconsin joined the St. Paul province of the Sisters of St. Joseph of Carondelet, who then assumed sponsorship over all health-care facilities.

While collaboration continues between congregations of like charism, willingness on the part of groups of different charism to collaborate in the form of transfer of sponsorship or affiliation has also increased. Often the motivation appears to be market-share considerations and service potential. Yet the preservation of religious presence in a given area is a strong motivator as well. In 1983, the Dominicans [1070] of Edmonds, Washington, conducted a very intensive study before transferring their two hospitals to the Sisters of Providence in Seattle [3350]. History has shown that this action opened up new opportunities for church ministry. Within the past few years, the Sisters of St. Joseph of Carondelet and the Daughters of Charity of St. Vincent de Paul assumed sponsorship of diocesan hospitals in Tucson and Austin, respectively. Both of these hospitals had previously been transferred from religious congregations. In North Dakota, the Sisters of St. Joseph of Carondelet transferred sponsorship of one of their hospitals to a Franciscan group. In Pennsylvania, the Missionary Sisters of the Sacred Heart [2860] transferred one of their hospitals to the Daughters of Charity in order to concentrate their personnel and efforts in three other facilities. In 1987, the School Sisters of St. Francis [1680] of Milwaukee transferred their acute-care facility in Waupun to the Sisters of the Congregation of St. Agnes [3710], which sponsored several hospitals in Wisconsin. In the same year, the Religious Hospitallers of St. Joseph [3440] affiliated their hospital in Vermont with the Covenant system, located in Boston and sponsored by another Canadian congregation, the Sisters of Charity of Montreal, the "Gray Nuns" [0490]. It is significant to note that after several years of study, the Sisters of Mercy of the Holy Cross [2630] in Wisconsin transferred sponsorship of their Wisconsin and North Dakota facilities to the Catholic Health Corporation in Omaha while they transferred their Illinois facility to the Hospital Sisters of the Third Order of St. Francis [1820] in Springfield. Obviously, regional interest received priority here. Both the Mercy Collaborative out of Farmington and the Catholic Health Association have assisted several congregations to seek new sponsors for their facilities. The Catholic Health Association of Wisconsin sponsored a special several-year-long project called Collaborative Sponsorship Design for the sixteen major superiors with facilities in Wisconsin. (At the end of this chapter appears a list of selected transfers to illustrate the scope of sponsorship transfers.)

One of the most outstanding innovations in intercongregational collaborative projects was the creation in 1980 of the Catholic Health Care Corporation of Omaha. While founded and directed by the Sisters of Mercy of Omaha [2580] it offers a partnership arrangement to congregations who seek assistance in fulfilling their corporate sponsorship responsibility. In 1987, the corporation owned by eight religious congregations served over thirty facilities located principally in the Midwest and Northwest. While the corporation has limited its geographic sphere of influence, it has positioned itself in a strongly expansionary model.

This type of joint ownership arrangement is very attractive to some single-facility sponsors who fear losing their own identity and control in a system dominated by one congregation. The exclusion of the word *mercy* from the title of the intercongregational corporation in Nebraska and California symbolically welcomes other congregations and signals equality.

Another type of intercongregational collaboration ignores charism lines and unites congregations with different spirits in one health system. A major venture in this regard occurred early in 1987 when the Sisters of Charity [0440] Health Care System, located primarily in Cincinnati, Ohio, joined forces with the Franciscan Health Care Corporation of Colorado Springs, Colorado [1640]. This collaborative model consists of cosponsorship within a single multi-institutional system, with the congregations retaining sponsorship rights and control of their own assets. A modified version of this occurred when the smaller Saint Benedict System [0230] in Utah joined the larger Holy Cross System [1910] in Indiana. Such system mergers will probably occur along regional lines with greater frequency. In 1987, the Benedictine Health System [0230] of Yankton, South Dakota, and the Presentation System of Sioux Falls formed an alliance for developing programs in rural areas. Earlier, the Presentation System had joined Mercy Collaborative from Farmington, Michigan, in a project enhancing Catholic health ministry in the north-central United States.

Ecumenical collaboration is also appearing. In a very much publicized arrangement, a Catholic hospital sponsored by the Daughters of Charity of St. Vincent de Paul and a Baptist hospital in Nashville bought a community hospital and now operate it under joint ownership. In Minneapolis, the Fairview Lutheran System is collaborating with St. Mary's Hospital sponsored by the Sisters of St. Joseph of Carondelet.

In a 1988 transfer situation, the Sisters of St. Mary of the Third Order of St. Francis [3970] (now Franciscan Sisters of Mary) sold St. Mary's Hospital in Kansas City to Trinity Lutheran Hospital because of declining admissions and already existing joint ventures between the two facilities.

In 1987, another type of regional intercongregational and interinstitutional collaboration appeared to increase. Two hospitals of the St. Joseph Sisters and the Bon Secours collaborated on the St. John/Bon Secours Continuing Care Center in Detroit, a complex that includes skilled nursing- and residential-care facilities as well as independent living units. In Denver, a Mercy hospital and a Franciscan hospital, both of which belong to large hospital systems, have formed their own local system which will encompass over one thousand hospital beds, several clinics, and related health activities. Examples of such collaboration are numerous and encompass both nonprofit and for-profit activities.

In a parallel development, some congregations are expanding their ministry by assuming ownership or management responsibility for public or community facilities. This trend, which began in earnest in the early 1980s in the Midwest and South, now appears in many parts of the country. At times these acquisitions and contracts require intensive negotiations because the Catholic facility must hold out for ethical controls. The recent acquisition of the French Hospital and Health Plan of San Francisco by the Daughters of Charity involved heavy debates with regulators. At a slower rate, Catholic systems and facilities are expanding by acquiring for-profit or physician-owned facilities and services. This trend may well accelerate as the economic benefits of proprietary health-care investments decrease. Although the for-profit sector of health care has lost some of the attractiveness it had in the early 1980s as a prize investment on Wall Street, it is still not certain what percentage of the provider share the for-profit sector will finally retain. It is possible that, as local municipalities and counties withdraw from hospitals because of the increasing tax burden and the for-profit sector experiences economic disincentives, religious-oriented hospitals may once again be the primary provider in many areas.

Even as one cites the acquisitions and expansions, one must also note that Catholic facilities continue to be lost by closure or sale to secular entities. In most cases these have been the single facility of a congregation or small, rural facilities. In some cases, the congregations have been motivated to withdraw their equity from facilities and secure their retirement situation or maintain a long-term lease for the same economic purpose. In two recent cases concerning Hôtel Dieu in El Paso, Texas, and St. Anne's in North Lake, Illinois, the sponsoring congregations had to withdraw because of the economic liabilities of their respective facilities. In the case of Hôtel Dieu, the Daughters of Charity of St. Vincent de Paul have decided to remain in the area to provide alternative types of health care. The Ancilla Domini Sisters (Poor Handmaids of Jesus Christ [3230]) who sponsored St. Anne's, will redirect their resources to other facilities. Several years ago the Benedictine Sisters [0230] of San Antonio sold their only health-care facility to a for-profit company and established the Health Care Resource Center, which now serves Catholic facilities in a variety of ways. Catholic Health Corporation of Omaha,

Nebraska, lost two of its member congregations recently when the Sisters of Humility of Mary [2100] sold St. Joseph Health Center in Ottauma, Iowa, and the Benedictines [0230] of Watertown, South Dakota, merged St. Ann's Hospital with the local community hospital. The Benedictines, because they are generally single-facility sponsors, are particularly vulnerable, but they are showing signs of collaboration. In 1988, for example, the Benedictine Health System of Duluth, which already has four facilities, assumed sponsorship of a facility run by the Crookston Minnesota Benedictines [0230].

There have been some cases of divestiture in which Catholic systems that sought to assist struggling congregations were unable to negotiate satisfactory arrangements to secure the Catholic identity of the facility. In one specific case, the Sisters of St. Francis of the Providence of God [1660] initially were unable to gain the assistance of Catholic systems and were forced to lease their two Illinois facilities to a for-profit company. Other divestitures have been attended by a great deal of publicity and controversy. St. Joseph Hospital of Creighton University and St. Mary's Hospital of the Mayo Clinic, both major teaching facilities, were the subject of much discussion when each was denied membership in the Catholic Health Association when it was determined that they were no longer "Catholic." In the St. Joseph case, the hospital was sold to a for-profit company but retained a relationship with the university. In the St. Mary's situation, a unique sponsorship arrangement was effected to ensure the Catholic identity of the hospital, which the Sisters of St. Francis [1720] of Rochester sponsored for ninety-seven years. Although this arrangement fell outside the accepted modes of sponsorship because it appeared to separate mission from business responsibilities (and, thus, was judged adversely), its corporate documents leave no doubt as to its intended Catholic identity. Both cases, nevertheless, remind the observer that, just as the canonical innovations of association of the faithful and private juridic person can be considered, so too new arrangements can be undertaken if extreme vigilance and superb communication have tested their overall compatibility with standards. Enforcement is not easy when aspects of governance are split, but perhaps the type of sponsorship desired at the Mayo Clinic may yet be considered an acceptable modality. The ability to continue to influence policy at a major medical center such as Mayo is a good that cannot be too quickly overlooked. It is important at this time to develop studies of each of these experiments so that their effectiveness can be evaluated accurately.

The oldest example of success in intra- and intercongregational collaboration can be traced to the very obvious benefits derived from group purchasing projects. When a few congregations began to unify their services as far back as 1940, purchasing usually became the first shared service to be implemented. In recent years, several major multicongregational and multisystem purchasing programs have been established and provide services for a major portion of the ministry. Some of the Catholic systems with major purchasing components which serve a number of congregations and systems are the Peoria Franciscans [1770], the Daughters of Charity, and Holy Cross. Mercy National Purchasing, based in Chicago, encompasses five systems, three of which comprise Mercy congregations. CROSS, a comprehensive purchasing program created by six Catholic systems in 1985, now negotiates contracts for one hundred and eighty institutions.

More recently, joint insurance-benefit programs are replacing purchasing as the focal point of business collaboration. These will undoubtedly yield the same kind of advantages as purchasing once they are fully developed and implemented. A few examples will suffice to show the type of insurance collaboration occurring in recent years. In Washington State, four Catholic groups, which together have fourteen hospitals, formed Washington Health Network, which writes PPO contracts. The Sisters of Mercy of Sacramento [2570], now part of Catholic Care Health West, acquired minority interest in Health Plan of American, an HMO operated by the Sisters of St. Joseph of Orange [2570] system. In Texas, five Catholic hospital systems with twenty-two hospitals in the state formed an insurance network. Just two of these five systems are based in Texas (Houston and San Antonio); the others are in Missouri, California, and Ohio. Two Illinois Franciscan hospital systems—in Peoria and Springfield—have formed a joint venture for an HMO for fourteen markets in their own home state. In Philadelphia, nine Catholic hospitals under five different sponsors formed an alliance to operate a local HMO that subsequently was bought out by the Franciscan Health System of Chadds Ford, Pennsylvania. Eleven Catholic systems, all members of Consolidated Catholic Health Care, a union of twenty-two Catholic multihospital systems, have formed Consolidated Catholic Casualty. In the East, six multihospital systems—Franciscans of Chadds Ford, Allegheny Franciscans, Franciscans of the Poor, Daughters of Charity, Dallas Mercys, and Eastern Mercy Network—have formed Eastern Health Care Consortium to develop Managed Care Strategies.

Other forms of intercongregational collaboration, both local and national, are appearing regularly. On the local level, the Missionary Sisters of the Sacred Heart in the Lake Shore area of Chicago and the Daughters of Charity of Evansville are seeking to collaborate so that their neighboring medical centers will not compete. Along with two other area hospitals, the two facilities have collaborated in a Magnetic Resonance Imaging Center. In the Chicago area as well, the Little Company of Mary Hospital [2270] and Palos Community Hospital sponsored by the Religious Hospitallers have joined in a medical-technology facility. On a broader base, the Incarnate Word Sisters of Houston [0470], the Sisters of Charity of Cincinnati, and the Daughters of Charity of St. Louis have collaborated in a risk-management education project for obstetrical services.

Consolidated Catholic Health Care, located in the Chicago area and referred to earlier in this chapter, represents a unique effort at intercongregational and intersystem collaboration. Founded in 1985 as an outgrowth of the System CEO Forums conducted by the Catholic Health Association, this organization is free standing and provides programs such as managed care, insurance, and marketing services to its twenty-two Catholic system members who account for fifty-nine thousand beds in over three hundred facilities. Because it is primarily a service organization, and many of the larger systems provide the same services themselves, it may not be positioned to assume the role of the United States megasystem mentioned earlier. It could, however, become a competitor to the Catholic Health Association as membership dues to both groups increase and cost-benefit studies are conducted. The Consolidated Catholic Health Care has, however, clearly demonstrated the need to have sponsors, systems, and local boards involved in unified planning for the ministry and has directly influenced the formation of the Commission on Catholic Health Care Ministry.

In addition to Consolidated Catholic Health Care, several other specialized organizations have encouraged communication on a broad base. Thus, there is a special-interest organization of chief executive officers of urban hospitals; the sister chief executive officers of fifteen systems meet regularly to discuss issues of system management as well as to provide support to one another. The latter group has expanded from a small group of five system executives, formed in the St. Louis area in 1984, into an expanded group of fifteen system executives from several states who meet monthly at rotating sites.

St. Louis can serve as an example of a city where effective programmatic collaboration among health-care sponsors at the local level has made an impressive difference. In the mid-1970s fourteen women's religious congregations in that area established Corporate Action for Care of the Elderly (CACE) with the archdiocese of St. Louis. This arrangement provides quality nursing care for the sick and elderly who could not otherwise afford the high cost of a private nursing home. Today 60 percent of its two hundred residents are Medicaid recipients. In 1986, the Daughters of Charity, Vincentian Fathers, and Catholic Charities opened the Rosati Stabilization Center in St. Louis, which provides a wide range of human services to the homeless. During the same period, eight religious congregations organized Emmaus House for the personal growth of sisters who are suffering from emotional fatigue or adjustment problems; now fourteen congregations collaborate on the project.

Retirement centers for sisters can also be cited as an arena for growing intercongregational collaboration. At St. Joseph Hospital and Health Care Center in Chicago thirty-one congregations of women religious are developing a plan for the long-term retirement needs of aging sisters in Illinois, where one out of two religious is over sixty and one out of three is retired or semiretired.

Examples of intercongregational and diocesan-congregational collaboration can be found throughout the United States, but it is important to note that while some persons herald joint ventures by religious congregations as a great advance toward church unity, others are more concerned that the homogenization of religious charisms will be a greater loss. The latter group point out that the church is enriched by diverse congregations who choose to focus on and practice one particular aspect of Jesus' ministry even as they seek to live out the entire Christian message. They are of the opinion that a health ministry that does not highlight, for example, the Mercy spirit of compassion, the St. Joseph spirit of unity and reconciliation, the Franciscan spirit of joy and simplicity, and the Ancilla Domini attitude of servanthood will be a poorer church. However, supporters of collaboration remind critics that as religious personnel retire from ministry and replacements are not available, the focus on charism could be counterproductive and, if maintained for its own sake, could serve merely to confuse the laity.

Another example of collaboration is the growing custom of appointing members of different congregations to serve on the corporate staff or boards of facilities of other congregations. In 1987, for example, three religious served as chief executive officers of systems sponsored by a congregation different from their own. The boards of systems and institutions reveal much interchange of congregational personnel. At the staff level the same collaboration exists: in one case, fourteen different congregations serve at an archdiocesan hospital in New York.

Greater Corporatization

The post–Vatican II period witnessed a strong move to establishing sophisticated legal structures to facilitate stewardship and safeguard sponsorship rights. In the early 1980s the development of systems and local corporate reorganization absorbed congregational sponsors' time as much as service issues did. In 1979, only twenty-eight multihospital systems were identified but in 1987 fifty-five systems encompassed over two-thirds of Catholic hospitals. As independent free-standing facilities began to be incorporated into or affiliated with multihospital systems, resistance to building superstructures was growing. This marked resistance characterized some religious who advocated that "small is beautiful," but it also surfaced among local boards who recognized that success in health care is as much dependent on securing the local market share and local support as it is in participating in cost-reduction programs. For these reasons, the expression "lean and mean" emerged as the shibboleth of system design and operations after 1983. Until retrospective payment systems began to disappear in 1983, there was little incentive to economize at the local or corporate level and thus useful, but not always essential, activities and staff were added to the corporate level without a great deal of reaction from the local dues-payer because the costs were passed on to third-party payers.

In the prospective-pricing era, systems are deemed more necessary but are receiving greater scrutiny. In the 1990s, as the overall inpatient system continues to shrink in some places and regroup in others, and as competitive pricing becomes more stringent, economic accountability demands from the local to the regional to the national system will become much more stringent. Cost-benefit documentation will be required and systems may have to concentrate on those services and issues that require high volume or large constituency support. Identifying and measuring such services will absorb system leaders in the nineties so that at the opening of the twenty-first century the systems that exist will be highly productive and carefully structured corporate entities. This type of cost-benefit dialogue will replace "the institutional autonomy versus system authority" discussions that dominated the 1980s as systems developed and expanded. Sponsors will indeed require the wisdom of Solomon to lead their institutions through these discussions. Short-term economic gains may distract participants from the long-term goal of mission integrity through corporate structures.

Another focus for corporatization efforts will be the "governance gridlock" created by the series of interlocking boards between levels of a system or between levels of a single corporation and its subsidiaries. Much of the convoluted corporate reorganization that developed in the 1970s and 1980s to maximize reimbursement and segregate revenues will be totally reversed. Very clean models of governance will probably emerge in the late 1990s that will ultimately simplify sponsorship responsibilities. The speed with which governance and management decisions will have to be made will necessitate this type of decision making. Some even suggest that, because of the tax-status situation, the nineties will find Catholic health care once again a pristine service, providing only health and medical services and divorcing itself from the wide range of diversified activities engaged in during the earlier decade. Whatever the model, the sponsors will demand responsive and responsible structures.

To advance this purification, sponsors will require much smaller boards with congregational leadership and outsider board members dominating the parent corporations while internal board members guide subsidiaries. These new models will accommodate the reality of fewer religious to fill top governance roles and exercise reserved powers. This will necessitate ongoing emphasis in ministry education and trustee formation for sponsoring congregations. Because of the small percentage of the membership of multiministry congregations prepared in health care, trusteeship may well become the principal ministry of some religious sponsors. Members will prepare for that service with the same time and study commitments formerly given to the traditional service ministries.

While corporatization is both inevitable and valuable, congregations will have to assure that the corporate life-style is based upon the Gospel and not on the secular models. Some women religious are now challenging the corporate style of health care institutions and systems. With increasing frequency some religious, sensitive to the great disparities among people, are asking health-care managers to justify such things as executive salaries, executive "perks," boardroom furnishings, and resort locations for professional meetings. With resources shrinking, many question the legitimacy and morality of religious maintaining in their facilities a corporate style that witnesses to secular values. While this issue will remain controversial through the nineties because of the need for the Catholic hospitals and systems to be competitive and to attract personnel, the attention given to stewardship and the increasing overall concern for a simple life-style could cause a major shift in the priorities of the ministry. The tension could become more acute in multiministry congregations, where the life-styles of some sister-executives and sister-trustees in health care appear to be higher than those of sister-executives and managers in other ministries.

Increasing Advocacy Efforts to Achieve Justice in Health Care

The ministry came full circle in the 1980s, as sponsors provided leadership in seeking justice for the poor. In the nineteenth century it was the need for medical care for the poor that had inspired the first sisters to begin the work. The neglected poor motivated religious congregations to establish clinics and hospitals as they followed the immigration patterns across the nation. Until relatively recent years, the rich could be cared for in their homes by paid physicians and servants, but the poor had to have institutional services. This basic orientation toward the poor that marked the foundation of most religious congregations has focused the justice concerns raised by Vatican II and given them priority as we move toward the millennium.

In the early 1980s, religious sponsors questioned seriously and publicly the integrity of a Catholic system if the poor were not its major concern. As the universal access promised by the 1965 Medicare and Medicaid legislation began to elude more and more people, sponsors questioned their remaining in the ministry if they were not addressing the health and medical needs of the poor. The American bishops shared this dilemma. In surveys conducted by the Catholic Health Association in 1982 and published in *Health Progress*, the bishops admitted that the hospitals probably could not increase their service to the poor and elderly because of economic constraints; but at the same time the bishops questioned the value of such hospitals continuing if total service could not be extended. On the same question, the chief executive officers of the hospitals showed just a slightly higher level of commitment to continuing Catholic facilities if, in fact, the possibilities of expanding service to the poor could not be realized. All concurred that Catholic identity required commitment to the poor.[10]

In response to these concerns, principally those expressed by sponsors who recognized their advocacy potential and responsibility, the 1981–1984 stewardship task force of the Catholic Health Association recommended that this topic receive more attention from the national association. As a result of this, a survey was conducted and a book published on the topic of *Justice and Health Care*. In addition, the task force recommended that a broad-base interdisciplinary task force be convened to follow through on the materials developed by the stewardship task force. This recommendation was presented to the Catholic Health Association board of directors in April 1984 and was implemented in the fall; congregational leaders assumed a major role in these deliberations. As a result of that particular project, the publication *No Room in the Marketplace* appeared in 1986 and contained several specific recommendations in regard to health-care justice for the poor. In addition, the Catholic Health Association became one of the major promoters of federal legislation to establish a National Council on Access to care.

Other health-care groups, generally at the prompting of sponsors, developed their own value and policy statements on the care of the poor. The California Catholic Health Association published a detailed statement and the Wisconsin Catholic Health Association sponsored a major educational undertaking on the subject. The Sisters of Mercy of Detroit produced a policy statement and the Bon Secours sisters undertook the development of principles. Unfortunately each of these groups worked in isolation and no group adopted or expanded the National Catholic Conference of Bishops' statement of six principles articulated in their health pastoral published in 1981 or the fifteen basic policy guidelines developed by the Catholic Health Association's stewardship task force. Many practical actions did follow, however: the Holy Cross System developed alternative delivery projects for the poor, and the Alexian Brothers [0120] and the Daughters of Charity of St. Vincent de Paul implemented a charity-care policy to guide hospital budgeting. These efforts for the poor, like many others in the ministry, call for greater communication and collaboration so that the size and quality of the Catholic ministry can be used effectively.

The ongoing concern of the sponsors and their successful insistence on care of the poor as central to mission ensures the importance of social-justice advocacy in the 1990s. The possibility of approaching this issue from the perspective of the whole church also appears strong at the moment. Charities USA adopted the topic of "Access to Care" as the subject of its 1988 policy statement and invited health-care leaders to participate in its development along with representatives from Catholic Charities. As such interministry collaboration becomes the more natural way of responding to issues within the church, it may well be possible to activate the church's corporate clout. Such a unified concerted effort will be necessary if the poor are to achieve justice in this nation. While many initiatives for the poor have already been developed and implemented by various congregations and various institutions, the magnitude and complexity of the issue demand more. Congregational sponsors appear committed to launch an effective education campaign so that consensus can be developed and political strength mobilized in behalf of the more than forty million United States residents who do not have access to medical care, a human right articulated in John XXIII's *Pacem in terris.*

Greater International Assistance

Finally, sponsors of health facilities in the United States are increasingly viewing their stewardship responsibilities as extending far beyond their facilities and this nation. After the Second Vatican Council the noted German theologian Karl Rahner wisely observed that power in the church would shift dramatically, from the Western World and Northern Hemisphere to the third-world nations. A similar shift is occurring as a result of the awareness that we truly live in that "global village" described by Marshall McLuhan. This consciousness has caused many to question the continued advance of high-technology care in this nation and other first-world countries when so many persons throughout the world still do not have the most basic necessities of food, shelter, and basic care.

While these issues are being discussed very seriously in church groups and in many health-care groups, many congregations are taking specific actions to assist their less fortunate brothers and sisters. Assistance is being offered in the form of medical and nursing expertise as well as by donations of equipment and supplies. Several congregations have enlisted the help of supply companies and transportation executives to assist in this endeavor. The multi-institutional health systems have a distinct advantage in this regard and are able to develop effective programs by drawing on resources in many facilities. Furthermore, many congregations have members who have served in these needy areas. Their knowledge of the cultures and languages makes them effective and trusted liaisons.

As news of these ventures appears in various modes of communication and congregations become more assertive in this new type of "missionary endeavors," it is certain they will challenge many current assumptions about health care and resource allocation so that greater stewardship responsibility will be exercised. The leadership exercised by the congregations of women will be a major determinant of the attitudes toward overall stewardship that develop among the over one-half million persons who collaborate with them in ministry in this nation of affluence.

Conclusion

For over a century and a half, women religious have guided the Catholic health ministry to respond in a Gospel spirit to the health and medical needs of persons throughout this nation. Their facilities have grown from log cabins to skyscraper medical towers; their services have developed from simple emergency and palliative care to a broad spectrum of preventive, restorative, and rehabilitative procedures; their management methods have evolved from simple individualistic leadership to elaborate governance and administrative structures: their staffs have grown from a single physician with a few sister-nurses to thousands of employees with an array of medical specialists and support personnel. While much has changed, the ministry of these women has consistently been marked by quality, innovation, optimism, nondiscrimination, responsibility, and, most important, creative faith. The record is clear and documentable: it continues to find women religious in the forefront as health-care providers.

The implications of this illustrious and consistent history were cited by the American bishops in their 1981 pastoral when they observed, "These examples of the healing ministry form a rich heritage which we must confidently and gratefully renew and adapt to the needs of today." Faithful to "the spirit of their founders and foundresses" and responsive to "the signs of the times," the post–Vatican II women religious are aware, grateful, and confident. They also appear to possess the competence and determination to meet the challenges of the next decade with no less commitment and no less resourcefulness than did their foremothers, who have bequeathed this legacy. With an increasing willingness to collaborate, with greater understanding of their mission, and with broader patterns of partnership, they will face the new millennium, witnessing that Catholic health ministry is secure in its role of "leaven and leverage" in this nation and is responsive to the health and medical needs of those beyond our borders.

NOTES

1. The following health-care and congregational leaders assisted in the development of this chapter by sharing their thoughts on the current status and the future of the Catholic health-care ministry. The author is greatly indebted to the spirit of cooperation and collaboration each manifested in responding to an opinionnaire distributed in April 1987: Ronald Aldrich, president of the Franciscan Health System, Chadds Ford, PA; Edward T. Connors, president of Mercy Health Services, Farmington, MI; Sister Bernice Coreil, DC, provincial of the Daughters of Charity, St. Louis, MO; Sister Justine Cyr, provincial of the Bob Secours sisters,

Baltimore, MD, and chairperson of the Commission on Catholic Health Care; Michael F. Doody, president of Consolidated Health Care, Westchester, IL; Theodore J. Druhot, executive vice president of St. Vincent's Medical Center, New York, NY; Sister Mary Kevin Ford, CSJ, president of the Health Care Corporation of the Sisters of St. Joseph of Carondelet, St. Louis, MO; Sister Caritas Geary, SP, president of Mercy Hospital, Springfield, MO; Sister Mary Rose McPhee, DC, president of the Daughters of Charity Health System—West Central, St. Louis, MO; A. Diane Moeller, president of the Catholic Health Corporation, Omaha, NE; Sister Kathleen Popko, SP, president of the Sisters of Providence, Springfield, MO, and chairman of Consolidated Catholic Health Care; Sister Mary Roch Rochlage, RSM, chief executive officer of the Sisters of Mercy Health System, St. Louis, MO; Sister Mary Maurita Sengelaub, RSM, president of the Mercy Collaborative, Livonia, MI; and Sister Joan Winkler, OSF, chief executive officer of the Catholic Health Association of Wisconsin.

2. *On Health and Health Care: A Pastoral Letter of the American Catholic Bishops* (Washington, D.C.: United States Catholic Conference, 1981).

3. The archdioceses of Boston, Hartford, Kansas City, Kansas, Milwaukee, New York, and Newark, and the dioceses of Bridgeport, Brooklyn, Buffalo, Covington, Manchester, Memphis, Metuchen, Owensboro, Providence, and Wheeling-Charleston.

4. Adam J. Maida, *Ownership, Control and Sponsorship of Catholic Institutions: A Practical Guide* (Harrisburg, PA: Catholic Conference, 1975).

5. John McGrath, *Catholic Institutions in the United States: Civil and Canonical Implications* (Washington, D.C.: Catholic University, 1968).

6. *Evaluative Criteria for Catholic Health Facilities* (St. Louis, MO: Catholic Health Association, 1980).

7. *The Dynamics of Catholic Identity in Healthcare: A Working Document* (St. Louis, MO: Catholic Health Associates, 1987).

8. Ursula Stepsis, CSA, "Congregations in Health Care," an unpublished survey commissioned by the Catholic Health Association, St. Louis, MO, 1981.

9. *Stewardship Task Force Report: Future Directions for the Catholic Health Ministry* (St. Louis, MO: Catholic Health Associates, 1984).

10. Thomas Callahan and Margaret Kelly, DC, *Views of the Catholic Health Ministry and Summary* (St. Louis, MO: Catholic Health Association, 1983).

Table 1: Samples of Congregational Transfers of Sponsorship[*]
1980–1987

Facility	Transferred from	Transferred to
St. Helen Hospital, Chehalis, WA (104)[**]	Dominicans, Edmonds, WA	Sisters of Providence, Seattle, WA
St. Joseph Hospital, Aberdeen, WA (163)[**]		
St. Joseph Hospital, Concordia, KS (132)[**]	Sisters of St. Joseph, Concordia, KS	Sisters of St. Joseph, Wichita, KS
St. Mary Hospital, Manhattan, KS (100)[***]	Sisters of St. Joseph, Concordia, KS	Sisters of St. Joseph, Wichita, KS
St. John's Hospital, Salina, KS (173)[**]	Sisters of St. Joseph, Concordia, KS	Sisters of St. Joseph, Wichita, KS
St. Joseph Hospital, Belvidere, IL (100)[**]	Sisters of St. Joseph of Wichita, KA	Sisters of St. Francis, Peoria, IL
Holy Cross Hospital, Merrill, WI (73)[**]	Sisters of Mercy of Holy Cross, Merrill, WI	Catholic Health Corporation, Omaha, NB
St. Joseph Hospital, Dickinson, ND (140)[**]	Sisters of Mercy of Holy Cross, Merrill, WI	Catholic Health Corporation
St. Joseph Hospital, Breese, IL (93)[**]	Sisters of Mercy of Holy Cross, Merrill, WI	Sisters of St. Francis, Springfield, IL
St. Mary's Hospital, Detroit Lakes, MN (87)[**]	Benedictines, Crookston, MN	Benedictines of Duluth, MN
St. Francis Medical Center, Shakopee, MN (126)[**]	Franciscans of St. Paul, MN	Benedictines of Duluth, MN
St. Theresa, Waukegan, IL (400)[**]	Sisters of Holy Spirit	Sisters of St. Francis, Mokena, IL
St. Joseph Hospital, Polson, MT (40)[**]	Hospitallers of St. Joseph	Sisters of Presentation, Aberdeen, SD
Waupun Memorial Hospital, Waupun, WI (70)[**]	Franciscan School Sisters of Milwaukee	Congregation of St. Agnes, Fond du Lac, WI
St. Elizabeth Hospital, Houston, TX (120)[**]	Missionary Sisters of Immaculate Conception, Patterson, NJ	Sisters of the Incarnate Word, Houston, TX
Holy Cross Hospital, Austin, TX (130)[**]	Diocese of Austin to CCVI, Houston, TX	Daughters of Charity, St. Louis, MO

Table 1: continued

Facility	Transferred from	Transferred to
St. Mary's Hospital, Ozaukee, WI (94)**	Sisters of Sorrowful Mother	Daughters of Charity, Evansville, IN
Good Samaritan Hospital, Pottsville, PA (204)**	Missionary Sisters of Sacred Heart	Daughters of Charity, Albany, NY
St. Francis Hospital, Lynwood, CA (515)**	Sisters of St. Francis of Penance & Charity, Redwood, CA	Daughters of Charity, Los Altos, CA
Lourdes Hospital, Paducah, KY (385)**	Franciscans of Tiffin, OH	Diocese of Owensboro, KY
Holy Cross Hospital, Nogales, AZ (80)**	Minim Daughters of Immaculate Heart (1981) to Diocese of Tucson, AZ (1986)	Sisters of St. Joseph Carondelet
St. John's Hospital, Fargo, ND (205)**	Sisters of St. Joseph Carondelet	Franciscan Sisters of Little Falls, MN
Trinity Hospital, Boudette, MN (35)**	Sisters of St. Joseph, Medaille	Franciscans Sisters of Little Falls, MN
St. Joseph Hospital, Park Rapids, MN (50)**	Sisters of St. Joseph, Medaille	Franciscans Sisters of Little Falls, MN
St. Clare's Hospital, New York, NY (200)**	Sisters of St. Francis of Alleghany to Missionary Sisters of Sacred Heart	Archdiocese of New York

*Because there is no central information source this listing can be considered representative but not exhaustive.
**Number of Beds.

✦ Profiles of Unique Service by Women Religious in Health Care

Introduction

Thousands of women religious have made and continue to make an impact on society. Values transmitted through each contact with patients, their families, physicians, employees, and others affect and change the lives of countless individuals. In the course of the preparation of this book, a request was made to all the congregations of women in health care to submit a short biographical sketch of sisters who have made a unique contribution in the field at the national or local level. Many congregations responded, but in the end, for reasons of space and balance, only nine could be included in the book. Among those singled out in the responses received were leaders in the fields of gerontology and care of the mentally ill, founders of various health organizations, sister-physicians who are currently serving the poor in rural areas throughout the United States, and one sister who attained the position of state health commissioner.

Two sisters included in the "Profiles" deserve special mention. They are Hilda Rita Brickus, FSM, and Mary Antona Ebo, FSM, who were among the first black women admitted to a congregation in health care, and both of whom made outstanding contributions to the field. The first and only Catholic School in the United States for black nursing students was established in St. Louis, Missouri, in 1933 by the Sisters of St. Mary of the Third Order of St. Francis (now the Franciscan Sisters of Mary). The school was located at St. Mary's Infirmary for the Negro, which the sisters had opened that same year to serve the black population of St. Louis. In 1946, the Sisters of St. Mary began to accept black candidates, and Sister Hilda and Sister Antona were among the first three black postulants received.

Sister Hilda Rita Brickus, FSM

Sister Hilda Rita Brickus was born on July 17, 1926, in Brooklyn, New York, the daughter of Eugene and Etta Brickus. She was baptized on August 22, 1926, at the Church of St. Peter Claver in Brooklyn. Both of her parents were Roman Catholic converts. Her father, a railroad porter, came from Solstice Creek, Virginia; her mother came from Newport News, Virginia. Sister Hilda had two sisters: Doris Douyon, now deceased, and Eleanor, who still lives in Brooklyn.

By the time she was nine, Hilda already knew that she wanted to enter a convent and become a nun ministering to the sick. Her sister Eleanor recalls that as a child Hilda had always shown interest in children from families poorer than her own. It was not uncommon for her to bring hungry children home for meals.

When she was about twelve years old, Hilda's right leg was amputated following an accident. This experience is thought to have deepened her desire to help others during sickness. After attending public elementary schools in New York, Hilda entered Brooklyn High School and later enrolled in St. Joseph's High School in St. Louis, Missouri. During her teenage years, Hilda wrote to a priest, Father Schwitalla, in St. Louis, who gave her letter to Mother Mary Concordia, Superior General of the Sisters of St. Mary of the Third Order of St. Francis, now the Franciscan Sisters of Mary. Hilda and Mother Concordia corresponded for the next year and a half.

At Mother Concordia's suggestion, Hilda moved to St. Louis in 1943, when she was seventeen, and enrolled at a local Catholic high school, St. Joseph's. She was graduated from St. Joseph's in 1945. Hilda had learned from Mother Concordia of the congregation's plans to begin a novitiate for black postulants. While attending high school and waiting for the opening of the novitiate, she lived at St. Mary's Infirmary for the Negro. On July 26, 1946, Sister Hilda was one of the first three black candidates accepted by the Sisters of St. Mary. Two years later she took her vows and served as a member of the Sisters of St. Mary for the remainder of her life.

Sister Hilda received her bachelor of science degree in radiologic technology in 1954 and her master's degree in education research in 1968, both from St. Louis University. She also undertook postgraduate studies in human relations at St. Louis University.

Sister Hilda began her work in the health-care field as a radiologic technician. After receiving her bachelor's degree, she was appointed administrative supervisor of the department of radiology and educational director of the School of Radiologic Technology of St. Mary's Infirmary Hospital. She held these positions from 1954 until 1963. Sister Hilda was a member of the staff in 1958 when the infirmary began to accept both black and white patients.

From 1963 until 1966, Sister Hilda was administrative supervisor of the Department of Radiology at St. Joseph's Hospital (now St. Joseph Health Center–Hospital West), in St. Charles, Missouri. While at St. Joseph's, she founded a two-year diploma program in radiologic technology and served as the program's educational director.

For a little more than a quarter of a century, Hilda Brickus was an innovative instructor and faculty member at St. Louis University. It was in teaching, in preparing her students, that Sister Hilda found her greatest challenge and sense of accomplishment in the health-care field.

From 1955 until 1965, while holding positions at St. Mary's Infirmary and St. Joseph's Hospital, she was a part-time instructor at St. Louis University. In 1965, after she entered graduate school at St. Louis University, she was elevated to full instructor. Then, after she received her master's degree in education research, Sister Hilda became a full-time faculty member at St. Louis University School of Nursing and Allied Health Professions in radiologic technology. In 1972 she became an assistant professor, and in 1977 an associate professor with tenure in the department of radiologic sciences.

Sister Hilda was also an adjunct professor in radiologic technology at St. Louis Community College at Forest Park from 1976 to 1978.

In 1981, Sister Hilda's ministry took a new focus as she studied pastoral ministry at St. Louis University, later serving at St. Francis Xavier's (the "College Church") and at St. Matthew's in St. Louis in a pastoral capacity serving the homebound.

Sister Hilda's lifelong concern for the welfare of those in need is reflected by her community activities—local, state, and national. She was chairperson of the St. Louis Human Relations and Equal Opportunity Enforcement Commission; a member of the St. Louis Archdiocesan Commission on Human Rights; secretary of the Missouri

Association for Social Welfare; vice president of the St. Louis Lead Poisoning Council; and a member of the National Black Sisters Conference.

During the last years of her life, Sister Hilda focused her efforts on helping persons with physical disabilities. In 1985, she was appointed chairperson of the ethics committee of the National Catholic Office for Persons with Disabilities. She also served on the national board of the Healing Community, an ecumenical advocacy group for persons with disabilities.

Sister Hilda has been listed in more than a dozen who's who biographical compilations. On one biographical form, she wrote:

> My involvement in the numerous community action and social justice organizations is due to a firm belief in the dignity of the person. Every person has certain basic human rights. Where some may fail due to their own neglect, they can change and are deserving of assistance to better their lives. Where inequities and oppressions are socially imposed resulting in deprivation, I wish to be in a position to assist in improving these conditions. Therefore, as one who can reach resources and well afford to speak out and stand as an advocate for the oppressed, underserved and neglected, and invisible persons, I will work towards changing systems, alleviating crises, and helping others to recognize and articulate their own needs. As a Christian, I take the Gospel seriously.

Sister Hilda Brickus died following heart surgery on March 18, 1987. The impact she had had on the lives of thousands of persons from all walks of life was evident during her wake and funeral. Priests, young and old; sisters; family members; friends; and colleagues all came to pay their respects. But so did many of those whom Sister Hilda had helped: the elderly, handicapped, sick, and poor persons. They came with walkers and wheelchairs; one person was connected to an I.V. stand.

Carol Bales

Sister Mary Antona Ebo, FSM

Sister Mary Antona Ebo was born Elizabeth Louise Ebo on April 10, 1924, in Bloomington, Illinois, the daughter of Daniel and Louise Teale Ebo. She has an older brother, Walter Ralph Ebo, and an older sister, Mary Jeanette Ebo Washington. The surname Ebo is authentically Nigerian.

When Elizabeth Louise, called "Betty," was four years old, her mother died suddenly at age twenty-nine during pregnancy. In the two years that followed, the family felt the impact of the Great Depression, as Betty's father lost his employment and then the family home. When she was six, Betty and her older brother and sister were placed in the McLean County Home for Colored Children in Bloomington. She resided at the Home from December 1930 until September 1942.

While living at the children's home, Betty, who had been born into a Baptist family, met the first black Catholic she had ever known—a young man the other children nicknamed "Bishop." She and Bishop became friends and together visited a Catholic church. These experiences made an indelible impression upon Betty.

When she was seventeen and a junior in high school, Betty became very ill with an infected thumb, which had to be amputated. She was then transferred from the hospital to the Fairview County sanatorium for treatment of tuberculosis. While a patient at the sanatorium, Betty began to talk with a Catholic priest and decided to convert to Roman Catholicism. She was baptized as a Roman Catholic on December 19, 1942, when she was eighteen.

Betty lived with a family friend, Mrs. Nettie Mounts, in Bloomington while completing her junior and senior years at Holy Trinity, a local Catholic high school (now called Central Catholic High School). She was the first black student to graduate from Holy Trinity.

Having decided that she wanted to become a nurse, Betty next sought admission to a nearby Catholic school of nursing, but was turned down because: "We've never taken a colored student." Determined to attend a

Catholic nursing school, she continued to pray and to search, but without success. Then, a friend of the family told Betty about St. Mary's Infirmary School of Nursing in St. Louis.

In 1944, Betty enrolled in the United States Cadet Corps program at St. Mary's Infirmary School. This program provided federal funds for professional nursing students who agreed to serve, if needed, during World War II. She was a student nurse from September 1944 until 1946. On July 26, 1946, Betty Ebo was one of the first three black women to be received as postulants of the Sisters of St. Mary of the Third Order of St. Francis, now the Franciscan Sisters of Mary. In religious life, she took the name Mary Antona Ebo.

Sister Antona received her bachelor of science degree in medical records administration in 1962 and her master's degree in hospital administration in 1970, both from St. Louis University. She served as medical records administrator at St. Mary's Infirmary from 1961 to 1967 and at St. Mary's Health Center in St. Louis from 1966 to 1967.

Sister Antona was one of six nuns among the fifty-four interfaith delegates from St. Louis to go to Selma, Alabama, on March 10, 1965 to support blacks seeking the right to vote. She was one of two sisters chosen to represent the Sisters of St. Mary. Sister Antona, the only black nun present, was singled out to march, along with the five other nuns, in the vanguard of five hundred civil rights demonstrators and to be the group's spokesperson. She is quoted as saying, "I am here because I am a Negro, a nun, a Catholic, and because I want to bear witness." Sister Antona's presence on that historic day was recorded and her words disseminated throughout the world.

In 1967, Sister Antona was appointed executive director of St. Clare Hospital in Baraboo, Wisconsin—the first black woman in this country to be appointed administrator of a Catholic hospital. From 1970 to 1974, she served as assistant executive director at St. Mary Hospital Medical Center in Madison, Wisconsin. She was executive director of the Wisconsin Conference of Catholic Hospitals (Catholic Health Association of Wisconsin) from 1974 to 1976.

Between 1976 and 1978, Sister Antona studied for the pastoral ministry. She received two certificates in clinical pastoral education: one from Alexian Brothers Medical Center in Elk Grove Village, Illinois, in 1976, and another from the Mendota Mental Health Institute in Madison, Wisconsin, in 1977. In 1978, she received her master's degree in theology of health-care ministry from the Aquinas Institute of Theology in St. Louis, then located in Dubuque, Iowa.

Sister Antona served as chaplain at St. Mary Hospital Medical Center in Madison, Wisconsin, from 1978 to 1981, and as chaplain at the University of Mississippi Medical Center in Jackson, Mississippi, from 1981 to 1987.

In August 1987, Sister Antona was elected a councillor of her congregation at a special refounding chapter that completed the process of reunification of the Sisters of St. Mary of the Third Order of St. Francis, St. Louis, and the Sisters of St. Francis of Maryville, Missouri. The refounded and reunified congregation has changed its name to the Franciscan Sisters of Mary. Sister Antona also serves on the board of directors of the SSM Health Care System, which the Franciscan Sisters of Mary sponsor.

Sister Antona is a member and former president of the National Black Sisters' Conference Board of Directors, and in 1987 was appointed to the Commission on Catholic Health Care Ministry by the national group's steering committee. In addition, Sister Antona has served as vice president of the Catholic Hospital Association of Wisconsin and the Wisconsin Health Facilities Authority; vice chairperson of the Madison, Wisconsin, Housing Authority Commission; vice chairperson of the Madison Urban League; a delegate to the National Black Catholic Congress in 1987 from the Jackson, Mississippi, diocese; and a member of the St. Louis Archdiocesan Human Rights Commission. She is also a member of the National Association of Catholic Chaplains. Sister Antona was listed in the 1976 bicentennial edition of the *American Catholic Who's Who*.

Throughout her life—as a child, a sister, and a health-care professional—Sister Antona Ebo has striven to bridge the distances that sometimes separate human beings of different races and religions.

Carol Bales

Mother Mary Francis Clare, CSJP

Margaret Anna Cusack was born to an aristocratic family of English origin at Coolak, county Dublin, in 1829. Her father, a doctor dedicated to the service of the poor, imbued his daughter with the virtues of caring at a very tender age. Margaret writes that she "took pleasure in going to the back lanes and byways to serve the needy."

While still very young her life in Ireland ended abruptly. His labors during a cholera epidemic resulted in a serious illness for Dr. Cusack that forced him to give up his profession. The family separated, and Margaret returned to England with her mother and brother. There she settled down in the town of Exeter, and under the auspices of "Grannie" received the benefits of wealth and education.

But for all her comforts and education, Margaret Anna never forgot her early lessons in serving the needy. With each passing year she became more keenly aware of the great social inequities that surrounded her. Developing an avid interest in social and political reform, she kept the company of other young reformers of equally serious purpose.

As a devout Christian, raised under the exacting precepts of the Church of England, Margaret Anna viewed social justice through Christian concepts. She wrote, "A Christian must have a very vocal political character . . . seek out justice, make peace . . . feed the hungry to live out the Gospel of Jesus Christ." Peace to her meant relief from pain and suffering, the dispensation of justice, and a social structure that cared for all God's children.

Her purpose in life took shape: to serve . . . to make peace. To this end she joined in 1853 the Angelican Sisterhood, but was soon disillusioned. For five years, she witnessed concern with petty matters supersede her primary goal—relief of human deprivation. In parting company from them, she commented, "I do not believe in offering the Gospel of small talk to starving people." In 1858, she became a convert to the Roman Catholic Church, and one year later took the name of Mother Francis Mary Clare on entering the Order of the Poor Clare nuns.

The Nun of Kenmare

The year 1861 brought Mother Clare to Kenmare, in Ireland, where she was a founding member of a new convent. Here she determined to start her life's work in earnest—to make peace—not merely by feeding the hungry but by striking at the causes of injustice. A gifted writer, she brought the weight of her talent to bear against those whom she considered righteous, greedy, and complacent. Deluging the newspapers far and near with letters and columns, she openly demanded equality for all, especially women. For them, she advocated equal pay for equal work, opportunities for equal education, and reforms to give women control of their own property. Supported by the press, she won many friends to her cause, and her influence spread through England, Europe, and the United States. She became known as the Nun of Kenmare.

Famine

The Irish famine of 1879 plunged the already poor Irish into even greater misery. Finding government aid wholly inadequate, Mother Clare appealed to her supporters for help. And help came in the sizable sum of twenty thousand dollars. With this she fed the starving—Catholic and Protestant alike. At first, her fund-raising success brought much praise, only to be dampened by accusations from local authorities. Afraid of her power with the people, some of those who controlled local offices viewed her as a threat to the prevailing social structure. A mere woman was interfering in politics. To a society geared to the wealthy and privileged, the idea of equal rights was unthinkable. The Nun of Kenmare had to be silenced. Her life was threatened.

Rejection

Showing his disapproval of her, the archbishop of Kenmare closed down her Famine Relief Fund and refused to see her. Following his example, her sister nuns began to ignore her as well. She remained alone in her room for almost a year with a heart condition. In her plight, she wrote: "As long as your Christianity is merely theoretical, they are well pleased with you, but once they find you are practical in carrying it out, they part company from you angrily. . . . "

She departed Kenmare on November 17, 1861, and returned to Newry, the home of her novitiate period. From there she went to Knock, county

Mayo, where at the invitation of the parish priest she established a convent. She then proposed an industrial school for women, with a day-care center for their children. The fund-raising she took upon herself.

Confrontation

It was not long before she again came under the heavy censure of the local clergy, who did not know how to cope with a noncomformist and a peoples' liberator in the form of a woman . . . still less a nun! Her suggestion that there were alternatives to the archbishop's education program, and her proposal that the Irish Poor Clares change their rule to include social work, induced a bitter confrontation, which resulted in an edict prohibiting further contact with her sister nuns. Henceforth spiritual guidance for her novices would come from other sources. Finally overwhelmed by frustration and a feeling of helplessness, Mother Clare left Ireland forever in November 1883, much to the relief of the Irish clergy. She left behind the living testimony of the many thousands of people she had helped and loved.

This time, however, she was not alone. A nucleus of sisters of like mind followed her to England, and through their support, a community was born, the St. Joseph Sisters of Peace.

To form a new community, papal dispensation was needed and for this purpose Mother Clare, accompanied by one of her sisters— Evangelista Gaffney—went to Rome in 1884. There she met with Pope Leo XIII, who commented favorably on the many books she had written on history, social issues, and causes of the church. Urging her to continue to write he gave his blessings on the new community, and assured her that not one word of the complaints against her had ever been substantiated.

Overjoyed, she incorporated the new community in Nottingham under Bishop Edward Gilpin Bagshawe. Almost at once, the sisters moved to bring some relief to squalor, sickness, and lack of housing, education, and food in the aftermath of England's Industrial Revolution. They nursed the sick, visited the poor, opened schools for children, and taught adults in the evenings. In countless ways they gave solace and help to those in need. Soon other dedicated young women joined their ranks, and as the little band of sisters began to grow, their services spread into neighboring towns.

Welcomed by local officials and encouraged by a sympathetic clergy, Mother Clare and her sisters were at last allowed to perform their good works unobstructed.

Rejection

On her arrival in New York, Mother Clare promptly set out with high hopes to meet with Archbishop Corrigan to present her letters of approval from Pope Leo XIII and Bishop Bagshawe. The Archbishop was not available. In fact, he was not available to see her for three years. Her reputation as a reformer and liberal had preceded her, and the ultraconservative archbishop was not about to let her into his diocese.

New Jersey

Hurt and bewildered, she retreated to New Jersey, where she was received with kindness by Bishop Wigger. Here she incorporated her community and once more devoted her energies to writing, establishing a home for girls, teaching, and aiding the needy.

In March 1886, she conceived the idea that institutions for training the blind were needed throughout the United States. Obtaining permission from her bishop, she set out to the major cities on the East Coast to make her proposal, only to meet with denial after denial. Archbishop Corrigan saw to this. Requests she had received for her services were soon withdrawn, even from as far away as Tacoma on the West Coast. To keep her out of New York, a ban prohibiting her from purchasing any property on the New York side of the Hudson River was issued. The archbishop clearly intended to keep the St. Joseph Sisters of Peace confined to New Jersey.

At last she reached the end of her endurance. Obstructed and disillusioned with the church of her choice, the Nun of Kenmare realized that her presence was a detriment to the growth of the community she had founded. She decided she would not stand in its way.

To Stay or Leave

In her dilemma, she hesitated for several months, not wanting to be parted from her sisters, whom she dearly loved. But, silently, she prepared the way for her departure, making such provision as she could for her community.

On November 17, 1887, three years after her arrival in the United States, Mother Clare met with Archbishop Corrigan for the first and last time. Her first book had recently appeared in print without the imprimatur of the church. In it she struck out boldly against the archbishop, who had expelled a priest for his liberalism. She wrote, "The

Monsigneur has been vindicated by the downfall of the priest, who loved the poor exceedingly . . . what matter? Obedience has been maintained, discipline has been supported. The poor are kept in their proper place. . . . " At the meeting, no mention was made of the book. Instead, the archbishop accused her of soliciting funds in his territory, a charge she denied. He then terminated the meeting by telling her that he never wanted to see her again.

Eight months later on July 11, 1888, Mother Francis Mary Clare arranged for a trip to New York. She left in a taxi and never again returned to her New Jersey community.

After twenty-nine years of dedication to the Roman Catholic cause, Margaret Anna Cusack returned to her Protestant friends and embraced the Church of England once more. The remainder of her years she spent in writing and lecturing, first in the United States and then in England.

On June 5th, 1899, Margaret Anna Cusack went to her final rest. She was seventy years old.

After the sudden departure of Mother Francis Clare, Bishop Bagshawe, original sponsor of the order, declared himself to be its spiritual guide. Later, the motherhouse was transferred from Nottingham to Newark, New Jersey, and the order became known as the Sisters of St. Joseph of Newark. The bright blue habit with its cross and dove insignia eventually gave way to the plain black habit, and in time the name of Mother Francis Mary Clare quietly faded into the past. Those sisters who knew her will realize the pain her decision to leave them must have cost.

"God alone knows what this sacrifice will cost me, but I make it willingly, as I see that it is the only way to secure permanence and prosperity to this work."

Under the diligence of Sister Evangelista Gaffney, lifelong friend of Mother Clare, the shattered pieces were put together. Within eighteen months the ecclesiastical doors were opened to the community and the sisters moved West.

But it was not until 1961, when the Second Vatican Council urged religious communities "to return to the original spirit of the institutes," and to study their "founders' spirit and special aims," that the memory of Mother Francis Clare was restored to its rightful place. In the light of twentieth-century freedom, a new generation of sisters recognize the great role played by their foundress in planting the seed of liberty and equality for women, which was to subsequently grow and flourish.

They see, too, with appreciation the rich inheritance that she has left them of service and justice to all.

A new statement of direction was accepted by the community; it is called "Peace through Justice": "We believe that in accord with our original charism as peacemakers, the promotion of justice is integral to our mission and spirituality as Sisters of St. Joseph of Peace." The order's original title, "Sisters of St. Joseph of Peace," was restored in 1970.

Terri Pollard

Sister M. Ignatia Gavin, CSA

On June 10, 1985, well more than one million people gathered in one hundred and fourteen countries around the world to celebrate the fiftieth anniversary of the founding of the Fellowship of Alcoholics Anonymous. In Akron, Ohio, where it all began, hundreds of AA members and their families, shunning publicity, met in undisclosed locations for a three-day celebration. The phenomenal growth of AA and the countless support groups patterned after its program might not have been a surprise to Bill W., one of the cofounders. His wife, Lois, recounts: "Bill never had any small ideas, you know, and his expectations for AA were certainly no exception."[1] For Sister M. Ignatia Gavin, perhaps the greater miracle would have been the decision by the AMA in 1954 to accept alcoholism as a treatable disease. When she received the Catherine of Siena Medal from Theta Pi Alpha Sorority in Cincinnati that year, the award given by the National Catholic Women's Colleges to a woman who has made a distinctive contribution to Catholic life in the United States, she noted that from the beginning, the cofounders of AA believed that the solution to the problem of alcoholism for many was to be found in the merger of the forces of medicine and religion:

> With this union, what could be more conducive to the regeneration of the whole person than the atmosphere of a Catholic hospital, the professional medical care administered there affording the spiritual, physical, mental, and moral therapy.[2]

A proponent of holistic health care long before it became fashionable, Delia Gavin entered the congregation of the Sisters of Charity of Saint Augustine in 1914. A graduate of the Wolfram School of Music in Cleveland, Ohio, she was a skilled musician and a teacher of piano. She had emigrated to the United States from Ireland with her parents and her brother in 1896, at the age of seven. On exploring the call to religious life, one of her concerns was the care of her parents. Who would look

after them should their health fail in their old age? Traditional spirituality and the teaching congregations of the diocese provided one answer: "Whoever loves father or mother, son or daughter, more than me
is not worthy of me" (Matthew 11:37). When she learned from clergymen and friends, however, that the Sisters of Charity in their hospital
ministry had the resources with which to care for their own elderly
family members, and when she was encouraged by Mother M. Helena
Burke not to let such a worry hinder her, she eagerly sought admission
to the community.[3]

During her novitiate and after her profession of vows in 1916, Sister
Ignatia's musical talents were well utilized. She directed the convent
choirs; taught fourth grade at St. Vincent's Orphanage, organizing an
orchestra and a band there; and established a music studio on the
motherhouse grounds. She gave private piano lessons and traveled from
the motherhouse to the local convents to help the sisters with liturgical
celebrations on the missions. In 1925, she graduated from the University
of Notre Dame with a bachelor's degree in music, specializing in voice,
piano, and organ. When the bishop of the diocese began pressuring the
congregation to expand their ministry to include classroom teaching in
the parish schools, it became clear that Sister Ignatia's musical talents
would be even more taxed. Her health began to fail, and in 1927, a
physician recommended a permanent change of occupation.

Because the congregation had engaged in a variety of health and
social-service ministries from its beginning, this posed less of a problem
than it would have for other orders. Sister Ignatia moved from the
motherhouse in Lakewood to St. John Hospital in Cleveland, a few
miles away. She began taking classes in medical terminology at the
nursing school there, and worked in the admitting office. In 1928, she
moved to Akron, Ohio, to help establish St. Thomas Hospital. It was
there, in the admitting office, that she met Bill W. and Dr. Bob Smith, the
cofounders of AA.

Bill Wilson was a Wall Street broker and Dr. Bob Smith was an Akron
proctologist with courtesy privileges at the hospital. Both were alcoholics whose attempts at self-treatment had ended in failure. Beginning in
1935, the two men met frequently at Dr. Bob's West Akron home, finding that somehow when they were together, sobriety seemed an achiev-
able goal. For long hours that included prayer, reflection, discussion, and
sharing of daily experience, the two men and others who eventually
joined them identified their struggles, and thus the first AA group was

born. That same year, in 1935, a group of alcoholics was taking shape in New York City, and by 1939, a third group had appeared in Cleveland. The groups struggled with many questions: What is alcoholism? What is sobriety? How do I know my problem is alcoholism? What do you mean by recovery? How do you pray? How do you deal with resentment? What is surrender? How do you handle the past? How long does it take? Who is God?[4]

"Dr. Bob was on our staff for five years before we knew he had a drinking problem," Sister Ignatia revealed in an interview at the CHA convention in Philadelphia in 1951. "We would not have known it then if he had not volunteered the information."

"He often discussed the problem of alcoholism with us," she continues. "After talking with the members of the families of these compulsive drinkers, and realizing the misery, suffering, and sorrow brought into the homes and lives of the afflicted ones because of drink, we became deeply interested."[5]

Speaking to a convocation at that convention, Sister Ignatia recalled the early days of AA in Akron:

> It was 1939, just about the time when we were pulling out of the Depression. Hospital beds were at a premium, without any prospect of adding to out-bed capacity. There was very little enthusiasm around the hospital about admitting people who were imbibing too freely in those days.
>
> However, prompted by the grace of God, we very cautiously admitted one patient, with the diagnosis of acute gastritis, under the care of Dr. Bob. The patient was placed in a two-bed room. The next morning, Dr. Bob came to the admitting office and very timidly requested that the patient be moved to a spot where the men who came to visit him might talk privately. The only available space we could think of was a small room the hall called the "Flower Room," where patients' flowers were changed and arranged. We pushed the alcoholic's bed into this room. It was there that he received his first AA visitors.[6]

From the secreted space in a closet the ward expanded and St. Thomas Hospital in Akron, Ohio, became the first private hospital in the country to provide for the care and treatment of alcoholics. First, a two-bed room was set aside; then four beds; later, six; and finally, eight beds, along with a meeting-space lounge, complete with a "bar" stocked with plenty of milk, fruit juice, and a bottomless pot of coffee. A corridor that led to the gallery of the hospital chapel permitted the patients to attend Mass daily if they chose to, and to make visits to the Blessed Sacrament, all in complete seclusion. "Bear in mind, that the alcoholic is a person who is sick spiritually as well as physically," Sister Ignatia wrote. "The ready access he is given to the Source of spiritual healing is a powerful factor in his recovery."[7]

Controversy surrounded the work in the ward from the beginning. Long hours of work on the floor, being completely available to the patients and AA visitors, led many of the sisters to fear for Sister Ignatia's health, which was frail at best. The need to provide for seclusion and to maintain confidentiality meant that the area had to be largely self-operating. Patients ministered to patients, AA members and sponsors helped the nurses aides with cleaning chores. Because the congregation saw AA as "too priceless a gift and too providential a remedy to withhold from the needy,"[8] no alcoholic was refused admittance because of inability to pay. This meant that the ward would operate at a constant deficit, patients being told by the sisters that they could "pay later," much to the consternation of administrators, treasurers, and trustees. Miraculously, however, the work continued, supported by the generosity of recovering members. More miraculously, the commitment of the congregation expanded. In 1941, a five-bed ward was opened in Cleveland at St. Vincent Charity Hospital under the direction of Sister M. Victorine Keller (1905–1988) and two beds were set aside at St. John Hospital in the care of Sister M. Mercedes Pervorse (1892–1975).

In 1952, after spending twenty-four years in Akron, Sister Ignatia was transferred to St. Vincent Charity Hospital in Cleveland. A shortage of hospital space and financial difficulties there had caused the discontinuation of the alcoholic ward a few years before. With the permission of the major superior, an enthusiastic committee of AA members raised more than sixty thousand dollars, obtained union permits, and contributed long days and nights of skilled labor to modernize an old wing at the hospital. A new seventeen-bed floor, Rosary Hall, was opened in October of 1952. Thirty-five years later, the area has expanded to include women's unit, an outpatient treatment center, and a family therapy program; more than thirty thousand alcoholics have been treated.

Characteristic of Sister Ignatia in her years of ministry to AA was her sincere desire to receive no particular notice for her contributions. This, coupled with AA's stance as a nonsectarian movement accounts for the relative lack of recognition she has received as a collaborator in the early days with the cofounders. A letter from Bill Wilson, dated October 13, 1949, attests to her status, however:

> The pioneering time of Alcoholics Anonymous is over. When one day the history of our fellowship is written, the great work done at St. Thomas Hospital will surely be its brightest page. Its alcoholic ward, where our infant movement was cradled, will become a place of intense interest and an object of thankful reminiscence and affection. For there, Dr. Bob labored untiringly with Sister Ignatia and other sisters who served as no others could.[9]

In 1966, at the age of seventy-seven, Sister Ignatia died. Two years before, celebrating her fiftieth anniversary as a Sister of Charity of St. Augustine, she received this tribute from the worldwide fellowship of AA. It reads:

> We of Alcoholics Anonymous look upon you as the finest friend and the greatest spirit we may ever know.
> We remember your tender ministrations to us in the days when AA was very young. Your partnership with Dr. Bob in that early time has created for us a spiritual heritage of incomparable worth.
> In all the years since, we have watched you at the bedside of thousands. So watching, we have perceived ourselves to be the beneficiaries of that wonderous light which God has always sent through you to illumine our darkness. You have tirelessly tended our wounds; you have nourished us with your unique understanding and matchless love. No greater gifts of Grace than these shall we ever have.[10]

Cheryl Keehner, CSA

Notes

1. Lois Wilson, Letter to Father Sam Ciccolini, July 1984 (Interval Brotherhood Home, Akron, OH).

2. Sister M. Ignatia Gavin's acceptance of the Catherine of Siena Medal, Cincinnati, OH, 1954 (Archives of the Sisters of Charity of Saint Augustine, Richfield, OH).

3. Sister M. Frances Seibold, Oral History of Sister Ignatia (Archives of the Sisters of Charity).

4. *God, A.A. and Akron.* A Golden Anniversary Tribute, 1985.

5. Interview with Sister M. Ignatia (Archives of the Sisters of Charity).

6. Sister M. Ignatia Gavin, "The Care and Treatment of Alcoholics," a paper delivered to the Catholic Hospital Association of United States and Canada (Philadelphia, June 2–5, 1951).

7. Letter from Sister Ignatia, undated (Archives of the Sisters of Charity).

8. Unsigned history of AA distributed at the opening of Rosary Hall, 1952.

9. Bill Wilson, Letter to Sister M. Ignatia, October 13, 1949 (Archives of the Sisters of Charity).

10. Fellowship of AA scroll to Sister M. Ignatia, March 25, 1964, Rosary Hall Solarium, St. Vincent Charity Hospital, Cleveland, OH.

Sister M. Olivia Gowan, OSB

It has been said that one can measure a person by his or her ability to persuade people to think the same way. This measure of one great woman is preserved in a beautiful book of testimonials and tributes presented to Sister Olivia Gowan, who devoted twenty-four years as architect and builder of the prestigious School of Nursing Education at the Catholic University of America. Her zeal for promoting a high standard of achievement in nursing education was recognized by thirty-one university and college schools of nursing education, twenty-five associations, twelve government-related health institutions, and eighty individuals who contributed testimonials or letters to the volume. The occasion was a testimonial luncheon in her honor sponsored by the Catholic University Alumni Association, a chapter of Sigma Theta Tau, and the Olivian Society during the twenty-fifth anniversary celebration of the nursing school, on Saturday, April 19, 1958.

The story of Sister Olivia Gowan's career as an inspiring educator of leaders in the nursing profession begins in Stillwater, Minnesota, where she was born to Margaret Lawlor and William Gowan in 1888. When Mary was eight years old, her father, a lumberman, found it imperative to move with the timber industry to the forests of northeastern Minnesota near the town of Virginia. It was a difficult decision for the parents to make. The children would be deprived of a parochial-school education, which was available to them in Stillwater, but the conscientious parents were well able to give them homespun character training and to instruct them in their Catholic religion.

The rigors of northern winters soon affected Mrs. Gowan's health, so Mary was taught by her father those responsibilities she was to carry out during his absence in the camps. Mr. Gowan was a firm believer that an eldest daughter's first duty was in the home. He taught her to purchase provisions wisely and to balance the family checkbook. To develop her mind, he expected her to be informed on the events of the times so as to bring him up-to-date on political and current affairs.

Mary was obedient and devoted to her father, but with her mother's approval she went out to help sick people in the neighborhood. When he learned of these activities, he disapproved. According to his judgment, Mary's care of her frail mother and of six brothers and sisters at home was sufficient responsibility. However, while he was away, Mary's sense of social responsibility led her to respond to occasional emergency calls. Mary graduated from Roosevelt High School, in Virginia, Minnesota, in 1908.

From childhood she wanted to become a nun, but her mature decision was to become a nurse first. She remained at home for another year before announcing her decision to enter the training school for nurses that would open at St. Mary's Hospital in Duluth in 1909. She graduated with the first class of nurses in 1912, and took examinations to qualify as a registered nurse. A month later she entered the novitiate at Villa St. Scholastica, the motherhouse of the Sisters of St. Benedict. After making temporary vows for three years in 1913, she was assigned as a nurse and teacher at the Villa, St. Mary's Hospital, and St. Joseph's Hospital in Brainerd.

In 1916 she made perpetual vows. Her qualifications, including administrative abilities and, of greater importance, the spiritual qualities required of one to be entrusted with extraordinary responsibility, induced her superiors to give her a year of internship as assistant superintendent. The following year she became the superintendent of St. Mary's Hospital. At that time the American College of Surgeons had devised a series of criteria for examining and classifying hospitals. Sister Olivia succeeded in bringing all of the departments at St. Mary's up to the minimum standards. When the hospitals were notified about their ratings, St. Mary's was one of eighty hospitals among seven thousand in the country to receive qualifying certificates. During the ten years Sister Olivia served at St. Mary's Hospital she intermittently took courses at the College of St. Scholastica. She was granted a baccalaureate degree in 1925, and became one of the relatively few nurses holding a nurse's diploma, an R.N., and a college degree.

In 1926 Dr. Thomas Verner Moore, OSB, finalized arrangements with the Duluth Benedictine community to staff a school for educable retarded girls in Brookland, D.C., in connection with his work in the Department of Psychology and Psychiatry at Catholic University. Sister Olivia was asked to undertake the venture and with three other sisters she pioneered the special school.

About this time the graduate schools of the only pontifical university in the United States were in the process of reorganization. By 1930 various departments were merged into the Graduate School of Arts and Sciences and the College of Arts and Sciences. The administrators of Catholic hospitals and schools of nursing, becoming aware that the sisters on their faculties lacked the educational opportunities open to lay nurses, feared the imminent threat of being subjected to examination by national nursing boards. Lay nurses in increasing numbers were obtaining graduate degrees in nursing education at secular universities; thus national standards were being raised. Catholic hospitals and training-school faculties were deprived by the fact that Catholic University, to which they would normally turn, did not offer graduate courses in nursing education. Hence demands for such university courses began to multiply among the superiors of religious communities.

Monsignor Ryan, moved by the increasing interest of the superiors, nurse educators, members of the clergy, and faculties of other universities, looked into the matter. Since the reorganization of the graduate schools made it possible to introduce courses in nursing education into the Graduate School of Arts and Science, he initiated an experimental program during a summer session, when coeducation was permitted on the campus. Such an experiment would also test the response of religious communities to the program.

Monsignor Ryan engaged Sister Olivia Gowan, recently graduated with a Master of Arts degree from Teachers College, Columbia University, to teach courses in administration, supervision, and ward teaching. Sister convinced her mentor, Mrs. Eugenia Spalding, to join her in the experiment for the summer of 1932. Dr. Thomas Verner Moore was the sole head of a graduate department who would accept the summer experiment, which became part of his Department of Psychology and Psychiatry. The nursing courses were scheduled but no classroom space was provided on campus. Dr. Roy Deferrari, dean of the graduate schools and a strong influence behind the eventual development of a graduate school of nursing education, loaned his office as a meeting place for the nursing classes. There was considerable opposition by those who disapproved and by others who expected the project to fail as other experiments had. They did not anticipate Sister Olivia's power of endurance.

The summer experiment was so successful that Monsignor Ryan granted permission for courses in nursing to continue during the regular academic session of 1933. Sister Berenice Beck, OSF, was hired to assist

Sister Olivia. In 1934 the special school of nursing became independent, with its own quarters in the Music Building. At their November meeting, the board of trustees voted in favor of granting provisional approval to the School of Nursing Education. In April 1936, Sister Olivia was appointed dean of the Provisional School of Nursing. The next year Dean Deferrari informed Sister Olivia that he had recommended to the rector the establishment of a permanent School of Nursing Education. Representing the School of Nursing in the senate, Sister Olivia would be the only woman dean of a graduate school in the university.

There were great hurdles for those administrators who favored the development of the School of Nursing. Each step of the way to creating a prestigious university-based School of Nursing Education called for the indefatigable stamina of Sister Olivia. Her strength of purpose came from her father, but her mother endowed her with the key—gracious womanliness—to the hearts of her colleagues, faculty, and students. Her success can be attributed to her ability to bring to each personal contact her full absorption, depth of interest, and overflowing kindness, in addition to her deep devotion to the alleviation of human suffering through the service of dedicated nurses.

Through the years, her professional leadership role beyond the university was phenomenal. It included active membership in six nursing associations in which she served as president, treasurer, or trustee. She held active membership in the American Hospital Association, the American College of Hospital Administrators, and the Postgraduate Board of Review of the National Nursing and Accrediting Service. She was an honorary consultant to the Bureau of Medicine and Surgery of the Department of the Navy; a member of the Health and Medical Committee, World War II Council on National Defense; a member of the Advisory Committee of the Veterans Administration; and consultant in mental hygiene to the National Institute of Mental Health. Sister Olivia's wise counsel was sought by numerous organizations and associations in the vicinity of the District of Columbia.

It is impossible to do justice to Sister Olivia's accomplishments; yet her development of a university school of nursing stands as a symbol of all that is finest in service to humanity. Through it her influence continues to touch people all over the world. The book presented to her in 1958 by two thousand alumnae, *A Tribute to Sister Olivia Gowan, OSB*, reveals the magnanimity of this great woman for the care of the sick in the spirit of Christ—the Benedictine foundation of her philosophy of nursing. The tribute paid her by the twenty-nine faculty members of the school of nursing synthesizes the general content of one hundred forty-eight testimonials and letters included in the aforementioned book:

> We, the Faculty of the School of Nursing, The Catholic University of America, welcome the opportunity on this happy occasion to extend our felicitations and gratitude to:
>
> SISTER OLIVIA GOWAN, OSB
>
> Exemplified in your life and works, Sister Olivia, are the qualities of the truly great:
>
> Your courage to pioneer in the Founding of our School of Nursing, with remarkable endurance, to persist in a struggle that we, who are its beneficiaries can only remotely imagine and never duplicate.
>
> Your vision of the future of nursing, supported by deep faith and translated into practical action with a supernatural prudence, an unfailing graciousness, a delightful sense of humor, and a penetrating intelligence that both differentiated issues and promoted unity.
>
> Your respect for the individual that made contact with you a source of inspiration and motivation to realize one's potential, and resulted in nursing leaders who carry on throughout the land with loyalty to your ideals, but with unique performance.
>
> Your humility, nourished by love, that gave credit where it was due, accepted others with warmth and understanding, permitted a difference of opinion, saw some good in the least of us, and made of all of us your co-workers in the never-ending task of bringing light into the dark places of man's mind and relieving suffering, that the will of Our Father be done and His Kingdom extended throughout the earth.

When Sister Olivia returned to Minnesota in 1957, she gave her assistance as a consultant to St. Mary's Hospital in Duluth, St. Cloud Hospital in Saint Cloud, Minnesota, and St. Mary College in Bismarck, North Dakota.

On the occasion of the thirty-fifth anniversary of the School of Nursing Education in 1969, the Catholic University conferred on Sister Olivia an Honorary Degree of Doctor of Education.

In 1970 Sister Olivia retired to the motherhouse, St. Scholastica Priory. She continued her research and writing for some time. In her later years her natural quality of gracious appreciation inspired the love of those devoted to her care. The news of her death on April 2, 1977, again brought many tributes, and the presence of friends and admirers at the funeral Mass celebrated by Bishop Paul Anderson.

In December 1981, on the recommendation of President Edmund D. Pellegrino, M.D., and the nursing school's dean, Sister of Charity Rosemary Donley, the Catholic University's board of trustees named the nursing building Olivia Gowan Hall.

M. Emmanuel Hanley, OSB

BIBLIOGRAPHY

Sister Olivia Gowan, OSB, R.N., and Sister Rita Marie Bergeron OSB, R.N., *The Development of Professional Nursing at the Catholic University of America 1932–1958: Relationship to the National Scene* (Duluth, MN: the college of St. Scholastica Nursing Department, 1967).

Edna Yost, *American Women of Nursing* (New York: Lippincott, 1947).

Sister Agnes Somers, Community History Manuscripts, (Archives of the St. Scholastica Priory).

Sister Olivia Gowan's personal file (Archives of the St. Scholastica Priory).

"A Tribute to Sister Olivia Gowan, OSB," an album of testimonials, tributes, and letters of congratulation and commendation, 1958 (Archives of the St. Scholastica Priory).

Sister Grace Marie Hiltz, SC

"Sister Grace touched the lives of so many in the health-care field in sharing generously and genuinely. She was always responsive to a request for guidance on an issue. She combined a no-nonsense manner with warm, cheerful good humor."[1] This handwritten note lies among the many testimonials and tributes of corporations, multihospital systems, and prestigious individuals received by the Sisters of Charity of Cincinnati following Sister Grace Marie Hiltz's sudden death on March 29, 1985. Here was a woman whose life had touched many others, not only in the health-care field but in a wide range of activities and organizations.

Born Mary Elizabeth Hiltz, on April 20, 1920, she grew up in Covington, Kentucky, attending parochial schools and Notre Dame Academy. Following high school graduation, she attended Good Samaritan Hospital School of Nursing in Cincinnati, Ohio, graduating in 1941. Also, in February 1941 she entered the congregation of the Sisters of Charity of Cincinnati and received the religious name of Sister Grace Marie.

Upon completion of the novitiate, this sister-nurse worked at Good Samaritan Hospital in Dayton, Ohio, from 1942–1955. Initially she was assigned as head nurse, then supervisor of obstetrics, and finally, from 1950–1955, assistant administrator. During these years she designed and supervised the building of a new maternity wing and designed "Madonna Crib," a bassinet for newborns that was later sold by a well-known national hospital supplier. Sister Grace also completed a postgraduate program in obstetrics at Margaret Hague Maternity Hospital in Jersey City, New Jersey, and received her bachelor's degree from the College of Mount St. Joseph.

The following year, Sister Grace Marie was assigned to study at St. Louis University, where she completed a master's in hospital administration. The same year she became a member of the American College of Hospital Administrators. Her association with St. Louis University did not cease in 1956: she was active in the Hospital Administration Alumni Association, serving as treasurer and later as president (1967–1968). In addition, in 1980 she received the Silver Alumni Award and in 1985 the Distinguished Alumni Award.

After graduation, Sister Grace Marie was assigned to Pueblo, Colorado, as an administrator of two hospitals. Historical circumstances found the Sisters of Charity in possession of two aging facilities in Pueblo in the 1950s. The community decided to merge St. Mary's and Corwin hospitals and build a new facility on the site of Corwin. Sister Grace Marie was appointed overseer. For the first time in the history of hospital construction, a hospital was built over and around an existing structure. The construction went on without interruption of hospital routine and was completed in July 1957. In addition to the construction, Sister Grace Marie saw to the human element as well, convincing the people of Pueblo and the two medical staffs that this merger was in everyone's best interests. She often referred to herself as the "dash" between St. Mary's and Corwin.

While in Colorado, Sister Grace began a long history of involvement in state, regional, and national hospital associations. She served as president of the Colorado Conference of Catholic Hospitals and the secretary-treasurer of the Western Conference of Catholic Hospitals.

In 1962, this experienced administrator was assigned to Cincinnati, Ohio, to Good Samaritan Hospital, the largest of the Sister of Charity hospitals, with seven hundred beds. One of her great joys, she remarked, was returning to the site of her beginnings in health services and "meeting electricians, nurses, and nutrition personnel who had known me as a student so many years before."[2]

In her tenure at Good Samaritan as administrator (1962–1974) and later as president (1975–1979), Sister Grace Marie became widely known in the Cincinnati community as a leader in health care. A 1974 newspaper article noted that she "readily confronts such issues as rising costs, the possibility of increasing government intervention, the demand by hospital consumers' for a role in policy making, and medical-moral issues of abortion, sterilization, euthanasia."[3] Sister Grace raised some eyebrows in Cincinnati when she agreed to participate in the area's first Health Maintenance Organization in 1973. "The Blue Cross approached us two years ago, " she said, "and began to talk about HMO. Admittedly it was an experiment. It must be explored. We have to try something to get down the cost of delivery of health care."[4] The head of the Greater Cincinnati Hospital Association at the time commented, "She can see what the picture will be in five to ten years. HMO is a huge commitment to the future and she is the only one in town who can do it."[5]

Sister Grace was responsible for many innovations in her years at Good Samaritan. She reorganized the administration by appointing a medical director and securing full-time department heads in the major medical-service areas. She introduced the concept of the emergency room operated by a group of physicians, a move later adopted by other area hospitals. The first hospital rehabilitation unit in Hamilton County was established during her tenure, as was a new-born intensive care unit. She was active in the expansion of the medical education program and personally participated in hospital-administration education by serving as preceptor for thirty-six hospital administrative residents.

Not one to be caught up in the technological or administrative aspects of health-care delivery, Sister Grace Marie frequently emphasized that most of all it's "personal patient care—that's what we're all about." "The old nurse in me keeps coming out." Hospital personnel are there to do more than "just bandage the wound." She stressed the need for a love of people and a belief in the need to minister to "the soul as well as the body." That includes "helping people to die well, accept suffering, and know what they're facing, and helping to promote a Christian attitude toward all these things."[6]

As an administrator, Sister Grace Marie was known for her foresight, innovation, courage, and strong leadership. She respected her staff and counted on them to oversee many facets of their work together. "People ask me what's going on," she said. "I tell them I don't know. I just hope everyone else does. I've been called 'the great delegator.' "[7] She valued the diversification of personality and talents that existed among her coworkers and tried to create an atmosphere where each could function well.

> She saw with clarity and honesty her strengths and weaknesses. She saw herself as a product of God's creative handiwork with limitations and talents as part of her endowment and heritage . . . She could show anger, stubborness, and impatience. Of her own admission, "I never want to give up my right to be wrong . . . You learn something from every mistake. Once you're always right you give up the ability to learn new things and move forward with your life."[8]

As a person she was known for her enthusiasm, warmth, and caring. In a hospital that employed more than two thousand people, she "like[d] to be around people at the hospital and know many of the employees by their first name."[9] She was known to acknowledge every favor by her persistent note writing. She was concerned about racial injustice, about slum dwellers, about just wages, about delivering health care in a substantial manner to the poor. At the time of her death, stories surfaced about food, clothing, and shelter provided through her instigation to the poor in times of desperation. One mother told of her providing help for mothers to come to the hospital to deliver their children when they had neither money nor insurance. "We named our babies after her— why, there are four Grace Maries in our neighborhood alone."[10]

This busy, active woman was always ready to participate in a good laugh even on herself and was known for her witty comments. She was an ardent baseball fan, and on one occasion enthusiasm ran so high in her party that holy water was sprinkled on the Astroturf. In one interview she commented, "I love life and I love people. If you make that come out, you've said everything."[11]

Sister Grace Marie did not confine herself to Good Samaritan Hospital or the Greater Cincinnati area where she was active as a board member in several health-care organizations. On the state level, she participated in the Ohio Conference of Catholic Hospitals and the Ohio Hospital Association. In the latter she was active on several committees as well as being a member of the board of trustees 1966–1972, serving as chair for the 1970–1971 term. Nationally, she participated in the Catholic Hospital Association's speaker's bureau, the editorial advisory panel for *Health Progress*, and various committees and task forces. She was a member of the CHA board for ten years, serving as chair in 1974–1975. Also active in the American Hospital Association on committees and panels, she was on that board from 1976–1980. The American College of Hospital Administrations was also the beneficiary of her talents: she participated in the administration of their oral examinations over a period of eight years.

Not only was this woman active in health care, she was a devoted member of the Sisters of Charity and energetically participated in congregational affairs. "I entered the convent when I was twenty-two to dedicate my life to the church and to God," she once said, "and I've never regretted it."[12] She realized the activity of her life could work against her. "It seems to me that for the past many years I have been more in the world than out of it, to the point that I'm sure I can see the

Good Lord shaking his finger at me and saying, 'Martha, Martha.' "
She emphasized the importance of prayer for staying on track. "We
must start with the premise that you cannot give what you do not
possess yourself," she said, "[we] must turn to the anatomy of spiritual
growth in unrelenting terms."[13] Sister Grace participated on various
committees in the community and from 1968–1973 was Health Services
coordinator and a member of the governing board.

In 1979 this energetic leader saw the fulfillment of one of her visions
with the creation of the Sisters of Charity Health Care Systems
(SCHCS). She served as the first president of this corporation from its
foundation until the time of her death, in 1985. Beginning with a staff
of three, Sister Grace Marie set high goals for herself. The results were
soon seen in the growth of the corporate office and the dynamic direction set for SCHCS. Besides creating the entire organizational structure
for the new system, she oversaw the addition of two hospitals to the
system.

In this new endeavor, she continued her strong leadership as she laid
the groundwork for SCHCS to become one of the leading Catholic
systems in the United States. Typically, she "was recognized for her
vision in seeking collaboration among Catholic multihospital systems
through strong and meaningful organizational arrangements," according to Paul Donnelly, chair for SCHCS. "Her advice and counsel were
sought by Catholic religious congregations and multihospital systems
from coast to coast."[14]

It would be tedious to list the many organizational memberships,
boards, and honors in which she participated. Suffice it to say that:

> Sister Grace Marie managed to carve out a career in which she
> could be both involved in the caring and service of people and
> still work with the leaders who were making the rules about
> sophisticated technology, elaborate human organizations, and
> regulated public service . . . most of her professional life was
> spent in large institutions and she learned to make "big"
> beautiful—a major challenge for the twenty-first century."[15]

As one citation noted: "She has shown it is possible to advance from the
role of bedside nurse to nationally respected and recognized health-care
leader. Is it any wonder that she is known by hundreds of people as
'Amazing Grace'."[16]

Judith Metz, SC

NOTES

1. Archives of the Sisters of Charity, Mount St. Joseph, OH.

2. Autobiography, Archives of the Sisters of Charity, Mount St. Joseph, OH.

3. Judy Ball, "Hospital Head's Concern—People," *Catholic Telegraph* (July 26, 1974).

4. Mary Lynn White, "Good Sam's 'SGM'—The Woman Behind HMO," *Cincinnati Post* (December 20, 1973): 40.

5. *Ibid.*

6. *Catholic Telegraph* (July 26, 1974).

7. *Cincinnati Post* (August 17, 1974).

8. Sisters of Charity Health Care Systems Staff, "A Tribute to Sister Grace Marie Hiltz" (April 1985): 5, 7.

9. *Catholic Telegraph* (July 26, 1974).

10. "A Tribute to Sister Grace Marie Hiltz," p. 5.

11. *Cincinnati Post* (August 17, 1974).

12. *Ibid.*

13. "Nuns Feel Need to Consider Changes," *Catholic Telegraph* (March 27, 1964).

14. "Sister Hiltz Dedicated Life to Health Care," *Cincinnati Enquirer* (March 31, 1985).

15. Sisters of Charity Health Care Systems Newsletter, *System Scope* 4, no. 6 (February/March 1985): 1.

16. Citation, "YWCA Career Women of Achievement" (May 18, 1982).

Sister Chrysostom Moynahan, DC

On October 28, 1982, Sister Chrysostom Moynahan, a Daughter of Charity of St. Vincent de Paul, was recognized for her great contribution in the health ministry of the church and the state of Alabama, when she was inducted into Alabama Women's Hall of Fame at Judson College, Marion, Alabama. Born Honora Moynahan on August 18, 1862, in County Kerry, Ireland, as a child she emigrated with her parents and settled in Massachusetts. After completing high school, she entered the religious community of the Daughters of Charity in Emmitsburg, Maryland. After her death, she was honored with other "women native to or identified most closely with the state of Alabama who have made significant contributions on a state, national, or international scale within their professional or personal fields of activity and concern."

Sister Chrysostom's life indeed bears witness to every aspect of this honor. After serving in assignments in Massachusetts, Indiana, and Virginia, where she treated burn patients and victims of yellow fever, she was assigned to St. Vincent's Hospital, Birmingham, Alabama. She served the state of Alabama during two assignments. The first period of eighteen years began in March 1899 when she was appointed administrator of St. Vincent's, Birmingham, the city's only hospital after the infirmary of the United Charities had been destroyed by fire. The second period was from 1933 to 1941 in Mobile, Alabama, where she was the adminstrator of Providence Hospital.

While at St. Vincent's she cared for patients during the dreaded blacksmallpox epidemic, helped to restore a hospital partially destroyed by a cyclone, and directed a hospital whose financial status was chronically troubled. During all these crisis, patients were served regardless of their ability to pay.

Sister Chrysostom was the first registered nurse licensed in Alabama. She established one of the first schools of nursing in the state, at St. Vincent's Hospital in 1900. In 1901, Sister Chrysostom also organized Montgomery's first public health-care facility, a temporary service in the

Watts Mansion. At the same time, she supervised the construction of St. Margaret's Hospital, which opened in 1903.

In 1918, Sister Chrysostom left Birmingham to respond to a request to lead nine Daughters of Charity and a group of nurses to serve in Italy during World War I, a mission for which she was later decorated. This group was known as the Loyola unit and was the only one of its kind that went abroad during the war. Traveling across the Atlantic Ocean in a coverted freighter was only the beginning of a venture of a lifetime. Even during the first voyage, work had begun. While on the high seas, Sister Chrysostom's group had to nurse survivors from another craft that had been torpedoed.

But the real nursing duty began at the United States Base Hospital 102, attached to the 332nd Regiment from Ohio, brigaded with the Italian armies. This unit was established near Vicenza, about fifteen miles from the firing lines. In addition to witnessing the horrors of war, the group suffered from exposure to the elements, and the danger of death from the worldwide scourge of Spanish influenza. At times, the sisters and nurses became patients.

The members of the base hospital 102 remained at their posts well after the armistice was signed, departing only at the end of March 1919. While in Italy, the nursing group received a decoration from the Italian government and returned to a heroes' welcome in New York and a citation from the United States government signed by President Woodrow Wilson.

After returning to the United States, Sister Chrysostom received assignments at Mullamphy Hospital in St. Louis, Missouri, where she served until 1927, when she assumed leadership at St. Joseph's Hospital, St. Joseph, Missouri. In 1933, Sister Chrysostom received her last assignment, when she returned to Alabama as administrator of Providence Hospital, Mobile. There she ministered with the same expert care of the sick and concern for duty.

Sister Chrysostom's life was dramatized for radio in a program about the Loyola unit's service in Italy. On her fiftieth year as a Daughter of Charity, she received congratulations from the pope, the president of the United States, and the governor of Alabama.

After fifty-three years as a Daughter of Charity, and having served well her church and nation in the health field, she died from a lingering illness at Providence Hospital, Mobile, Alabama, on February 15, 1941, at age seventy-eight. She was buried with military honors in Mobile's

Catholic Cemetery. Her tombstone noted that she belonged to the Army Nurse Corps. Today that tombstone also notes that Sister Chrysostom Moynahan was installed in the Alabama Women's Hall of Fame, October 28, 1982.

Margaret Flynn, DC

Sister Mary Maurita Sengelaub, RSM

Sister Mary Maurita Sengelaub—nurse, educator, administrator, project director, initiator—was born Katherine Marie Sengelaub near Reed City, Michigan, where she received her early education. Later she entered Mercy Central School of Nursing, St. Mary's Unit, in Grand Rapids, Michigan, graduating in 1940. During World War II, and after two years' experience as a staff and head nurse, she accepted a position as clinical instructor of the Mercy Hospital, Bay City Unit, of Mercy Central School of Nursing, then heavily involved in educating nurses for the Cadet Corps.

At the end of the war, Katherine Sengelaub entered the Sisters of Mercy, Detroit Province, and in 1949 graduated from Mercy College, Detroit, with a B.S.N. in education. There she became an instructor and director in the nursing-arts department. In 1954, Sister Mary Maurita (as she was now known) earned a master's degree in hospital administration at St. Louis University, and, after finishing a year's residency, filled two successive administrative positions.

In 1961, Sister Mary Maurita became assistant provincial of the Sisters of Mercy in Detroit, and coordinator of hospitals, homes, and health-care facilities for the twenty-seven hospitals in the province, an area including Michigan and sections of Iowa and Indiana.

As coordinator, her initiative and creativity became even more evident. Under her leadership studies were conducted to determine the needs of the twenty-seven hospitals in the province. Acting on the results of these studies, she brought together administrators, financial officers, personnel directors, and medical directors of education to develop policies and improve services. She also initiated a study to identify religious women with potential to become administrators.

In 1965, Sister Mary Maurita was elected to the general council, the central governing body of the Sisters of Mercy of the Union located in Bethesda, Maryland. While holding this position, she served as consultant to the hospitals and health facilities throughout the nine provinces of the Sisters of Mercy. In addition to this full-time position, in 1969 she became assistant to the head of the Division of Health Affairs of the United States Catholic Conference, located in Washington, D.C. Her activities there—serving on various committees, working on projects, and other assignments—besides her involvement as a member and chairperson of a key task force of Conference of Major Superiors of Religious Women (in 1969–1970), eminently prepared her for the role of president of the Catholic Hospital Association (now the Catholic Health Association). She was the first woman elected to this post.

Under her leadership (1970–1976) new ideas were activated and shaped to meet the conditions of the period. A special initiative undertaken during her first year as chief executive officer of the association was to give direction and encouragement to the development of a program of service, the Catholic Health Services Leadership Program. This program was an attempt to develop the concept of sponsorship through leadership and influence exerted by religious congregations to bring a sense of interdependence and unity between and among the acute-care institutions owned by the congregations. The concept was a forerunner of more formal systems that other religious congregations began a decade later. Under Sister Mary Maurita's leadership the association also established an Office of Government Relations in Washington, D.C.; an internal legal department; a Department of Medical Ethics; a Department of Services for the Aging; and a Department of Pastoral Care. A subsidiary corporate organization was developed, the Pope John XXIII Center for Medical-Moral Issues and Research, which had as its mission the addressing of emerging moral issues, such as genetic engineering and organ transplants.

A sequence of serious illnesses ended Sister Mary Maurita's tenure as president of the CHA in 1976, but not before she had traveled to almost every state for participation in Catholic hospital activities. She was also a board member of the Canadian Catholic Hospital Association and in 1972 represented the CHA in India.

Meanwhile, in the Detroit Province a new health system was emerging, the Sisters of Mercy Health Corporation. Sister Mary Maurita was appointed to serve as a member of the newly created board of trustees and prior to July 1, 1976, provided consultation services when the SMHC was being created and organized.

In July, 1972, Sister Mary Maurita was elected to a three-year term as provincial councilor. She was also appointed chairperson of the SMHC, a position she held until July 1, 1983.

An evaluation of SMHC and a corporate restructuring study in 1981–82 resulted in the formation of a holding company, Mercy Health Services. On July 1, 1984, Sister Mary Maurita became president and chief executive officer of Mercy Collaborative, a new subsidiary providing services to religious congregations and Catholic hospitals in areas of governance, management, sponsorship, technology, education, and international health. Its primary purpose is to enhance and ensure the viability and continuity of the healing mission of the Catholic church. Sister Mary Maurita held this leadership position until July 1987, when she resigned to become senior advisor to the president of Mercy Health Services and a senior consultant of Mercy Collaborative.

Sister Mary Maurita's deep love for people and her desire to be of service to others, especially the poor, neglected, and forgotten, prompted her work to improve conditions for migrants in the United States. This she has been doing for over twenty years. Together with other religious women she founded the National Migrant Worker's Council of the Conference of Major Superiors of Women, co-chairing the council and spearheading its incorporation in 1978. This organization recruits professional personnel—nurses, health aides, and others—who can serve migrants during the winter at the migrants' home base in Florida. Through her efforts substantial funds for the project have been appropriated by the Division of Community Health Services of the U.S. Department of Health and Human Services and by other organizations. Founded more recently by Sister Mary Maurita and the council is the Midwest Migrant Health Project, which operates out of the Midwest Migrant Health Information Office and is making significant contributions to migrant health. Four Catholic health systems are presently involved and contribute annual funds to this initiative.

During her years of dedicated service in the Catholic health ministry, many honors and awards have come to Sister Mary Maurita, and many of her more than fifty addresses to health organizations have been published in professional health magazines. In 1965 she received the Key Award for Meritorious Service from the American Hospital Association, and the Newcomer Award as Medical Administrator of the Year from the American Academy of Medical Adminstrators. In 1979 she received an honorary doctoral degree from St. Michael's College in Winooski, Vermont, and in 1984 an honorary doctoral degree in humane letters from College Misericordia, Dallas, Pennsylvania. The Alumni Association of the Department of Hospital and Health Care

Administration presented her with the Distinguished Alumni Award in 1985. Recently her oral history was published as part of the Hosptial Administration Oral History Collection, sponsored by the AHA and Hospital Research and Education Trust.

"Because her life has been an example of openness to others," St. Mary's Hospital, Grand Rapids (where her distinguished career of service began), in 1983 considered it appropriate that a newly renovated Mercy Center in the hospital be dedicated to her.

Besides her present advisory position with MHS, Sister Mary Maurita continues to serve on national, regional, and local boards and is a member of several professional organizations. Her summation of her life's career, "leaving works I love for other works I grow to love," will undoubtedly hold as she continues to dedicate her services to God and humanity.

Edna Marie LeRoux, RSM

Sister Dorothy Peterson, SCN

A new direction in health care for the rural population was taken by Dorothy Peterson and Sally Griffin in 1971, when they founded Community Health Services–Nazareth Home Health Agency and Nazareth Community Clinic. I feel most privileged to have known and walked along the way with these Sisters of Charity of Nazareth, Kentucky.

I stand in awe of the courage and strength of these women who were co-creators with God in giving birth, not without pain, to a new entity that has served so many people over the years. They never failed to hear the cries of the poor or respond to the voiceless, even when faced by obstacles and the power of the secure. They conceived, gave birth, nourished, enabled growth and development, guided through adolesence, and let go of a well-established agency and clinic. I continue to be inspired and renewed in spirit when I remember what can be done when the Spirit calls. They had only a dream—no money, no personnel, no property, and little support, but they had faith, courage, dared to risk, and most of all they had a strong sense of justice and great love.

In 1970, while the two women were employed at the Visiting Nurse Association (VNA) in Louisville as registered nurses, they became aware of the great need for in-home health services, especially among the rural poor and elderly of Kentucky. Dorothy, in particular, sensed a strong call to take such services to these people, realizing at the same time the risks, challenges, opposition, and struggles she would face in setting this idea in motion. After resigning their positions at VNA in April 1971 they began to put in place a strategy for organizing such a service. With the blessing of their major superiors, they donated their time and services to the development of this project.

Statistics revealed that one-fourth of families in the surrounding area had incomes below Social Security Administration's poverty level. The federal Department of Health, Education, and Welfare had also determined that the majority of the poor counties in the U.S. were rural. They began by visiting physicians in two adjoining counties to ascertain their perceived need for such services. Despite a disappointing reception, they moved ahead, contacting one of the county judges about their plans and solicitng his support. He proved most helpful in promoting the concept in a variety of ways over the next several years. They introduced their ideas and plans to local human-service agencies and were given names of clients in need of health-related services. Immediately they followed up on these referrals by offering services gratis and knocking on doors of homes to explain their work.

During 1971 they also applied for monies from the U.S. Catholic Bishops Campaign for Human Development—War on Poverty Program for initiating rural health services to the poor and elderly through home visits and the purchase of a mobile health unit to take into remote areas. Their proposal was among the first fifty-three projects to be funded in the country. In early 1972 they opened their rural office on the Nazareth motherhouse campus in converted space formerly occupied by their religious community's college, which had closed the previous year. During that year three other SCNs joined the staff as secretary-bookkeeper, home health aide, and registered nurse. The state certified and licensed the home health agency on July 31 for two counties. This meant that they were approved for reimbursement by Medicare and Medicaid.

In the first quarter of 1972 the mobile health unit was initiated with the purchase of a twenty-five-foot recreational motor-home vehicle that was adapted to clinical purposes for ambulatory health care. It was operated through standing written orders of several local physicians. It was driven to remote community centers, schools, or churches in the late afternoon or early evening. Many of the sites were forty miles round trip. Two examining rooms were used to treat minor illnesses, provide routine and emergency care, and perform initial screening and health evaluations for referral to physicians and health-care facilities or agencies.

Three norms were used in selection of the sites: (1) inaccessability of health services, (2) shortage of health-care personnel, and (3) transportation problems to towns and cities for health care. Prevention of health problems was a major thrust for provision of this service. Health counseling and teaching basic health habits proved to be a necessity. Through the on-site visits they also learned of persons in need of home health services, and word of the two-pronged ministry spread quickly. The mobile unit was operated for two years, but because of more stringent state standards for license requirements, a shortage of qualified personnel, and inadequate funding sources, the services were discontinued. However, they continued health screening at senior centers and nutrition sites upon request. During the two-year period they had traveled 1,132 miles, treated and/or advised 375 clients during 436 visits, and distributed 412 free medications. It is still Dorothy's belief that the concept has merit and could be viable as a means of improving health services, particularly in remote rural areas.

Another adjunct of the Campaign for Human Development funding request was for a two-way radio communication system. This was put into operation by placing radios in the automobiles of the nurses, so that there was contact between them and their office while they made home visits. This proved valuable in relaying messages to and from physicians relative to the condition of patients. It likewise prevented unnecessary travel, as they could visit clients who needed assistance while they were already in the geographical area for the day. A four-wheel-drive jeep was also purchased with the bishops' funds for visits to homes difficult to reach in a conventional automobile.

By 1973 physical-therapy services were added to the registered nursing skills and home health aides already being provided, and the service area was expanded to include two additional counties. In 1974, because of great demand, two more counties were included for provision of in-home health care, bringing the total to six counties and serving a population over one hundred thousand.

The organization also served as an educational experience for nursing students in several Kentucky-area colleges and universities, as well as for students in other health fields who opted to spend a clinical rotation at Nazareth, and was widely used as a community health learning center.

During this same period because of the rapid expansion and demands for services, an application was made for federal seed monies and $87,280 was approved for dispensation over a three-year period, after which time the agency would be expected to be totally self-supporting. Eventually, because of federal cuts, a total of only $63,592 was received over a two-year span toward hiring additional field staff and purchasing of medical supplies and equipment. After this time, the Nazareth Home Health Agency became a strong, viable, respected health-care provider.

Dorothy Peterson became a leader in the home health-care field and was active in the formation of the Kentucky Home Health Association, serving as its first president for two years. Her agency was considered a role model for newly organized home-health agencies and her staff was called upon to assist them in their early stages of formation. Her expertise was also recognized by many other health groups and she was appointed by the governor to serve on the newly created Kentucky

Certificate of Need and Licensure Board for Health Care Facilities and Health Services, from 1972 to 1980. She also served on two regional health planning councils in her geographic service area. The governor of Kentucky in 1984 appointed Sister Dorothy to the Task Force for Older Kentuckians. Throughout her tenure on these various committees and boards she found herself the only religious woman among the various memberships.

In 1976 and 1977 the home-health agency added an SCN nutritional consultant (a registered dietitian), speech pathologist, occupational therapist, and medical social worker, creating a full multidiscipline staff. Other federal grant monies were applied for through the state: the Older American's Act Title III program allowed the agency to offer services to people not meeting guidelines for third-party reimbursement. Such things as homeworker services, respite for families, nutritional evaluations, diet counseling in the home, and personal care and hygiene services were provided. A shelf-stable meal program was begun by the SCN dietitian for the elderly homebound. These meals were also needed on weekends when the sites were closed or bad weather prevented their opening. Initially, privately donated funds were used to start the project and later Title III funds were received to expand the program.

In 1979 a SCN pastoral care team member was brought on staff on a part-time basis to meet more fully the total needs of the clients. At the same time, a need for a geriatric nurse practitioner was recognized and cofounder Sally Griffin took a leave to enroll in the University of Miami's nurse-practitioner program. On her return she set up a rural health clinic on the motherhouse campus to offer health services, not only to our elderly sisters but also to the lay elderly living in low-income housing on the campus complex. Despite much opposition from some local physicians and health-planning groups, a certificate of need and licensure was granted by the state. The clinic, the first in Kentucky to be licensed, was named Nazareth Community Clinic and was an arm of the original home-health agency. The history of the clinic's struggles and achievements was published in the National League for Nursing's February 1986 issue of *Nursing and Health Care,* having been coauthored by Dorothy Peterson, Sally Griffin, and H. Terri Brower, the project director of the GNP Program at the School of Nursing and Medicine at the University of Miami. The SCN religious community partially funded the clinic services on an ongoing basis. Sally practiced under approved protocols of a medical doctor who visited the clinic monthly to treat an average of more than twenty-five clients at each visit. The same physician treated some of the clinic patients in his own office as deemed necessary between clinic visits.

Continued efforts were made to expand services at the home health agency. A federal grant was received from the Department of Health, Education, and Welfare to provide an intake planner to strengthen relationships with hospitals and physicians and provide continuity of health care from the hospital to the patient's home. The grant also provided for a family nurse practitioner to support staff development and improve the quality of nursing services. Still another grant was awarded by the Honorable Order of Kentucky Colonels to implement a management information system toward the purchase of computer services.

By 1984 an extended care service was begun to provide live-in companions, sitters, and nursing personnel for private paying patients in their own homes. Nurses for the home-health agency began to be on call twenty-four hours a day to meet the demand for around-the-clock services. Plans were also laid to establish an urban office for referrals. A Louisville satellite office was set up in one of our SCN hospitals and has been a great success. Other grant monies from the state have been used to offer a personal-care attendant program and Independent Living project in eleven other counties. An office to administer this program was set up in Lexington. A second satellite office was established for home health services in a small town twenty-five miles from the base office to be more readily available for referrals and to save travel time for management and field staff as well as for convenience of replacing medical supplies. At the close of 1987 the caseload averaged more than seven hundred clients with approximately one-hundred sixty-five personnel. The anticipated total for fiscal year 1988 is fifty-six thousand visits. The rapidly increasing older population (due to persons living longer) and attempts to provide for them in their own homes promises that this agency, which began as a small nucleus, will continue a vital service for many citizens of Kentucky.

Ann Murphy, SCN

APPENDIX 2

◆ Statistics

Ursula Stepis, CSA

Table 1: Religious Congregations in Health Care in the United States

OCD Code	Official Name and Location of Congregation	Country of Origin	Established in U.S.	Generalate	1985 Professed Membership	Number in Acute Health Care 1960	Number in Acute Health Care 1985	1985 Sponsored Hospitals
[0100]	(ASC) ADORERS OF THE BLOOD OF CHRIST Province of Ruma Provincial House Rt. 1, Box 115 Red Bud, IL 62278	Italy	1870 1876	Rome	298	139	31	4
	Province of Wichita Provincial House 1400 Smith Sheridan Wichita, KS 67213		1929		287			
[0210]	(OSB) MISSIONARY BENEDICTINE SISTERS Immaculata Convent 300 N. 18th St. Norfolk, NE 68701	Bavaria	1923	Rome	62	24	7	2

Table 1: *continued*

OCD Code	Official Name and Location of Congregation	Country of Origin	Established in U.S.	Generalate	1985 Professed Membership	Number in Acute Health Care		1985 Sponsored Hospitals
						1960	1985	
[0230]	(OSB) BENEDICTINE SISTERS St. Walburga Priory 851 N. Broad St. Elizabeth, NJ 07208	United States	1868	United States	98	15	10	1
[0230)	(OSB) BENEDICTINE SISTERS St. Walburga Monastery Villa Madonna 2500 Amsterdam Rd. Covington, KY 41016	United States	1859	United States	144	19	NR*	1
[0230]	(OSB) BENEDICTINE SISTERS Mother of God Priory Watertown, SD 57201	United States	1961	United States	106	49	13	2
[0230]	(OSB) BENEDICTINE SISTERS Sacred Heart Convent 1005 W. 8th St. Yankton, SD 57078	United States	1874	United States	225	83	45	4
[0230]	(OSB) BENEDICTINE SISTERS Mount St. Benedict East Summit Ave. Crookston, MN 56716	United States	1919	United States	210	28	9	3
[0230]	(OSB) BENEDICTINE SISTERS Convent of the Immaculate Conception 802 E. 10th St. Ferdinand, IN 47562	United States	1867	United States	276	10	10	1

* Not reporting.

Table 1: *continued*

OCD Code	Official Name and Location of Congregation	Country of Origin	Established in U.S.	Generalate	1985 Professed Membership	Number in Acute Health Care		1985 Sponsored Hospitals
						1960	1985	
[0230]	(OSB) BENEDICTINE SISTERS Priory of St. Gertrude Cottonwood, ID 47532	Switzerland	1930	United States	110	28	8	1
[0230]	(OSB) BENEDICTINE SISTERS St. Scholastica Convent Albert Pike and Rogers Ave. Fort Smith, AR 72913	United States	1879	United States	179	22	6	1
[0230]	(OSB) BENEDICTINE SISTERS St. Benedict's Convent St. Joseph, MN 56374	United States	1857	United States	673	116	26	3
[0230]	(OSB) BENEDICTINE SISTERS St. Scholastica Priory Kenwood Ave. Duluth, MN 55811	United States	1892	United States	254	47	17	3
[0230]	(OSB) BENEDICTINE SISTERS Annunciation Priory 7520 University Dr. Bismarck, ND 58501	United States	1947	United States	140	31	20	1
[0230]	(OSB) BENEDICTINE SISTERS St. Paul's Priory 2675 Larpenteur Ave. E. St. Paul, MN 55109	United States	1948	United States	133	2	2	2

Table 1: *continued*

OCD Code	Official Name and Location of Congregation	Country of Origin	Established in U.S.	Generalate	1985 Professed Membership	Number in Acute Health Care 1960	1985	1985 Sponsored Hospitals
[0240]	(OSB) OLIVETAN BENEDICTINE SISTERS Holy Angels Convent P.O. Drawer 130 Jonesboro, AR 72403	United States	1887	United States	80	17	10	1
[0270]	(CBS) CONGREGATION OF BON SECOURS 1525 Marriottsville Rd. Marriottsville, MD 21104	France	1881	Rome	72	90	3	7
[0370]	(OCD) CARMELITE SISTERS OF THE MOST SACRED HEART 920 E. Alhambra Rd. Alhambra, CA 91801		1904	United States	144	51	62	1
[0440]	(SC) SISTERS OF CHARITY OF CINCINNATI, OH Cincinnati Region College of Mt. St. Joseph Mt. St. Joseph, OH 45051 Dayton Region 3045 Far Hills Ave. Kettering, OH 45429 Great Lakes Province Region 22851 Lexington Ave. East Detroit, MI 48021 Central Region Mt. St. Joseph, OH 45051	United States	1852	United States	920	217	63	8

Table 1: *continued*

OCD Code	Official Name and Location of Congregation	Country of Origin	Established in U.S.	Generalate	1985 Professed Membership	Number in Acute Health Care		1985 Sponsored Hospitals
						1960	1985	
[0440]	(SC) continued							
	Western Region 1661 Mesa Ave. Colorado Springs, CO 80906							
[0460]	(CCVI) CONGREGATION OF THE SISTERS OF CHARITY OF THE INCARNATE WORD San Antonio Province Incarnate Word Convent 4515 Broadway San Antonio, TX 78209	United States	1869	United States	462	102	58	8
	United States Province 2128 Stone Mose Rd. Grapevine, TX 76051							
[0470]	(CCVI) CONGREGATION OF THE SISTERS OF CHARITY OF THE INCARNATE WORD Villa de Matel 6510 Lawndale Ave. Houston, TX 77023	Ireland	1866	United States	348	300	158	15
[0480]	(SCL) SISTERS OF CHARITY OF LEAVENWORTH 4200 S. 4th St. Leavenworth, KS 66048	United States	1858	United States	561	153	73	8

Table 1: *continued*

OCD Code	Official Name and Location of Congregation	Country of Origin	Established in U.S.	Generalate	1985 Professed Membership	Number in Acute Health Care		1985 Sponsored Hospitals
						1960	1985	
[0490]	(SGM) SISTERS OF CHARITY OF MONTREAL (Grey Nuns) USA Province Provincial Administrator 10 Pelham Rd. Lexington, MA 02173	Canada	1855	Canada	83	57	13	2
[0500]	(SCN) SISTERS OF CHARITY OF NAZARETH Nazareth Campus Service Nazareth, KY 44048	United States	1812	United States		125	72	7
	Louisville Province I Provincial Office 676 Atwood P.O. Box 17545 Louisville, KY 40217				174			
	Louisville Province II Provincial Office P.O. Box 17545 Louisville, KY 40217				151			
	Southern Province Provincial Office 904 Hawthorne St. Memphis, TN 38107				127			
	Nazareth Province Provincial House 1590 Harrodsburg Rd. No. 6 Lexington, KY 40504				226			

Table 1: *continued*

OCD Code	Official Name and Location of Congregation	Country of Origin	Established in U.S.	Generalate	1985 Professed Membership	Number in Acute Health Care 1960	Number in Acute Health Care 1985	1985 Sponsored Hospitals
[0500]	(SCN) continued Eastern Province Provincial House 169 Fenno St. Quincy, MA 02170				120			
[0510]	(OLM) SISTERS OF CHARITY OF OUR LADY OF MERCY P.O. Box 12410 424 Fort Johnson Rd. James Island, Charleston, SC 24812	United States	1829	United States	55	18	8	2
[0520]	(SCMM) SISTERS OF CHARITY OF OUR LADY OF MERCY 520 Thompson Ave. East Haven, CT 06512	Holland	1874	Netherlands	28	10	8	1
[0540]	(SCO) SISTERS OF CHARITY OF OTTOWA, CANADA American Province 975 Varnum Ave. Lowell, MA 01855	Canada	1857	Canada	197	26	13	1
[0570]	(SC) SISTERS OF CHARITY OF SETON HILL Mt. Thor Rd. Greensburg, PA 15601	United States	1870	United States	496	8	10	1

Table 1: *continued*

OCD Code	Official Name and Location of Congregation	Country of Origin	Established in U.S.	Generalate	1985 Professed Membership	Number in Acute Health Care		1985 Sponsored Hospitals
						1960	1985	
[0580]	(CSA) SISTERS OF CHARITY OF ST. AUGUSTINE 5232 Broadview Rd. Richfield, OH 44286	United States	1851	United States	172	109	43	4
[0590]	(SC) SISTERS OF CHARITY OF ST. ELIZABETH Convent of St. Elizabeth Convent Station, NJ 07961	United States	1859	United States		120	81	5
	Northern Province Provincial House 41 Emery St. Jersey City, NJ 07304				309			
	Southern Province Provincial House 139 Gregory Ave. West Orange, NJ 07052				343			
	Western Province Western Provincial House 31 Jackson St. Paterson, NJ 07501				347			
[0610]	(SCSH) SISTERS OF CHARITY OF ST. HYACINTHE U.S. Administration 98 Campus Ave. Lewiston, ME 04240	Canada	1878	Canada	67	18	2	1

Table 1: continued

OCD Code	Official Name and Location of Congregation	Country of Origin	Established in U.S.	Generalate	1985 Professed Membership	Number in Acute Health Care		1985 Sponsored Hospitals
						1960	1985	
[0650]	(SC) SISTERS OF CHARITY OF ST. VINCENT DE PAUL OF NEW YORK Mount Saint Vincent-on-Hudson Bronx, NY 10471	United States	1817	United States	765	103	42	4
[0660]	(SCC) SISTERS OF CHRISTIAN CHARITY North American Eastern Province Mallinckrodt Convent Mendham, NJ 07945	Germany	1873	Rome	402	43	60	2
[0760]	(DC) DAUGHTERS OF CHARITY OF ST. VINCENT DE PAUL	United States	1809	France		455	349	37
	Emmitsburg Province (Southeast) St. Joseph's Provincial House Emmitsburg, MD 21727		1809		446			
	West Central Province Marillac Provincial House 7800 Natural Bridge Rd. St. Louis, MO 63121		1910		374			
	East Central Province Mater Dei 9400 New Harmony Rd. Evansville, IN 47712		1969		260			
	Northeast Province DePaul Provincial House 96 Menands Rd. Albany, NY 12204		1969		248			

Table 1: *continued*

OCD Code	Official Name and Location of Congregation	Country of Origin	Established in U.S.	Generalate	1985 Professed Membership	Number in Acute Health Care 1960	Number in Acute Health Care 1985	1985 Sponsored Hospitals
[0760]	(DC) continued							
	Province of the West Seton Provincialate 26000 Altamont Rd. Los Altos Hills, CA 94022				188			
[0860]	(DM) DAUGHTERS OF MARY OF THE IMMACULATE CONCEPTION 314 Osgood Ave. New Brittain, CT 06053	United States	1904	United States	107	20	9	1
[0920]	(DSF) DAUGHTERS OF ST. FRANCIS OF ASSISI St. Joseph Convent 507 North Prairie St. Lacon, IL 61540	Hungary	1946	United States	34	8	12	1
[0930]	(FSJ) RELIGIOUS DAUGHTERS OF ST. JOSEPH U.S. Foundation Santa Marta Hospital 319 N. Humphrey Ave. Los Angelos, CA 90022	Spain		Spain	16	NR	12	1
[0940]	(DSMP) DAUGHTERS OF ST. MARY OF PROVIDENCE St. Mary of Providence Institute 4200 N. Austin Ave. Chicago, IL 60634	Italy	1913	Rome	100	39	8	1

Table 1: *continued*

OCD Code	Official Name and Location of Congregation	Country of Origin	Established in U.S.	Generalate	1985 Professed Membership	Number in Acute Health Care		1985 Sponsored Hospitals
						1960	1985	
[0960]	(DW) DAUGHTERS OF WISDOM Provincial House P.O. Box 430 Islip, NY 11751	France	1904	France	190	86	NR	4
[0990]	(CDP) SISTERS OF DIVINE PROVIDENCE St. Peter's Province 9000 Babcock Blvd. Allison Park, PA 15101	Germany	1876	Rome	381	41	25	2
	St. Louis Province Mount Providence 8351 Florissant Rd. St. Louis, MO 63121		1930		78			
[1020]	(SDR) SISTERS OF DIVINE REDEEMER American Province 999 Rock Run Rd. Elizabeth, PA 15037	France	1912	Rome	89	14	8	1
[1030]	(SDS) SISTERS OF DIVINE SAVIOR 4311 N. 100th St. Milwaukee, WI 53222	Italy	1895	Rome	177	24	5	1
[1070]	(OP) CONGREGATION OF ST. MARY OF THE SPRINGS St. Mary of the Springs Motherhouse Columbus, OH 43219	United States	1830	United States	479	34	12	1/2 co-sponsorship with 1440
[1070]	(OP) CONGREGATION OF THE MOST HOLY NAME 1520 Grand Ave. San Rafael, CA 94901	United States	1850	United States	200	23	14	2

Table 1: *continued*

OCD Code	Official Name and Location of Congregation	Country of Origin	Established in U.S.	Generalate	1985 Professed Membership	Number in Acute Health Care		1985 Sponsored Hospitals
						1960	1985	
[1070]	(OP) CONGREGATION OF THE HOLY CROSS Albany Ave. Amityville, NY 11701	United States	1853	United States	944	34	NR	1
[1070]	(OP) CONGREGATION OF OUR LADY OF THE SACRED HEART 1237 W. Monroe St. Springfield, IL 62704	United States	1873	United States	430	25	27	2
	CONGREGATION OF THE MOST HOLY ROSARY 1257 Siena Heights Dr. Adrian, MI 49221	United States	1878	United States	225	20	10	2
[1070]	(OP) DOMINICAN SISTERS OF GREAT BEND Immaculate Conception Convent 3600 Broadway Great Bend, KS 67530	United States	1902	United States	176	51	32	3
[1070]	(OP) CONGREGATION OF DOMINICAN SISTERS 4600 93rd St. Kenosha, WI 53142	Portugal Ireland	1911	United States	70	50	32	4
[1070]	(OP) DOMINICAN SISTERS INSTITUTE OF ST. DOMINIC Province of the Immaculate Heart of Mary W 3102 Ft. George Wright Dr. Spokane, WA 99204	Germany	1893	Germany	45	34	12	3

Table 1: continued

OCD Code	Official Name and Location of Congregation	Country of Origin	Established in U.S.	Generalate	1985 Professed Membership	Number in Acute Health Care 1960	Number in Acute Health Care 1985	1985 Sponsored Hospitals
[1100]	(OP) DOMINICAN SISTERS OF CHARITY OF THE PRESENTATION OF THE BVM Provincial House The Heights 3012 Elm St. Dighton, MA 02715	France	1906	France	77	34	12	1
[1170]	(CSSF) FELICIAN SISTERS Presentation of the Blessed Virgin Province 36800 Schoolcraft Rd. Livonia, MI 48150	Poland	1874	Rome	393	187	116	9
	Mother of Good Counsel Province Felician Sisters Convent 3800 Peterson Ave. Chicago, IL 60659				445			
	Immaculate Conception Province Immaculate Conception Convent 260 S. Main St. Lodi, NJ 07644				396			
	Our Lady of the Sacred Heart Province Felician Sisters 1500 Woodcrest Ave. Coraopolis, PA 15108				212			

Table 1: continued

OCD Code	Official Name and Location of Congregation	Country of Origin	Established in U.S.	Generalate	1985 Professed Membership	Number in Acute Health Care 1960	1985	1985 Sponsored Hospitals
[1170]	(CSSF) continued							
	Assumption of the Blessed Virgin Mary Province Box 15096 4210 Meadowlark Ln. S.E. Rio Rancho, NM 87174				106			
	Our Lady of the Angels Province Our Lady of the Angels Convent 1315 Enfield St. Enfield, CT 06082							
[1180]	(OSF) FRANCISCAN SISTERS OF ALLEGANY, NY St. Elizabeth Motherhouse Allegany, NY 14706	United States	1859	United States		124	54	6
	Region I, Franciscan Sisters of Allegany 1627 St. Agnes Ave. Utica, NY 13501				233			
	Region II, Franciscan Sisters of Allegany 142 Second St. Woodridge, NJ 07075				143			
	Region III, Franciscan Sisters of Allegany 3001 W. Buffalo Ave. Tampa, FL 33607				147			

Table 1: *continued*

OCD Code	Official Name and Location of Congregation	Country of Origin	Established in U.S.	Generalate	1985 Professed Membership	Number in Acute Health Care		1985 Sponsored Hospitals
						1960	1985	
[1210]	(OSF) FRANCISCAN SISTERS OF CHICAGO Our Lady of Victory Convent 1220 Main St. Lemont, IL 60439	United States	1894	United States	207	61	14	1
[1220]	(OSF) FRANCISCAN SISTERS OF THE BLESSED VIRGIN MARY OF THE HOLY ANGELS Franciscan Regional Center 1388 Prior Ave. S. St. Paul, MN 55116	Germany	1863	Germany	25	32	6	1
[1230]	(OSF) FRANCISCAN SISTERS OF CHRISTIAN CHARITY Holy Family Convent 2409 South Alverno Rd. Manitowoc, WI 54220	United States	1869	United States	761	84	12	3
[1240]	(OSF) THE FRANCISCAN SISTERS, DAUGHTERS OF THE SACRED HEARTS OF JESUS AND MARY St. Clara's Province P.O. Box 667 Wheaton, IL 60189	Germany	1872	Rome	200	189	39	8
[1290]	(OSF) FRANCISCAN SISTERS OF THE IMMACULATE CONCEPTION OF THE ORDER OF ST. FRANCIS St. Mary of the Angels Convent 1000 30th St. Rock Island, IL 61202	United States	1901	United States	20	19	6	1

Table 1: *continued*

OCD Code	Official Name and Location of Congregation	Country of Origin	Established in U.S.	Generalate	1985 Professed Membership	Number in Acute Health Care		1985 Sponsored Hospitals
						1960	1985	
[1310]	(OSF) FRANCISCAN SISTERS OF LITTLE FALLS, MN St. Francis Convent Little Falls, MN 56345	United States	1891	United States	312	81	25	5
[1350]	(OSF) FRANCISCAN SISTERS OF THE IMMACULATE CONCEPTION 11306 Laurel Canyon Blvd. San Fernando, CA 91340	Mexico	1926		98			2
[1380]	(FMM) THE FRANCISCAN MISSIONARIES OF MARY U.S. Province 225 E. 45th St. New York, NY 10017	India	1904	Rome	227	82	3	1
[1380]	(OSF) FRANCISCAN MISSIONARIES OF OUR LADY 4200 Essen Ln. Baton Rouge, LA 70809	France	1913	France	36	15	22	3
[1440]	(SFP) FRANCISCAN SISTERS OF THE POOR Community Service Center 191 Joralemon St. Brooklyn, NY 11201	Germany	1858	United States	297	194	63	11 1/2 co-sponsorship with 1770
[1450]	(OSF) FRANCISCAN SISTERS OF THE SACRED HEART St. Francis Woods, RR 4 Mokena, IL 60448	Germany	1876	United States	259	136	67	5

Table 1: *continued*

OCD Code	Official Name and Location of Congregation	Country of Origin	Established in U.S.	Generalate	1985 Professed Membership	Number in Acute Health Care		1985 Sponsored Hospitals
						1960	1985	
[1470]	(FSSJ) FRANCISCAN SISTERS OF ST. JOSEPH Immaculate Conception Convent 5286 S. Park Ave. Hamburg, NY 14075	United States	1897	United States	312	26	1	1
[1490]	(OSF) SISTERS OF THE THIRD FRANCISCAN ORDER St. Anthony Convent 1024 Court St. Syracuse, NY 13208	United States	1860	United States	454	64	50	4
[1510]	(OSF) SISTERS OF ST. FRANCIS Immaculate Conception Motherhouse Hastings-on-Hudson, NY 10706	United States	1893	United States	141	36	2	2
[1530]	(OSF) SISTERS OF ST. FRANCIS OF THE CONGREGATION OF OUR LADY OF LOURDES 6832 Convent Blvd. Sylvania, OH 43560	United States	1916	United States	408	46	55	5
[1570]	(OSF) SISTERS OF ST. FRANCIS OF THE HOLY FAMILY General Motherhouse Dubuque, IO 52001	United States	1875	United States	625			1
[1590]	(OSF) SISTERS OF ST. FRANCIS OF THE IMMACULATE HEART OF MARY Province of Hankinson Hankinson, ND 58041	Bavaria	1913	Rome	110	49	20	3

Table 1: *continued*

OCD Code	Official Name and Location of Congregation	Country of Origin	Established in U.S.	Generalate	1985 Professed Membership	Number in Acute Health Care		1985 Sponsored Hospitals
						1960	1985	
[1600]	(OSF) SISTERS OF ST. FRANCIS OF THE MARTYR ST. GEORGE St. Francis Convent 2120 Central Ave. Alton, IL 62002	Germany	1923	Germany	52	42	20	1
[1610]	(OSF) SISTERS OF ST. FRANCIS Mt. Alverno Convent RR 3, Box 64 Maryville, MO 64468	United States	1894	United States	45	41	18	2
[1620]	(OSF) SISTERS OF ST. FRANCIS OF MILLVALE St. Francis Convent 146 Hawthorne Rd. Millvale P.O. Pittsburgh, PA 15209	United States	1865	United States	323	36	71	2
[1630]	(OSF) SISTERS OF ST. FRANCIS OF PENANCE AND CHRISTIAN CHARITY Holy Name Province 4421 Lower River Rd. Stella Niagara, NY 14144	Holland	1874	Rome	302	87	29	5
	Sacred Heart Province Marycrest 2851 W. 52nd Ave. Denver, CO 80221				108			

Table 1: *continued*

OCD Code	Official Name and Location of Congregation	Country of Origin	Established in U.S.	Generalate	1985 Professed Membership	Number in Acute Health Care		1985 Sponsored Hospitals
						1960	1985	
[1630]	(OSF) continued							
	St. Francis Province Mt. Alverno 3910 Bret Harte Dr. P.O. Box 1028 Redwood City, CA 94064				137			
[1640]	(OSF) SISTERS OF ST. FRANCIS OF PERPETUAL ADORATION Province of the Immaculate Heart of Mary St. Francis Convent Box 766 Mishawaka, IN 46544	Germany	1863	Germany	264	254	65	16
	Province of St. Joseph Mt. St. Francis P.O. Box 1060 Colorado Springs, CO 80901				187			
[1650]	(OSF) THE SISTERS OF ST. FRANCIS OF PHILADELPHIA Convent of Our Lady of Angels Glen Riddle—Aston, PA 19014	United States	1855	United States	1694	326	157	10
	Immaculate Conception Province St. Anthony Convent 1715 Sproul Rd. Springfield, PA 19064				407			

Table 1: *continued*

OCD Code	Official Name and Location of Congregation	Country of Origin	Established in U.S.	Generalate	1985 Professed Membership	Number in Acute Health Care		1985 Sponsored Hospitals
						1960	1985	
[1650]	(OSF) continued							
	Sacred Heart Province Convent of Our Lady of Angels 0858 S.W. Palatine Hill Rd. Portland, OR 97219				195			
	St. Joseph Province 4500 Franford Ave. Baltimore, MD 21206				407			
	St. Anthony Province 75 Leonard Ave. Trenton, NJ 08610				254			
[1660]	(OSF) SISTERS OF ST. FRANCIS OF THE PROVIDENCE OF GOD St. Francis Convent Mount Providence Grove and McRoberts Rd. Pittsburgh, PA 15234	United States	1922	United States	152	32	18	2
[1680]	(OSF) SCHOOL SISTERS OF ST. FRANCIS St. Joseph Convent 1515 S. Layton Blvd. Milwaukee, WI 53215	United States	1874	United States	1541	10	NR	2
[1720]	(OSF) SISTERS OF THE THIRD ORDER REGULAR OF ST. FRANCIS OF THE CONGREGATION OF OUR LADY OF LOURDES Assisi Heights Rochester, MN 55903	United States	1877	United States	595	138	65	2

Table 1: *continued*

OCD Code	Official Name and Location of Congregation	Country of Origin	Established in U.S.	Generalate	1985 Professed Membership	Number in Acute Health Care		1985 Sponsored Hospitals
						1960	1985	
[1760]	(OSF) SISTERS OF THE THIRD ORDER OF ST. FRANCIS OF PENANCE AND CHARITY St. Francis Convent St. Francis Ave. Tiffin, OH 44883	United States	1869	United States	186	7	12	1
[1770]	(OSF) SISTERS OF THIRD ORDER OF ST. FRANCIS St. Francis Lane Edgewood Hills East Peoria, IL 61611	United States	1877	United States	118	176	61	6
[1780]	(FSPA) CONGREGATION OF THE SISTERS OF ST. FRANCIS OF PERPETUAL ADORATION 912 Market St. LaCrosse, WI 54601	United States	1849	United States	676	58	26	5
[1800]	(OSF) SISTERS OF ST. FRANCIS OF THE THIRD ORDER REGULAR St. Mary of the Angels Convent 400 Mill Street P.O. Box 275 Williamsville, NY 14221	United States	1855	United States	203	23	18	2
[1810]	(OSF) BERNARDINE SISTERS OF THE THIRD ORDER OF ST. FRANCIS 647 Spring Mill Rd. Villanova, PA 19085 Sacred Heart Province Mt. Alvernia Reading, PA 19607	United States	1894	United States	356	89	49	3

Table 1: *continued*

OCD Code	Official Name and Location of Congregation	Country of Origin	Established in U.S.	Generalate	1985 Professed Membership	Number in Acute Health Care		1985 Sponsored Hospitals
						1960	1985	
[1810]	(OSF) continued							
	Heart of Mary Province Villa Maria 159 Sky Meadow Drive N. Stamford, CT 06903				179			
[1820]	(OSF) HOSPITAL SISTERS OF THE THIRD ORDER OF ST. FRANCIS St. Francis Convent Box 19431 Springfield, IL 62794	Germany	1875	Germany	404	477	163	13
[1840]	(GNSH) GREY NUNS OF THE SACRED HEART General Motherhouse 1750 Quarry Rd. Yardley, PA 19067	United States	1921	United States	248	25		1
[1920]	(CSC) CONGREGATION OF THE SISTERS OF THE HOLY CROSS Sisters of the Holy Cross Generalate Saint Mary's Notre Dame, IN 46556	France	1843	United States		123	75	10
	Eastern Region Regional House 3706 Rhode Island Ave. Mt. Rainier, MD 20712				218			

Table 1: *continued*

OCD Code	Official Name and Location of Congregation	Country of Origin	Established in U.S.	Generalate	1985 Professed Membership	Number in Acute Health Care 1960	Number in Acute Health Care 1985	1985 Sponsored Hospitals
[1920]	(CSC) continued							
	Southern Region Regional House 2301 East Side Dr. Austin, TX 78704				35			
	Midwestern Region Regional House 52700 Shellbark Ave. South Bend, IN 46628				229			
	Western Region Regional House 900 S. El Camino Real San Mateo, CA 99402				201			
[1970]	(CSFN) SISTERS OF THE HOLY FAMILY OF NAZARETH	Italy	1885	Rome		148	80	6
	Sacred Heart Province 353 N. River Rd. Des Plaines, IL 60016		1885		342			
	Sacred Heart Vice Province 1814 Egyptian Way Box 530959 Grand Prairie, TX 75053		1962		54			
	Immaculate Conception Province Grant and Torresdale Ave. Torresdale, Philadelphia, PA 19114		1918		256			

Table 1: *continued*

OCD Code	Official Name and Location of Congregation	Country of Origin	Established in U.S.	Generalate	1985 Professed Membership	Number in Acute Health Care		1985 Sponsored Hospitals
						1960	1985	
[1970]	(CSFN) continued St. Joseph Province 285 Bellevue Rd. Pittsburgh, PA. 15229		1918		231			
[2000]	(CSR) SISTERS OF THE HOLY REDEEMER Province of the Immaculate Conception Huntington Valley, PA 19006	Germany	1924	Germany	80	49	1	1
[2100]	(CHM) CONGREGATION OF THE HUMILITY OF MARY Humility of Mary Center Davenport, IA 52804	France	1864	United States	237	23	7	1
[2110]	(HM) SISTERS OF THE HUMILITY OF MARY Villa Maria Community Center Villa Maria, PA 16155	France	1864	United States	362	70	45	3
[2160]	(IHM) SISTERS, SERVANTS OF THE IMMACULATE HEART OF MARY Marywood Scranton, PA 18509	United States	1871	United States	881	72	24	1
[2200]	(IWBS) CONGREGATION OF THE INCARNATE WORD AND BLESSED SACRAMENT Incarnate Word Convent 1101 N.E. Water St. Victoria, TX 77901	France	1853	United States	181	10	2	1

Table 1: *continued*

OCD Code	Official Name and Location of Congregation	Country of Origin	Established in U.S.	Generalate	1985 Professed Membership	Number in Acute Health Care		1985 Sponsored Hospitals
						1960	1985	
[2230]	(CIJ) CONGREGATION OF THE INFANT JESUS 310 Prospect Park West Brooklyn, NY 11215	France	1947	United States	102	40	1	1
[2270]	(LCM) SISTERS OF THE LITTLE COMPANY OF MARY Province of the Immaculate Conception 9350 S. California Ave. Evergreen Park, IL 60642	England	1893	Rome	47	63	38	3
[2450]	(SMP) SISTERS OF MARY OF THE PRESENTATION Maryvale Valley City, ND 58072	France	1903	France	82	32	43	4
[2570]	(RSM) SISTERS OF MERCY Sisters of Mercy Generalate S 5245 Murphy Ave. Orchard Park, NY 14127	Ireland	1858	United States	278	61	3	3
[2570]	(RSM) SISTERS OF MERCY Sacred Heart Convent Belmont, NC 28016	Ireland	1869	United States	157	33	16	2
[2570]	(RSM) SISTERS OF MERCY Sacred Heart Convent 1125 Prairie Drive N.E. Cedar Rapids, IA 52402	Ireland	1879	United States	152	36	14	1

Table 1: *continued*

OCD Code	Official Name and Location of Congregation	Country of Origin	Established in U.S.	Generalate	1985 Professed Membership	Number in Acute Health Care 1960	1985	1985 Sponsored Hospitals
[2570]	(RSM) continued							
[2570]	SISTERS OF MERCY Convent of Mercy 634 New Scotland Ave. Albany, NY 12208	Ireland	1863	United States	240	29	29	1
[2570]	(RSM) SISTERS OF MERCY Sisters of Mercy Motherhouse Marion, PA 19066	Ireland	1861	United States	540	21	22	1
[2570]	(RSM) SISTERS OF MERCY 333 Fifth Ave. Pittsburgh, PA 15213	Ireland	1843	United States	312	51	52	1
[2570]	(RSM) SISTERS OF MERCY St. Joseph Convent 605 Stevens Ave. Portland, ME 04103	Ireland	1865	United States	227	53	15	1
[2570]	(RSM) SISTERS OF MERCY Motherhouse of Sisters of Mercy 1435 Blossom Rd. Rochester, NY 14610	Ireland	1857	United States	260	20	6	1
[2570]	(SM) SISTERS OF MERCY Convent of Our Lady of Mercy 535 Sacramento St. Auburn, CA 95603	Ireland	1857	United States	113	25	32	3

Table 1: *continued*

OCD Code	Official Name and Location of Congregation	Country of Origin	Established in U.S.	Generalate	1985 Professed Membership	Number in Acute Health Care		1985 Sponsored Hospitals
						1960	1985	
[2570]	(RSM) SISTERS OF MERCY Generalate 2300 Adelome Dr. Burlingame, CA 94010	Ireland	1854	United States	289	126	65	5
	SISTERS OF MERCY Sisters of Mercy Motherhouse 444 East Grandview Blvd. Erie, PA 16504	Ireland	1854	United States				
[2580]	(RSM) SISTERS OF MERCY OF THE UNION IN THE UNITED STATES OF AMERICA Mercy Center Washington 1320 Fenwick IN Suite 610 Silver Springs, MD 20910					1223	538	85
	Province of Baltimore Sisters of Mercy Provincialate P.O. Box 11448 Baltimore, MD 21239	Ireland	1843	United States	332			
	Province of Chicago Province Center 10024 S. Central Park Ave. Chicago, IL 60642				531			
	Province of Cincinnati Sisters of Mercy Provincialate 2301 Grandview Ave. Cincinnati, OH 45206				555			

Table 1: *continued*

OCD Code	Official Name and Location of Congregation	Country of Origin	Established in U.S.	Generalate	1985 Professed Membership	Number in Acute Health Care 1960	Number in Acute Health Care 1985	1985 Sponsored Hospitals
[2580]	(RSM) continued							
	Province of Detroit Sisters of Mercy Provincialate 29000 Eleven Mile Rd. Farmington Hills, MI 48018				375			
	Province of New York Provincialate 541 Broadway Dobbs Ferry, NY 10522				232			
	Province of Omaha Provincial House 1801 S. 72nd St. Omaha, NE 68124				339			
	Province of St. Louis Sisters of Mercy Provincialate 2039 N. Geyer Rd. St. Louis, MO 62131				508			
	Province of Scranton Provincialate Dallas, PA 18612				540			
[2680]	(SM) MISERICORDIA SISTERS U.S. Address: 820 Jungles Ave. Aurora, IL 60505	Canada	1887	Canada	38	20	8	1

Table 1: *continued*

OCD Code	Official Name and Location of Congregation	Country of Origin	Established in U.S.	Generalate	1985 Professed Membership	Number in Acute Health Care		1985 Sponsored Hospitals
						1960	1985	
[2790]	(MSBT) MISSIONARY SERVANTS OF THE MOST BLESSED TRINITY Motherhouse 3502 Solly Ave. Philadelphia, PA 19136	United States	1912	United States	340	NR	15	1
[2800]	(MCS) MISSIONARY SISTERS OF THE MOST SACRED HEART OF JESUS OF HILTRUP St. Michael's Convent Hyde Park Reading, PA 19605	Germany	1908	United States	216	99	19	3
[2860]	(MSC) MISSIONARY SISTERS OF THE SACRED HEART OF JESUS Eastern Province 222 E. 19th St. 5B New York, NY 10003 Western Province 434 West Deming Pl. Chicago, IL 60614	Italy	1889	Rome	NR	164	90	5
[2990]	(SND) SISTERS OF NOTRE DAME Covington Province 1601 Dixie Highway Covington, KY 41011	Germany	1874	Rome	252	22	10	1
[3150]	(SAC) SISTERS OF THE PALLOTINE MISSIONARY SOCIETY Pallotine Renewal Center Rt. 2 15270 Old Halls Ferry Rd. Florissant, MO 63034	Rome	1912	Rome	84	69	24	2

Table 1: *continued*

OCD Code	Official Name and Location of Congregation	Country of Origin	Established in U.S.	Generalate	1985 Professed Membership	Number in Acute Health Care		1985 Sponsored Hospitals
						1960	1985	
[3230]	(PHJC) POOR HANDMAIDS OF JESUS CHRIST Convent, Ancilla Domini Donaldson, IN 46513	Germany	1868	Germany	309	200	40	8
[3320]	(PBVM) SISTERS OF THE PRESENTATION OF THE BLESSED VIRGIN MARY Sacred Heart Convent 1101 32nd Ave. South Fargo, ND 58103	Ireland	1854	United States	84	20	8	3
[3320]	(PBVM) SISTERS OF THE PRESENTATION OF THE BLESSED VIRGIN MARY Presentation Convent Aberdeen, SD 57401	Ireland	1854	United States	225	107	37	5
[3340]	(SP) SISTERS OF PROVIDENCE Convent of Our Lady of Victory Holyoke, MA 01040	Canada	1873	United States	235	187	44	5
[3350]	(SP) SISTERS OF PROVIDENCE Province of the Sacred Heart P.O. Box C-11038 Seattle, WA 98111	Canada	1856	Canada	234	204	106	17
	Province of St. Ignatius 9 E. 9th Ave. Spokane, WA 99202				151			

Table 1: *continued*

OCD Code	Official Name and Location of Congregation	Country of Origin	Established in U.S.	Generalate	1985 Professed Membership	Number in Acute Health Care		1985 Sponsored Hospitals
						1960	1985	
[3440]	(RHSJ) RELIGIOUS HOSPITALLERS OF ST. JOSEPH U.S. Address: Holy Family Convent 438 College St. Burlington, VT 05401	France	1894	Canada	70	51	24	2
[3480]	(CR) SISTERS OF THE RESURRECTION Western Province Provincial House 7432 Talcott Ave. Chicago, IL 60631	Italy	1900	Rome	134	43	19	1
[3520]	(SSCM) SERVANTS OF THE HOLY HEART OF MARY Provincial House 145 S. Fourth Ave. Kankakee, IL 60901	France	1889	Canada	93	42	33	2
[3530]	(SSpS) MISSIONARY SISTERS, SERVANTS OF THE HOLY SPIRIT Convent of the Holy Spirit Techny, IL 60082	Holland	1901	Rome	203	152	22	2
[3640]	(SMG) POOR SERVANTS OF THE MOTHER OF GOD American Foundation Holy Spirit Convent 1800 Geary St. Philadelphia, PA 19145	London	1947	London	27	8	9	1

Table 1: *continued*

OCD Code	Official Name and Location of Congregation	Country of Origin	Established in U.S.	Generalate	1985 Professed Membership	Number in Acute Health Care 1960	Number in Acute Health Care 1985	1985 Sponsored Hospitals
[3710]	(CSA) CONGREGATION OF THE SISTERS OF ST. AGNES St. Agnes Convent 475 Gillett St. Fond du Lac, WI 54933	United States	1858	United States	564	112	21	3
[3740]	(SSC) SISTERS OF ST. CASIMIR General Motherhouse 2601 W. Marquette Rd. Chicago, IL 60629	United States	1907	United States	380	28	35	2
[3830]	(CSJ) SISTERS OF ST. JOSEPH Motherhouse 637 Cambridge St. Brighton, MA 02135	France	1873	United States	1124	NR	61	1
[3830]	(CSJ) Motherhouse of the Sisters of St. Joseph of Orange 480 S. Batavia St. Orange, CA 92668	France	1912	United States	300	81	41	8
[3830]	(CSJ) Sisters of St. Joseph Mt. St. Mary Convent Generalate 3700 E. Lincoln St. Wichita, KS 67218	France	1888	United States	274	83	40	12
[3830]	(CSJ) Generalate of the Sisters of St. Joseph 23 Agassiz Circle Buffalo, NY 14214	France	1854	United States	236	23	11	1

Table 1: *continued*

OCD Code	Official Name and Location of Congregation	Country of Origin	Established in U.S.	Generalate	1985 Professed Membership	Number in Acute Health Care		1985 Sponsored Hospitals
						1960	1985	
[3830]	(CSJ) Motherhouse of the Sisters of St. Joseph Villa Maria 819 W. 8th St. Erie, PA 16502	France	1860	United States	256	58	20	1
[3830]	(CSJ) Sisters of St. Joseph St. Joseph Motherhouse RR #3, Box 291A Tipton, IN 46072	France	1888	United States	71	44	8	2
[3830]	(CSJ) Sisters of St. Joseph Motherhouse Nazareth, MI 49074	France	1889	United States	479	84	36	5
[3830]	(CSJ) SISTERS OF ST. JOSEPH Nazareth-on-the-Lake Motherhouse 1412 E. 2nd St. Superior, WI 54880	United States	1907	United States	61	7	2	1
	Sisters of St. Joseph St. Joseph Convent Brentwood, NY 11717	United States		United States	1261			1
[3830]	(CSJ) Sisters of St. Joseph Motherhouse 4095 East Ave. Rochester, NY 14610	France	1864	United States	562	53	2	1

Table 1: *continued*

OCD Code	Official Name and Location of Congregation	Country of Origin	Established in U.S.	Generalate	1985 Professed Membership	Number in Acute Health Care		1985 Sponsored Hospitals
						1960	1985	
[3830]	(CSJ) Sisters of St. Joseph Motherhouse of Mt. St. Joseph Pogue Run Rd. Wheeling, WV 26003	France	1853	United States	151	20	11	2
[3840]	(CSJ) SISTERS OF ST. JOSEPH OF CARONDELET Generalate 2307 S. Lindbergh Blvd. St. Louis, MO 63131	France	1836	United States		322	69	14
	Province of St. Louis St. Joseph Provincial House 6400 Minnesota Ave. St. Louis, MO 63111		1836		905			
	Province of St. Paul St. Joseph Provincial House 1884 Randolph Ave. St. Paul, MN 55105		1851		638			
	Province of Albany St. Joseph Provincial House 385 Watervliet-Shaker Rd. Latham, NY 12110		1858		770			
	Province of Los Angeles St. Mary Provincialate 1199 Chalon Rd. Los Angeles, CA 90049		1878		642			

Table 1: *continued*

OCD Code	Official Name and Location of Congregation	Country of Origin	Established in U.S.	Generalate	1985 Professed Membership	Number in Acute Health Care 1960	Number in Acute Health Care 1985	1985 Sponsored Hospitals
[3850]	(CSJ) SISTERS OF ST. JOSEPH OF CHAMBERY Convent of Mary Immaculata 27 Park Rd. West Hartford, CT 06119	France	1885	Rome	257	99	50	3
[3890]	(CSJP) SISTERS OF ST. JOSEPH OF PEACE Sisters of St. Joseph of Peace Generalate, Inc 1225 Newton St. N.E. Washington, D.C. 20017								
	St. Joseph Province Shalom Center P.O. Box 1053 Englewood Cliffs, NJ 07632	England	1885	United States	203	96	35	3
	Our Lady's Province St. Mary's Provincialate 1655 Killarney Way, Box 248 Bellevue, WA 98009					135			
[3900]	(SSJ) SISTERS OF ST. JOSEPH OF AUGUSTINE, FLORIDA St. Joseph Convent 241 St. George St. P.O. Box 3506 St. Augustine, FL 32085	France	1866	United States	148	15	14	1

Table 1: *continued*

OCD Code	Official Name and Location of Congregation	Country of Origin	Established in U.S.	Generalate	1985 Professed Membership	Number in Acute Health Care		1985 Sponsored Hospitals
						1960	1985	
[3930]	(SSJ-TOSF) SISTERS OF ST. JOSEPH OF THE THIRD ORDER OF ST. FRANCIS Central Administration Sherland Building, Rm. 312–105 East Jefferson St. P.O. Box 688 South Bend, IN 46624	United States	1901	United States				
	Marymount Province Marymount Convent 12215 Granger Avenue Garfield Heights, OH 44125		1936		719	49	20	2
	Province of the Immaculate Conception Immaculate Convent 801 W. Bartlett Rd. Bartlett, IL 60103		1936					
[3970]	(FSM) FRANCISCAN SISTERS OF MARY Convent of St. Mary of the Angels 1100 Bellevue Ave. St. Louis, MO 63117	United States	1872	United States	283	372	92	14
[4100]	(SSM) SISTERS OF THE SORROWFUL MOTHER (Third Order of St. Francis) Denville Province Our Lady of Sorrows Convent 9 Pocono Rd. Denville, NJ 07834	Italy	1889	Rome	335	289	78	10

Table 1: *continued*

OCD Code	Official Name and Location of Congregation	Country of Origin	Established in U.S.	Generalate	1985 Professed Membership	Number in Acute Health Care 1960	Number in Acute Health Care 1985	1985 Sponsored Hospitals
[4100]	(SSM) continued							
	Tulsa Province Tulsa Provincialate 17600 East 51st St. South Broken Arrow, OK 74012							
	Milwaukee Province Mother of Sorrows Convent 6618 N. Teutonia Ave. Milwaukee, WI 53209							
[4160]	(VSC) VINCENTIAN SISTERS OF CHARITY General Motherhouse St. Vincent Hill 8200 McKnight Rd. Pittsburgh, PA 15237	United States	1902	United States	287	8	1	1
No Code	SISTERS OF ST. FRANCIS OF OUR LADY OF GUADALUPE Gettysburg Memorial Hospital 606 E. Garfield Ave. Gettysburg, SD 57442						5	1

Table 2: Membership of Congregations in Acute Health Care

Year	Total Religious Membership in United States	Professed	Novices	Candidates	Religious in Health Ministry	Catholic Hospitals
1965	181,421	89,596	5,691	4,303	13,618 (15.1%)	803
1966	178,671	91,889	4,385	2,772		
1967	176,341	90,498	3,650	1,986		
1968	176,358	88,009	2,583	1,155	15,897 (18.0%)	777
1969	160,931	84,676	1,603	609		
1970	153,821	81,868	903	477	11,202 (13.7%)	737
1971	146,914	78,123	670	427		
1972	143,189	74,572	514	371	10,958 (14.6%)	707
1973	139,963	71,348	482	293	10,321 (14.5%)	
1974	135,362	71,673	418	261	8,772 (12.2%)	671
1975	130,995	69,089	469	272	8,980 (12.9%)	
1976	130,929	70,247	421	294		649
1977	129,391	67,378	438	339		
1978	128,499	65,938	440	335	8,243 (12.5%)	634
1979	126,517	64,559	449	341		
1980	122,771	62,200	555	471	7,131 (11.5%)	633
1981	121,370	59,964	487	354	7,259 (12.1%)	633
1982	120,699	56,650	374	234	5,762 (10.2%)	628
1983	118,027	55,503	331	182	5,592 (10.0%)	623
1984	115,386	51,376	327	180	5,455 (10.6%)	620
1985	113,658	51,125	357	180	5,051 (9.8%)	620
1986	112,489	48,302	333	192	4,919 (10.2%)	613

Sources: Kenedy's *Official Catholic Directory* and religious congregations in health

Table 3: Demographic Changes among 179 Congregations or Provinces in the United States, 1960–1985

	1–99	100–199	200–399	400–499	500–999	1000+
			MEMBERS			
1960	14	23	39	29	36	15
1965	12	21	44	28	41	16
1970	15	29	53	29	35	9
1975	17	39	69	22	25	3
1980	27	37	73	14	22	2
1985	28	42	68	13	19	2

Individual congregations but no provinces	107
22 congregations with provinces	72
Total	179

Of the 72 provinces, 65 give a separate membership. However, 7 of the 72 provinces include their membership in the total congregational membership.

Sources: Kenedy's *Official Catholic Directory* and religious congregations in health

Table 4: Membership in Various Ministries

MEMBERSHIP IN CONGREGATIONS SPONSORING
AT LEAST ONE ACUTE GENERAL HOSPITAL

	Professed	Novices	Candidates			
1960	94,407	4,655	3,599	Professed	1960–1980	34.1% decrease
1970	81,868	903	477	Novices	1960–1980	88.1% decrease
1980	62,200	555	388	Candidates	1960–1980	86.9% decrease

MEMBERSHIP IN RELIGIOUS CONGREGATIONS INVOLVED IN NONACUTE FACILITIES

	Professed	Novices	Candidates			
1960	13,880	850	720	Professed	1960–1980	20.7% decrease
1970	13,337	239	150	Novices	1960–1980	87.3% decrease
1980	10,999	108	78	Candidates	1960–1980	89.2% decrease

MEMBERSHIP IN RELIGIOUS CONGREGATIONS IN EDUCATIONAL MINISTRIES

	Professed	Novices	Candidates			
1960	51,932	3,239	2,568	Professed	1960–1980	18.5% decrease
1970	52,068	827	335	Novices	1960–1980	87.0% decrease
1980	42,347	422	170	Candidates	1960–1980	93.4% decrease

Sources: Kenedy's *Official Catholic Directory* and religious congregations in health

Table 5: Religious Congregations' Acute Hospitals Established, by Decade

Decade	Number of Hospitals	Number of Congregations
1820–1829	2	1
1830–1839	1	1
1840–1849	8	6
1850–1859	22	9
1860–1869	41	19
1870–1879	35	12
1980–1889	49	39
1890–1899	89	59
1900–1909	59	45
1910–1919	43	34
1920–1929	44	30
1930–1939	51	41
1940–1949	73	53
1950–1959	6	6
1960–1969	31	27
1970–1979	18	18

Table 6a: Total Membership of
Six Original Religious Congregations in the United States in 1850[*]

	Membership	Left	
Daughters of Charity [0760]	680	206	30.3%
Sisters of Loretto [2360]	215	9	4.2%
Sisters of Charity of Nazareth [0500]	198	74	37.4%
Dominican Sisters of Kentucky [1070]	49	9	18.4%
Oblates of Providence [3040]	27	10	24.4%
Sisters of Charity of Our Lady of Mercy [0510]	41	10	24.4%

Table 6b: Number of Women Who Entered
the Six Original Congregations, 1800–1850*

OCD	Congregation	1800–1809	1810–1819	1820–1829	1830–1839	1840–1850
[0760]	Daughters of Charity	13	50	78	246	277
[2360]	Sisters of Loretto		48	80	28	58
[0500]	Sisters of Charity of Nazareth		24	70	38	66
[1070]	Dominican Sisters of Kentucky			20	13	16
[3040]	Oblates of Providence			3	20	4
[0510]	Sisters of Charity of Our Lady of Mercy			4	17	20

Table 6c: Religious Who Left the Six Congregations,
1800–1850, and Years in Community*

DAUGHTERS OF CHARITY		LORETTO		NAZARETH	
Departures	206	Departures	9	Departures	74
Unknown	162	Unknown	2	Unknown	5
1–5 years	23	1–5 years	3	1–5 years	49
6–10 years	5	8 years	1	6–10 years	11
11–15 years	5	12 years	1	11–15 years	6
17 years	1	16–20 years	2	16–20 years	3
21–25 years	3				
26–33 years	6				
38 years	1				

DOMINICANS		OBLATES OF PROVIDENCE		SISTERS OF CHARITY OF OUR LADY OF MERCY	
Departures	9	Departures	5	Departures	10
Unknown	6	Unknown	3	Unknown	4
1 year	2	1 year	1	1–5 years	3
3 years	1	10 years	1	7 years	1
				29 years	1
				34 years	1

*Source: Barbara Misner, A Comparative Social Study of the Members and Apostolate of the First Eight Permanent Communities of Women Religious within the Original Boundaries of the United States, 1791–1850 (Ann Arbor, MI: University Microfilm International, 1980). The two other congregations studied in the dissertation, but not listed here, were the Carmelites and the Visitation Sisters.

APPENDIX 3

◆ Milestones in Health Care

URSULA STEPSIS, CSA

Year	OCD	
1790		First Federal Census: 3,929,314 American white and black population was spread across various settlements. There were approximately 35,000 Catholics. Only five out of thirteen colonies had given Catholics equal citizenship.
Early 1800s		The Almshouse was the accepted method of taking care of persons needing institutionalized relief in the United States. Unclassified persons were herded together, the aged, the infirm, the insane, the feebleminded, the sick and dependent and neglected children.
		The education of physicians was usually two years but much of their medical knowledge was gleaned through their apprenticeship.
		Before the sisters established mission hospitals, Indians suffered due to inadequate medical and surgical treatment.
1804		By act of Congress, every seaman in the merchant service paid twenty cents per month, which was deducted from his wages, for support of the sick and disabled.
1808		The United States government prohibited the importation of slaves from Africa.
1809	[0760]	SISTERS OF CHARITY OF ST. JOSEPH: Founded by St. Elizabeth Seton and was the first sisterhood founded in America.
1812	[2360]	SISTERS OF LORETTO AT THE FOOT OF THE CROSS: The first act of the superior elected was the purchase of the land on which their cabins stood. For this she paid seventy-five dollars, the money being from the sale of her negro slave for whom she received two hundred dollars.

Year	OCD	
1823		BALTIMORE INFIRMARY: One of the early regulations was that the Bible be read aloud each day in each ward.
	[0760]	DAUGHTERS OF CHARITY: Came to Baltimore to take charge of the Marine hospital.
1829	[0510]	SISTERS OF CHARITY OF OUR LADY OF MERCY: During the Civil War their convent was burned.
	[0760]	DAUGHTERS OF CHARITY: Mullanphy Hospital in St. Louis was the first Catholic Hospital in the United States.
	[1960] [3040]	SISTERS OF THE HOLY FAMILY OF NEW ORLEANS and OBLATES OF PROVIDENCE OF BALTIMORE: Two black congregations were initiated due to the fact that black applicants as a rule were not accepted in white congregations.
1830	[1070]	DOMINICAN SISTERS, CONGREGATION OF ST. MARY OF THE SPRINGS, Columbus, OH: This community was established by four sisters from the Dominican Sisters of St. Catharine (KY) in Somerset, OH. Later the community moved to Columbus. Focus is on education; newer thrusts include health care.
1832	[3040]	OBLATE SISTERS OF PROVIDENCE: The sisters went out to nurse cholera victims in the city's almshouse. No record of public acknowledgement of their service (as was given to the white sisters).
1833	[0400]	CONGREGATION OF OUR LADY OF MOUNT CARMEL: The congregation was founded in France in 1825. The Revolution of 1830, aimed at destroying the church in France, forced the community to disperse. The founder sought refuge in New Orleans. The American congregation was established in 1833 and was involved in health care.
	[0760]	DAUGHTERS OF CHARITY: Requested by the state of Maryland to take charge of the Maryland Hospital for the Insane.
1834	[0510]	SISTERS OF CHARITY OF OUR LADY OF MERCY, Charleston, SC: The sisters devoted themselves to the education of female children and particularly children of color. They attended the sick. They sponsor two hospitals.
1836	[0500]	SISTERS OF CHARITY OF NAZARETH, Louisville, KY: The Sisters opened St. Joseph Hospital in Louisville, KY. The occupations listed of patients included: slaves, peddlers, boat captain, sheriff, and judge. The first record of a mental patient being cared for in the infirmary of Louisville was in 1845.
1839	[0510]	SISTERS OF CHARITY OF OUR LADY OF MERCY: The Hospital of the Society of Working Brotherhood of St. Marino was founded by Bishop England for homeless

Year	OCD	
		men and immigrant mechanics. The hospital was staffed by the sisters. The mechanics supported the hospital for their own benefit through contributions.
1842	[1960]	SISTERS OF THE HOLY FAMILY: Founded in New Orleans. They were touched by the wretched condition of the Negroes in the United States. Young women dedicated their lives to God for the uplifting of their own people.
1844		St. Louis Medical School Department: There were seven physicians as faculty members and the school had thirty-one medical students and nine "took" the degree. Honorary degree in Medicine was conferred on "two gentlemen."
1845	[2160]	SISTERS, SERVANTS OF THE IMMACULATE HEART OF MARY, Scranton, PA: Stem from the congregation founded in Michigan in 1845. In 1858 the congregation was established in Pennsylvania. When Scranton became a separate diocese in 1871, the Scranton congregation was established. They sponsor two hospitals.
	[2580]	SISTERS OF MERCY: Converted three log cabins into a free hospital for the poor in Detroit.
1846		The great Irish potato famine brought more than one million immigrants to the United States. A large migration from Germany and France occurred the same year.
1847	[2570]	SISTERS OF MERCY OF PITTSBURGH: The sisters established an "outdoor clinic." Advice was given free of charge to "outdoor" patients on Tuesdays and Fridays.
1847		Formation of the American Medical Association for the reform and advancement of medicine. The AMA created a permanent Committee on Education in 1904 that became the AMA Council on Medical Education in 1906.
1848	[2570]	SISTERS OF MERCY OF PITTSBURGH: The sisters founded Mercy Hospital. A small pantry on the second floor became the drug room. In the early days, Sister Augustine Shuck, daughter of a pharmacist and surgeon, took charge of the drug room. With all that she had learned from her father, she was able to assist doctors in instructing medical students in pharmacology.
1849	[1780]	CONGREGATION OF THE SISTERS OF THE THIRD ORDER OF ST. FRANCIS OF PERPETUAL ADORATION, La Crosse, WI: A small group in Germany decided to band together to begin a new religious community in the United States. Arriving in Wisconsin in 1849, the new community eventually settled in La Crosse. The small group began to respond to the health needs of immigrant families in the Midwest.

Year	OCD	
1850		The Hospital of Woman's Medical College of Pennsylvania: Founded as the first college in the United States for the medical education of women.
	[0760]	THE EMMITSBURG COMMUNITY OF THE SISTERS OF CHARITY: Affiliated with the Daughters of Charity in France and passed under the authority of the superior general of that order, assuming the garb of the French sisterhood. The headdress was the celebrated white linen coronette as given by St. Vincent de Paul.
1851	[0650]	SISTERS OF CHARITY OF ST. VINCENT DE PAUL, NY: Cost of hospitalization was three dollars per week. The sisters were willing to admit the sick poor and to give them of their time and kindness. However, they indicated that since they had no funds or endowment little medical treatment could be done at this time.
	[3840]	SISTERS OF ST. JOSEPH OF CARONDELET, St. Paul, MN: When they arrived in 1851 they found no provision for taking care of the sick of the city and immigrants did not have an institution to meet their health needs. They opened St. Joseph Hospital in 1853.
1852	[1070]	CONGREGATION OF THE MOST HOLY NAME, San Rafael, CA: The sisters experienced many hardships during their years in California when their butter had to come from Ireland and their flour from Chile. In the famine year of 1852, flour cost eighty dollars a barrel.
	[0580]	SISTERS OF CHARITY OF ST. AUGUSTINE, Cleveland, OH: Their first general hospital originated in a small brick building of St. Vincent's Orphan Asylum at Willet and Monroe streets. On August 5, the sisters opened the doors of St. Joseph's Hospital (forerunner of St. Vincent Charity Hospital) to the community. The hospital was closed in 1859 due to a large influx of orphans.
1853	[3840]	SISTERS OF ST. JOSEPH OF CARONDELET, St. Paul, MN: A Sioux chieftain furnished lumber to build a church. Before completion, a cholera epidemic spread rapidly. The log church was converted into a hospital where the sisters taught amateur nurses to take care of the cholera patients.
1854	[3830]	SISTERS OF ST. JOSEPH, Buffalo, NY: An autonomous congregation grew from the Sisters of St. Joseph of Carondelet in St. Louis. Focus: education and health.
	[2570]	SISTERS OF MERCY, Burlingame, CA: The sisters arrived from Ireland and placed themselves at the disposal of the city of San Francisco to care for victims of the cholera epidemic.
1855	[1490]	SISTERS OF ST. FRANCIS OF THE THIRD ORDER REGULAR: John Neuman, on the advice of Pope Pius X, gave approbation to the first mother general to establish this community.

Year	OCD	
1856	[1650]	SISTERS OF ST. FRANCIS, Philadelphia, PA: A small community of sisters were visiting the sick and supplying medication and nourishment to the poor and destitute. As the demands for charity increased, a larger facility was needed. A large dwelling was procured. The residence was spacious and in good condition but it was believed to be haunted. The sisters leased the place for five years. When the lease expired the owner, perceiving that the story about the ghosts had not interfered with the progress of the institution, increased the rent from five to seven hundred dollars a year. The sisters, however, decided to put their money into a permanent location.
	[3250]	SISTERS OF PROVIDENCE: Led by Mother Joseph of the Sacred Heart, a group of five sisters arrived in Vancouver, Washington, on December 8 after a forty-five-day journey on land and water from Montreal. She established many hospitals in the West before her death in 1902. She was a carpenter, architect, fund raiser, religious superior, and one of five women and the only nun honored in the statuary hall in Washington, DC.
	[3830]	SISTERS OF ST. JOSEPH OF BRENTWOOD: Three sisters formed the congregation. One sister came from Philadelphia, one from New York, and one from St. Louis. In 1903 the motherhouse was moved to Brentwood, NY. A sister physician gave professional care to members of the congregation and to private patients.
1857	[2570]	SISTERS OF MERCY, Auburn, CA: A group of eight sisters from Ireland established a congregation in San Francisco. From this congregation five sisters under the leadership of Mother Mary Gabriel Brown established a new community at Auburn in 1857. They sponsor three hospitals.
	[2570]	SISTERS OF MERCY, Pittsburgh, PA: From the very beginning the sisters faced financial difficulties. There were 232 patients of whom 172 were classified as "no pay." Other difficulties had to be faced. When the city decided to pipe water into the eighth ward, no provision was made for Mercy Hospital. For more than a year, the sisters had to draw every drop of water for cooking, laundry and department use from a well dug on the grounds. Even when the city water was pumped into the hospital, it was unfiltered. Filtered water was not available until 1907.
	[2570]	SISTERS OF MERCY OF ORCHARD PARK, NY: Many Irish immigrants had settled south of Buffalo, where they could find work in the grain mills and on the railroad. Their great poverty was made even more severe by the famine in 1857. The sisters did what they could to help.

Year	OCD	
	[0760]	DAUGHTERS OF CHARITY, Rochester, NY: St. Mary's Hospital: two small stables were secured to receive the suffering poor. Those who heard of the founding of a hospital in the old stables laughed at the idea. The sisters had no funds but with courage and faith succeeded in erecting a building from the two stables.
1858	[3350]	SISTERS OF PROVIDENCE, Vancouver, WA: The sisters, who came to Washington three years after it became a territory, opened St. Joseph's Hospital in a log cabin vacated by Indians.
		The early accounts are somewhat vague, but the first black physician in America appears to have established his practice in Cleveland about three years prior to the Civil War.
1859	[2580]	SISTERS OF MERCY, Chicago, IL: Mercy Hospital admitted its first medical intern.
		BENEDICTINE SISTERS, Covington, KY: The sisters from St. Benedict's Convent in Erie, PA, composed the foundation of Benedictines which began to labor in Covington, KY. This was only six years after the establishment of the Diocese of Covington. Focus: Health Care and Education.
		SISTERS OF ST. BENEDICT OF ST. JOSEPH, MN: From a congregation founded by St. Benedict in Italy in 1529, sisters from the priory in Bavaria established the first community in the United States at St. Mary's, PA, in 1852. Five years later six members of that community established a priory at St. Cloud, MN, which became autonomous in 1859. The priory was relocated in St. Joseph in 1863. Focus: Education and Health Care.
1860	[1440]	FRANCISCAN SISTERS OF THE POOR, Covington, KY: St. Elizabeth Hospital opened in a remodeled grocery store.
	[1490]	SISTERS OF THE THIRD FRANCISCAN ORDER: Seven Franciscans were working in two schools in central New York when Bishop James Wood separated this small community from their motherhouse in Philadelphia. Thus they were destined to be pioneers in the new community of the Sisters of St. Francis in Syracuse, NY. Major health problems for the people of Syracuse were caused by the poor water supply and the prevalence of swampland.
	[2570]	SISTERS OF MERCY OF PITTSBURGH: No school for the training of nurses was available before this time. The general classroom for the beginning nurse was the ward. She learned from the doctor at the bedside of the patients. She observed, learned the techniques, and through practice under the direction of the supervisor became an efficient nurse.

Year	OCD
	[3830]

[3830] SISTERS OF ST. JOSEPH, Erie, PA: Founded in France in 1650 by Jean Pierre Medaille, S.J., the first congregation in the U.S. was established in Carondelet, St. Louis, and from there the sisters established a congregation in Erie in 1860. Focus: health care and education.

1861 [1920] CONGREGATION OF THE SISTERS OF THE HOLY CROSS: An urgent appeal came from General Grant for sister-nurses. Six sisters volunteered their services and reported to General Grant.

SISTERS OF CHARITY OF MONTREAL, St. Vincent Hospital, Toledo, OH: Through funds furnished by local churches and the bishops of Montreal, the main section of the building was completed. A debt of $70,000 was incurred for building purposes. The motherhouse assumed the entire financial responsibility. A dispensary, one of the original buildings, was placed at the disposal of the Government when the United States entered World War I.

1862 [1920] CONGREGATION OF THE SISTERS OF THE HOLY CROSS: Three sisters became the forerunners of today's Navy nurses when they boarded the *Red River*, the first naval hospital ship.

[1440] FRANCISCAN SISTERS OF THE POOR: At the start of the Civil War members of the community were placed in charge of the marine hospital in Cincinnati. Some nursed the wounded on the steamer *Superior*, and large numbers of wounded soldiers and sailors were cared for in general wards.

1863 [0580] SISTERS OF CHARITY OF ST. AUGUSTINE, Cleveland, OH: Bishop Rappe had proposed to the Cleveland city council that a hospital should be built in Cleveland for the care of wounded soldiers, with nursing care being provided by the sisters. Newspaper editorials opposed a hospital under Catholic auspices since nine-tenths of the tax payers were Protestant.

1864 [2110] SISTERS OF THE HUMILITY OF MARY, Villa Marie, PA: The congregation was founded in France by a priest and Mother Magdalene Potier but after her death in 1864 the entire community moved to America, where teachers were needed in French settlements in the Diocese of Cleveland. Focus: health care and education.

[3830] SISTERS OF ST. JOSEPH, Rochester, NY: Toward the end of the Civil War, the bishop of Buffalo sent three sisters to Rochester to open an asylum for soldiers' children. After the diocese was separated, the congregation became autonomous. As the number of sisters increased, St. Joseph's Hospital and Training School opened in Elmira, NY, in 1902.

Year	OCD	
	[0760]	In Alton, Illinois, a prison hospital housing about four thousand Confederate and one thousand Union soldiers was taken over by the Daughters of Charity.
1865	[0440]	SISTERS OF CHARITY OF CINCINNATI: St. Vincent's Sanitarium and Hospital in Sante Fe was established at the instigation of the bishop, who requested that the Sisters of Charity of Cincinnati operate a hospital and orphanage in the West. The building erected by the United States government for a marine hospital at a cost of three hundred thousand dollars was purchased by the sisters for ninety thousand dollars.
		SISTERS OF ST. FRANCIS OF MILLVALE, Pittsburgh, PA: Stem from the congregation founded by Bishop John Neumann. From the congregation established in Buffalo, NY, three sisters established the congregation in Pittsburgh, PA, in 1865. They work with the poor in Appalachia and New Mexico.
	[2570]	SISTERS OF MERCY, Portland, ME: Two sisters from the motherhouse in Manchester, NH, established the congregation in Bangor, ME, and then moved to Portland in 1873. The sisters sponsor one hospital.
1866	[1010]	SISTERS OF DIVINE PROVIDENCE, Helotes, TX: The congregation was founded in France in 1762 and was established in Austin, TX. Focus: health and education.
1867	[2570]	SISTERS OF MERCY, Albany, NY: Mother Agnes O'Connor established an independent branch in Greenbush, NY. The community became independent in 1868. Focus: health ministry and urban and rural nursing.
	[1920]	CONGREGATION OF THE SISTERS OF THE HOLY CROSS: During the Civil War the sisters operated the military hospital at Mound City and also cared for wounded and ill soldiers in Cairo, IL, and Memphis, TN. Mother Angela, returning from the South, found a number of persons who were put off the boat at Cairo with fever and immediately sent sisters to open a hospital in Cairo.
	[0230]	SISTERS OF ST. BENEDICT, Ferdinand, IN: The foundation was made in 1867 by Benedictine sisters from Covington, KY. The congregation became autonomous in 1867. Newer thrusts include hospital and health services.
	[0230]	BENEDICTINE SISTERS, Elizabeth, NJ: This community was founded by the Sisters of St. Benedict from Newark, NJ. The sisters are engaged in health care and sponsor Benedictine Hospital in Kingston, NY.
	[1600]	SISTERS OF ST. FRANCIS OF THE MARTYR ST. GEORGE: The community was founded in Germany. The foundress, facing the danger of an epidemic of typhoid

Year	OCD	

fever then raging, with three other women resolved to take vows of Franciscan rule. They traveled from home to home nursing the sick. The vice provincialate in the United States was established in 1923.

[1760] SISTERS OF THE THIRD ORDER OF ST. FRANCIS OF PENANCE AND CHARITY, Tiffin, OH: The order was founded by a pastor and a widow. Focus: education and health care. They work also with the elderly.

[1230] FRANCISCAN SISTERS OF CHRISTIAN CHARITY: The sisters formally began their community with the reception of the habit. Originally, there were five sisters. these five instructed children in a neighboring parish. In 1875 a small group of Franciscan Sisters from Germany joined them and the two communities amalgamated in 1878. Focus: health care and education.

According to a report of the American Medical Association, as early as 1869 the sisterhoods were the only organized groups in the United States that realized the importance of nursing.

[2570] SISTERS OF MERCY, Belmont, NC: The sisters were brought by Mother Frances Warde in 1843 to Pittsburgh. From a later foundation at Charleston, SC, the Belmont congregation was established. Work began immediately after the Civil War, pioneering in hospital work and education.

1870 Up to about this time, the Catholic hospital was entirely an institution of charity. The wealthy and middle class had deep prejudice against it.

Many of the Catholic hospitals established in the 1870s owed their origin to German sisterhoods coming to the United States.

[0480] SISTERS OF CHARITY OF LEAVENWORTH: In the mining and railroad centers the Catholic hospital was particularly in demand for workers disabled by accidents, so the St. John Hospital in Helena, MT, was organized by the sisters.

[0610] SISTERS OF CHARITY OF ST. HYACINTHE, Lewiston, ME: St. Mary's Hospital is a unit of a group of hospitals operated by the Sisters of Charity, who came to Lewiston in 1870. St. Mary's was founded in 1888.

1871 The beginning of the Kulturkampf in Germany. The so-called "May Laws," which sought to transform bishops and priests into state officials, were passed 1873–1875.

[1650] SISTERS OF ST. FRANCIS OF PHILADELPHIA: When the sisters from Philadelphia came to Trenton, the need for a hospital was so great that they undertook to establish

Year	OCD	

one shortly after their arrival. Due to lack of financial support and considerable opposition, construction progressed slowly. In 1874 the sisters occupied the unfinished structure.

1872   [1240]   FRANCISCAN SISTERS, DAUGHTERS OF THE SACRED HEARTS OF JESUS AND MARY, Wheaton, IL: Originated in Germany in 1860. Three sisters came to the United States in 1872, to St. Louis. The original sisters returned to Germany. The American province was formed in 1877 and moved to Wheaton. Newest thrust is management of low-cost housing units.

          [1450]   FRANCISCAN SISTERS OF THE SACRED HEART: The sisters did strenuous work to help thousands of Italian immigrants.

1873   [0520]   SISTERS OF CHARITY OF OUR LADY, MOTHER OF MERCY, East Haven, CT: The congregation was founded in Holland for the purpose of engaging in all works of mercy. In 1873, in response to the invitation of Bishop MacFarland of Hartford, the sisters came to the United States. Sponsor one hospital in Connecticut.

          [0480]   SISTERS OF CHARITY OF LEAVENWORTH, Deer Lodge, MT: St. Joseph's Hospital was opened in a log cabin. After the bloody and desperate battle at Big Hole, General Gibbon moved his command toward Deer Lodge in order to place his wounded men in the care of the sisters.

          [3830]   SISTERS OF ST. JOSEPH, Brighton, MA: In 1873 four sisters at the request of the bishop came to serve in Boston. Focus: education and health care.

          [1570]   SISTERS OF ST. FRANCIS OF THE HOLY FAMILY, Dubuque, IA: The congregation was founded in Germany and was compelled to leave due to the cruel "May Laws." The small community was reestablished in Iowa City in 1875. In 1878 the bishop invited them to Dubuque and the community became autonomous in 1925. Health care is included in the ministries.

          [1070]   DOMINICAN SISTERS, CONGREGATION OF OUR LADY OF THE SACRED HEART, Springfield, IL: President Grant requested that the honor of unveiling a monument be conferred on a sisterhood as a token of gratitude for the sacrificed service of all sisterhoods during the Civil War. Two sisters who had ministered to the wounded and dying on the battlefield shared the honors of this day as they unveiled the statue of the martyred President Lincoln.

          [3340]   SISTERS OF PROVIDENCE, Holyoke, MA: This congregation was founded in Canada in 1861. The first foundation in the United States was in 1873 and became

Year	OCD	
		an independent foundation in 1892. At first they took care of orphans and soon afterward became involved in ministry to the sick in hospitals.
	[0660]	SISTERS OF CHRISTIAN CHARITY: When the "May Laws" of 1871 compelled all Catholic teaching orders to abandon their activities, the church in the United States was at the time greatly in need of religious teachers and this community arrived to assist. Focus: health care and education.
1874	[2580]	SISTERS OF MERCY, Baltimore, MD: The sisters assumed control of Baltimore City Hospital, a department of Washington University. Deplorable conditions prevailed in the hospital.
		BENEDICTINE SISTERS OF YANKTON, SD: Originally the foundation was located in Missouri and then transferred to Yankton, SD; in addition to educational work, sponsors two hospitals.
	[0760]	DAUGHTERS OF CHARITY OF ST. VINCENT DE PAUL, Saginaw, MI: St. Mary's Hospital began in a former hotel. To finance the institution in pioneer days, the sisters visited lumber camps and sold all-inclusive hospital service, the beginning of hospital insurance. Tickets were five dollars.
	[1170]	FELICIAN SISTERS: Five sisters sailed for America, responding to the invitation of Father Joseph Dabrowski, who was convinced that the welfare of the Polish people required the presence of religious congregations of their own nationality. The sisters are active in health care and education; in six of their provinces sponsor health-care institutions.
	[1630]	SISTERS OF ST. FRANCIS OF PENANCE AND CHRISTIAN CHARITY, New York, NY; Denver, CO; Redwood, CA: The congregation was established in the Netherlands in 1835 and spread throughout Europe. From the congregation founded in Germany, four sisters established the first United States foundation in Buffalo. Engaged in the ministry of health.
1875	[1920]	CONGREGATION OF THE SISTERS OF THE HOLY CROSS, Salt Lake City, UT: Holy Cross Hospital opened in 1875. Miners paid one dollar per month for access to free hospital care when needed.
	[2570]	SISTER OF MERCY, Cedar Rapids, IA: The community of Sisters of Mercy in Davenport established a branch house in Cedar Rapids. Focus: Health Care and Education.
	[3350]	SISTERS OF PROVIDENCE: In 1875 the Jesuit missionaries who labored among Yakima Indians pleaded for the

Year	OCD	
		sisters to assist them. To help in a great irrigation project financed by the United States and destined to bring under cultivation thousands of acres of productive land, the government petitioned the sisters to open a hospital in Yakima, WA.
	[2990]	SISTERS OF NOTRE DAME, Covington, KY: The congregation was founded in Germany in the 1850s and came to the United States in 1875. The Covington province sponsors one hospital.
1876	[0100]	ADORERS OF THE BLOOD OF CHRIST, Ruma, IL: Mother Clementine Zerr led a group of 48 sisters from Germany. The community split in 1875, and the original group relocated at Ruma in 1876. Focus: education, health care, and aging.
	[2100]	SISTERS OF THE HOLY HUMILITY OF MARY: The sisters began to minister to the sick in Ottumwa and continued until facilities were provided by other agencies of welfare. When a new motherhouse and school were completed, Mother M. Liguori supported the plan for the establishment of a hospital in the old structure.
1877	[1440]	FRANCISCAN SISTERS OF THE POOR: To take charge of hospital drugs, one sister was chosen to study pharmacy; she received a certificate as a registered pharmacist.
1878	[0580]	SISTERS OF CHARITY OF ST. AUGUSTINE, Cleveland, OH: The relationship between St. Vincent Charity Hospital in Cleveland and Western Reserve School of Medicine began when Western Reserve first used the hospital for teaching purposes.
	[0230]	BENEDICTINE SISTERS, Fort Smith, AZ: From Bavaria, first came to the United States in 1852, to Saint Mary's, Pennsylvania. From there other communities were established. Nine sisters from Ferdinand are considered the founders in Fort Smith; they eventually returned to their Indiana community. Traditional focus is on education and health care.
1879	[1450]	FRANCISCAN SISTERS OF THE SACRED HEART: To meet and solve some of the problems of cutting bread when the labor required an almost unimaginable amount of time, the procurator devised a plan by which a bread cutter in one operation might be made to cut a whole loaf into portions.
	[3230]	POOR HANDMAIDS OF JESUS CHRIST: Patients from the poor farm were accepted by the sisters of St. Joseph Hospital, Fort Wayne, IN, as a doctor was obtained to take care of them. The city and county authorities gave

Year	OCD	

the hospital three dollars a week for their care. The going rate for patients who could pay was six dollars a week.

1880 [1770] SISTERS OF THE THIRD ORDER OF ST. FRANCIS, Peoria, IL: In response to the request of laymen and physicians, the sisters bought a residence and converted it into a hospital.

[3320] SISTERS OF THE PRESENTATION OF THE B.V.M., Fargo, ND: Established in Fargo, ND, by Mother Mary Agnes Hughes and Mother Mary Saint John Hughes, who came to the United States from Ireland in 1880. Focus: education and health care.

1882 [0230] BENEDICTINE SISTERS, Cottonwood, ID: The sisters stem from the abbey in Switzerland from which Mother Mary Johanne Zumstein came to Uniontown, WA. The priory became autonomous in 1899. Focus: education and health care.

[0510] SISTERS OF CHARITY OF OUR LADY OF MERCY, Charleston, SC: A hospital ambulance in the early days was a horse-drawn covered wagon: a circus in town had donated two old dance horses to the sisters, who in turn used them to draw the ambulance. One day while transporting a patient, a band began to play and the horses started to dance. The patient was not hurt.

[1450] FRANCISCAN SISTERS OF THE SACRED HEART, St. Elizabeth Hospital, Danville, IL: The sisters began their work by taking care of the sick in private homes. The small frame building in which they lived could not accommodate patients. When the sisters' home burned down, a larger home was built and a small number of patients could be received.

[1820] HOSPITAL SISTERS OF THE THIRD ORDER OF ST. FRANCIS: Three sisters kept nightly vigil with President Lincoln's widow until she died.

1883 [0760] DAUGHTERS OF CHARITY OF ST. VINCENT DE PAUL, Norfolk, VA: St. Vincent's Hospital had a home for invalids. An advertisement indicated that the home was heated by steam with an open fire. It also specialized in Russian and Turkish baths.

[1640] SISTERS OF ST. FRANCIS OF PERPETUAL ADORATION: The sisters were sent from Omaha to Grand Island, NE, to collect funds for a hospital. Owing to droughts, grasshopper plague, and poor soil, the scattered and struggling population's resources were not sufficient to provide funds and the sisters returned to Omaha. They returned to Grand Island in 1884 and completed building a hospital in 1887.

Year	OCD

[4100] SISTERS OF THE SORROWFUL MOTHER (THIRD ORDER OF ST. FRANCIS): The sisters, whose order was founded in Rome, sent two sisters to the United States to establish a hospital and to begin the spread of the order in the New World. The sisters journeyed to Wichita, KS. The bishop needed sisters to open an abandoned hospital building. The sisters took over the hospital project and rented the vacated hospital building for fifty dollars a month. During the first year the sisters were also obliged to do home nursing, for which they were paid fifty cents per day.

[1720] SISTERS OF THE THIRD ORDER REGULAR OF ST. FRANCIS OF THE CONGREGATION OF OUR LADY OF LOURDES: St. Mary's Hospital of Rochester, MN—known as the Mayo Brothers Institution—owed its origin to a terrible tornado which partially destroyed the city of Rochester. The Academy of the Franciscan Sisters of Rochester was temporarily remodeled for a hospital and the sisters came at the request of Dr. Mayo.

[3830] SISTERS OF ST. JOSEPH, Wichita, KA: The community was established from the Concordia congregation and became autonomous in 1888. Traditional focus is on education and health care, including hospitals for miners and migrant workers.

1886   [0460] CONGREGATION OF THE SISTERS OF CHARITY OF THE INCARNATE WORD, San Antonio, TX: The sisters were engaged to work in a hospital owned by the International and Great Northern Railroad. The sisters had to contend with much opposition and bigotry. They left the hospital at the request of the board, which asked for a total change of sisters or withdrawal.

[1070] CONGREGATION OF THE MOST HOLY ROSARY, Adrian, MI: The Rev. Casimir Rahowski, CPPS, pastor of Saint Joseph's Church, needed sisters to staff a hospital for railroad-accident cases. The hospital was in existence only for four years and it became clear that it was a refuge for the aged and afflicted. There was seldom an accident case and the railroad companies apparently found no reason to offer permanent support. The hospital closed and it became the provincial house in 1892 and later the motherhouse of the sisters.

[1820] HOSPITAL SISTERS OF THE THIRD ORDER OF ST. FRANCIS: These sisters opened the first Catholic hospital school of nursing just for sisters.

[1180] FRANCISCAN SISTERS OF ALLEGANY, NY: St. Elizabeth Hospital and Eye Infirmary of Boston: 210 patients were received during the year, of whom 175 were charity

Year	OCD	
		patients. The sisters visited "out door" patients. In the eye department, 400 outpatients were treated gratuitously.
	[3320]	SISTERS OF THE PRESENTATION OF THE BLESSED VIRGIN MARY: This order was founded in Ireland in 1776 and was established in Canada in 1833. The Aberdeen congregation was established in 1886. The diptheria epidemic of 1900 prompted the building of the first hospital, known as St. Luke's, in Aberdeen, SD.
	[3840]	SISTERS OF ST. JOSEPH OF CARONDELET: The first cholecystectomy ever attempted in the United States was performed in St. Joseph's Hospital in St. Paul, MN. The patient survived.
1887	[2580]	SISTERS OF MERCY, Council Bluff, IA: The Reverend Bernard P. McManamy, pastor of St. Francis Xavier Church, requested the Sisters of Mercy to establish an institute of their own in Council Bluff. In 1888 the sisters received a deed for three acres for St. Bernard's Hospital. In 1890 the sisters entered into a contract with the county for the care of the county's mental cases with the provision that the sisters erect a suitable building for income patients. Mercy Hospital was opened as a general hospital in 1903 and St. Bernard's hospital took care of psychiatric patients.
	[2680]	MISERICORDIA SISTERS: The congregation was founded in Canada in 1848. The foundation of a mission in New York was instituted and hospitals were established in the United States.
	[3830]	SISTERS OF ST. JOSEPH OF NAZARETH, Kalamazoo, MI: The Reverend Francis A. O'Brien, pastor of St. Augustine's Church, spoke to the city council about the need for a hospital in Kalamazoo. At that time, the only place in Kalamazoo with a spare bed and round-the-clock attention was the city jail. After a young man died in the jail, Father O'Brien stepped up his campaign for a hospital. In 1889 Borgess Hospital opened its doors for the people of Kalamazoo in a two-story frame house with twenty beds and a nursing staff of five members of the Sisters of St. Joseph.
	[3840]	SISTERS OF ST. JOSEPH OF CARONDELET, Minneapolis, MN: St. Mary's Hospital opened in an old mission. Minor surgery was performed in the patients' rooms or in the upper hallway, which was screened off during surgery. Major operations were performed on the table in the sisters' dining room. The sisters ate in the pantry. The kitchen was the only place to boil water or sterilize instruments.
1888	[0230]	BENEDICTINE SISTERS, Duluth, MN: The sisters opened the city's first hospital, known as St. Mary's of Duluth. This hospital was to serve the lumbermen of northern

Year	OCD

Minnesota. The nationalities of the first 730 patients were listed as 478 Swedes and Norwegians, 177 Irish, 74 Americans, and 1 Yankee.

[0240] OLIVETAN BENEDICTINE SISTERS: The sisters opened the first school for colored students, with thirty-six pupils. The community began with seventy-five cents in Mother Beatrice's purse. A malarial fever epidemic led to the community being involved in health; they opened St. Bernard's Hospital in Jonesboro, AK, in 1900.

[4100] SISTERS OF THE SORROWFUL MOTHER (THIRD ORDER OF ST. FRANCIS): The first two sisters came from Germany to collect funds and to look for activities that might ensure the congregation's continuance.

[3830] SISTERS OF ST. JOSEPH, Tipton, IN: The congregation was established in Tipton from other foundations of the Sisters of St. Joseph. They have been involved in health care since 1904.

[3890] SISTERS OF ST. JOSEPH OF PEACE: Mother Clare, the foundress, resigned as leader of the community because she saw that the bishops' animosity toward her, due to her pointed social writings, would retard the growth of her order. She then joined the Episcopal Church.

1889 [3530] MISSIONARY SISTERS, SERVANTS OF THE HOLY SPIRIT: Blessed Arnold Jannssen founded the congregation in Holland in 1889. The first foundation in the United States was in Techny, IL, in 1901. They sponsor two hospitals.

[2860] MISSIONARY SISTERS OF THE SACRED HEART: Mother Francis Xavier Cabrini sailed to New York to work among impoverished Italian immigrants. She became an American citizen in 1909 and, but for a period during World War I spent working among Italian wounded, she devoted the rest of her life to immigrants in American cities. She died in 1917 of malaria and was buried in New York. She was canonized on July 7, 1946, as the first United States citizen to be a saint. She is called "the Saint of the Immigrants."

[3520] SERVANTS OF THE HOLY HEART OF MARY, Kankakee, IL: The community was first established in 1889. The United States province is located in Kankakee, IL with its generalate in Montreal. Focus is on health and education.

[3710] CONGREGATION OF THE SISTERS OF ST. AGNES, Fond du Lac, WI: The community was founded in Wisconsin. One outstanding work had been cooperation with the St. Raphael Society in Germany in maintaining the Leo House in New York as a shelter for immigrants.

Year	OCD	
	[3830]	SISTERS OF ST. JOSEPH OF NAZARETH, MI: In the first years, the sisters provided all hospital services—nursing, cooking, laundry, and maintenance at Borgess Hospital, as well as home nursing. By 1895, one of the sisters had earned a medical degree and assisted the other sisters in opening a school to prepare nurses for the developing hospital.
1890	[0470]	CONGREGATION OF THE SISTERS OF CHARITY OF THE INCARNATE WORD, Houston, TX: St. Joseph's Hospital. There was a smallpox epidemic, 1890–1891. The city pesthouse was located in an old cemetery. The sisters lived in pesthouse tents. The first superior died of yellow fever at the age of thirty-four.
	[2630]	THE SISTERS OF MERCY OF THE HOLY CROSS, Breese, IL: Elizabeth Speckman willed nine lots of land and one thousand five hundred dollars for the erection of a hospital. The Poor Handmaids of Jesus Christ managed the institution from 1898 to 1917. It was closed until 1921, when at the request of the Reverend F. Marfuss the sisters of Mercy assumed control.
	[3230]	POOR HANDMAIDS OF JESUS CHRIST, East St. Louis, IL: St. Mary's Hospital is located in an economically depressed area. The hospital provides a high quality of general and specialized services to a disadvantaged community.
	[2570]	SISTERS OF MERCY, Burlingame, CA: St. Joseph Hospital and Medical Center was begun when two Sisters of Mercy saw a tubercular man on a rooming-house porch struggling for breath. They took him in and made him comfortable. He died the following day. This shock made the sisters aware of the need for nursing care for people coming to the desert in search of health. In the same year, Mother M. Michael, with fifty dollars in her pocket, arrived in San Diego, a depressed town, and opened a dispensary/hospital.
	[2570]	SISTERS OF MERCY, Rochester, NY: Father Early came to Hornellsville in 1879 and was long aware of the need for a place to care for the ill and injured. On a cold Friday he was called to administer spiritual care to a badly injured man being treated by a doctor on the floor of a tavern. The next day he made a decision and bought a large farmhouse with his own funds. Part of the house is occupied as St. James Mercy Hospital. The will of Father Early indicated that the Sisters of Mercy have perpetual charge of the hospital and at least two positions on the hospital's board.
	[3840]	SISTERS OF ST. JOSEPH OF CARONDELET, Menominee, WI: The sisters staffed the Indian hospital.

Year	OCD	
	[3890]	SISTERS OF ST. JOSEPH OF PEACE: Two members of the Sisters of St. Joseph of Newark set out from their New Jersey home to the Pacific Northwest. Traveling by train across the continent, they arrived in Tacoma, WA, and there boarded a ferry to their destination in the town of Fairhaven, WA. Fairhaven, a lumbering town with its share of accidents and sickness, was without a hospital. At the invitation of the Fairhaven Land Company, the sisters immediately began to collect building funds for the needed hospital.
1891	[1310]	FRANCISCAN SISTERS, Little Falls, MN: In the center of the lumber industry, serious injuries and contagious diseases were commonplace. Orphans arrived by train with no home or families to care for them. All of these needs called the sisters to build a multifaceted structure and begin their ministries in health and education.
1893	[2270]	THE LITTLE COMPANY OF MARY NURSING SISTERS, Evergreen Park, IL: This congregation was founded in England in 1877 specifically for the work of nursing the sick and praying for the dying. In 1893 Chicago was chosen as the first site for the United States foundation.
1894	[1210]	FRANCISCAN SISTERS, Chicago, IL: The Franciscan Sisters of Chicago were founded by Mother Mary Theresa (Josephine) Dudzik and Mother Mary Ann (Rosalie) Wisinki in Chicago. Their focus is on the care of the sick, aged, and poor.
	[1610]	SISTERS OF ST. FRANCIS, Maryville, MO: Established by seven sisters, formerly from the Congregation of the Sisters of the Third Order of St. Francis from St. Louis. Focus: education and health service in private homes. Sponsors two hospitals.
	[1970]	SISTERS OF THE HOLY FAMILY OF NAZARETH: The sisters extended themselves to the service of others, helping the sick who called upon them and visiting them in hospitals and at home. Immigrants from Poland had difficulty communicating with hospital personnel and felt keenly the lack of ministration of their faith. They proposed to the sisters the idea of establishing an ethnic hospital in Chicago. On May 6, 1894, Archbishop Feehan dedicated a twenty-four bed hospital known as Holy Family Hospital. Today the hospital is known as St. Mary of Nazareth Hospital Center.
	[3840]	RELIGIOUS HOSPITALLERS OF ST. JOSEPH: Fanny Allen Hospital was established by the sisters, even though the outlook seemed hopeless, with absolutely no funds. However, with the help of the people, the sisters succeeded in opening the hospital.

Year	OCD	
1895	[0570]	SISTERS OF CHARITY OF SETON HALL, Greensburg, PA: Plans for the first hospital in the East End of Pittsburg were in the hearts and minds of the sisters. The sisters spent endless hours looking at property. With two local doctors, they opened their first hospital in 1897 in a small house that had been vacated by a neighborhood family. There were beds for ten patients.
	[1030]	SISTERS OF THE DIVINE SAVIOR, Milwaukee, WI: This congregation was founded in Rome in 1888. The sisters came to the United States in 1895 to do nursing in private homes. The North American province was formed in 1926 with its own administration. Focus is on health care and education.
	[2570]	SISTERS OF MERCY, Davenport, IA: St. John of God Hospital was intended for cholera and smallpox patients. The building was erected at the expense of the city of Davenport and turned over under special contract to the Sisters of Mercy with the understanding that such patients would be cared for by them.
1898	[0580]	SISTERS OF CHARITY OF ST. AUGUSTINE, Cleveland, OH: With an enrollment of six, the school of nursing was founded under the direction of Sister M. Charles, Superior of St. Vincent Charity Hospital. The school motto was "Charity is kind."
	[2570]	SISTERS OF MERCY, Burlingame, CA: The sisters were asked to nurse United States military personnel during the Spanish-American War.
1899	[0230]	BENEDICTINE SISTERS, Watertown, SD: Five Sisters of St. Benedict came to Pierre from Yankton to start a school. The morning after they arrived, they were called upon by local physicians who insisted that a hospital was urgently needed. To emphasize their point, a sick person was brought to the sisters in the afternoon. Their first task was to prepare the old Park Hotel for the care of the sick.
	[0760]	DAUGHTERS OF CHARITY, Norfolk, VA: Norfolk's citizens opened their newspaper to a devastating front-page headline, "St. Vincent Hospital Totally Destroyed." The night after the fire, even before most of Norfolk could grasp the enormity of the loss, several of the city's leading citizens sat down to devise ways to rebuild.
	[1820]	HOSPITAL SISTERS OF THE THIRD ORDER OF ST. FRANCIS: The first book on nursing to be published by a religious in the United States was called *Nursing Sister*.
	[3900]	SISTERS OF ST. JOSEPH, St. Augustine, FL: First established in the United States in 1866, when eight sisters founded a community in St. Augustine. The

Year	OCD

Florida province became autonomous in 1899 and became a diocesan congregation. Focus is on education and health care.

1900 [3480] SISTERS OF THE RESURRECTION, Chicago, IL: The congregation originated in 1891 in Rome and was established in the United States in 1900. Originally came to the Diocese of Chicago to conduct Polish schools but branched out into health and nursing homes.

[3830] SISTERS OF ST. JOSEPH, Wheeling, WV: St. Joseph Hospital in Wheeling was initially housed in a convent. Five sisters and two nurses provided health care in the twenty-one bed hospital.

1901 [1290] FRANCISCAN SISTERS OF THE IMMACULATE CONCEPTION OF THE THIRD ORDER OF ST. FRANCIS, Rock Island, IL: The congregation was founded in the United States. Sponsor one hospital and one convalescent hospital.

[3930] SISTERS OF ST. JOSEPH OF THE THIRD ORDER OF ST. FRANCIS: Founded at Stevens Point, WI. Forty-six School Sisters of St. Francis of Milwaukee formed the initial congregation to fill a crucial need for religious teachers to instruct children of Polish immigrants. As the congregation grew, the sisters entered the health field.

1902 [1530] SISTERS OF ST. FRANCIS OF THE CONGREGATION OF OUR LADY OF LOURDES, Sandusky, OH: Providence Hospital was established in 1902 as a small emergency hospital conducted for a short period of time by the Visiting Nurses Association. Financial trouble curtailed the usefulness of the hospital and in 1902 ownership was transferred to the Sisters of Charity of St. Augustine. With a change in the boundaries of the diocese, the Sisters of Charity were withdrawn. Since 1923, the Sister of St. Francis sponsor the hospital.

[4160] VINCENTIAN SISTERS OF CHARITY, Pittsburgh, PA: From the congregation of St. Vincent de Paul, established in Romania in 1842, they came to the United States in 1902. As there was already a congregation of Sisters of Charity in the diocese, the name was changed to the Vincentian sisters of Charity. Focus: health and education. The sisters were pioneers in home nursing.

1904 [0470] SISTERS OF CHARITY OF THE INCARNATE WORD, Houston, TX: The constitution of these sisters adopted a new provision that made it possible for the sisters to nurse in public institutions when emergencies arose. Three religious lived in the pesthouse during the cholera epidemic, working twenty hours each day when others could not be induced to work at any price. Burial was at night. Transfer of patients to City Hospital was

Year	OCD	

accomplished by placing fever patients on their mattresses and carrying them to the hospital.

[1070] SISTERS OF ST. CATHERINE OF SIENA, St. Catherine, KY: One night sufficed to wipe out the work of eighty years when flames spent their force and then there was "not a stone left upon a stone."

[1370] FRANCISCAN MISSIONARIES OF MARY, New York, NY: This missionary community has been active in the United States since 1904 and sponsors two hospitals.

[1680] SCHOOL SISTERS OF ST. FRANCIS, Milwaukee, WI: The sisters were asked by a priest to work in a small parochial hospital in Galina, IL. The hospital accommodated eleven patients. The pastor closed the hospital in 1910 because of financial problems.

[0860] DAUGHTERS OF MARY OF THE IMMACULATE CONCEPTION: The congregation is an American community founded in New Brittain, CT, by the Rev. Luucian Bojnowski. The community sponsors one hospital.

[0990] SISTERS OF DIVINE PROVIDENCE, Granite City, IL: Granite City Hospital (St. Elizabeth Hospital) was established by Lutherans. Due to financial difficulties, it was turned over to a company that found the responsibility for the deficit too burdensome and persuaded a priest of Venice, IL, to seek a solution for the problem. The priest tried to get an order interested but the request was declined. Finally, the Sisters of Divine Providence took over the hospital, paying fifty thousand dollars for the property and spending another forty five thousand to put it into useable condition.

1905 [1100] DOMINICAN SISTERS OF CHARITY OF THE PRESENTATION OF THE BLESSED VIRGIN MARY, Dighton, MA: The sisters first came to the United States in 1905 from Tours, France, and established a congregation in Fall River. They opened a hospital the following year. Traditional emphasis is on pastoral care in hospitals and homes for the aged.

[2230] CONGREGATION OF THE INFANT JESUS, Brooklyn, NY: The sisters continue to respond through a system of health and human services to the many social needs of the time. In order to sensitize society to needs, the sisters involve themselves in civic, political, and ecclesiastical matters on the local, state, and national levels.

1906 [0590] SISTERS OF CHARITY OF ST. ELIZABETH, Convent Station, NJ: The Hospital of St. Raphael owes its existence to a generous impulse of Catholic physicians to provide New Haven, CT, with an institution to which members of their creed might have a resource without restriction. A

Year	OCD	
		meeting of the city's Catholic physicians was called to form an organization known as the Catholic Health Association of New Haven. The sisters were asked to assume the management of the proposed hospital.
	[1070]	DOMINICAN SISTERS, CONGREGATION OF THE IMMACULATE CONCEPTION, Great Bend, KS: The community met an evident need in this city by opening a hospital known as St. Rose's Hospital.
	[2570]	SISTERS OF MERCY, Burlingame, CA: The San Francisco earthquake and fire struck St. Mary's Hospital. The hospital was safely evacuated hours before burning down. Within a week the Sisters of Mercy opened a tent hospital near Golden Gate Park.
	[2570]	SISTERS OF MERCY, Philadelphia, PA: A group of physicians met with Dr. E. Clarence Howard, first Negro graduate of Hahnemann University Medical School, to discuss the advisability of establishing an institution that would permit Negro physicians' patients to enter under their direct care. It would also provide interns and Negro medical graduates and train young Negro women in the art of nursing.
1907	[3970]	THE SISTERS OF ST. MARY OF THE THIRD ORDER OF ST. FRANCIS (FRANCISCAN SISTERS OF MARY): A nursing program was established for the sisters at St. Mary's Infirmary in St. Louis. Some sisters obtained licensure by waiver but after 1917 the sisters took the state Board of Nursing Examination.
	[3830]	SISTERS OF ST. JOSEPH, Superior, WI: The Sisters of St. Joseph of Carondelet in St. Louis branched out to various sections of the country and were established in Wisconsin as an autonomous congregation. Sponsor one hospital.
1908	[2800]	MISSIONARY SISTERS OF THE MOST SACRED HEART OF JESUS, Reading, PA: The congregation was founded in Germany in 1900 and came to the United States in 1908. Sponsor hospitals.
	[2450]	SISTERS OF ST. MARY OF THE PRESENTATION, Spring Valley, IL: A hospital was founded in 1903 by the sisters in a building known as "Power Homestead." The hospital was moved to a new building in 1908 and named St. Margaret's Hospital in honor of Mrs. Mary Power, mother of Father Power.
	[0580]	SISTERS OF CHARITY OF ST. AUGUSTINE, Canton, OH: Timken Mercy Hospital was established in the remodeled home of the late President McKinley. It proved inadequate soon after opening and in 1911 an adjoining building was opened for service. The McKinley home was used as an annex until 1931 as a

Year	OCD	
		children's unit known as the "Little Flower Hospital" operated under the jurisdiction of Mercy Hospital.
1909	[3850]	SISTERS OF ST. JOSEPH OF CHAMBERY, Waterbury, CT: St. Mary's Hospital was founded in 1909 by the Rt. Rev. Msgr. William Slocum. The entire personnel consisted of six sisters. At the end of the first year, the hospital had cared for 980 patients.
1910	[0230]	BENEDICTINE SISTERS, Jonesboro, AR: The sisters planned St. Bernard's Hospital. When Negroes were treated some of the doctors resigned. A special section was set aside for the Negro patients.
		The Flexner Report was a damning indictment of medical education and brought foundation money to the higher quality medical schools while the weaker ones were forced out of existence.
1911	[1070]	CONGREGATION OF ST. CATHERINE OF SIENA, Kenosha, WI: During the Portuguese revolution in 1910, the sisters were expelled from Portugal and stayed a short time in Ireland, from where the first congregation in the United States was established. A small band of sisters were received in the Archdiocese of Milwaukee. The provincial house was established in Kenosha, WI. The hospital in Kenosha has developed programs for people with drug problems.
1912	[1020]	SISTERS OF DIVINE REDEEMER, Elizabeth, PA: The first sisters to come to the United States were from the convent in Hungary. They settled in McKeesport, PA, and then moved to Elizabeth, PA. The focus is on health care, especially of the elderly, and education.
	[2860]	MISSIONARY SISTERS OF THE SACRED HEART: Columbus Hospital in Seattle was established by St. Francis Cabrini, foundress of this order. The original purpose of the institution was the care of chronic and convalescent patients. With the rapid growth of the community, it admitted other patients.
	[3150]	SISTERS OF THE PALLOTTINE MISSIONARY SOCIETY, Florissant, MO: The Pallottine Fathers asked for sister co-workers to assist them in missionary endeavors. The congregation was founded in the United States. The sisters were engaged in nursing in various hospitals.
		The American College of Surgeons was organized to elevate the standards of surgical practice.
1913	[1380]	FRANCISCAN MISSIONARIES OF OUR LADY, Baton Rouge, LA: Founded in Calais, France, in 1854. The first American foundation was established in Monroe, LA, in 1913. In 1923, the community relocated to Baton Rouge, where a hospital was opened by the sisters. Traditional focus is on health care.

Year	OCD	
	[1590]	SISTERS OF ST. FRANCIS OF THE IMMACULATE HEART OF MARY, Hankinson, ND: The congregation was founded in Germany in 1241; the first American congregation was established in Collegeville, MN, in 1913. The provincial motherhouse was established in Hankinson in 1927. Focus is in areas of health and education, with work among migrants and the poor.
	[0940]	DAUGHTERS OF ST. MARY OF PROVIDENCE, Chicago, IL: The congregation was founded in Italy in 1872 and has been in the United States since 1913. The sisters engage in health work.
1914	[3350]	SISTERS OF PROVIDENCE: St. Ignatius Hospital was established at the request of the United States government to provide/a hospital for workers on a local irrigation project.
	[2680]	MISERICORDIA SISTERS, Canada: A non-Catholic physician, Jacob L. Huber, bequeathed twenty thousand dollars to endow a hospital for the community, directing his wife to execute his wishes. The Sisters of Misericordia were invited to take charge of Huber Memorial Hospital in Pana, IL.
		A historic meeting between Mothers Esperance and Madeleive Lyons of the Sisters of St. Joseph of Carondelet with Jesuit Father Moulinier, SJ, resulted in the formation of the Catholic Hospital (Health) Association the following year.
1915		The Catholic Health (Hospital) Association was organized in 1915 to promote the general welfare of the Catholic health system and to assist its personnel.
1917		The Rt. Rev. Joseph Schrembs, newly appointed bishop of Toledo, established Mercy Hospital as his contribution to hospital work in the diocese.
	[1820]	HOSPITAL SISTERS OF THE THIRD ORDER OF ST. FRANCIS, Springfield, IL: St. John's Hospital was established by twenty sisters who arrived from the motherhouse of the community in Germany. The Rt. Rev. Peter James Baltes sent them to Springfield to begin hospital work.
	[1440]	FRANCISCAN SISTERS OF THE POOR, Brooklyn, NY: World War I was a difficult time for the sisters. Many were recruited from Germany and were torn between patriotism for the United States and love for those in Germany.
1918	[2790]	MISSIONARY SERVANTS OF THE MOST BLESSED TRINITY, Gadsden, AL: Holy Name of Jesus Hospital was established as Gadsden General Hospital by a local physician in 1918. The same year the hospital was sold by the founder to the Sisters of Divine Providence of Pittsburgh. The Missionary Servants acquired the hospital in 1925.

Year	OCD	
1919	[0230]	BENEDICTINE SISTERS, Crookston, MN: Branching off from Duluth, this independent priory began in Crookston and absorbed the health-care institutions within the Crookston diocese.
	[0270]	SISTERS OF BON SECOURS, Baltimore, MD: It was thirty-eight years from the time the first sisters arrived in Baltimore in 1881 to the opening of their first American hospital in 1919. During the years before the hospital opened, the sisters became well-known in Baltimore for their work in caring for the sick in homes. In the early days, the sisters lived on donations.
	[0960]	DAUGHTERS OF WISDOM, Islip, NY: At the beginning of the century, when religious congregations were expelled from France, the community spread to North and South America. The sisters nursed in hospitals and children's clinics for orthopedic cases, and cared for those afflicted with cerebral palsy.
1922	[0210]	MISSIONARY BENEDICTINE SISTERS, Norfolk, NB: The sisters, founded in Bavaria in 1885, came to the United States in 1922 with a mission to teach. Two years later, they were asked to take over the operation of the Sacred Heart Hospital in Lynch, NE. This began a new health-care mission in America.
		SISTERS OF ST. FRANCIS OF OUR LADY OF GUADALUPE: Generalate in Gettysburg, SD. Staff one hospital.
	[1660]	SISTERS OF ST. FRANCIS OF THE PROVIDENCE OF GOD, Pittsburgh, PA: When America was flooded with immigrants in the 1920s, a group of dedicated women turned to meet their needs. Centering on the plight of exiles from Lithuania, these women founded a Franciscan community.
	[0930]	RELIGIOUS DAUGHTERS OF ST. JOSEPH, Los Angeles, CA: This congregation was founded in Spain in 1875. Santa Marta Hospital and Clinic was established in 1922.
1923	[1220]	FRANCISCAN SISTERS OF THE BLESSED VIRGIN MARY OF THE ANGELS, St. Paul, MN: The community was founded in Germany in 1863. The first foundation in the United States was established in 1923. The sisters, who are engaged in nursing the sick, sponsor one hospital.
1924	[2000]	SISTERS OF THE HOLY REDEEMER, Huntingdon Valley, PA: From the Congregation founded in Alsace in 1849, the first foundation in the United States was made in 1924. Focus is on health ministry with emphasis on home health care.
1925	[1070]	DOMINICAN SISTERS, INSTITUTE OF ST. DOMINIC, Spokane, WA: Twelve Sisters emigrated from Germany in 1925. They came to Mount St. Charles, where they

Year	OCD	
		took charge of the domestic needs of Carroll College. In 1947 the community was established as a formal American province. In 1978 Dominican Health Services was developed to manage the sisters' health-care ministry. This way the sisters were able to continue in their sponsorship role in spite of fewer members. They sponsor three hospitals. In 1985, the small community of forty-two members separated from the generalate in West Germany to become a diocesan congregation.
1928	[3740]	SISTERS OF ST. CASIMIR, Chicago, IL: Before the inception of the Holy Cross Hospital in Chicago, the Lithuanian Catholic Alliance, a community organization, was dedicated to caring for poor and needy Lithuanian immigrants in the United States. As a result, this group wanted to provide an orphanage for the community. Cardinal George Mudelein suggested the idea of building a local hospital as a revenue-producing instrument for the Lithuanian Catholic Alliance's projects. He enlisted the help of the Sisters of St. Casimir and negotiated a loan for the hospital project, which the sisters funded. Because of the efforts of the people and businesses, Holy Cross Hospital opened in 1928.
1929	[2580]	SISTERS OF MERCY OF THE UNION IN THE UNITED STATES OF AMERICA: Convoked by the apostolic delegate to the United States, the Most Rev. P. Fumasoni-Biondi, at the command of the Sacred Congregation of Religious, there was held in Cincinnati, OH, during the last week in August 1929, the first general chapter of the Sisters of Mercy in the United States. Each of the communities of the Sisters of Mercy that had signified a desire to enter the generalate was represented at the general chapter by its mother superior and two delegates. At this meeting the election of the mother general and other administrative officers took place.
1930	[0230]	CONGREGATION OF ST. SCHOLASTICA: Eleven motherhouses of the Benedictine Sisters formed this confederation. There is no general motherhouse. There were 641 Catholic Hospitals in the United States: 13,500 sisters were employed (average of 21 sisters for each hospital); the sisters belonged to 154 different orders or congregations; 139 of the sisterhoods divided their activities between teaching and nursing; 60 percent of the sisterhoods in acute health care migrated from Europe and 79 percent originated in the United States or Canada.
	[1820]	HOSPITAL SISTERS OF ST. FRANCIS, Springfield, IL: One sister recalled that the Knights of the Road had a saying, "If you are sick or need help, stop in Springfield and go

Year	OCD	
		to St. John's Hospital and see Sister Juanaria and she will take care of you." She would provide food, a bath, and clean clothes. If they were sick, she would give them medicine and have a doctor friend look at them before they went on the road again.
	[3830]	SISTERS OF ST. JOSEPH OF ORANGE, CA: The sisters established four hospitals during the depression. While ethnic and racial prejudices were common, the sisters devised many ways to provide service to minority groups.
1939		The March of Dimes was founded to finance research that would combat polio.
1940	[1470]	FRANCISCAN SISTERS OF ST. JOSEPH: The congregation was founded in Trenton, NJ for the education of children of immigrant families. In 1928, the motherhouse was located in Hamburg, NY. The sisters opened a hospital in 1940.
1941	[0440]	Sister Eugene Marie Carpe, SC, directed the first exchange transfusion in a "blue baby" ever performed in Cincinnati. In 1961 she was selected president of the Ohio Hospital Association, the first sister-administrator ever to be president of the association.
1943	[1810]	BERNARDINE SISTERS OF THE THIRD ORDER OF ST. FRANCIS: The community accepted its first hospital in Hoven, SD. The hospital remained the property of the city of Hoven until 1946, when it was turned over to the sisters and renamed Holy Infant Hospital.
	[3740]	SISTERS OF ST. CASIMIR, Chicago, IL: A new twenty-three bed psychiatric unit was set up at Loretto Hospital. This was the first of its kind to be established by a Catholic general hospital in Chicago.
1944	[0230]	BENEDICTINE SISTERS, Bismarck, ND: The first congregation was established in the United States from Bavaria in 1852. With successive foundations, the sisters established a new community in Bismarck in 1944 that became autonomous in 1947. Continued to work in the health field.
		Helen Brooke Taussig, M.D.: her major work was with Dr. Alfred Blalock. she was the codeveloper on the clinical side of the "blue baby" operation and was the first to demonstrate that changes in the heart and lungs could be diagnosed by X ray and fluoroscope.
1946	[0920]	DAUGHTERS OF ST. FRANCIS OF ASSISSI: Mother M. Bruenner founded the congregation in Austria in 1890. The American province originated in 1946 when fifteen sisters came from Slovacia and settled in Peru, IL. Later the provincialate was transferred to Lacon, IL. They sponsor one hospital and one nursing home.

Year	OCD	
	[0460]	CONGREGATION OF THE SISTERS OF CHARITY OF THE INCARNATE WORD, San Antonio, TX: When the city sued the Santa Rosa Hospital for taxes, both for the current year and for back taxes (amounting to approximately half a million dollars), Mother Robert in the name of the hospital fought the lawsuit. As a result of the Texas Supreme Court's decision, all hospitals and other charitable institutions were assured like exemptions.
1947	[1070]	CONGREGATION OF THE MOST HOLY ROSARY, Adrian, MI: Bishop Gorman of Reno, NV, asked Mother Gerald to accept a hospital that during World War II had served government employees. The government preferred sisters. Cost of one dollar per year on a lease for two years and no government control was offered. At the end of the two years, the hospital became a gift.
	[3640]	POOR SERVANTS OF THE MOTHER OF GOD, NC: The congregation was founded by Mother Magdaline, who had been a volunteer with Florence Nightingale in Crimea in 1854. In 1947, the sisters came to the United States. They sponsor one hospital.
1948	[0230]	BENEDICTINE SISTERS, St. Paul, MN: The first priory was established in the United States in 1852. Five years later, a priory was established in St. Joseph, MN, from which a group of sisters left to establish an autonomous priory at St. Paul. Focus is on health and education.
1953	[1070]	DOMINICAN SISTERS, CONGREGATION OF THE HOLY CROSS, Amityville, NY: The congregation was established by four sisters from the Holy Cross cloister in Germany. Focus is on education and health care. Newer thrusts are works among the poor and minority groups.
Early 1950s		Hospital administration was recognized as a profession and programs in hospital administration became available in various universities throughout the United States.
Late 1950s		The Leadership Conference of Women Religious was organized in the late 1950s as the Conference of Major Superiors of Women. The name was changed in 1971 and approved by the Congregation for Religious and Secular Institutes on June 13, 1962. Its purpose is to promote the spiritual and apostolic calling and works of sisterhoods in the United States. Membership is approximately seven hundred.
1960s		Drug therapy was refined and synthetic drugs were developed. Major surgery was improved and new procedures were instituted, such as open-heart surgery, bypass surgery, brain surgery, and replacement and prosthesis for orthopedic cases. Research and

Year	OCD	

educational opportunities multiplied, systems (versus individual hospitals) became prevalent, and new methods of financing health care came into existence along with marketing and competition.

Drastic changes occured in religious congregations, such as the great exodus of religious and lack of vocations, professionally preparation for religious instead of self-preparation, restructuring of institutional sponsorship, merger and divestiture of Catholic health institutions, and new ethical and religious directives. There was also challenge to ownership, and issues of private property and public interest.

1968 [0270] CONGREGATION OF BON SECOURS, Baltimore, MD: The sisters worked in poverty-stricken Harlem. They supported themselves as part-time nurses in a local hospital. Ministry to the poor was carried out in cooperation with existing health agencies.

1969 [2570] SISTERS OF MERCY, Orchard Park, NY: The first sister-administrator received a graduate degree in administration. Following this, additional sisters qualified in the field. In 1984, the Sisters of Mercy continue to serve as chief executive officers in their hospitals.

"Study of the Future Role of Health-Care Facilities under Catholic Auspices in the United States" was sponsored by the Catholic Health Association in St. Louis.

1972 [0370] CARMELITE SISTERS OF THE MOST SACRED HEART, Los Angeles, CA: The congregation was founded in Mexico in 1904. During religious persecution in Mexico, the sisters came to the United States. Their apostolic activities include nursing and the sponsorship of one hospital.

[1310] THE FRANCISCAN SISTERS, Little Falls, MN: The sisters began inviting laypeople to be members of the governing boards of the congregation's facilities. There were a number of factors that led to the move, including the call of the Vatican for more collaboration between religious and laity, a decreasing number of sisters in health care, and the growing complexities of health care. The congregation sponsors several health-care institutions.

1973 [0230] BENEDICTINE SISTERS, Ferdinand, IN: After a year of meetings with the Huntingburg Airport manager and the state police, application was made on March 10, 1973, to the Federal Aviation Administration to establish a heliport at St. Joseph's Hospital in Huntingburg for heliocopter service. On July 18, 1973, approval was received.

Year	OCD	
1977	[1820]	HOSPITAL SISTERS OF ST. FRANCIS, Springfield, IL: Sister Jane Marie, OSF, founded the SHARE program. The basic reason for SHARE is the comfort and mutual reassurance that parents who have had the experience of a loss of a newborn or miscarriage can offer to each other. In 1982, there were fifty SHARE groups in seventeen states.
		On September 15, 1977, the Rev. John J. Flanagan, SJ, former executive director of the Catholic Hospital (Health) Association, died. He was executive director from 1947 through 1968.
1978		A pilot project to refine evaluation criteria for determining the Catholicity of Catholic health-care facilities was launched at a September 1978 meeting in St. Louis under the sponsorship of the Catholic Health Association.
1979	[0760]	Sisters Irene Kraus, DC, became chairperson of the American Hospital Association's board of trustees, having been elected in 1978. She was the first woman and first religious to be chairperson in the history of the American Hospital Association.
1970s	[2580]	SISTERS OF MERCY OF THE UNION, Detroit Province: In the 1970s Mercy Hospitals set aside a percentage for charity. For example: some hospitals now require no other payment for the elderly beyond what Blue Cross/Blue Shield, Medicare, or other insurance will pay. Mercy Hospitals have set up health centers in deprived areas and offer other services to small health institutions.
1980	[3350]	SISTERS OF PROVIDENCE: National attention was focused on the pioneer Sisters of Providence in May where a bronze statue of Mother Joseph was installed in the National Statuary Hall in Washington, DC. Mother Joseph became the first nun and the fifth woman to be honored in the hall as a great American. She joined Marcus Whitman as the second representative from Washington State. (The Statuary Hall began more than one hundred years ago, when President Lincoln invited each state to send a statue of a distinguished citizen to be displayed in the nation's capital.)
	[2580]	SISTERS OF MERCY OF THE UNION: The sisters sold their 346-acre national headquarters in Potomac, MD, to the United States Postal Service for $6.8 million. Proceeds from the sale are to be used to shelter the homeless.
1981		Colloquium I sponsored by the Catholic Health Association, entitled "Leaven and Leverage," was held in Dallas, TX, on May 28 through 30. Sponsored for Religious Congregations and Health-Care Facilities.

Year	OCD	
1982		Colloquium II sponsored by the Catholic Health Association, entitled "Commitment and Collaboration," was held in St. Louis on February 15 through 17. Sponsored for Religious Congregations and Health-Care Facilities.
	[0760]	DAUGHTERS OF CHARITY: Sister Hilary Ross, DC, one of the eminent scientific pioneers in the field of leprosy, published over forty papers on her investigations.
1984	[3840]	SISTERS OF ST. JOSEPH OF CARONDELET, St. Paul, MN: St. Joseph Hospital Parish Community Network Program provides communication between the parish and discharged patient and provides area parishes with information regarding hospital programs available in the community. The goal is "to provide a system of interaction between the hospital parish and discharged patient."
1985	[3830]	SISTERS OF ST. JOSEPH OF CONCORDIA: This congregation had been in the health apostolate from the beginning of the twentieth century to July 1, 1985. Their hospitals were transferred to the Sisters of St. Joseph of Wichita, KS. Many thanks for so many years of dedicated service to the church through your health ministry.
		Loss of acute health-care institutions: From 1960 to 1985 the number of Catholic hospitals in United States decreased from 838 to 620, for a loss of 16 percent.
		Bishop Anthony M. Pilla of Cleveland meets regularly with the representatives of the Catholic hospitals of the diocese. He emphasizes the importance of this cooperative effort in keeping administration informed. He meets with the major superiors and chief executive officers of the hospitals sponsored by the religious congregations in the diocese.
		Life for the medically afflicted, the handicapped, and the elderly is being made better today through the use of new medical systems and therapeutic procedures that incorporate advanced technologies initially developed for national aeronautics and space programs.
1986	[2200]	CONGREGATION OF THE INCARNATE WORD AND BLESSED SACRAMENT, Victoria, TX: Recently terminated the lease of their last health facility and wish to record in the chronology the following hospital-staff activities: Burns Hospital, Cuero, TX 1934–1970; Huth Memorial, Yoakum, TX 1933–1983; and Mercy Hospital, Juordanton, TX 1956–1986. Many thanks for all of your past service.
1987	[0760]	DAUGHTERS OF CHARITY, Birmingham, AL: St. Vincent's Hospital in has been selected by the University of Kentucky to serve as a clinical outreach facility for

Year	OCD	
		patient screening, treatment, and research on a cancer-fighting substance called "Biological Response."
	[3930]	SISTERS OF ST. FRANCIS OF THE MISSION, NY: St. Francis Certified Home Health Services, a new nonprofit corporation of St. Francis Hospitals, Poughkeepsie and Beacon, has begun providing certified health care following approval by the New York State Department of Health.
	[1920]	CONGREGATION OF THE SISTERS OF THE HOLY CROSS: Holy Cross Hospital has been the first hospital in Maryland to ask the state for permission to include an AIDS unit in the plans to build a nursing home. The hospital is proposing to build a $5.5 million dollar nursing home with a fifteen-bed AIDS unit.
	[2860]	MISSIONARY SISTERS OF THE SACRED HEART: Cabrini Medical Center treats about fifty AIDS patients a day, which is 10.5 percent of the entire hospital population. The clinic associated with the hospital treats about fifteen patients a week and has had a total of six hundred AIDS patients since 1981.
		President and Chief Executive Officer John E. Curly, Jr., of the Catholic Health Association (St. Louis, MO), delivered a seven-minute address to the Holy Father during the pope's visit to the United States. The address focused on the ministry's challenges in bringing God's healing presence to the people of the United States: "Few religious and the fact that the religious congregations are reassessing whether they will maintain health-care apostolates are challenges to the ministry. We must transform the uncertainties and discomforts of the present by our continued fidelity to the stewardship of this essential ministry."
1980s	[1840]	GREY NUNS OF THE SACRED HEART: Sisters work individually in various health services outside of the institution: hospice, psychiatric intensive care unit, medical physician, family practice, home health co-ordinator, geriatric center, and others. Sister Rosalie Bartell, director of the Institute of Concern for Public Health, has achieved international recognition.
	[3970]	SISTERS OF ST. MARY OF THE THIRD ORDER OF ST. FRANCIS (now FRANCISCAN SISTERS OF MARY): A relatively large population of AIDS patients treated at the University Hospital of St. Louis are hemophiliac with transfusion-associated AIDS. These transfused patients are from nearby Cardinal Glennon Hospital, which has a program for hemophiliacs.

Contributors

Judith G. Cetina, PhD, is manager, chief archivist, and curator of county manuscripts of the Cuyahoga County Archives, Ohio, and is the author of numerous papers and articles devoted to the history of Ohio and the Midwest.

Mary Carol Conroy, SCL, PhD, RN, a member of the Sisters of Charity of Leavenworth, Kansas, is assistant dean and chair of the Graduate Nursing Program, School of Nursing and Health Sciences, Spalding University, Louisville, Kentucky.

James Hennesey, SJ, PhD, is Professor of the History of Christianity, Boston College, and past president of the American Catholic Historical Association. Father Hennesey is the author of over 140 articles and four books, including *American Catholics: A History of the Roman Catholic Community in the United States.*

Margaret John Kelly, DC, PhD, is provincial of the Daughters of Charity in the Northeast Province, Albany, New York, as well as director of the Daughters of Charity National Health System, chairman of the board of the Daughters of Charity Health System, Northeast, and consultor to the Pontifical Commission on Health Affairs. Sister Margaret John's articles have appeared in a range of journals from *Hospitals* and *Health Progress* to *Sisters Today* and *Cross and Crown*. She also edited the volume *Justice and Health Care* for the Catholic Health Association.

Carlan Kraman, OSF, MA, is a member of the Sisters of Saint Francis in Rochester, Minnesota. After many years of teaching at the high-school and college levels, Sister Carlan has devoted her time to historical research and writing. She is the author of *Reflections on the Renewal Years, 1964–1967*, published on the occasion of her congregation's centennial, and *A Portrait of Saint Labre Indian Mission through One*

321

Hundred Years (1884–1977).

Judith Metz, SC, MA, is currently on the administrative staff of the Sisters of Charity of Cincinnati. Sister Judith has done extensive research on the history of the Sisters of Charity in the United States, leading to several articles and a book, and is currently a member of the board of Good Samaritan Hospital in Cincinnati.

Edna Marie LeRoux, RSM, PhD, is director of archives for the Sisters of Mercy, Detroit Province, and a member of the board of trustees of Mercy Hospital, Muskegon, Michigan.

Dolores Ann Liptak, RSM, PhD, a member of the Sisters of Mercy of West Hartford, Connecticut, and historical editor of this volume, is an archival and historical consultant for religious organizations, congregations, and dioceses throughout the United States. Sister Dolores serves on the board of the *U.S. Catholic Historian* and is the author of the recently published monograph, *European Immigrants and the Catholic Church in Connecticut.*

Duncan Neuhauser, PhD, is Professor of Epidemiology and Community Health and Keck Foundation Senior Research Scholar at the School of Medicine, Case Western Reserve University. Professor Neuhauser is the author of numerous books and scientific papers and also the editor of the journal *Health Matrix* and coeditor of the journal *Medical Care.*

Ursula Stepsis, CSA, FACHE, project director and general editor of this volume, has had an extensive career as a health-care executive in the Catholic health field as well as at the municipal (Cincinnati) and federal levels.

Index